PRAISE FOR JONATHAN SCHELL

THE FATE OF THE EARTH
"The most important book of the decade, perhaps of the century."
—Harrison E. Salisbury

"There have been thousands of commentaries on what this new destructive power of man means; but my guess is that Schell's book . . . will become the classic statement of the emerging consciousness." —Max Lerner, *New Republic*

THE TIME OF ILLUSION
"By persuasively connecting the Nixon years to the larger dilemmas of our time, Mr. Schell has elevated a shabby political story to the level of tragedy. And one closes his deeply intelligent book not with feelings of vindication or outrage, but with a sense of understanding and equanimity that only tragedy can evoke."
—Christopher Lehmann-Haupt, *The New York Times*

THE UNCONQUERABLE WORLD
"Schell, in this profoundly important book, wants us to being thinking about how we can use democracy—the actions of people, rather than governments— to bring about a peaceful world." —Howard Zinn, *The Boston Globe*

"*The Unconquerable World* is Mr. Schell's most ambitious, and over time will be regarded as his most significant work. . . . The book mounts perhaps the most impressive argument ever made that there exists a viable and desirable alternative to a continued reliance on war and that the failure to seize this opportunity will bring catastrophic results to America and the world."
—Richard Falk, *The New York Times*

"Wise, passionate, eloquent, and infused with historical vision rare in these dark times, Jonathan Schell's new book makes a powerful case for the realism of idealism in breaking the cycles of violence that threaten to destroy us all."
—John Dower, Pulitzer Prize-winning author of *Embracing Defeat*

The Jonathan Schell Reader

ON THE UNITED STATES AT WAR,
THE LONG CRISIS OF THE AMERICAN REPUBLIC,
AND THE FATE OF THE EARTH

Jonathan Schell

NATION BOOKS   New York

THE JONATHAN SCHELL READER
ON THE UNITED STATES AT WAR,
THE LONG CRISIS OF THE AMERICAN REPUBLIC,
AND THE FATE OF THE EARTH

Copyright © 2004 Jonathan Schell

Published by
Nation Books, An Imprint of Avalon Publishing Group
245 West 17th St., 11th Floor
New York, NY 10011

AVALON
publishing group incorporated

Nation Books is a co-publishing venture of the Nation Institute and Avalon Publishing
Group Incorporated.

The material in this book originally appeared in *The New Yorker, Harper's, Newsday, and The
Nation*. It was later published in the following volumes. *The Village of Ben Suc*, (Knopf,
1967); *The Military Half* (Knopf 1968); *The Time of Illusion* (Knopf, 1976); *The Fate of the
Earth* (Knopf 1982); *The Abolition (Knopf 1984); Observing the Nixon Years* (Pantheon 1989);
Writing in Time (Moyer Bell Ltd, 1997); The Unfinished Twentieth Century (Verso, 2001); *The
Unconquerable World* (Metropolitan, 2003).

"March 15, 1992" "March 17, 1994" "June 23, 1994" from *The Time of Illusion*. Reprinted by
permission of Moyer Bell.
Excerpt from *The Unconquerable World* by Jonathan Schell. Copyright © 2003 by Jonathan
Schell. Reprinted by arrangement with Henry Holt & Co.

Library of Congress Cataloging-in-Publication Data is available.

ISBN 1-56025-407-6

9 8 7 6 5 4 3 2 1

Book design by Simon M. Sullivan & Maria E. Torres
Printed in the United States of America
Distributed by Publishers Group West

Contents

THE REPUBLIC IN CRISIS || III

"Notes and Comment" from *The New Yorker*

The Time of Illusion

Columns from *Newsday*

TOWARD PEACE || IV

Introduction

Jonathan Schell

THESE PAGES OPEN with an excerpt from the first article I ever wrote (with the exception of juvenilia), an account of my arrival on helicopter 48 (there were sixty in all) into the village of Ben Suc, some thirty miles north of Saigon, in the so-called Iron Triangle, in South Vietnam, on January 8, 1967. They end with commentary on the American war in Iraq more than three decades later. In between is reporting and reflection on, among other things, the rest of the Vietnam War, the constitutional crisis brought about by the Nixon administration, the nuclear dilemma, the transformation of American politics by the expansion of the electronic news media, the rise of the Solidarity movement in Poland and the fall of the Soviet Union, and the "war on terror" that followed the attacks of September 11. Almost all of the writing was first published in magazines or newspapers and only later in books, so, with the exception of the introduction to Adam Michnik's *Letters from Prison* and the passage from *The Unconquerable World,* each excerpt has been identified by the name and date of the publication rather than the book title.

The main character in this collection is the United States of America. Its plot (as I can see now) meshes several running themes that cannot easily be separated. The first is "limited war"—thus named because in high theory it was designated as the alternative to "general war," which meant nuclear war, which meant annihilation. The limited war in question in the real world was of course the one in Vietnam. I reported on it for *The New Yorker* in 1967, and then commented on it until the war's end in the magazine's *Notes and Comment* section. A second theme is nuclear war itself. Sometime in the early 1970s, I arrived at a conviction, which I hold to this day, that the gravest danger of our age—or, for that matter, of any age, since it threatens to end the entire order of the ages—is nuclear destruction. It stood and still stands at the apex of the collection of new threats that the human species, grown powerful through scientific discovery, poses to itself and its earthly home. The peril of nuclear destruction is a bass note that sounds through these pages, as it did through the era. Yet just as the pitch of certain dog-whistles is too high for human hearing, so the pitch of this bass note has on the whole been, so to speak, *too low* for human hearing. The very enormity of the danger has rendered it inapprehensible. It seems to infect or stun the human faculties that try to take stock of it. It is so pervasive that it cannot not easily be seen, so immense that it cannot not readily be grasped by the intellect, so deeply buried in the psyche that it cannot easily be felt. Yet precisely because, though indisputably real, it has remained largely unheard, unseen, unapprehended, and unfelt—in a word, denied—it has, like an undiagnosed neurosis, paradoxically shaped our time (so it seems to me) more powerfully and deeply than any other influence.

A third theme is a protracted crisis of the American Republic, strained to the breaking point by a concentration of power in the executive branch and abuse of that power by a series of presidents. The crisis became so severe in the early 1970s that it was necessary to draw up articles of impeachment against President Nixon and drive him out of office before his term was over. This grand drama, in which the misbegotten limited war in Vietnam, pervasive nuclear danger, and the crisis of the republic were tangled inextricably together, was the subject of my *New Yorker* piece *The Time of Illusion*, represented here by it's sixth part, called "Credibility."

A fourth theme that runs through the whole story is the takeover and corruption of the political process by the rise of the communication industry, which by now I think might be better called the obfuscation industry.

In looking back over one's own writing, there is a dangerous, almost irresistible temptation to do, however circuitously, what a writer should never do—review his own work: to reheat old polemics, point up correct predictions, try to gloss over or excuse old mistakes. Resisting this temptation as best I can, I'll instead offer a few retrospective thoughts on the questions touched upon in the *Reader*. Of course, retrospection also has its dangers. It's perhaps all too easy to impose sense and continuity on events afterward, much as the ancients, looking up at the randomly distributed stars, were able to connect the dots to find crabs, ladles, and porpoises. Certainly, the patterns of history were obscure to forward-looking glances. The fact is that almost none of most important things that happened in this period was foreseen in the conventional wisdom of the time. For example, as I look through the door of my office into the main workspace, I see people gazing all day into screens and clicking away at keyboards. True, the first computers were already in existence in 1967. But the idea of the personal computer was widely dismissed. The World Wide Web was undreamed of. Who in 1967 would have imagined this ubiquitous staring and clicking life, connecting people all over the world instantaneously, but at the same time harnessing them to screens, like horses in stalls?

In 1967, the phrase "the environment" was fresh on people's lips (the first Earth Day was held on 1969), and seemed to have mainly to do with DDT and the life of birds; today, we know that all continents, all

seas, the air, and life itself, are fatally vulnerable to human intervention. Global warming, a slower way of ruining the ecosphere than
nuclear war, has emerged to rival it in importance. In 1967, no human
foot had ever been planted on any heavenly body; in 1969, human beings
walked on the moon. But the greatest of the surprises, perhaps, was the
fall of the Soviet Union. In 1967, this great empire, represented to the
world every year on May Day by the familiar lineup of leaders standing
on the Kremlin wall, like a row of granite statues, seemed the embod-
iment of everything that was unchanging and unchangeable in human
affairs. Yet in 1991, to general astonishment, it evaporated like the
morning dew.

And on September 10, 2001, how many observers foresaw the global
war on terror that has now come to dominate the policies of the United
States, and, through them, the politics of the world? Proudhon's statement, quoted by Hannah Arendt, that "the fecundity of the unexpected
far exceeds statesman's prudence" seems more true of our time than ever.
In the last century, the powers at the disposal of human beings—and now
not just of governments but of private groups as well—have become
greater than at any time in history, and their use or abuse, often sudden,
has taken on the role once played by earthquakes and other natural catastrophes. In these circumstances, the unpredictability of human events
acquires a new and more unnerving aspect.

The upheavals in the world have been so surprising and deep that one would
expects the politics of the United States today also to have been revolu-
tionized. Yet as I looked over these writings, it became clear that it was not
so. A remarkable continuity emerged. Encountering the United States of
today is like meeting the country of 1967 in disguise—wearing different
clothes, perhaps glasses and a beard—yet distinctly the same character.

Here with us still—or again—are new variations on exactly the same complex of themes that roiled the country in the earlier period.

I confess to having been a bad prophet. When Nixon was driven from office, I imagined that the constitutional crisis might be over. When the Cold War ended, I imagined that the nuclear dilemma, too, might head toward a resolution. When "world communism" disappeared, I dared to hope that "limited war," if not war itself, might at least become rare. Each time, I was ready for history's page to turn, and it did not; it seemed to remain stuck.

"Limited war" has reappeared as the war on terror. In 1967 it was Vietnam; now it is Iraq. Then it was the Iron Triangle; now it is the Sunni Triangle. Then the threat was global communism; now it is global Islamic fundamentalism. The "hearts and minds" being lost then were Vietnamese; now they are Iraqi.

Nuclear danger, which everyone did his best to forget when the Cold War ended, has returned to the foreground, in the shape of nuclear proliferation, both to nations and, potentially, to terrorist groups. Once again, the relationship of conventional to nuclear war preoccupies the strategists, though each has assumed a new form. In 1967, the problem was escalation of conventional war to nuclear war. Today, the problem is the relationship of conventional war to proliferation. What are the sources of proliferation? Can it be stopped? Should the United States wage conventional military campaigns against terrorists and states that support them, as the United States has done in Iraq, or should it instead move diplomatically and politically in concert with allies to forge an international consensus against proliferation and for disarmament, as called for in the global Nuclear Non-Proliferation Treaty?

The crisis of the republic is also back, with a vengeance. The war on terror has been used to suspend basic liberties, and has unbalanced the constitution. The concentration of power in the White House is greater even than during the Cold War.

Finally, the pervasive influence of the communications revolution on politics is deeper than ever, accelerating the detachment from reality that was such an important aspect of Richard Nixon's method of governing.

To try to explain this surprising continuity of troubling themes in American life would be beyond the scope of these comments. But what we seem to be dealing with in part is one of those cases in which a country is forced to repeat history because it has failed to remember it. More than amnesia appears to be involved. There has been active rejection of important lessons of the recent American past. For example, a deliberate erasure of the lessons of Vietnam—lessons soon called a "syndrome," which is to say an illness—contributed to the fiasco in Iraq. Effective denial in the late twentieth century of the persistence of the Cold War nuclear arsenals after the end of the Cold War set the stage for proliferation in the twenty-first, leaving the United States foolishly surprised to find itself facing danger from smaller nuclear powers as well as terrorist groups. Blind to the dangers it posed to the world, it was also blind to the world's response. For more than a half century, denial has been the dominant American response to nuclear danger. Can a country deal effectively with a problem that it cannot see?

Denial of reality, when indulged in too much, in regard to too many things that are too important, becomes habit-forming. Some comments by a senior adviser to President George W. Bush to the *New York Times* writer Ron Suskind show where the habit can lead. The adviser informed Suskind that he and others like him lived "in what we call the reality-based community." The adviser went on, "That's not the way the world really works anymore. We're an empire now, and when we act, we create our own reality. And while you're studying that reality—judiciously, as you will—we'll act again, creating other new realities, which you can study too, and that's how things will sort out. We're history's actors . . . and you, all of you, will be left to just study what we do."

The bid for a global American empire mentioned by the official has been long in the making. Has reality become passé in the new American order? Has the creation of that new empire truly made the study of reality obsolete? If the pages presented here offer any clue, the answer is no.

New York City
October 2004

LIMITED WAR ‖ I

The Village of Ben Suc

The New Yorker, JULY 15, 1967

UP TO A FEW months ago, Ben Suc was a prosperous village of some thirty-five hundred people. It had a recorded history going back to the late eighteenth century, when the Nguyen Dynasty, which ruled the southern part of Vietnam, fortified it and used it as a base in its campaign to subjugate the natives of the middle region of the country. In recent years, most of the inhabitants of Ben Suc, which lay inside a small loop of the slowly meandering Saigon River, in Binh Duong Province, about thirty miles from the city of Saigon, were engaged in tilling the exceptionally fertile paddies bordering the river and in tending the extensive orchards of mangoes, jackfruit, and an unusual strain of large grapefruit that is a famous product of the Saigon River region. The village also supported a small group of merchants, most of them of Chinese descent, who ran shops in the marketplace, including a pharmacy that sold a few modern medicines to supplement traditional folk cures of herbs and roots; a bicycle shop that also sold second-hand motor scooters; a hairdresser's; and a few small restaurants, which sold mainly noodles. These merchants were far wealthier than the other villagers; some of them even owned second-hand cars for their businesses. The village had no electricity and little machinery of any kind. Most families kept pigs, chickens, ducks, one or two cows for milk, and a team of water buffaloes for labor, and harvested enough rice and vegetables to sell some in the market every year. Since Ben Suc was a rich village, the market was held daily, and it attracted farmers from neighboring villages as well as the Ben Suc farmers. Among the people of Ben Suc, Buddhists were more numerous than Confucianists, but in practice the two religions tended to resemble each other more than they differed, both conforming more to locally developed village customs practiced by everyone than to the requirements of the two doctrines. The Confucianists prayed to Confucius as a Buddha-like god, the Buddhists regarded their ancestors as highly as any Confucianist did, and everyone celebrated roughly the same main holidays. In 1963, Christian missionary teams, including both Vietnamese and Americans, paid several visits to the village. One of these groups began its missionary work by slowly driving its car down the narrow main streets of the village, preaching through a loudspeaker mounted on the top of the car, and singing hymns accompanied by an accordion. Then, in the center of the village, a Vietnamese minister gave a sermon. He argued for the existence of God by pointing out that Vietnamese spontaneously cry out *"Troi oi!"* ("Oh God!") when they fall or get hurt, and told the villagers that their sins were as numerous as the particles of red dust that covered the leaves of the trees in the dry season. (The soil around Ben Suc is of a reddish hue.) Just as only God could wash every leaf clean by sending down a rainstorm, only God could wash away their countless sins. At the end of the sermon, he asked the villagers to kneel and pray, but none did. When he asked for questions, or even for arguments against what he had said, only the old village fool stepped forward to challenge him, to the amusement of the small group of villagers who had assembled to listen. Ordinarily, to entertain themselves, small groups of men would get together in the evening every two weeks or so to drink the

local liquor—sometimes until dawn—and occasionally they would go
fishing in the river and fry their catch together at night. Some of the
marriages in the village were arranged and some were love matches.
Although parents—particularly the girls' parents—didn't like it, cou-
ples often sneaked off in the evenings for secret rendezvous in the tall
bamboo groves or in glades of banana trees. At times, there were
stormy, jealous love affairs, and occasionally these resulted in fights
between the young men. Parents complained that the younger generation was rebellious and lazy, and sometimes called their children *hu
gao*—rice pots—who did nothing but eat.

Troops of the Army of the Republic of Vietnam (usually written
"ARVN" and pronounced "Arvin" by the Americans) maintained an outpost in Ben Suc from 1955 until late 1964, when it was routed in an
attack by the National Liberation Front (or N.L.F., or Vietcong, or
V.C.), which kidnapped and later executed the government-appointed
village chief and set up a full governing apparatus of its own. The
Front demanded—and got—not just the passive support of the Ben
Suc villagers but their active participation both in the governing of
their own village and in the war effort. In the first months, the Front
called several village-wide meetings. These began with impassioned
speeches by leaders of the Front, who usually opened with a report of
victories over the Americans and the "puppet troops" of the government, emphasizing in particular the downing of helicopters or planes
and the disabling of tanks. Two months after the "liberation" of the
village, the Front repelled an attack by ARVN troops, who abandoned
three American M-113 armored personnel-carriers on a road leading
into the village when they fled. The disabled hulks of these carriers
served the speakers at the village meetings as tangible proof of their
claimed superiority over the Americans, despite all the formidable and
sophisticated weaponry of the intruders. Occasionally, a badly burned

victim of an American napalm attack or an ex-prisoner of the government who had been tortured by ARVN troops was brought to Ben Suc to offer testimony and show his wounds to the villagers, giving the speakers an opportunity to condemn American and South Vietnamese–government atrocities. They painted a monstrous picture of the giant Americans, accusing them not only of bombing villages but also of practicing cannibalism and slitting the bellies of pregnant women. The speeches usually came to a close with a stirring call for support in the struggle and for what was sometimes called "the full cooperation and solidarity among the people to beat the American aggressors and the puppet troops." The speeches were often followed by singing and dancing, particularly on important National Liberation Front holidays, such as the founding day of the Front, December 20th, and Ho Chi Minh's birthday, May 19th. At one meeting, the dancers represented the defeat of a nearby "strategic hamlet." Usually, some of the women from Ben Suc itself danced, after being instructed by dancers from the Front. During the first year of Front government, a group of village teenagers formed a small band, including a guitar, a trumpet, and various traditional Vietnamese instruments, and played for the meetings, but toward the end of 1965 they were replaced by a professional itinerant band. In all its meetings to boost morale and rally the villagers, the Front attempted to create an atmosphere combining impassioned seriousness with an optimistic, energetic, improvised gaiety that drew the villagers into participation. At every opportunity, it attempted to make the villagers aware of their own collective power and of the critical necessity of their support in winning the war.

The Front organized the entire village into a variety of "associations" for the support of the war effort. The largest were the Youth Liberation Association, the Farmers' Liberation Association, and the

Women's Liberation Association. Each of these three associations met twice a month, and in times of emergency they met more often. At the meetings, leaders again reported news of recent victories and also delivered instructions from higher authorities for the coming month. The Youth Liberation Association exacted dues of one piastre (about three-quarters of a cent) a month. The usual duties of its members were to carry supplies and rice for the troops, build blockades to make the roads impassable to jeeps and slow for armored personnel-carriers, and dig tunnels, usually as bomb shelters for the village but sometimes as hideouts or hospitals for the Front's troops. Every once in a while, the members were called to the scene of a battle to remove the dead and wounded. The Farmers' Liberation Association asked for dues of two piastres a month. The farmers also had to pay the Front a tax of up to ten per cent of their harvest. Taxes were assessed on a graduated scale, with the richest farmers paying the most and the poorest paying nothing, or even receiving a welfare allotment. In its propaganda, the Front emphasized the fact that rich peasants, who had the most to lose from the Front's policy of favoring the poor as a "priority class," would not be allowed to slip out of their obligations to the war effort or to play a merely passive role in it. Soldiers were recruited from both the Youth Association and the Farmers' Association, with members of the priority class most often entrusted with positions as officers and leaders. In one case, the Front supported a young orphan on welfare until he became established as a farmer, and then made him a soldier and promoted him to the rank of squad commander within a few months. Generally speaking, rich families and families with relatives in ARVN were mistrusted and kept under close watch. The duties of members of the Women's Liberation Association were not fixed. They supported the war effort through a number of miscellaneous jobs, among them making clothes. A few young women served as nurses, helping roving Front doctors at a large underground hospital in the jungle, only a few miles from the village. On the non-military side, the Women's Association took a strong stand on the need to break the bonds imposed on women by the "dark feudal society" and to raise women to an equal position with men. There was no Front organization for old people—formerly the most influential group in village life. As an ex-member of the Farmers' Association has put it, the Front's policy toward old people was to "recruit them if they were smart" and otherwise leave them alone with their old ways. The activities of the three large associations were coordinated by the Village Committee, a group of three men in close contact with higher officials of the Front. The three men on the Village Committee were the village chief, who dealt with military and political matters; the village secretary, who dealt with taxes and supplies; and the education officer, who was responsible for the schools and the propaganda meetings. The Front was particularly diligent in establishing schools where the children, along with reading and their multiplication tables, learned anti-American slogans. In short, to the villagers of Ben Suc the National Liberation Front was not a band of roving guerrillas but the full government of their village.

In the two years between the Front's victory at Ben Suc and the beginning of 1967, both the war on the ground and what the Americans call the "air war" escalated rapidly throughout the area of Binh Duong Province bordering on the Saigon River. This was the period of the extensive American buildup in Vietnam, and at the villages of Di An, Lai Khé, Ben Cat, and Dau Tieng—all in the vicinity of Ben Suc—American and ARVN bases were either established or greatly expanded. Following its initial failure to retake Ben Suc, ARVN ran several more campaigns in the area, but in these it either failed to make contact with the enemy or was beaten back. A push by the American

173rd Airborne Brigade in October, 1965, failed to engage the enemy significantly. In late 1965, the Front permitted a team of ARVN troops to come into Ben Suc and attempt their own version of the Front's village meetings. This kind of ARVN meeting, which the Americans call a Hamlet Festival, is, like so many of the techniques employed by the South Vietnamese government and the United States Army, a conscious imitation of the Front's programs. (In a full-scale Hamlet Festival, troops will surround a village and order everyone into the center. Then, while intelligence men set up a temporary headquarters to interrogate the males caught in the roundup, searching for draft dodgers as well as for the enemy, a special team of entertainers will put on a program of propaganda songs and popular love songs for the women and children. Sometimes a medical team will give shots, hand out pills, and offer medical advice. Lunch is usually served from a mess tent. In the most abbreviated version of the Hamlet Festival, only a medical team will go into a village.) The fact that the Front allowed an ARVN medical team to enter the village in 1965 was quite consistent with the Front's continuing policy of deriving whatever benefit it can from government programs and facilities. One American official has noted, "If they don't try to blow up a certain power station, it usually means they're drawing power off it for themselves."

Between 1965 and 1967, American bombing of every kind increased tremendously throughout the Saigon River area. There were strikes with napalm and phosphorus, and strikes by B-52S, whose bombs usually leave a mile-long path of evenly spaced craters. As the American bases grew, the amount of large artillery also increased. There is apparently a policy in Vietnam of never letting any big gun remain silent for more than twenty-four hours, and the artillery on many bases fires a certain number of rounds every evening. Ordinarily, before bombing or shelling, an American pilot or artillery man must obtain permission from the province chief, or district chief, who, as a Vietnamese, is presumed to be more familiar with the surroundings than the Americans and able to restrain them from destroying populated areas. However, in the case of Binh Duong Province in January of 1967 the province chief, himself a colonel in ARVN, who was from outside the province, had taken his post only three months before, and had never controlled most of the areas being bombed, so he knew less about the area than most of the Americans. In South Vietnam, certain areas have been designated Free Strike Zones, which means that no permission is needed to fire into them. These are usually unpopulated jungle areas in which the Front is suspected of operating at night. Most of the routine nightly fire is lobbed into these zones, where it blows up jungle trees and—the Americans hope—the caves and bunkers of the Front. As there was at least one Free Zone within a few miles of Ben Suc, the thump of incoming artillery shells jarring the ground became a regular feature of life in the village.

In the daytime, pilots of fighter-bombers are shown their targets by troops on the ground or by small propeller planes called bird dogs, which spot promising targets from the air. The fliers adhere to a policy of bombing populated areas as little as possible, but sometimes beleaguered ground troops will call in planes or artillery fire to destroy a village that is being defended by the Front. In such cases, if there is time, an attempt is made to warn the villagers, either by airborne loudspeakers or by leaflets dropped on the village. The United States Army's Psychological Warfare Office has many hundreds of different leaflets, designed for subtly different situations. On one side of Leaflet No. APO-6227, for instance, a cartoon drawing represents the long trajectory of a large shell from a ship at sea to an inland village, where a human figure has been blown into the air and a grass-roofed house is bursting into pieces under the impact of the explosion. On the other side is a message in Vietnamese, reading, "Artillery from our ships will soon hit your village. You must look for cover immediately. From now on, chase the Viet-cong away from your village, so the government won't have to shell your area again."

The center of Ben Suc was bombed one morning in mid-1965. The bombs destroyed several two-story brick-and-mortar houses and wounded or killed more than twenty people, including several children. Some months before the bombing, the Front, to protect the center of the village, had made a mocking use of a new policy of the South Vietnamese government. Around that time, the government had publicly offered a guarantee that Allied troops would refrain from attacking any building or vehicle showing the government flag of three red stripes on a yellow ground. The purpose, as an American officer explained it, was to encourage the people to "associate safety with the national flag," for "it means something when everybody's going around carrying the national flag." In Ben Suc, however, the Front, moved by a spirit of irreverent humor quite typical of it at times, raised the government flag over a rice-storage house—more as a prank than as a serious preventive measure against bombings. For several months, it fluttered at the top of the storehouse—a bold joke, known through the whole village, and a brazen taunt to the government. The joke had a bitter ending when the center of the village was bombed and the rice storehouse destroyed. After this bombing, the Front government in Ben Suc moved about a hundred people from the center of the village to the outskirts, where they lived with relatives. It also laid explosive booby traps in various spots outside the village. The job of warning villagers away from these spots was entrusted to teams of teenage girls. In addition, the Front encouraged families to dig out rooms beneath their houses as bomb shelters. Later, there were many bombings, and many casualties, in the fields outside the village—particularly near the river, where the bombing was most frequent. From Ben Suc halfway to the provincial capital of Phu Cuong, about fifteen miles down the river, the riverside fields were polkadotted with craters of every size. At least a third of the small fields had been hit at least once, and some of the craters had turned entire fields into ponds. The bombing and the artillery fire were at their most intense in the early morning, when the Americans considered anything that moved highly suspicious, so the farmers took to starting work in the fields around eight or nine o'clock instead of at seven, as their custom had been. Not only the destruction but the crashing of bombs and shells nearby and in the distance made life continuously nerve-racking, with everyone tensely ready to run to a bomb shelter at a second's notice. The Psychological Warfare Office sought to make the most of the fear and tension by stepping up the volume of the leaflets dropped on the area. In a booklet describing the leaflets available for these purposes, Leaflet No. AVIB-246, whose "theme" is listed as "scare," has a cartoon drawing on one side showing a soldier of the Front dying, his hands futilely clutching the air in front of him and his face in the dirt, while jet planes fly overhead, dropping bombs. The message on the other side reads, "Each day, each week, each month, more and more of your comrades, base camps, and tunnels are found and destroyed. You are shelled more often, you are bombed more often. You are forced to move very often, you are forced to dig deeper, you are forced to carry more loads away. You are tired, you are sick. Your leaders tell you victory is near. They are wrong. Only DEATH is near. Do you hear the planes? Do you hear the bombs? These are the sounds of DEATH: your DEATH. Rally now to survive." Another leaflet shows a photograph of the mutilated corpse of a young man. His stomach and intestines are flowing out of him onto the ground. The message on the other side reads, "If you continue to follow the

Viet-cong, and destroy villages and hamlets, sooner or later you will be killed, like Colonel Iran Thuoe Quong. Colonel Quong will never need his belt again. He is DEAD." The word "dead" is written in large block letters that drip with blood. Some leaflets depict American weapons with the teeth and claws of beasts, killing or torturing people in the manner of the fantastic devils in medieval paintings of Hell. The drawing on one leaflet shows a tank with evil, slitted eyes, fangs, and long mechanical arms with metal talons that reach out toward the viewer. The tank crushes one man under its treads, squeezes drops of blood from a screaming second man in its talons, and engulfs a third man in a column of flame that spurts from between its dragonlike fangs.

People from many villages around Ben Suc who had been left homeless after ground battles, bombing, and shelling migrated to the comparative safety of other villages, to live with relatives or just fend for themselves. When the small village of Mi Hung, across the river from Ben Suc, was heavily bombed, at least a hundred of its people moved into Ben Suc. During 1966, a scattering of refugees from other bombed villages had also found their way there. Then, in the second week of the month of January, 1967—when the population of Ben Suc was further swollen by relatives and friends from neighboring villages who had come to help with the harvest, which was exceptionally abundant that season, despite the war—the Americans launched in Binh Duong Province what they called Operation Cedar Falls. It was the largest operation of the war up to that time.

For the Americans, the entire Saigon River area around Ben Suc, including particularly a notorious forty-square-mile stretch of jungle known as the Iron Triangle, had been a source of nagging setbacks. Small operations there were defeated; large operations conducted there turned up nothing. The big guns shelled and bombed around the clock but produced no tangible results. The enemy "body count" was very low, and the count of "pacified" villages stood at zero. In fact, a number of villages that had been converted into "strategic hamlets" in Operation Sunrise, launched three years earlier, had run their government protectors out of town and reverted to Front control. Late in 1966, the American high command designed the Cedar Falls operation as a drastic method of reducing the stubborn resistance throughout the Iron Triangle area. Named after the home town, in Iowa, of a 1st Division lieutenant who had been posthumously awarded the Medal of Honor, Operation Cedar Falls involved thirty thousand men, including logistical support, and it was planned and executed entirely by the Americans, without the advance knowledge of a single Vietnamese in the province. The decision that *no* Vietnamese was a good enough security risk was based on previous experiences, in which the enemy had learned about operations ahead of time and had laid traps for the attackers or simply disappeared. It also reflected the Army's growing tendency to mistrust all Vietnamese, regardless of their politics. On several American bases, entrance is forbidden to all Vietnamese, including ARVN soldiers, after a certain hour in the evening. During Cedar Falls, security was particularly tight.

A plan was made to attack Ben Suc, but Ben Suc was regarded as an objective quite separate from the operation's principle target—the Iron Triangle. The Iron Triangle is a patch of jungle bounded on the west, for about thirteen miles, by the Saigon River; on the east, also for about thirteen miles, by National Route No. 13; and on the north, for six miles, by a nameless smaller road. Ben Suc lay just beyond the northwest corner of the Triangle. Until the Cedar Falls operation, the Triangle long had a reputation as an enemy stronghold impenetrable to government troops, and had been said to shelter a full division of enemy troops and also a vast system of bunkers and tunnels issued by the Front as headquarters for its Military Region IV, which surrounds the city of Saigon. American intelligence had also received reports of a twelve-mile tunnel running the length of the Triangle from north to south. The operation was the first move in a newly devised long-term war strategy in which large American forces would aim primarily at engaging the main forces of the enemy and destroying their jungle bases one by one, while ARVN troops would aim primarily at providing security for the villages thus freed from Front control. General Earle G. Wheeler, chairman of the Joint Chiefs of Staff, who visited the area later, said, in an interview, "We must continue to seek out the enemy in South Vietnam—in particular, destroy his base areas where the enemy can rest, retrain, recuperate, resupply, and pull up his socks for his next military operation. . . . Primarily, the American units are engaged in search-and-destroy operations. In other words, they don't stay permanently in any given locale. . . . The Vietnamese military and paramilitary units are the ones which are used in the permanent security operations. The situation being what it is, General West-moreland's first effort is to engage the Viet Cong main-force units and the North Vietnamese Army units and defeat them." He added, "The South Vietnamese forces are not ample enough to cope with the main-force units throughout the country. . . . I don't wish to imply that the South Vietnamese are not going to participate in the operations there. Of course they will. . . . This does not mean that all of the Vietnamese forces are going to be devoted to pacification. They can't be. And there's no intent for them to be. I just said a substantial portion."

According to the Cedar Falls plan, the Triangle was to be bombed and shelled heavily for several days both by B-52s and by fighter-bombers, and then blocked off around its entire thirty-two-mile perimeter with elements of the 1st Infantry Division along the northern edge, elements of the 196th Light Infantry Brigade along the river, on the west side, and elements of the 173rd Airborne Brigade along Route 13, on the east side. Together, these troops would man a hundred and sixty pieces of artillery. After the jungle had been heavily shelled and bombed, the 1st Division troops were to flatten the jungle in fifty-yard swaths on both sides of the road, using sixty bulldozers airlifted in by the huge, two-rotor Chinook helicopters. Then they were simultaneously to destroy the villages of Rach Bap, Bung Cong, and Rach Kien, evacuate the villagers, and start cutting broad avenues in the jungle with special sixty-ton bulldozers nicknamed hogjaws. These drives would be supported by air strikes and artillery barrages against the jungle. American troops would enter the Triangle behind the bulldozers, in an attempt to engage the enemy division that was rumored to be there and destroy the enemy headquarters.

The attack on Ben Suc was planned for January 8th—the day before the thrust into the Triangle. I joined a group of six newsmen outside a field tent on the newly constructed base at the village of Lai Khé, to hear Major Allen C. Dixon, of the 173rd Airborne Brigade, outline the plan and purpose of this part of the operation. "We have two targets, actually," he explained, pointing to a map propped on a pile of sandbags. "There's the Iron Triangle, and then there's the village of Ben Suc. This village is a political center, as far as the V.C. is concerned, and it's been solid V.C. since the French pulled out in '56. We haven't even been able to get a census taken in there to find out who's there." Most of the American officers who led the operation were not aware that ARVN had had an outpost in Ben Suc for the nine years preceding 1964. They saw the village as "solid V.C. as long as we can remember." Major Dixon continued, "Now, we can't tell you whether A, B, and C are at their desks or not, but we *know* that there's important infrastructure there—what we're really after here is the infrastructure of the V.C. We've run several operations in this area before with ARVN, but it's always been hit and run—you go in there, leave the same day, and the V.C. is back that night. Now, we realize that you can't go in and then just abandon the people to the V.C. This time we're really going to do a thorough job of it: we're going to clean out the place completely. The people are all going to be resettled in a temporary camp near Phu Cuong, the provincial capital down the river, and then we're going to move *everything* out—livestock, furniture, and all of their possessions. The purpose here is to deprive the V.C. of this area for good. The people are going to Phu Cuong by barge and by truck, and when they get there the provincial government takes over—it has its own Revolutionary Development people to handle that, and U.S. aid is going to help."

A reporter asked what would happen to the evacuated village.

"Well, we don't have a certain decision or information on that at this date, but the village may be levelled," Major Dixon answered, and went on to say, "The attack is going to go tomorrow morning and it's going to be a complete surprise. Five hundred men of the 1st Infantry Division's 2nd Brigade are going to be lifted *right into* the village itself in sixty choppers, with Zero Hour at zero eight hundred hours. From some really excellent intelligence from that area, we have learned that the perimeter of the village is heavily mined, and that's why we'll be going into the village itself. Sixty choppers is as large a number as we've ever used in an attack of this nature. Simultaneous with the attack, choppers with speakers on them are going to start circling over the village, telling the villagers to assemble in the center of the town or they will be considered V.C.s. It's going to be hard to get the pilots on those choppers to go in low to make those announcements audible, but everything depends on that. Also, we're going to drop leaflets to the villagers." (Later, I picked up one of these leaflets. On one side, the flags of the Republic of Vietnam, the United States, the Republic of Korea, New Zealand, and Australia were represented in color; on the other side was a drawing of a smiling ARVN soldier with his arm around a smiling soldier of the National Liberation Front. The text, written in English, Vietnamese, and Korean, read, "Safe conduct pass to be honored by all Vietnamese Government Agencies and Allied Forces." I learned that the Chieu Hoi, or Open Arms, program would be in operation during the attack. In an attempt to encourage defections from the Front, the government was opening its arms to all *hoi chanh*, or returnees who turned themselves in. Hence the unusually friendly tone of the leaflets.)

About the encirclement of the village, Major Dixon said, "There are going to be three landing zones for the choppers. Then the men will take up positions to prevent people from escaping from the village. Five minutes after the landing, we're going to bring artillery fire and air strikes into the whole area in the woods to the north of the village to prevent people from escaping by that route. At zero eight thirty hours, we're going to lift in men from the 2nd Brigade below the woods to the south to block off that route. After the landing is completed, some of our gunships are going to patrol the area at treetop level to help keep the people inside there from getting out. After the area is secure, we're lifting a crew of ARVN soldiers into the center of the village to help us with the work there. We want to get the Vietnamese dealing with their own people as much as we can here. Now, we're hoping that opposition is going to be light, that we're going to be able to get this thing over in one lightning blow, but if they've got intelligence on this, the way they did on some of our other operations, they could have something ready for us and this *could* be a hot landing. It could be pretty hairy."

For several reasons, the plan itself was an object of keen professional satisfaction to the men who devised and executed it. In a sense, it reversed the search-and-destroy method. This time, they would destroy first and search later—at their leisure, in the interrogation rooms. After all the small skirmishes and ambushes, after months of lobbing tons of bombs and shells on vague targes in Free Strike Zones, the size, complexity, and careful coordination of the Cedar Falls operation satisfied the military men's taste for careful large-scale planning. Every troop movement was precisely timed, and there would be full use of air support and artillery, in a design that would unfold over a wide terrain and, no matter what the opposition might be, would almost certainly produce the tangible result of evacuating several thousand hostile civilians, thereby depriving the V.C. of hundreds of "structures," even if the "infrastructure" was not present. This time, unless the entire village sneaked off into the forest, the objective of the operation could not wholly elude the troops, as it had in previous campaigns. Thus, a measure of success was assured from the start. In concluding his briefing to the newsmen, Major Dixon remarked, "I think this really ought to be quite fascinating. There's this new element of surprise, of going right into the enemy village with our choppers and then bringing in our tremendous firepower. Anyway, it ought to be something to see."

That evening, I was sent by helicopter to a newly constructed base ten miles north of Ben Suc, at Dau Tieng, where Colonel James A. Grimsley, commanding officer of the and Brigade, 1st Infantry Division, was winding up his briefing of his officers on the next morning's attack on Ben Suc. The officers were assembled in a tent, in which a single lightbulb hung from the ceiling. "The purpose of this operation is to move in there absolutely as fast as we can get control of the situation," Colonel Grimsley said. "I want to emphasize that you're going to have only about ten seconds to empty each chopper, because another chopper will be coming right in after it. A last word to men landing below the southwest woods: Your job is to keep anyone from escaping down that way. Now, of course, if it's just a bunch of women and children wandering down through the woods, who obviously don't know what they're doing, don't fire, but otherwise you'll have to take them under fire. The choppers will be taking off at zero seven twenty-three hours tomorrow morning. Are there any questions?" There were no questions, and the officers filed out of the tent into the darkness.

The men of the 1st Division's 2nd Brigade spent the day before the battle quietly, engaging in few pep talks or discussions among themselves about the dangers ahead. Each man seemed to want to be alone with his thoughts. They spent the night before the attack in individual tents on the dusty ground of a French rubber plantation, now the Americans' new base at Dau Tieng. The airstrip was complete, but not many buildings were up yet, and construction materials lay in piles alongside freshly bulldozed roads. The men were brought in by helicopter in the afternoon from their own base and were led to their sleeping area among the rubber trees. Most of the transporting of American troops in Vietnam is done by helicopter or plane. So the men, hopping from American base to American base, view rural Vietnam only from the air until they see it through gunsights on a patrol or a search-and-destroy mission.

Darkness fell at about six-thirty. Thanks to a cloudy sky over the high canopy of rubber leaves, the area was soon in perfect blackness. A few men talked quietly in small groups for an hour or so. Others turned to their radios for company, listening to rock-'n'-roll and country-and-Western music broadcast by the American armed-services radio station in Saigon. The great majority simply went to sleep. Sleep that night, however, was difficult. Artillery fire from the big guns on the base began at around eleven o'clock and continued until about three o'clock, at a rate of four or five rounds every ten minutes. Later in the night, along with the sharp crack and whine of outgoing artillery the men heard the smothered thumping of bombing, including the rapid series of deep explosions that indicates a B-52 raid. Yet if the outgoing artillery fire had not been unusually near—so near that it sent little shocks of air against the walls of the tents—the sleepers would probably not have been disturbed very much. Because artillery fire is a routine occurrence at night on almost every American base in Vietnam, and because everyone knows that it is all American or Allied, it arouses no alarm, and no curiosity. Furthermore, because most of it is harassment and interdiction fire, lobbed into Free Strike Zones, it does not ordinarily indicate a clash with the enemy. It does make some men edgy when they first arrive, but soon it becomes no more than a half-noticed dull crashing in the distance. Only the distinctive sound of mortar fire—a popping that sounds like a champagne cork leaving a bottle—can make conversations suddenly halt in readiness for a dash into a ditch or bunker. Throughout that night of January 7th, the roaring of one of the diesel generators at the base served as a reminder to the men that they were sleeping on a little island of safety, encircled by coils of barbed wire and minefields, in a hostile countryside.

The men got up at five-thirty in the morning and were guided in the dark to a mess tent in a different part of the rubber grove, where they had a breakfast of grapefruit juice, hot cereal, scrambled eggs, bacon, toast, and coffee. At about six-thirty, the sky began to grow light, and they were led back to the airstrip. Strings of nine and ten helicopters with tapered bodies could be seen through the treetops, filing across the gray early-morning sky like little schools of minnows. In the distance, the slow beat of their engines sounded soft and almost peaceful, but when they rushed past overhead the noise was fearful and deafening. By seven o'clock, sixty helicopters were perched in formation on the airstrip, with seven men assembled in a silent group beside each one. When I arrived at the helicopter assigned to me—No. 47—three engineers and three infantrymen were already there, five of them standing or kneeling in the dust checking their weapons. One of them, a sergeant, was a small, wiry American Indian, who spoke in short, clipped syllables. The sixth man, a stocky infantryman with blond hair and a red face, who looked to be about twenty and was going into action for the first time, lay back against an earth embankment with his eyes closed, wearing an expression of boredom, as though he wanted to put these wasted minutes of waiting to some good use by catching up on his sleep. Two of the other six men in the team were also going into combat for the first time. The men did not speak to each other.

At seven-fifteen, our group of seven climbed up into its helicopter, a UH-1 (called Huey), and the pilot, a man with a German accent, told us that four of us should sit on the seat and three on the floor in front, to balance the craft. He also warned us that the flight might be rough, since we would be flying in the turbulent wake of the helicopter in front of us. At seven-twenty, the engines of the sixty helicopters started simultaneously, with a thunderous roar and a storm of dust. After idling his engine for three minutes on the airstrip, our pilot raised his right hand in the air, forming a circle with the forefinger and thumb, to show that he hoped everything would proceed perfectly from then on. The helicopter rose slowly from the airstrip right after the helicopter in front of it had risen. The pilot's gesture was the only indication that the seven men were on their way to something more than a nine-o'clock job. Rising, one after another, in two parallel lines of thirty, the fleet of sixty helicopters circled the base twice, gaining altitude and tightening their formation as they did so, until each machine was not more than twenty yards from the one immediately in front of it. Then the fleet, straightening out the two lines, headed south, toward Ben Suc.

In Helicopter No. 47, one of the men shouted a joke, which only one other man could hear, and they both laughed. The soldier who had earlier been trying to catch a nap on the runway wanted to get a picture of the sixty helicopters with a Minolta camera he had hanging from a strap around his neck. He was sitting on the floor, facing backward, so he asked one of the men on the seat to try to get a couple of shots. "There are sixty choppers here," he shouted, "and every one of them costs a quarter of a million bucks!" The Huey flies with its doors open, so the men who sat on the outside seats were perched right next to the drop. They held tightly to ceiling straps as the helicopter rolled and pitched through the sky like a ship plunging through a heavy sea. Wind from the rotors and from the forward motion blasted into the men's faces, making them squint. At five minutes to eight, the two lines of the fleet suddenly dived, bobbing and swaying from the cruising altitude of twenty-five hundred feet down to treetop level, at a point about seven miles from Ben Suc but heading away from it, to confuse enemy observers on the ground. Once at an altitude of fifty or sixty feet, the fleet made a wide U turn and headed directly for Ben Suc at a hundred miles an hour, the helicopters' tails raised slightly in forward flight. Below, the faces of scattered peasants were clearly visible as they looked up from their water buffalo at the sudden, earsplitting incursion of sixty helicopters charging low over their fields.

All at once, Helicopter No. 47 landed, and from both sides of it the men jumped out on the run into a freshly turned vegetable plot in the village of Ben Suc—the first Vietnamese village that several of them had ever set foot in. The helicopter took off immediately, and another settled in its place. Keeping low, the men I was with ran single file out into the center of the little plot, and then, spotting a low wall of bushes on the side of the plot they had just left, ran back there for cover and filed along the edges of the bushes toward several soldiers who had landed a little while before them. For a minute, there was silence. Suddenly a single helicopter came clattering overhead at about a hundred and fifty feet, squawking Vietnamese from two stubby speakers that stuck out, winglike, from the thinnest part of the fuselage, near the tail. The message, which the American soldiers could not understand, went, "Attention, people of Ben Suc! You are surrounded by Republic of South Vietnam and Allied Forces. Do not run away or you will be shot as V.C. Stay in your homes and wait for further instructions." The metallic voice, floating down over the fields, huts, and trees, was as calm as if it were announcing a flight departure at an air terminal. It was gone in ten seconds, and the soldiers again moved on in silence. Within two minutes, the young men from No. 47 reached a little dirt road marking the village perimeter, which they were to hold, but there were no people in sight except American soldiers. The young men lay down on the sides of embankments and in little hollows in the small area it had fallen to them to control. There was no sign of an enemy.

For the next hour and a half, the six men from No. 47 were to be the masters of a small stretch of vegetable fields which was divided down the center by about fifty yards of narrow dirt road—almost a path— and bounded on the front and two sides (as they faced the road and, beyond it, the center of the village) by several small houses behind copses of low palm trees and hedges and in back by a small graveyard giving onto a larger cultivated field. The vegetable fields, most of them not more than fifty feet square and of irregular shape, were separated by neatly constructed grass-covered ridges, each with a path running along its top. The houses were small and trim, most of them with one side open to the weather but protected from the rain by the deep eaves of a thatch-grass roof. The houses were usually set apart by hedges and low trees, so that one house was only half visible from another and difficult to see from the road; they were not unlike a wealthy American suburb in the logic of their layout. An orderly small yard, containing low-walled coops for chickens and a shed with stalls for cows, adjoined each house. Here and there, between the fields and in the copses, stood the whitewashed waist-high columns and brick walls of Vietnamese tombs, which look like small models of the ruins of once-splendid palaces. It was a tidy, delicately wrought small-scale landscape with short views—not overcrowded but with every square foot of land carefully attended to.

Four minutes after the landing, the heavy crackle of several automatic weapons firing issued from a point out of sight, perhaps five hundred yards away. The men, who had been sitting or kneeling, went down on their bellies, their eyes trained on the confusion of hedges, trees, and houses ahead. A report that Mike Company had made light contact came over their field radio. At about eight-ten, the shock of tremendous explosions shattered the air and rocked the ground. The men hit the dirt again. Artillery shells crashed somewhere in the woods, and rockets from helicopters thumped into the ground. When a jet came screaming low overhead, one of the men shouted, "They're bringing in air strikes!" Heavy percussions shook the ground under the men, who were now lying flat, and shock waves beat against their faces. Helicopter patrols began to wheel low over the treetops outside the perimeter defended by the infantry, spraying the landscape with long bursts of machine-gun fire. After about five minutes, the explosions became less frequent, and the men from the helicopters, realizing that this was the planned bombing and shelling of the northern woods, picked themselves up, and two of them, joined by three soldiers from another helicopter, set about exploring their area.

Three or four soldiers began to search the houses behind a nearby copse. Stepping through the doorway of one house with his rifle in firing position at his hip, a solidly build six-foot-two Negro private came upon a young woman standing with a baby in one arm and a little girl of three or four holding her other hand. The woman was barefoot and was dressed in a white shirt and rolled-up black trousers; a bandanna held her long hair in a coil at the back of her head. She and her children intently watched each of the soldier's movements. In English, he asked, "Where's your husband?" Without taking her eyes off the soldier, the woman said something in Vietnamese, in an explanatory tone. The soldier looked around the inside of the one-room house and, pointing to his rifle, asked, "You have same-same?" The woman shrugged and said something else in Vietnamese. The soldier shook his head and poked his hand into a basket of laundry on a table between him and the woman. She immediately took all the laundry out of the basket and shrugged again, with a hint of impatience, as though to say, "It's just laundry!" The soldier nodded and looked around, appearing unsure of what to do next in this situation. Then, on a peg on one wall, he spotted a pair of men's pants and a shirt hanging up to dry. "Where's *he?*" he asked, pointing to the clothes. The woman spoke in Vietnamese. The soldier took the damp clothing down and, for some reason, carried it outside, where he laid it on the ground.

The house was clean, light, and airy, with doors on two sides and the top half of one whole side opening out onto a grassy yard. On the table, a half-eaten bowl of rice stood next to the laundry basket. A tiny hammock, not more than three feet long, hung in one corner. At one side of the house, a small, separate wooden roof stood over a fireplace with cooking utensils hanging around it. On the window ledge was a row of barley sprouting plants, in little clods of earth wrapped in palm leaves. Inside the room, a kilnlike structure, its walls and top made of mud, logs, and large stones, stood over the family's bedding. At the rear of the house, a square opening in the ground led to an underground bomb shelter large enough for several people to stand in. In the yard, a cow stood inside a third bomb shelter, made of tile walls about a foot thick.

After a minute, the private came back in with a bared machete at his side and a field radio on his back. "Where's your husband, huh?" he asked again. This time, the woman gave a long answer in a complaining tone, in which she pointed several times at the sky and several times at her children. The soldier looked at her blankly. "What do I do with her?" he called to some fellow-soldiers outside. There was no answer. Turning back to the young woman, who had not moved since his first entrance, he said, "O.K., lady, you stay here," and left the house.

Several other houses were searched, but no other Vietnamese were found, and for twenty minutes the men on that particular stretch of road encountered no one else, although they heard sporadic machine-gun fire down the road. The sky, which had been overcast, began to show streaks of blue, and a light wind stirred the trees. The bombing, the machine-gunning from helicopters, the shelling, and the rocket firing continued steadily. Suddenly a Vietnamese man on a bicycle appeared, pedalling rapidly along the road from the direction of the village. He was wearing the collarless, pajamalike black garment that is both the customary dress of the Vietnamese peasant and the uniform of the National Liberation Front, and although he was riding away from the center of the village—a move forbidden by the voices from the helicopters—he had, it appeared, already run a long gantlet of American soldiers without being stopped. But when he had ridden about twenty yards past the point where he first came in sight, there was a burst of machine-gun fire from a copse thirty yards in front of him, joined immediately by a burst from a vegetable field to one side, and he was hurled off his bicycle into a ditch a yard from the road. The bicycle crashed into a side embankment. The man with the Minolta camera, who had done the firing from the vegetable patch, stood up after about a minute and walked over to the ditch, followed by one of the engineers. The Vietnamese in the ditch appeared to be about twenty, and he lay on his side without moving, blood flowing from his face, which, with the eyes open, was half buried in the dirt at the bottom of the ditch. The engineer leaned down, felt the man's wrist, and said, "He's dead." The two men—both companions of mine on No. 47—stood still for a while, with folded arms, and stared down at the dead man's face, as though they were giving him a chance to say something. Then the engineer said, with a tone of finality, "That's a V.C. for you. He's a V.C., all right. That's what they wear. He was leaving town. He had to have some reason."

The two men walked back to a ridge in the vegetable field and sat down on it, looking off into the distance in a puzzled way and no longer bothering to keep low. The man who had fired spoke suddenly, as though coming out of deep thought. "I saw this guy coming down the road on a bicycle," he said. "And I thought, you know, Is this it? Do I shoot? Then some guy over there in the bushes opened up, so I cut loose."

The engineer raised his eyes in the manner of someone who has made a strange discovery and said, "I'm not worried. You know, that's the first time I've ever seen a dead guy, and I don't feel bad. I just don't, that's all." Then, with a hard edge of defiance in his voice, he added, "Actually, I'm glad. I'm glad we killed the little V.C."

THE VILLAGE OF BEN SUC || 29

Over near the copse, the man who had fired first, also a young soldier, had turned his back to the road. Clenching a cigar in his teeth, he stared with determination over his gun barrel across the wide field, where several water buffaloes were grazing but no human beings had yet been seen. Upon being asked what had happened, he said, "Yeah, he's dead. Ah shot him. He was a fuckin' V.C."

Quang Ngai & Quang Tin

The New Yorker, MARCH 6–MARCH 9, 1968

WHEN I ATTEMPTED to find a record of what the Marines had done in Quang Ngai during their two years of operation before Task Force Oregon arrived, I met with very little success. The Information Officers of the units in Task Force Oregon were unable to name any operations that had been conducted by the Marines, and they did not possess any record of casualties, enemy or friendly. Several times, in August, while I was flying over areas where the remnants of fields, forests, and villages were densely pockmarked with half-overgrown craters from the days of Marine operations, I asked the Forward Air Control pilots what operations had been launched in the areas, but they were unable to tell me when, or why, the areas had been bombed.

I met one man who had worked as a Psychological Warfare Officer with the Marines when they first arrived in Duc Pho. He said that for the first month they had been unable to travel five hundred yards beyond their camp without running into heavy enemy fire. After receiving reinforcements, they had moved out farther but had still been unable to penetrate many areas. When the Marines had developed a system in which they took reprisals against the rural people by bombing villages that were thought to be giving support to the National Liberation Front, Leaflet No. 244-286-67 announced this system to the villagers. Its title is listed in a catalogue of Psychological Warfare leaflets used by the Marines and by Task Force Oregon in Quang Ngai as "Marine Ultimatum to Vietnamese People," and its target is listed as "Civilian Population." The text of the leaflet, like that of all such leaflets, is printed, of course, in Vietnamese. On one side there are two cartoon drawings. The first shows several soldiers of the Vietcong setting up a mortar position near a thatch-roofed house while another soldier leans out of a window firing an automatic weapon. A woman holding a child by the hand stands next to the house. Under the picture, a caption reads, "If the Vietcong do this . . ." The second picture shows an Air Force jet pulling out of its dive over the house. An explosion in front of the house has thrown the soldiers and the woman and her child to the ground, and the house is aflame. In the foreground, a man lies on the earth, clutching his chest. Streams of blood flow from his eyes, nostrils, mouth, and ears. The rest of the pamphlet is in black and white, but this blood is printed in red ink. The second caption, completing the unfinished sentence of the first, reads, ". . . your village will look like this." On the other side is a text reading:

DEAR CITIZENS:

The U.S. Marines are fighting alongside the Government of Vietnam forces in Duc Pho in order to give the Vietnamese people a chance to live a free, happy life, without fear of hunger and suffering. But many Vietnamese have paid with their lives and their homes have been destroyed because they helped the Vietcong in an attempt to enslave the Vietnamese people. Many hamlets have been destroyed because these villages harbored the Vietcong.

The hamlets of Hai Mon, Hai Tan, Sa Binh, Tan Binh, and

many others have been destroyed because of this. We will not hesitate to destroy every hamlet that helps the Vietcong, who are powerless to stop the combined might the G.V.N. and its allies.

The U.S. Marines issue this warning: THE U.S. MARINES WILL NOT HESITATE TO DESTROY IMMEDIATELY, ANY VILLAGE OR HAMLET HARBORING THE VIETCONG. WE WILL NOT HESITATE TO DESTROY, IMMEDIATELY, ANY VILLAGE OR HAMLET USED AS A VIETCONG STRONGHOLD TO FIRE AT OUR TROOPS OR AIRCRAFT.

The choice is yours. If you refuse to let the Vietcong use your villages and hamlets as their battlefield, your homes and your lives will be saved.

Peaceful citizens, stay in your homes. Deny your support to the V.C.s.

After a reprisal bombing had been carried out against a village, the Marines sometimes showered it with Leaflet No. 244-068-68. Its title is listed as "Your Village Has Been Bombed," and its target, again, as "Civilian Population." The second picture on the leaflet entitled "Marine Ultimatum to Vietnamese People," which shows the house aflame and the people dead, occupies one whole side of this leaflet. The caption reads, "the vietcong caused this to happen!" On the other side, the text reads:

ATTENTION VILLAGERS:
1.—YOUR VILLAGE WAS BOMBED BECAUSE YOU HARBORED VIET-CONG IN YOUR VILLAGE.
2.—YOUR VILLAGE WAS BOMBED BECAUSE YOU GAVE HELP TO THE VIETCONG IN YOUR AREA.
3.—YOUR VILLAGE WAS BOMBED BECAUSE YOU GAVE FOOD TO THE VIETCONG.

4.—WE WARNED YOU ABOUT THE BOMBINGS BECAUSE WE DID NOT WANT TO HURT INNOCENT VILLAGERS.

5.—YOUR HOMES ARE DAMAGED OR DESTROYED BECAUSE OF THE VIETCONG.

6.—YOUR VILLAGE WILL BE BOMBED AGAIN IF YOU HARBOR THE VIETCONG IN ANY WAY.

7.—YOU CAN PROTECT YOUR HOMES BY COOPERATING WITH THE G.V.N. AND THE ALLIED FORCES.

8.—TELL THE G.V.N. AND THE ALLIED FORCES WHERE THE VIETCONG ARE, SO THEY CAN PROTECT YOU.

9.—THE G.V.N. AND THE ALLIED FORCES WILL DRIVE THE VIETCONG AWAY FROM YOUR VILLAGES.

10.—THE G.V.N. AND THE ALLIED FORCES WILL HELP YOU TO LIVE IN PEACE AND TO HAVE A HAPPY AND PROSPEROUS LIFE.

* * *

On August 19th, I flew in a "bubble," or OH-23, helicopter over the northern twenty kilometres of the coast of Duc Pho and Mo Duc Districts, and had a chance to view at firsthand the areas I had seen on the Duc Pho artillery maps and had been discussing with the men of the 3rd of the 4th for the last several days. The OH-23 seats two people inside a clear-plastic bubble that affords a view in all directions except through a small steel plate underfoot and through the seat backs. The engine sits, uncovered, directly behind the bubble, and supports the long rotor blades on a metal shaft; behind the engine a thin, sticklike tail supports a small rear rotor. The machine rests on narrow metal runners. Originally, the Army had brought the OH-23 to Vietnam strictly for reconnaissance flights, but the 3rd of the 4th had converted it into a gunship by dangling an automatic weapon by a piece of wire in the open doorway on one side of the bubble. The OH-23 pilots, who were Army men, went out daily over the destroyed, but still inhabited, areas on what they called "squirrel-hunting missions," to find the enemy and either kill them with the dangling machine gun or call for artillery fire. They informed me that in the course of three months their body count had reached fifty-two, which was more than the larger Huey gunships of the 3rd of the 4th could claim for that period. "The Huey has to start its run on a target from much farther away than we do, and has to pull off sooner, and it can't fly low at all," a young pilot told me while I was talking with a group of OH-23 pilots.

I asked whether they considered everybody who remained in the destroyed areas to be one of the enemy.

"They've had a chance to get out," the pilots' commanding officer answered. "But they're not *all* V.C., I guess. Sometimes they just go back to their fields. But anyone of military age is a pretty sure bet as a V.C. It's definitely a V.C.-controlled area. We've got shot at in that area ever since we got here. A lot of times, you see a guy taking a shot at you and a woman and kid are standing right nearby. I used to hesitate to call artillery strikes on them, but I'm getting over that now."

The purpose of the flight I went on was only to convey me from the Duc Pho base to the city of Quang Ngai, but the pilot offered to take me on a detour over the areas where he and his fellow-pilots hunted the enemy. Since there was go gunner aboard, it would not be possible to fire on anyone the pilot might identify as a Vietcong soldier during our flight. We left shortly after five o'clock—about half an hour before sunset. Flying in the bubble gives one an entirely different sensation from flying in any other aircraft. In contrast to the Huey helicopter, a ten-passenger craft that takes off and lands slowly and hesitantly, like a boat leaving or approaching a pier, the bubble seems to leap effortlessly into the air, like an elevator in a modern office building. Aloft, you find that as you face forward or to either side no part of the helicopter is visible except the control panel at the front, the tiny floor, and the edge of your seat, which sticks out several inches beyond the edge of the floor. Most helicopters fly over the landscape, above the treetops and house roofs, but the bubble flies *within* the landscape—often among the trees and level with the houses, when they are not too close together. Above rice fields, it easily skims along at an altitude of six or eight feet. Flying in this tiny, agile craft, with all the machinery out of sight behind you, you feel a tremendous freedom to go wherever you please—as though you could alight on a tree branch, like a bird, or fly right in at the door of someone's house and then out through a window.

As we flew east toward the coast, I saw that the destroyed area began on the outskirts of the base. Tracks made by tanks, bulldozers, and armored personnel-carriers crisscrossed the red-earth foundations of the houses; not even the ruins were left standing. We soon passed beyond these former villages and arrived over a wide belt of rice fields lying between Route 1 and the coast. The fields were covered with craters but were still cultivated; people wearing the loose black garment of the Vietnamese peasant were bent over at work in the rows of rice. The fields were littered with scraps of paper, which covered the field divides and had sunk into the shallow water between them. The pilot explained that these were Psychological Warfare leaflets. (An average of a million leaflets were being dropped on Quang Ngai Province every day.) We crossed a tree line at the eastern edge of the rice fields and entered an area where the homes of between twenty and thirty thousand people had been loosely grouped in villages along a coastal strip that was about twenty kilometres long and four kilometres wide. The houses along this strip had been destroyed almost without exception. In the coastal area of Duc Pho District, approximately two-thirds of the houses had clay-and-bamboo walls with thatched roofs, and the rest had stone walls with red tile roofs. Where soldiers had set fire to a house on the ground, the back-yard garden and fence, the well, the hedge, the stone gateposts, and the surrounding palm glade or bamboo grove remained standing, but the house that had provided a focus for this setting, and had received the shade of the trees, was missing; only a square of ashes and debris remained on the foundation. In places where the villages had been shelled, bombed, or strafed, the destruction had not been so selective. "General-purpose" bombs had sent out hails of steel fragments and shock waves, and, near their craters, the upward force of the blasts had torn off the leafy tops of the palm trees, leaving only the trunks standing, with their shattered tips pointing at the sky. Shrapnel had cut down many trees halfway up their trunks, or lopped off their branches, or, in places, thrown whole trees fifty or a hundred yards into adjacent fields. In places where napalm had been used, the yards and fields were blackened and leafless in large splotches. Many artillery and bomb craters were partly filled with leaflets that had been carried across the fields by winds. It did not appear that the destruction had been carried out systematically. The ruins of most of the villages displayed the marks of many methods of destruction. Knowing that the artillery often simply "covered" large areas several kilometres on a side with harassment-and-interdiction fire over a period of days, I found the senseless-looking pattern of craters-dotting the open fields as well as the tree lines and the villages—more understandable. Tanks and armored personnel-carriers had cut their own roads through the landscape. Apparently, the drivers had chosen to travel through the fields rather than use the existing roads, which were likely to be mined.

The families who had returned from the camps, or had just stayed on in the area, lived underground. The dark mouths of their caves dotted the tree lines of the back yards. As we flew overhead, whole families sitting in the yards of destroyed houses tilted their heads up and froze in position to watch us out of sight. It was nearly six o'clock now, and many families were crouching around fires, cooking their dinners. Pots, bedding, and a few pieces of furniture lay out in the yards. In some places, the spindly frames of tiny huts had appeared. Everywhere there were mounds of hay about three feet high, and I later found out that these were small, wall-less individual sleeping shelters consisting of straw thatching mounted on sticks. Some people had built their straw shelters out in the center of the fields, away from trees and bunkers—perhaps because they knew that our Army, believing all bunkers and caves to have been constructed by the Vietcong as fortifications, treated them as prime military targets. Firewood, most of it beams from the destroyed houses, lay about in piles. Children played in the dust, and generally there were far more children, women, and old people in sight than men. Small boys were riding in from the fields on the backs of water buffalo. The pilot noticed artillery shells sending up puffs of whitish smoke in several spots near one edge of these fields, and took care to skirt the area by about a kilometre. The people below continued to work outside their shelters and did not show any sign of noticing the artillery shells that were exploding nearby. The pilot flew the bubble out over the rice fields, and we raced across them at a height of fifteen feet. He pointed out a few scraps of twisted metal and machinery lying in a scorched circle in one of the fields and said that his helicopter had been shot down there a month before. He and his gunner had landed without injury. Once they were on the ground, guerrillas had shot at them from a tree line, and they had fired back. Fifteen minutes later, they had been rescued by another helicopter. A minute or so after he'd pointed out the spot where he crashed, he performed one of the bubble's many aerial stunts. He raced toward the tree line and then, when it seemed that we would crash into the trees, suddenly brought the helicopter sharply upward and arrested its forward motion, so that it rolled up over the trees and house ruins and came to a stop in the air as though it had been caught head on by a blast of wind. As we floated slowly just above the half-destroyed trees, the pilot exclaimed, "Look! There's one!" In a rising tone of tense excitement, he continued, "See? See? He's hiding!" I looked down and saw a youth crouching on a path next to a line of trees. The pilot wheeled the bubble and headed it back toward the youth, who then stood up and began to chop at a log with an axe. "See? Now he's pretending to be working!" the pilot said. An instant later, he cried out, "Look! There's another. She's hiding! See how she's hiding?" I looked down and saw that as our bubble drifted in a slow arc a woman in black edged carefully around a thin tree, always keeping on the opposite side of the trunk from the bubble.

We flew inland to the other side of Route 1, where the villages had also been destroyed. Rushing low across the darkening landscape, we passed over a field of tall grass, and the pilot said, "I killed four there. They ran for a bunker, but they didn't make it." We came to a destroyed village that had stood in the shade of rows of trees. A line of smoke rose from an orange dot of flame in a thicket, and the pilot said, "There's a V.C. havin' his supper. There shouldn't be anyone down there. He shouldn't be there." We began to fly a meandering seaward course down the Song Ve, which marked the boundary between the 3rd of the 4th's Area of Responsibility and the South Vietnamese Army's Tactical Area of Responsibility. A naked boy stood washing a smaller naked boy in a broad bend of the river, which was clear, with a sandy bottom. The two froze and watched as our helicopter passed over them. The spans of two bridges lay twisted in the river. On the south bank, where the 3rd of the 4th had been operating, piles of bricks and ashes and skeletons of blackened poles stood on the foundations of houses, and the fields were brown or black, or had gone wild, but on the north bank, where the South Vietnamese Army had been operating, the trees and fields were full and green—it might have been a different season there—and the houses remained standing, next to their vegetable gardens, yards, and palm trees. As we returned toward Route 1, we crossed over to the north bank. Smoke from supper fires rose from dark courtyards. People carrying loads on shoulder poles walked homeward down the sides of the road, and girls glided down other roads on bicycles. When the pilot set me down on a small helicopter pad within the American Advisory compound on the edge of Quang Ngai City, night had fallen. Inside the compound, all was American, and there was nothing to indicate that I had not magically been set down within the United States itself.

The buildings of the compound were of white clapboard, and neatly ordered, and the busy sound of conversation floated out of a brightly lit dining hall, where food was being served buffet style. Soldiers and civilian advisers with fresh shirts and neatly combed hair laughed and chatted as they entered an air-conditioned movie theatre. I went into the officers' bar and sat down next to a table of officers who were singing as they drank. Their voices were loud and unrestrained, and they banged their glasses on the table to keep time. The lyrics of one of the songs—a song that was apparently meant, in part, to ridicule the idea that civilians are unnecessarily killed by our air strikes, and one that I was to hear again, in many variations, during my stay in Quang Ngai—went:

> *Bomb the schools and churches.*
> *Bomb the rice fields, too.*
> *Show the children in the courtyards*
> *What napalm can do.*

On August 13, 1967, two days after Operation Hood River came to an end, Task Force Oregon launched Operation Benton. In Quang Ngai Province I had seen the results of the American bombing, shelling, and ground activity but, for the most part, I had not seen the destruction take place. Now I was about to observe in detail the process of destruction as it unfolded in Operation Benton, in which Task Force Oregon went over the northern border of Quang Ngai into Quang Tin Province. I spent several days flying in FAC planes attached to the 1st Brigade of the 101st Airborne. On August 12th, I flew over the area where Operation Benton was to be carried out. This was a three-hour reconnaissance mission, with a pilot whom I will call Major Ingersol. Major Ingersol was a few years older than the other pilots, and he was more reserved. At the FAC pilots' quarters on the base at Chu Lai, he often read paperback mysteries or other novels while the rest of the pilots joked together. When he did enter into the conversation, he ordinarily spoke in serious, measured tones, which did not quite fit in with the usual light banter. Once, when the other pilots were sitting around drinking and discussing the figures of Thai bar girls, his contribution to the conversation was "I've heard that there are some exquisite restaurants in Bangkok." Another time, while chatting with a captain in the FAC central control room, he expressed a keen appreciation of the natural beauty of Quang Ngai. "It's a lovely countryside," he said. "One of my favorite activities is following waterfalls up through the valleys. It's a shame we have to destroy it."

While Major Ingersol and I were flying to the area of the new operation, he described to me his method of distinguishing Vietcong soldiers from the rest of the population. "You know that they are V.C.s if they shoot at you or if you see them carrying a weapon. Those are about the only two ways," he said. In the matter of trails through the woods, he had subtler criteria. As we passed over the flank of a tall mountain, he pointed out a trail, almost as wide as a small road, that ran up the mountainside from the valley. The trees were tall and dense, and the path was visible as an occasional gap in the jungle foliage. About halfway up the mountain, this large, clearly distinguishable trail began to get narrower. For a stretch, it apparently continued under the dense foliage, because farther up the mountain it became visible once again, but then it was lost to sight altogether, "This is the kind of thing we look for," Major Ingersol said. "See how that trail disappears up there? That indicates to us that there is probably a base camp up there. These trails that go up into the mountains and disappear are often V.C. trails. Also, we look to see if the trails have been freshly used."

I remarked that from fifteen hundred feet it must be very difficult to tell whether a trail that was mostly covered by dense jungle foliage had been used recently.

"Even then you can tell," Major Ingersol said. "You see, the V.C. use water buffalo and other large animals to carry their equipment around, and they leave marks. These trails often get hit by artillery fire at night." As we flew over a thirty-foot-wide crater that had eliminated one section of a footpath, Major Ingersol commented, "Now look down there. See how someone has built the trail *around* the crater? This is the kind of sign you look for." He said that he also looked for bunkers to recommend as bombing targets. And, as still another example of the kind of suspicious sign he looked for on his reconnaissance missions, he told me that in one small field high in the mountains there was a small herd of water buffalo that disappeared from sight every few days. "We speculate that the V.C. use those water buffalo to carry things," he said.

* * *

Early the next morning, Operation Benton was launched in the area I had just flown over with Major Ingersol. The men of the 1st Brigade of the 101st Airborne Division were beginning their fifth consecutive week in the field. On the evening of the twelfth, the FAC pilots for the 1st of the 101st had only one drink each before dinner and did not drink at all after dinner. During a final planning session at quarters that evening, the lower officers called their superiors "sir" regularly, for the first time in the two days I had spent with them. Their mission for the next day was to guide air strikes onto the four initial landing zones, or L.Z.s, for helicopters bearing the troops into the area. These air strikes were a general practice, and were termed "L.Z. preps." Just before the troops were landed, the landing zones were "hosed down" with machine-gun and rocket fire from helicopters.

During the first two days of the operation, the back seat of every FAC plane that went up was occupied by an artillery observer, so I was unable to fly, but in the evenings the FAC pilots told me something of what they had seen. They said that, at the last minute before the L.Z. preps were to start, one flight of planes had been cancelled, owing to mechanical failure, so one landing zone had received only the machine-gun and rocket fire from helicopters. At a second landing zone, the L.Z. prep had been applied to a plot of high fields, according to plan, but the troops had mistakenly landed a kilometre away, on a hilltop that had not been blown up for them in advance. Meanwhile, seven or eight kilometres away, at an artillery battery that was to give support to the L.Z. preps and to the operation itself as it got under way, a helicopter had crashed into an ammunition truck, setting off the ammunition and blowing up the battery and inflicting several casualties, so no further artillery support could be given to any of the landing zones from that position. The installation of the command post for the operation, on top of a small mountain just north of the

Song Tien at the point where it starts to bend north, had gone smoothly at first, but then a fire had broken out on the landing zone. (According to the FAC pilots, the air strikes they directed never started fires. It was the helicopters, they maintained, that started the fires, with their machine guns and their rockets.) When more than a hundred men, several artillery pieces, and several crates of ammunition had been landed, the fire had got out of control. Artillery shells had begun to explode in the flames, and the troops had evacuated the spot and set up a camp on a nearby hilltop, temporarily leaving several damaged artillery pieces and mortars behind. The men and equipment of the command post itself had been removed by helicopter to the top of a mountain about five kilometres to the east. Artillery shells had continued to explode sporadically on the flaming hilltop of the old command post for several hours. Over the next two days, seven more landings were completed without serious accident.

* * *

On the second day, the 1st of the 101st began to spread out into the countryside in small units; several of them met heavy resistance from the enemy and suffered casualties. That night, the FAC pilots said that the unit ground commanders had called for an unusually large number of air strikes throughout the area of operation. The pilots described the targets to each other in terms of topographical features, or by coordinates on their maps, because they did not know the names of any of the towns or rivers in the area. One FAC pilot remarked that the units involved in Operation Benton must be "really kill-hungry," for three of the companies had chosen as code designations for themselves the names Cutthroat, Marauder, and Assassin.

On the morning of the third day of Operation Benton, I flew over the 1st of the 101st's area of operation with Major Billings, whom I had flown with during Operation Hood River. I saw that, except for two or three houses, the village of Duc Tan, which had stood below the evacuated command post, had been destroyed. Some groups of houses in Duc Tan had been completely annihilated by bombs; the only traces of their former existence were their wells or back gardens. Other houses had been burned to the ground by napalm. Most of the fields around the destroyed village had been eliminated by the deep craters of delayed-fuse bombs or else had been covered with debris. More craters were scattered across other fields in the Chop Vum area and across mountainsides, and the gray squares of freshly burned individual houses dotted most of the landscape. Major Billings told me that these houses had been burned by phosphorus rockets fired from helicopter "gunship" patrols. A few minutes later, I watched a gunship cruise low over the landscape. It wheeled suddenly and fired several phosphorus rockets into a group of three houses that stood in a clump of palms. White smoke puffed up, and the houses burst into flames. The helicopter circled and then charged the houses again, firing more rockets into the fields and gardens. Several hilltops and small mountains that had been green and wooded when I saw them three days earlier were burned black by napalm. Fresh artillery craters were spattered over the fields around the landing zones. At that point, approximately twenty per cent of the houses in the Chop Vum area had been destroyed.

Major Billings had been assigned to guide a "preplanned strike," but before he could locate the target on the ground a ground commander called for an "immediate" strike, which meant a strike carried out a few hours, at most, after it was requested, whether by a ground commander or by a FAC pilot. "We picked up some sniper fire earlier this morning from a couple of hootches down below us, at about 384 297, and we'd like you to hit it for us," the ground commander said. Major Billings flew over the hundred-metre square described by the coordinates, and found that it included the two large stone churches along the road, in the village of Thanh Phuoc. The ground commander was in charge of a hilltop landing zone that was a little over half a kilometre from the churches. When he had received the sniper fire, he had apparently scanned the horizon, noticed the two church steeples, which were the only buildings that stuck up above the lines of trees, and decided that the snipers were firing from the churches. In front of one church, a white flag flew from the top of a pole as high as the church itself.

"Let's have a look and see what's down there," said Major Billings. He took our plane on a low pass over the churches. The churches were surrounded by twenty or thirty houses. About half of these had stone walls and red tile roofs. The others had clay-and-bamboo walls and thatched roofs. One thatch-roofed building was perhaps fifty feet long and thirty feet wide, and appeared to be some sort of gathering place. Flower gardens were in bloom in front of both churches. Behind both, plots of vegetables stretched back through glades of palm trees to rice fields. After climbing to fifteen hundred feet again, Major Billings got into contact with the ground commander and said, "Two of those structures seem to be structures of worship. Do you want them taken out?"

"Roger," the ground commander replied.

"There seems to be a white flag out front there," Major Billings said.

"Yeah. Beats me what it means," the ground commander replied.

An hour later, three F-4 fighter-bombers reached the target area, and the flight commander radioed to Major Billings—who had spent the time trying to spot suspicious activities—to say that they were prepared to strike with seven-hundred-and-fifty-pound bombs, rockets, and 20-mm.-cannon strafing fire.

"We can use all that good stuff," said Major Billings.

"What kind of a target is it?" asked the flight commander.

"They're military structures. You can tell by how they look that they're military structures," Major Billings answered. Just then a fleet of ten helicopters moving in tight formation arrived at the hilltop landing zone. Major Billings went on to say that he would have to wait until the helicopters left before he gave clearance to bomb.

I asked him whether he thought it was necessary to bomb the churches.

"Well, if the V.C. don't care and just go in there and use the place to fire on our troops, then we've got to wipe it out," Major Billings said. "And the V.C.—the V.C. are *the first ones to blow up a church.* They go after the churches on purpose, because the churches won't always go along with what the V.C. are doing. *They* don't care at all about blowing up a church and killing innocent civilians."

As the helicopters rose from the hilltop, Major Billings said to the flight commander, "Believe it or not, two of those big buildings down there are churches. I'll check with the ground commander again to see if he wants them taken out."

"No kidding!" said the flight commander.

"Say, do you want those two churches hit down there?" Major Billings asked the ground commander.

"That's affirmative," the ground commander replied.

"O.K., here goes," said the major. Then, addressing the F-4 pilots, he said, "Make your passes from south to north. I'll circle over here to the west."

The major brought the O-1 into a dive, aiming its nose at the village, and fired a phosphorus rocket. Its white smoke rose from a patch of trees fifty yards to the south of one church. "Do you see my smoke?" he asked the flight commander.

"Yeah, I got you," the flight commander said. "I'll make a dry run and then come in with the seven-hundred-and-fifty-pounders."

A minute later, an F-4 appeared from the south, diving low over the churches in a practice run. As it pulled out of its dive, it cut eastward and began to circle back for the next pass. A second F-4 made its dive in the same way, and released its bombs. A tall cloud of brown smoke rolled up from the vegetable garden in back of one of the churches.

"That's about a hundred metres off," Major Billings said. "See if you can move it forward."

"O.K. Sorry," the flight commander said.

The third plane also sent its bombs into the vegetable garden. The first plane, on its second pass, sent its bombs into rice fields about sixty yards to one side of the churches. Three pillars of brown smoke now rose several hundred feet in the air, dwarfing the churches and the houses. On the second plane's second pass, a bomb hit the back of one church directly—the church with the white flag on the pole in front.

"Oh, that's nice, baby, real nice," Major Billings said. "You're layin' those goodies right in there!"

When the smoke cleared, the church was gone except for its façade, which stood by itself, with its cross on top. The white flag still flew from its pole. The third plane sent its bombs into the rice fields to the side. The first plane fired rockets on its third pass, and they landed in the vegetable garden behind the destroyed church, leaving it smoking with dozens of small brown puffs. Several of the rockets from the next volley hit the other church, obliterating its back half and leaving two holes the size of doors in the roof of the front half. Four or five of the houses around the church burst into flame.

"That's real fine!" said Major Billings.

"Where do you want the twenty mike-mike?" asked the flight commander. ("Twenty mike-mike" is military slang for 20-mm.-cannon
strafing fire, which fires a hundred explosive shells per second.)

"Lay it right down that line you've been hitting," Major Billings
said. "Put it right down across those hootches, and we'll see if we can
start a few fires." (Strafing rounds often set houses on fire, whereas
bombs rarely do.)

As one of the F-4s made the first strafing run, the path of fire cut
directly through the group of houses around the churches, sparkling
for a fraction of a second with hundreds of brilliant flashes.

"Goody, goody! That's right down the line!" exclaimed Major
Billings. "Why don't you just get those hootches by the other church,
across the road, now?"

"Roger," answered the flight commander.

On the second strafing pass, the flashing path of shells cut across
the group of houses on the other side of the road.

"Real fine!" Major Billings said. "Now how about getting that
hootch down the road a bit?" He was referring to a tile-roofed house
that stood in a field about a hundred yards to the west of one church.
The path of fire from the third strafing pass—the final pass of the
strike—cut directly across the house, opening several large holes in
its roof.

"Right down the line!" Major Billings said. "Thanks, boys. You
did a real fine job. I'm going to give you ninety-per-cent Target
Coverage."

"Did I get any K.B.A.S?" the flight commander asked. (The
number of killings credited to each pilot is not kept as an official sta-
tistic, but most pilots try to keep track of their K.B.A.S informally.)

Major Billings, who told me he had not seen any people in the area, either before or during the strike, answered, "I don't know—you'll have to wait until ground troops go in there sometime. But I'd say there were about four."

As the two men were talking, perhaps a dozen houses in the strafed area began to burn. First, the flames ate holes in the roofs, and then they quickly spread to the walls, turning each house into a ball of flame. Most of the houses burned to the ground within a few minutes, leaving columns of black smoke rising from the ruins.

Major Billings called Chu Lai to give his Bomb Damage Assessment Report. "There were two Permanent Military Structures Destroyed, ten Military Structures Destroyed, and five Damaged," he said.

I asked him whether he considered the houses and the churches military structures.

"Oh, that's just what we call them," he replied.

A few minutes later, the ground commander on the hilltop got in touch with Major Billings to request another immediate strike. "There's a row of bunkers down below our hill here, along a tree line, and we've seen the V.C.s down there," the ground commander said. "We see their heads poppin' in and out. We'd like to get an air strike put in down there."

Major Billings flew over the spot the ground commander had indicated, and found a line of trees about half a kilometre from the hill. The dark openings of several bunkers showed on the near side, and a row of several houses was standing on the far side.

"I've got you," Major Billings said. "Do you want us to put 'em in along that tree line down there? There are a couple of hootches down there, too."

"Affirmative. We've been getting trouble from that whole general area down there."

"O.K.," said Major Billings wearily, pronouncing the first syllable long and high, and the second low. "We'll do that as soon as the fighters come in."

Three F-4s arrived in the area twenty minutes later, and the flight commander announced that they were carrying napalm and thousand-pound bombs, which are the largest normally used in South Vietnam.

The first bombs of the strike landed about a hundred metres off target. One bomb turned an entire rice field into a crater about thirty-five feet across and six feet deep, and splashed mud over the surrounding fields. The next two bombs annihilated two houses with direct hits. Two more bombs landed next to the tree line, breaking most of the trees in half and hurling one palm tree fifty or sixty metres into a field.

"O.K., you got that tree line real good," Major Billings said. "Now let's get some of those hootches to the south of it with the napes." He directed the pilots to a group of a dozen houses that stood about forty yards from the tree line. The first canister landed beside two houses, which were instantly engulfed in napalm. When the smoke cleared, only the broken, blackened frames of the houses remained in the intense blaze, which continued after the houses were burned to the ground, because the napalm itself had not yet finished burning.

"Beautiful!" cried Major Billings. "You guys are right on target today!"

The next canister did not land directly on any of the houses, but it landed close enough to splash napalm over four of them, and these houses immediately burned down.

With the strike completed, Major Billings told the fighter-bomber pilots, "I'm giving you a hundred-percent Target Coverage. Thank you very much. It's been a pleasure to work with you. See you another day."

"Thank *you,*" the flight commander answered.

Major Billings' three hours of flying time were up, and he turned the plane toward Chu Lai. Fifteen minutes later, we landed.

After we had taxied to a halt at the fuel pump, a young mechanic asked, "How'd it go, Major? Did you get some of 'em today?" He spoke with a nonchalance that failed to disguise his intense interest in getting an answer.

Instead of just replying "I dunno," or "Real fine," as he and the other pilots usually did, Major Billings burst out "We bombed two churches!" and gave a laugh that seemed to register his own surprise and wonderment at the act.

That afternoon, back at the FAC pilots' quarters, Major Billings, scratching his head and staring into the faces of the other pilots, exclaimed, again with a laugh, "I put in a strike on two churches!"

"No kidding," said one.

"They had a white flag in front of them. That damn white flag is still standing," the major said.

"Yeah, I saw the white flag when I was out today," Lieutenant Moore said. "We'll have to get that white flag. It's a matter of *principle.*"

The conversation turned to the subject of accidental bombings, and Major Billings, who had been a bomber pilot in both the Second World War and the Korean War, told of an ill-conceived bombing run he had once made over North Korea. "There was a big building right in the center of a town, and they told me it was a real important military headquarters," he said. "The target was so important that they sent two reconnaissance planes to guide me right to it. I laid my stuff all over it. About three days later, I found out that the place was really a school, and about a hundred children had been killed. They weren't going to tell me about the mistake, but I found out."

A man I have called Major Nugent said, "In early '65, there was a pilot who accidentally bombed an orphanage and killed a lot of kids. When he found out about it, he was so shook up that he voluntarily grounded himself for good. He said that he'd never fly again."

"That's the way you feel when something like that happens," said a man I have called Captain Reese, whom I'd also flown with during Operation Hood River.

"No—I mean, you can't let it get to you, or you couldn't go on," Major Billings objected. "It gets completely impersonal. After you've done it for a while, you forget that there are people down there."

"Yeah, everything looks so calm up where we are," Major Nugent said. "We can't even tell when we're getting shot at. We forget what's going on down on the ground. It's the guys on the ground—the ground troops—that really have it rough. They really know what's happening."

The extreme solemnity that had descended on the group seemed suddenly to generate an opposite impulse of hilarity, and small, irrepressible smiles began to appear on the pilots' faces.

Captain Reese turned to me and asked if I had ever heard the songs about the war that they occasionally sang.

I said that I had heard one such song.

"Shall we tell him?" he asked the other pilots. They all looked at each other, and before anyone could answer, Captain Reese sang rapidly:

Strafe the town and kill the people,
Drop napalm in the square,
Get out early every Sunday
And catch them at their morning prayer.

Major Billings then recited the words of another song:

Throw candy to the ARVN,
Gather them all around,
Take your twenty mike-mike
And mow the bastards down.

At dinner in the Marine dining hall that evening, after a few drinks, the pilots began to make jokes in which they ridiculed the idea that the bombings they guided were unnecessarily brutal by inventing remarks that might be made by men so bloodthirsty that they took delight in intentionally killing innocents. The joke-tellers appeared to bring out their remarks with considerable uneasiness and embarrassment, and some of the pilots appeared to laugh unduly long in response, as though to reassure the tellers. All the jokes seemed to deal, indirectly, with the conflicts of conscience that had arisen in the conversation at the pilots' quarters during the afternoon.

When the main course was nearly finished, Major Nugent asked Captain Reese, "Git any woman and children today?"

"Yeah, but I let a pregnant woman get away," Captain Reese answered.

Lieutenant Moore's heavy-browed, serious, wooden face began to reflect a struggle between his usual gravity and a rebellious smile. "When we kill a pregnant woman, we count it as two V.C.—one soldier and one cadet," he said.

Everyone laughed loudly.

"Bruce got a bunch of kids playing marbles," said Major Nugent.

The group laughed again.

"I got an old lady in a wheelchair," Lieutenant Moore said, and there was more laughter.

"You know, when I flew over Japan, *anything* was fair game," Major Billings said. "They really were merciless, and they shot at everything. I remember I once saw an old guy riding a bicycle down the road, and I came up behind him, putting my fire in the road. The guy's feet started going faster and faster on the pedals, and just before my fire caught up with him you would never believe how fast the old bugger's feet were flying!"

The idea that civilians were often killed in the bombings they guided rarely arose in the pilots' conversation, and now that it had come up—if only to be debunked—the pilots made their jokes in the casual, familiar tone that marked most of their conversations. Yet the laugh that followed Major Billings' story erupted with a sudden force that seemed to take the men themselves by surprise. I sensed that their laughter eased a tension that had been building up during the session of jokes—eased it, perhaps, because this usually straightforward, informal group of men had found it a strain to have a largely undiscussed subject standing between them. Lieutenant Moore was so severely racked with laughter that he could not swallow a mouthful of food, and for several seconds he was convulsed silently and had to bend his head low with his hands over his mouth. Tears came to his eyes and to Major Nugent's.

"Oh, my!" Lieutenant Moore sighed, exhausted by all the laughing. Then he said, "I didn't kill that woman in the wheelchair, but she sure bled good!"

Nobody laughed at this joke. A silence ensued. Finally, Captain Reese suggested that they find out what movies were playing on the base that night.

THE NUCLEAR DILEMMA | II

The Fate of the Earth

The New Yorker, FEBRUARY 1–FEBRUARY 15, 1982

THE YARDSTICKS BY which one can measure the destruction that will be caused by weapons of different sizes are provided by the bombings of Hiroshima and Nagasaki and American nuclear tests in which the effects of hydrogen bombs with up to sixteen hundred times the explosive yield of the Hiroshima bomb were determined. The data gathered from these experiences make it a straightforward matter to work out the distances from the explosion at which different intensities of the various effects of a bomb are likely to occur. In the back of the Glasstone book, the reader will find a small dial computer that places all this information at his fingertips. Thus, if one would like to know how deep a crater a twenty-megaton ground burst will leave in wet soil one has only to set a pointer at twenty megatons and look in a small window showing crater size to find that the depth would be six hundred feet—a hole deep enough to bury a fair-sized skyscraper. Yet this small circular computer, on which the downfall of every city on earth is distilled into a few lines and figures, can, of course, tell us nothing of the human reality of nuclear destruction. Part of the horror of thinking about a holocaust lies in the fact that it leads us to supplant the human world with a statistical world; we seek a human truth and come up with a handful of figures. The only source that gives us a glimpse of that human truth is the testimony of the survivors of the Hiroshima and Nagasaki bombings. Because the bombing of Hiroshima has been more thoroughly investigated than the bombing of Nagasaki, and therefore more information about it is available, I shall restrict myself to a brief description of that catastrophe.

On August 6, 1945, at 8:16 A.M., a fission bomb with a yield of twelve and a half kilotons was detonated about nineteen hundred feet above the central section of Hiroshima. By present-day standards, the bomb was a small one, and in today's arsenals it would be classed among the merely tactical weapons. Nevertheless, it was large enough to transform a city of some three hundred and forty thousand people into hell in the space of a few seconds. "It is no exaggeration," the authors of *Hiroshima and Nagasaki* tell us, "to say that the whole city was ruined instantaneously." In that instant, tens of thousands of people were burned, blasted, and crushed to death. Other tens of thousands suffered injuries of every description or were doomed to die of radiation sickness. The center of the city was flattened, and every part of the city was damaged. The trunks of bamboo trees as far away as five miles from ground zero—the point on the ground directly under the center of the explosion—were charred. Almost half the trees within a mile and a quarter were knocked down. Windows nearly seventeen miles away were broken. Half an hour after the blast, fires set by the thermal pulse and by the collapse of the buildings began to coalesce into a firestorm, which lasted for six hours. Starting about 9 A.M. and lasting until late afternoon, a "black rain" generated by the bomb (otherwise, the day was fair) fell on the western portions of the city, carrying radioactive fallout from the blast to the ground. For four hours at midday, a violent whirlwind, born of the strange meteorological conditions produced by the explosion, further devastated the city. The number of people who were killed outright or who died of their injuries over the next three months is estimated to be a hundred and thirty thousand. Sixty-eight per cent of the buildings in the city were either completely destroyed or damaged beyond repair, and the center of the city was turned into a flat, rubble-strewn plain dotted with the ruins of a few of the sturdier buildings.

In the minutes after the detonation, the day grew dark, as heavy clouds of dust and smoke filled the air. A whole city had fallen in a moment, and in and under its ruins were its people.

* * *

What happened at Hiroshima was less than a millionth part of a holocaust at present levels of world nuclear armament. The more than millionfold difference amounts to more than a difference in magnitude; it is also a difference in kind. The authors of *Hiroshima and Nagasaki* observe that "an atomic bomb's massive destruction and indiscriminate slaughter involves the sweeping breakdown of all order and existence—in a word, the collapse of society itself," and that therefore "the essence of atomic destruction lies in the totality of its impact on man and society." This is true also of a holocaust, of course, except that the totalities in question are now not single cities but nations, ecosystems, and the earth's ecosphere. Yet with the exception of fallout, which was relatively light at Hiroshima and Nagasaki (because both the bombs were air-burst), the immediate devastation caused by today's bombs would be of a sort similar to the devastation in those cities. The immediate effects of a twenty-megaton bomb are not different in kind from those of a twelve-and-a-half-kiloton bomb; they are only more extensive. (The proportions of the effects do change greatly with yield, however. In small bombs, the effects of the initial nuclear radiation are important, because it strikes areas in which

people might otherwise have remained alive, but in larger bombs—
ones in the megaton range—the consequences of the initial nuclear
radiation, whose range does not increase very much with yield, are
negligible, because it strikes areas in which everyone will have already
been burned or blasted to death.) In bursts of both weapons, for
instance, there is a radius within which the thermal pulse can ignite
newspapers: for the twelve-and-a-half-kiloton weapon, it is a little
over two miles; for the twenty-megaton weapon, it is twenty-five
miles. (Since there is no inherent limit on the size of a nuclear weapon,
these figures can be increased indefinitely, subject only to the limitations
imposed by the technical capacities of the bomb builder—and of the
earth's capacity to absorb the blast. The Soviet Union, which has
shown a liking for sheer size in so many of its undertakings, once detonated a sixty-megaton bomb.) Therefore, while the total effect of a
holocaust is qualitatively different from the total effect of a single
bomb, the experience of individual people in a holocaust would be, in
the short term (and again excepting the presence of lethal fallout
wherever the bombs were ground-burst), very much like the experience of individual people in Hiroshima. The Hiroshima people's
experience, accordingly, is of much more than historical interest. It is
a picture of what our whole world is always poised to become—a
backdrop of scarcely imaginable horror lying just behind the surface
of our normal life, and capable of breaking through into that normal
life at any second. Whether we choose to think about it or not, it is an
omnipresent, inescapable truth about our lives today that at every
single moment each one of us may suddenly become the deranged
mother looking for her burned child; the professor with the ball of
rice in his hand whose wife has just told him "Run away, dear!" and
died in the fires; Mr. Fukai running back into the firestorm; the naked
man standing on the blasted plain that was his city, holding his eyeball

in his hand; or, more likely, one of millions of corpses. For whatever our "modest hopes" as human beings may be, every one of them can be nullified by a nuclear holocaust.

One way to begin to grasp the destructive power of present-day nuclear weapons is to describe the consequences of the detonation of a one-megaton bomb, which possesses eighty times the explosive power of the Hiroshima bomb, on a large city, such as New York. Burst some eighty-five hundred feet above the Empire State Building, a one-megaton bomb would gut or flatten almost every building between Battery Park and 125th Street, or within a radius of four and four-tenths miles, or in an area of sixty-one square miles, and would heavily damage buildings between the northern tip of Staten Island and the George Washington Bridge, or within a radius of about eight miles, or in an area of about two hundred square miles. A conventional explosive delivers a swift shock, like a slap, to whatever it hits, but the blast wave of a sizable nuclear weapon endures for several seconds and "can surround and destroy whole buildings" (Glasstone). People, of course, would be picked up and hurled away from the blast along with the rest of the debris. Within the sixty-one square miles, the walls, roofs, and floors of any buildings that had not been flattened would be collapsed, and the people and furniture inside would be swept down onto the street. (Technically, this zone would be hit by various overpressures of at least five pounds per square inch. Overpressure is defined as the pressure in excess of normal atmospheric pressure.) As far away as ten miles from ground zero, pieces of glass and other sharp objects would be hurled about by the blast wave at lethal velocities. In Hiroshima, where buildings were low and, outside the center of the city, were often constructed of light materials, injuries from falling buildings were often minor. But in New York, where the buildings are tall and are constructed of heavy materials, the physical collapse of the city would certainly kill millions of people. The streets of New York are narrow ravines running between the high walls of the city's buildings. In a nuclear attack, the walls would fall and the ravines would fill up. The people in the buildings would fall to the street with the debris of the buildings, and the people in the street would be crushed by this avalanche of people and buildings. At a distance of two miles or so from ground zero, winds would reach four hundred miles an hour, and another two miles away they would reach a hundred and eighty miles an hour. Meanwhile, the fireball would be growing, until it was more than a mile wide, and rocketing upward, to a height of over six miles. For ten seconds, it would broil the city below. Anyone caught in the open within nine miles of ground zero would receive third-degree burns and would probably be killed; closer to the explosion, people would be charred and killed instantly. From Greenwich Village up to Central Park, the heat would be great enough to melt metal and glass. Readily inflammable materials, such as newspapers and dry leaves, would ignite in all five boroughs (though in only a small part of Staten Island) and west to the Passaic River, in New Jersey, within a radius of about nine and a half miles from ground zero, thereby creating an area of more than two hundred and eighty square miles in which mass fires were likely to break out.

If it were possible (as it would not be) for someone to stand at Fifth Avenue and Seventy-second Street (about two miles from ground zero) without being instantly killed, he would see the following sequence of events. A dazzling white light from the fireball would illumine the scene, continuing for perhaps thirty seconds. Simultaneously, searing heat would ignite everything flammable and start to melt windows, cars, buses, lampposts, and everything else made of metal or glass. People in the street would immediately catch fire, and would shortly be reduced to heavily charred corpses. About five seconds after the light appeared, the blast wave would strike, laden with the debris of a now nonexistent midtown. Some buildings might be crushed, as though a giant fist had squeezed them on all sides, and others might be picked up off their foundations and whirled uptown with the other debris. On the far side of Central Park, the West Side skyline would fall from south to north. The four-hundred-mile-an-hour wind would blow from south to north, die down after a few seconds, and then blow in the reverse direction with diminished intensity. While these things were happening, the fireball would be burning in the sky for the ten seconds of the thermal pulse. Soon huge, thick clouds of dust and smoke would envelop the scene, and as the mushroom cloud rushed overhead (it would have a diameter of about twelve miles) the light from the sun would be blotted out, and day would turn to night. Within minutes, fires, ignited both by the thermal pulse and by broken gas mains, tanks of gas and oil, and the like, would begin to spread in the darkness, and a strong, steady wind would begin to blow in the direction of the blast. As at Hiroshima, a whirlwind might be produced, which would sweep through the ruins, and radioactive rain, generated under the meteorological conditions created by the blast, might fall. Before long, the individual fires would coalesce into a mass fire, which, depending largely on the winds, would become either a conflagration or a firestorm. In a conflagration, prevailing winds spread a wall of fire as far as there is any combustible material to sustain it; in a firestorm, a vertical updraft caused by the fire itself sucks the surrounding air in toward a central point, and the fires therefore converge in a single fire of extreme heat. A mass fire of either kind renders shelters useless by burning up all the oxygen in the air and creating toxic gases, so that anyone inside the shelters is asphyxiated, and also by heating the ground to such high temperatures that the shelters turn, in effect, into ovens, cremating the people inside them. In Dresden, several days after the firestorm raised there by Allied conventional bombing, the interiors of some bomb shelters were still so hot that when they were opened the inrushing air caused the contents to burst into flame. Only those who had fled their shelters when the bombing started had any chance of surviving. (It is difficult to predict in a particular situation which form the fires will take. In actual experience, Hiroshima suffered a firestorm and Nagasaki suffered a conflagration.)

In this vast theatre of physical effects, all the scenes of agony and death that took place at Hiroshima would again take place, but now involving millions of people rather than hundreds of thousands. Like the people of Hiroshima, the people of New York would be burned, battered, crushed, and irradiated in every conceivable way. The city and its people would be mingled in a smoldering heap. And then, as the fires started, the survivors (most of whom would be on the periphery of the explosion) would be driven to abandon to the flames those family members and other people who were unable to flee, or else to die with them. Before long, while the ruins burned, the processions of injured, mute people would begin their slow progress out of the outskirts of the devastated zone. However, this time a much smaller proportion of the population than at Hiroshima would have a chance of escaping. In general, as the size of the area of devastation increases, the possibilities for escape decrease. When the devastated area is relatively small, as it was at Hiroshima, people who are not incapacitated will have a good chance of escaping to safety before the fires coalesce into a mass fire. But when the devastated area is great, as it would be after the detonation of a megaton bomb, and fires are springing up at a distance of nine and a half miles from ground zero, and when what used to be the streets are piled high with burning rubble, and the day (if the attack occurs in the daytime) has grown impenetrably dark, there is little chance that anyone who is not on the very edge of the devastated area will be able to make his way to safety. In New York, most people would die wherever the blast found them, or not very far from there.

If instead of being burst in the air the bomb were burst on or near the ground in the vicinity of the Empire State Building, the overpressure would be very much greater near the center of the blast area but the range hit by a minimum of five pounds per square inch of overpressure would be less. The range of the thermal pulse would be about the same as that of the air burst. The fireball would be almost two miles across, and would engulf midtown Manhattan from Greenwich Village nearly to Central Park. Very little is known about what would happen to a city that was inside a fireball, but one would expect a good deal of what was there to be first pulverized and then melted or vaporized. Any human beings in the area would be reduced to smoke and ashes; they would simply disappear. A crater roughly three blocks in diameter and two hundred feet deep would open up. In addition, heavy radioactive fallout would be created as dust and debris from the city rose with the mushroom cloud and then fell back to the ground. Fallout would begin to drop almost immediately, contaminating the ground beneath the cloud with levels of radiation many times lethal doses, and quickly killing anyone who might have survived the blast wave and the thermal pulse and might now be attempting an escape; it is difficult to believe that there would be appreciable survival of the people of the city after a megaton ground burst. And for the next twenty-four hours or so more fallout would descend downwind from the blast, in a plume whose direction and length would depend on the speed and the direction of the wind that happened to be blowing at the time of the attack. If the wind was blowing at fifteen miles an hour, fallout of lethal intensity would descend in a plume about a hundred and fifty miles long and as much as fifteen miles wide. Fallout that was sublethal but could still cause serious illness would extend another hundred and fifty miles . downwind. Exposure to radioactivity in human beings is measured in units called rems—an acronym for "roentgen equivalent in man." The roentgen is a standard measurement of gamma- and X-ray radiation, and the expression "equivalent in man" indicates that an adjustment has been made to take into account the differences in the degree of biological damage that is caused by radiation of different types. Many of the kinds of harm done to human beings by radiation—for example, the incidence of cancer and of genetic damage—depend on the dose accumulated over many years; but radiation sickness, capable of causing death, results from an "acute" dose, received in a period of anything from a few seconds to several days. Because almost ninety per cent of the so-called "infinite-time dose" of radiation from fallout—that is, the dose from a given quantity of fallout that one would receive if one lived for many thousands of years—is emitted in the first week, the one-week accumulated dose is often used as a convenient measure for calculating the immediate harm from fallout. Doses in the thousands of rems, which could be expected throughout the city, would attack the central nervous system and would bring about death within a few hours. Doses of around a thousand rems, which would be delivered some tens of miles downwind from the blast, would kill within two weeks everyone who was exposed to them. Doses of around five hundred rems, which would be delivered as far as a hundred and fifty miles downwind (given a wind speed of fifteen miles per hour), would kill half of all exposed able-bodied young adults. At this level of exposure, radiation sickness proceeds in the three stages observed at Hiroshima. The plume of lethal fallout could descend, depending on the direction of the wind, on other parts of New York State and parts of New Jersey, Pennsylvania, Delaware, Maryland, Connecticut, Massachusetts, Rhode Island, Vermont, and New Hampshire, killing additional millions of people. The circumstances in heavily contaminated areas, in which millions of people were all declining together, over a period of weeks, toward painful deaths, are ones that, like so many of the consequences of nuclear explosions, have never been experienced.

A description of the effects of a one-megaton bomb on New York City gives some notion of the meaning in human terms of a megaton of nuclear explosive power, but a weapon that is more likely to be used against New York is the twenty-megaton bomb, which has one thousand six hundred times the yield of the Hiroshima bomb. The Soviet Union is estimated to have at least a hundred and thirteen twenty-megaton bombs in its nuclear arsenal, carried by Bear intercontinental bombers. In addition, some of the Soviet SS-18 missiles are capable of carrying bombs of this size, although the actual yields are not known. Since the explosive power of the twenty-megaton bombs greatly exceeds the amount necessary to destroy most military targets, it is reasonable to suppose that they are meant for use against large cities. If a twenty-megaton bomb were air-burst over the Empire State Building at an altitude of thirty thousand feet, the zone gutted or flattened by the blast wave would have a radius of twelve miles and an area of more than four hundred and fifty square miles, reaching from the middle of Staten Island to the northern edge of the Bronx, the eastern edge of Queens, and well into New Jersey, and the zone of heavy damage from the blast wave (the zone hit by a minimum of two pounds of overpressure per square inch) would have a radius of twenty-one and a half miles, or an area of one thousand four hundred and fifty square miles, reaching to the southernmost tip of Staten

Island, north as far as southern Rockland County, east into Nassau County, and west to Morris County, New Jersey. The fireball would be about four and a half miles in diameter and would radiate the thermal pulse for some twenty seconds. People caught in the open twenty-three miles away from ground zero, in Long Island, New Jersey, and southern New York State, would be burned to death. People hundreds of miles away who looked at the burst would be temporarily blinded and would risk permanent eye injury. (After the test of a fifteen-megaton bomb on Bikini Atoll, in the South Pacific, in March of 1954, small animals were found to have suffered retinal burns at a distance of three hundred and forty-five miles.) The mushroom cloud would be seventy miles in diameter. New York City and its suburbs would be transformed into a lifeless, flat, scorched desert in a few seconds.

If a twenty-megaton bomb were ground-burst on the Empire State Building, the range of severe blast damage would, as with the one-megaton ground blast, be reduced, but the fireball, which would be almost six miles in diameter, would cover Manhattan from Wall Street to northern Central Park and also parts of New Jersey, Brooklyn, and Queens, and everyone within it would be instantly killed, with most of them physically disappearing. Fallout would again be generated, this time covering thousands of square miles with lethal intensities of radiation. A fair portion of New York City and its incinerated population, now radioactive dust, would have risen into the mushroom cloud and would now be descending on the surrounding territory. On one of the few occasions when local fallout was generated by a test explosion in the multi-megaton range, the fifteen-megaton bomb tested on Bikini Atoll, which was exploded seven feet above the surface of a coral reef, "caused substantial contamination over an area of more than seven thousand square miles," according to Glasstone. If, as seems likely, a twenty-megaton bomb ground-burst on New York would produce at least a comparable amount of fallout, and if the wind carried the fallout onto populated areas, then this one bomb would probably doom upward of twenty million people, or almost ten per cent of the population of the United States.

The "strategic" forces of the Soviet Union—those that can deliver nuclear warheads to the United States—are so far capable of carrying seven thousand warheads with an estimated maximum yield of more than seventeen thousand megatons of explosive power, and, barring unexpected developments in arms-control talks, the number of warheads is expected to rise in the coming years. The actual megatonnage of the Soviet strategic forces is not known, and, for a number of reasons, including the fact that smaller warheads can be delivered more accurately, it is very likely that the actual megatonnage is lower than the maximum possible; however, it is reasonable to suppose that the actual megatonnage is as much as two-thirds of the maximum, which would be about eleven and a half thousand megatons. If we assume that in a first strike the Soviets held back about a thousand megatons (itself an immense force), then the attack would amount to about ten thousand megatons, or the equivalent of eight hundred thousand Hiroshima bombs. American strategic forces comprise about nine thousand warheads with a yield of some three thousand five hundred megatons. The total yield of these American forces was made comparatively low for strategic reasons. American planners discovered that smaller warheads can be delivered more accurately than larger ones, and are therefore more useful for attacking strategic forces on the other side. And, in fact, American missiles are substantially more accurate than Soviet ones. However, in the last year or so, in spite of this advantage in numbers of warheads and in accuracy, American leaders have come to believe that the American forces are inadequate, and, again barring unexpected developments in arms-control talks, both the yield of the American arsenal and the number of warheads in it are likely to rise dramatically. (Neither the United States nor the Soviet Union reveals the total explosive yield of its own forces. The public is left to turn to private organizations, which, by making use of hundreds of pieces of information that *have* been released by the two governments, piece together an over-all picture. The figures I have used to estimate the maximum capacities of the two sides are taken for the most part from tables provided in the latest edition of *The Military Balance*, a standard yearly reference work on the strength of military forces around the world, which is published by a research institute in London called the International Institute for Strategic Studies.) The territory of the United States, including Alaska and Hawaii, is three million six hundred and fifteen thousand one hundred and twenty-two square miles. It contains approximately two hundred and twenty-five million people, of whom sixty per cent, or about a hundred and thirty-five million, live in various urban centers with a total area of only eighteen thousand square miles. I asked Dr. Kendall, who has done considerable research on the consequences of nuclear attacks, to sketch out in rough terms what the actual distribution of bombs might be in a ten-thousand-megaton Soviet attack in the early nineteen-eighties on all targets in the United States, military and civilian.

"Without serious distortion," he said, "we can begin by imagining that we would be dealing with ten thousand weapons of one megaton each, although in fact the yields would, of course, vary considerably. Let us also make the assumption, based on common knowledge of weapons design, that on average the yield would be one-half fission and one-half fusion. This proportion is important, because it is the fission products—a virtual museum of about three hundred radioactive isotopes, decaying at different rates—that give off radioactivity in fallout. Fusion can add to the total in ground bursts by radioactivation of ground material by neutrons, but the quantity added is comparatively small. Targets can be divided into two categories—hard and soft. Hard targets, of which there are about a thousand in the United States, are mostly missile silos. The majority of them can be destroyed only by huge, blunt overpressures, ranging anywhere from many hundreds to a few thousand pounds per square inch, and we can expect that two weapons might be devoted to each one to assure destruction. That would use up two thousand megatons. Because other strategic military targets—such as Strategic Air Command bases—are near centers of population, an attack on them as well, perhaps using another couple of hundred megatons, could cause a total of more than twenty million casualties, according to studies by the Arms Control and Disarmament Agency. If the nearly eight thousand weapons remaining were then devoted to the cities and towns of the United States in order of population, every community down to the level of fifteen hundred inhabitants would be hit with a megaton bomb—which is, of course, many, many times what would be necessary to annihilate a town that size. For obvious reasons, industry is highly correlated with population density, so an attack on the one necessarily hits the other, especially when an attack of this magnitude is considered. Ten thousand targets would include everything worth hitting in the country and much more; it would simply *be* the United States. The targeters would run out of targets and victims long before they ran out of bombs. If you imagine that the bombs were distributed according to population, then, allowing for the fact that the attack on the military installations would have already killed about twenty million people, you would have about forty megatons to devote to each remaining million people in the country. For the seven and a half million people in New York City, that would come to three hundred megatons. Bearing in mind what one megaton can do, you can see that this would be preposterous overkill. In practice, one might expect the New York metropolitan area to be hit with some dozens of one-megaton weapons."

In the first moments of a ten-thousand-megaton attack on the United States, I learned from Dr. Kendall and from other sources, flashes of white light would suddenly illumine large areas of the country as thousands of suns, each one brighter than the sun itself, blossomed over cities, suburbs, and towns. In those same moments, when the first wave of missiles arrived, the vast majority of the people in the regions first targeted would be irradiated, crushed, or burned to death. The thermal pulses could subject more than six hundred thousand square miles, or one-sixth of the total land mass of the nation, to a minimum level of forty calories per centimetre squared—a level of heat that chars human beings. (At Hiroshima, charred remains in the rough shape of human beings were a common sight.) Tens of millions of people would go up in smoke. As the attack proceeded, as much as three-quarters of the country could be subjected to incendiary levels of heat, and so, wherever there was inflammable material, could be set ablaze. In the ten seconds or so after each bomb hit, as blast waves swept outward from thousands of ground zeros, the physical plant of the United States would be swept away like leaves in a gust of wind. The six hundred thousand square miles already scorched by the forty or more calories of heat per centimetre squared would now be hit by blast waves of a minimum of five pounds per square inch, and virtually all the habitations, places of work, and other manmade things there—substantially the whole human construct in the United

States—would be vaporized, blasted, or otherwise pulverized out of existence. Then, as clouds of dust rose from the earth, and mushroom clouds spread overhead, often linking to form vast canopies, day would turn to night. (These clouds could blanket as much as a third of the nation.) Shortly, fires would spring up in the debris of the cities and in every forest dry enough to burn. These fires would simply burn down the United States. When one pictures a full-scale attack on the United States, or on any other country, therefore, the picture of a single city being flattened by a single bomb—an image firmly engraved in the public imagination, probably because of the bombings of Hiroshima and Nagasaki—must give way to a picture of substantial sections of the country being turned by a sort of nuclear carpet-bombing into immense infernal regions, literally tens of thousands of square miles in area, from which escape is impossible. In Hiroshima and Nagasaki, those who had not been killed or injured so severely that they could not move were able to flee to the undevastated world around them, where they found help, but in any city where three or four bombs had been used—not to mention fifty, or a hundred —flight from one blast would only be flight toward another, and no one could escape alive. Within these regions, each of three of the immediate effects of nuclear weapons—initial radiation, thermal pulse, and blast wave—would alone be enough to kill most people: the initial nuclear radiation would subject tens of thousands of square miles to lethal doses; the blast waves, coming from all sides, would nowhere fall below the overpressure necessary to destroy almost all buildings; and the thermal pulses, also coming from all sides, would always be great enough to kill exposed people and, in addition, to set on fire everything that would burn. The ease with which virtually the whole population of the country could be trapped in these zones of universal death is suggested by the fact that the sixty per cent of the population that lives in an area of eighteen thousand square miles could be annihilated with only three hundred one-megaton bombs—the number necessary to cover the area with a minimum of five pounds per square inch of overpressure and forty calories per centimetre squared of heat. That would leave nine thousand seven hundred megatons, or ninety-seven per cent of the megatonnage in the attacking force, available for other targets. (It is hard to imagine what a targeter would do with all his bombs in these circumstances. Above several thousand megatons, it would almost become a matter of trying to hunt down individual people with nuclear warheads.)

The statistics on the initial nuclear radiation, the thermal pulses, and the blast waves in a nuclear holocaust can be presented in any number of ways, but all of them would be only variations on a simple theme—the annihilation of the United States and its people. Yet while the immediate nuclear effects are great enough in a ten-thousand-megaton attack to destroy the country many times over, they are not the most powerfully lethal of the local effects of nuclear weapons. The killing power of the local fallout is far greater. Therefore, if the Soviet Union was bent on producing the maximum overkill—if, that is, its surviving leaders, whether out of calculation, rage, or madness, decided to eliminate the United States not merely as a political and social entity but as a biological one—they would burst their bombs on the ground rather than in the air. Although the scope of severe blast damage would then be reduced, the blast waves, fireballs, and thermal pulses would still be far more than enough to destroy the country, and, in addition, provided only that the bombs were dispersed widely enough, lethal fallout would spread throughout the nation. The amount of radiation delivered by the fallout from a ground burst of a given size is still uncertain—not least because, as Glasstone notes, there has never been a "true land surface burst" of a bomb with a yield of over one kiloton. (The Bikini burst was in part over the ocean.) Many factors make for uncertainty. To mention just a few: the relative amounts of the fallout that rises into the stratosphere and the fallout that descends to the ground near the blast are dependent on, among other things, the yield of the weapon, and, in any case, can be only guessed at; the composition of the fallout will vary with the composition of the material on the ground that is sucked up into the mushroom cloud; prediction of the distribution of fallout by winds of various speeds at various altitudes depends on a choice of several "models"; and the calculation of the arrival time of the fallout—an important calculation, since fallout cannot harm living things until it lands near them—is subject to similar speculative doubts. However, calculations on the basis of figures for a one-megaton ground burst which are given in the Office of Technology Assessment's report show that ten thousand megatons would yield one-week doses around the country averaging more than ten thousand rems. In actuality, of course, the bombs would almost certainly not be evenly spaced around the country but, rather, would be concentrated in populated areas and in missile fields; and the likelihood is that in most places where people lived or worked the doses would be many times the average, commonly reaching several tens of thousands of rems for the first week, while in remote areas they would be less, or, conceivably, even nonexistent. (The United States contains large tracts of empty desert, and to target them would be virtually meaningless from any point of view.)

These figures provide a context for judging the question of civil defense. With overwhelming immediate local effects striking the vast majority of the population, and with one-week doses of radiation then rising into the tens of thousands of rems, evacuation and shelters are a vain hope. Needless to say, in these circumstances evacuation before an attack would be an exercise in transporting people from one death to another. In some depictions of a holocaust, various rescue operations are described, with unafflicted survivors bringing food, clothes, and medical care to the afflicted, and the afflicted making their way to thriving, untouched communities, where churches, school auditoriums, and the like would have been set up for their care—as often happens after a bad snowstorm, say. Obviously, none of this could come about. In the first place, in a full-scale attack there would in all likelihood *be* no surviving communities, and, in the second place, everyone who failed to seal himself off from the outside environment for as long as several months would soon die of radiation sickness. Hence, in the months after a holocaust there would be no activity of any sort, as, in a reversal of the normal state of things, the dead would lie on the surface and the living, if there were any, would be buried underground.

To this description of radiation levels around the country, an addition remains to be made. This is the fact that attacks on the seventy-six nuclear power plants in the United States would produce fallout whose radiation had much greater longevity than that of the weapons alone. The physicist Dr. Kosta Tsipis, of M.I.T., and one of his students, Steven Fetter, recently published an article in *Scientific American* called "Catastrophic Releases of Radioactivity," in which they calculate the damage from a one-megaton thermonuclear ground burst on a one-gigawatt nuclear power plant. In such a ground burst, the facility's radioactive contents would be vaporized along with everything nearby, and the remains would be carried up into the mushroom cloud, from which they would descend to the earth with the rest of the fallout. But whereas the fission products of the weapon were newly made, and contained many isotopes that would decay to insignificant levels very swiftly, the fission products in a reactor would be a collection of longer-lived isotopes (and this applies even more strongly to the spent fuel in the reactor's holding pond), since the short-lived ones would, for the most part, have had enough time to reduce themselves to harmless levels. The intense but comparatively short-lived radiation from the weapon would kill people in the first few weeks and months, but the long-lived radiation that was produced both by the weapon and by the power plant could prevent anyone from living on a vast area of land for decades after it fell. For example, after a year an area of some seventeen hundred square miles downwind of a power plant on which a one-megaton bomb had been ground-burst (again assuming a fifteen-mile-an-hour wind) would still be delivering more than fifty rems per year to anyone who tried to live there, and that is two hundred and fifty times the "safe" dose established by the E.P.A. The bomb by itself would produce this effect over an area of only twenty-six square miles. (In addition to offering an enemy a way of redoubling the effectiveness of his attacks in a full-scale holocaust, reactors provide targets of unparalleled danger in possible terrorist nuclear attacks. In an earlier paper, Tsipis and Fetter observe that "the destruction of a reactor with a nuclear weapon, even of relatively small yield, such as a crude terrorist nuclear device, would represent a national catastrophe of lasting consequences." It can be put down as one further alarming oddity of life in a nuclear world that in building nuclear power plants nations have opened themselves to catastrophic devastation and long-term contamination of their territories by enemies who manage to get hold of only a few nuclear weapons.)

If, in a nuclear holocaust, anyone hid himself deep enough under the earth and stayed there long enough to survive, he would emerge into a dying natural environment. The vulnerability of the environment is the last word in the argument against the usefulness of shelters: there is no hole big enough to hide all of nature in. Radioactivity penetrates the environment in many ways. The two most important components of radiation from fallout are gamma rays, which are electromagnetic radiation of the highest intensity, and beta particles, which are electrons fired at high speed from decaying nuclei. Gamma rays subject organisms to penetrating whole-body doses, and are responsible for most of the ill effects of radiation from fallout. Beta particles, which are less penetrating than gamma rays, act at short range, doing harm when they collect on the skin, or on the surface of a leaf. They are harmful to plants on whose foliage the fallout descends—producing "beta burn"—and to grazing animals, which can suffer burns as well as gastrointestinal damage from eating the foliage. Two of the most harmful radioactive isotopes present in fallout are strontium-90 (with a half-life of twenty-eight years) and cesium-137 (with a half-life of thirty years). They are taken up into the food chain through the roots of plants or through direct ingestion by animals, and contaminate the environment from within. Strontium-90 happens to resemble calcium in its chemical composition, and therefore finds its way into the human diet through dairy products and is eventually deposited by the body in the bones, where it is thought to cause bone cancer. (Every person in the world now has in his bones a measurable deposit of strontium-90 traceable to the fallout from atmospheric nuclear testing.)

Over the years, agencies and departments of the government have sponsored numerous research projects in which a large variety of plants and animals were irradiated in order to ascertain the lethal or sterilizing dose for each. These findings permit the prediction of many gross ecological consequences of a nuclear attack. According to "Survival of Food Crops and Livestock in the Event of Nuclear War," the proceedings of the 1970 symposium at Brookhaven National Laboratory, the lethal doses for most mammals lie between a few hundred rads and a thousand rads of gamma radiation; a rad—for "roentgen absorbed dose"—is a roentgen of radiation that has been absorbed by an organism, and is roughly equal to a rem. For example, the lethal doses of gamma radiation for animals in pasture, where fallout would be descending on them directly and they would be eating fallout that had fallen on the grass, and would thus suffer from doses of beta radiation as well, would be one hundred and eighty rads for cattle; two hundred and forty rads for sheep; five hundred and fifty rads for swine; three hundred and fifty rads for horses; and eight hundred rads for poultry. In a ten-thousand-megaton attack, which would create levels of radiation around the country averaging more than ten thousand rads, most of the mammals of the United States would be killed off. The lethal doses for birds are in roughly the same range as those for mammals, and birds, too, would be killed off. Fish are killed at doses of between one thousand one hundred rads and about five thousand six hundred rads, but their fate is less predictable. On the one hand, water is a shield from radiation, and would afford some protection; on the other hand, fallout might concentrate in bodies of water as it ran off from the land. (Because radiation causes no pain, animals, wandering at will through the environment, would not avoid it.) The one class of animals containing a number of species quite likely to survive, at least in the short run, is the insect class, for which in most known cases the lethal doses lie between about two thousand rads and about a hundred thousand rads. Insects, therefore, would be destroyed selectively. Unfortunately for the rest of the environment, many of the phytophagous species—insects that feed directly on vegetation— which "include some of the most ravaging species on earth" (according to Dr. Vernon M. Stern, an entomologist at the University of California at Riverside, writing in "Survival of Food Crops"), have very high tolerances, and so could be expected to survive disproportionately, and then to multiply greatly in the aftermath of an attack. The demise of their natural predators the birds would enhance their success.

Plants in general have a higher tolerance to radioactivity than animals do. Nevertheless, according to Dr. George M. Woodwell, who supervised the irradiation with gamma rays, over several years, of a small forest at Brookhaven Laboratory, a gamma-ray dose of ten thousand rads "would devastate most vegetation" in the United States, and, as in the case of the pastured animals, when one figures in the beta radiation that would also be delivered by fallout the estimates for the lethal doses of gamma rays must be reduced—in this case, cut in half. As a general rule, Dr. Woodwell and his colleagues at Brookhaven discovered, large plants are more vulnerable to radiation than small ones. Trees are among the first to die, grasses among the last. The most sensitive trees are pines and the other conifers, for which lethal doses are in roughly the same range as those for mammals. Any survivors coming out of their shelters a few months after the attack would find that all the pine trees that were still standing were already dead. The lethal doses for most deciduous trees range from about two thousand rads of gamma-ray radiation to about ten thousand rads, with the lethal doses for eighty per cent of deciduous species falling between two thousand and eight thousand rads. Since the addition of the beta-ray burden could lower these lethal doses for gamma rays by as much as fifty per cent, the actual lethal doses in gamma rays for these trees during an attack could be from one thousand to four thousand rads, and in a full-scale attack they would die. Then, after the trees had died, forest fires would break out around the United States. (Because as much as three-quarters of the country could be subjected to incendiary levels of the thermal pulses, the sheer scorching of the land could have killed off a substantial part of the plant life in the country in the first few seconds after the detonations, before radioactive poisoning set in.) Lethal doses for grasses on which tests have been done range between six thousand and thirty-three thousand rads, and a good deal of grass would therefore survive, except where the attacks had been heaviest. Most crops, on the other hand, are killed by doses below five thousands rads, and would be eliminated. (The lethal dose for spring barley seedlings, for example, is one thousand nine hundred and ninety rads, and that for spring wheat seedlings is three thousand and ninety rads.)

When vegetation is killed off, the land on which it grew is degraded. And as the land eroded after an attack life in lakes, rivers, and estuaries, already hard hit by radiation directly, would be further damaged by minerals flowing into the watercourses, causing eutrophication—a process in which an oversupply of nutrients in the water encourages the growth of algae and microscopic organisms, which, in turn, deplete the oxygen content of the water. When the soil loses its nutrients, it loses its ability to "sustain a mature community" (in Dr. Woodwell's words), and "gross simplification" of the environment occurs, in which "hardy species," such as moss and grass, replace vulnerable ones, such as trees; and "succession"—the process by which ecosystems recover lost diversity—is then "delayed or even arrested." In sum, a full-scale nuclear attack on the United States would devastate the natural environment on a scale unknown since early geological times, when, in response to natural catastrophes whose nature has not been determined, sudden mass extinctions of species and whole ecosystems occurred all over the earth. How far this "gross simplification" of the environment would go once virtually all animal life and the greater part of plant life had been destroyed and what patterns the surviving remnants of life would arrange themselves into over the long run are imponderables; but it appears that at the outset the United States would be a republic of insects and grass.

In recent years, scientists in many fields have accumulated enough knowledge to begin to look on the earth as a single, concrete mechanism, and to at least begin to ask how it works. One of their discoveries has been that life and life's inanimate terrestrial surroundings have a strong reciprocal influence on each other. For life, the land, oceans, and air have been the environment, but, equally, for the land, oceans, and air life has been the environment—the conditioning force. The injection of oxygen into the atmosphere by living things, which led to the formation of an ozone layer, which, in turn, shut out lethal ultraviolet rays from the sun and permitted the rise of multicellular organisms, was only one of life's large-scale interventions. The more closely scientists look at life and its evolution, the less they find it possible to draw a sharp distinction between "life," on the one hand, and an inanimate "environment" in which it exists, on the other. Rather, "the environment" of the present day appears to be a house of unimaginable intricacy which life has to a very great extent built and furnished for its own use. It seems that life even regulates and maintains the chemical environment of the earth in a way that turns out to suit its own needs. In a far-reaching speculative article entitled "Chemical Processes in the Solar System: A Kinetic Perspective," Dr. McElroy has described the terrestrial cycles by which the most important elements of the atmosphere—oxygen, carbon, and nitrogen—are kept in proportions that are favorable to life. He finds that in each case life itself—its birth, metabolism, and decay—is chiefly responsible for maintaining the balance. For example, he calculates that if for some reason respiration and decay were suddenly cut off, photosynthesis would devour all the inorganic carbon on the surface of the ocean and in the atmosphere within forty years. Thereafter, carbon welling up from the deep ocean would fuel photosynthesis in the oceans for another thousand years, but then "life as we know it would terminate."

Dr. McElroy also observes that the amount of ozone in the strato-sphere is influenced by the amount of organic decay, and thus by the amount of life, on earth. Nitrous oxide is a product of organic decay, and because it produces nitric oxide—one of the compounds respon-sible for ozone depletion—it plays the role of regulator. In the absence of human intervention, living things are largely responsible for introducing nitrous oxide into the atmosphere. When life is excep-tionally abundant, it releases more nitrous oxide into the atmosphere, and may thus act to cut back on the ozone, and that cutback lets in more ultraviolet rays. On the other hand, when life is sparse and depleted, nitrous-oxide production is reduced, the ozone layer builds up, and ultraviolet rays are cut back. These speculative glimpses of what might be called the metabolism of the earth give substance to the growing conviction among scientists that the earth, like a single cell or a single organism, is a systemic whole, and in a general way they tend to confirm the fear that any large man-made perturbation of terrestrial nature could lead to a catastrophic systemic breakdown. Nuclear explosions are far from being the only perturbations in question; a heating of the global atmosphere through an increased greenhouse effect, which could be caused by the injection of vast amounts of carbon dioxide into the air (for instance, from the increased burning of coal), is another notable peril of this kind. But a nuclear holocaust would be unique in its suddenness, which would permit no observa-tion of slowly building environmental damage before the full—and, for man, perhaps the final—catastrophe occurred. The geological record does not sustain the fear that sudden perturbations can extin-guish all life on earth (if it did, we would not be here to reflect on the subject), but it does suggest that sudden, drastic ecological collapse is possible. It suggests that life as a whole, if it is given hundreds of mil-lions of years in which to recuperate and send out new evolutionary lines, has an astounding resilience, and an ability to bring forth new and ever more impressive life forms, but it also suggests that abrupt interventions can radically disrupt any particular evolutionary configuration and dispatch hundreds of thousands of species into extinction.

The view of the earth as a single system, or organism, has only recently proceeded from poetic metaphor to actual scientific investigation, and on the whole Dr. Thomas's observation that "we do not really understand nature, at all" still holds. It is as much on the basis of this ignorance, whose scope we are only now in a position to grasp, as on the basis of the particular items of knowledge in our possession that I believe that the following judgment can be made: Bearing in mind that the possible consequences of the detonations of thousands of megatons of nuclear explosives include the blinding of insects, birds, and beasts all over the world; the extinction of many ocean species, among them some at the base of the food chain; the temporary or permanent alteration of the climate of the globe, with the outside chance of "dramatic" and "major" alterations in the structure of the atmosphere; the pollution of the whole ecosphere with oxides of nitrogen; the incapacitation in ten minutes of unprotected people who go out into the sunlight; the blinding of people who go out into the sunlight; a significant decrease in photosynthesis in plants around the world; the scalding and killing of many crops; the increase in rates of cancer and mutation around the world, but especially in the targeted zones, and the attendant risk of global epidemics; the possible poisoning of all vertebrates by sharply increased levels of Vitamin D in their skin as a result of increased ultraviolet light; and the outright slaughter on all targeted continents of most human beings and other living things by the initial nuclear radiation, the fireballs, the thermal pulses, the blast waves, the mass fires, and the fallout from the explosions; and, considering that these consequences will all interact with one another in unguessable ways and, furthermore, are in all likelihood an incomplete list, which will be added to as our knowledge of the earth increases, one must conclude that a full-scale nuclear holocaust could lead to the extinction of mankind.

To say that human extinction is a certainty would, of course, be a misrepresentation—just as it would be a misrepresentation to say that extinction can be ruled out. To begin with, we know that a holocaust may not occur at all. If one does occur, the adversaries may not use all their weapons. If they do use all their weapons, the global effects, in the ozone and elsewhere, may be moderate. And if the effects are not moderate but extreme, the ecosphere may prove resilient enough to withstand them without breaking down catastrophically. These are all substantial reasons for supposing that mankind will not be extinguished in a nuclear holocaust, or even that extinction in a holocaust is unlikely, and they tend to calm our fear and to reduce our sense of urgency. Yet at the same time we are compelled to admit that there *may* be a holocaust, that the adversaries *may* use all their weapons, that the global effects, including effects of which we are as yet unaware, *may* be severe, that the ecosphere *may* suffer catastrophic breakdown, and that our species *may* be extinguished. We are left with uncertainty, and are forced to make our decisions in a state of uncertainty. If we wish to act to save our species, we have to muster our resolve in spite of our awareness that the life of the species may not now in fact be jeopardized. On the other hand, if we wish to ignore the peril, we have to admit that we do so in the knowledge that the species may be in danger of imminent self-destruction. When the existence of nuclear weapons was made known, thoughtful people everywhere in the world realized that if the great powers entered into a nuclear-arms race the human species would sooner or later face the possibility of extinction. They also realized that in the absence of international agreements preventing it an arms race would probably occur. They knew that the path of nuclear armament was a dead end for mankind. The discovery of the energy in mass—of "the basic power of the universe"—and of a means by which man could release that energy altered the relationship between man and the source of his life, the earth. In the shadow of this power, the earth became small and the life of the human species doubtful. In that sense, the question of human extinction has been on the political agenda of the world ever since the first nuclear weapon was detonated, and there was no need for the world to build up its present tremendous arsenals before starting to worry about it. At just what point the species crossed, or will have crossed, the boundary between merely having the technical knowledge to destroy itself and actually having the arsenals at hand, ready to be used at any second, is not precisely knowable. But it is clear that at present, with some twenty thousand megatons of nuclear explosive power in existence, and with more being added every day, we have entered into the zone of uncertainty, which is to say the zone of risk of extinction. But the mere risk of extinction has a significance that is categorically different from, and immeasurably greater than, that of any other risk, and as we make our decisions we have to take that significance into account. Up to now, every risk has been contained within the frame of life; extinction would shatter the frame. It represents not the defeat of some purpose but an abyss in which all human purposes would be drowned for all time. We have no right to place the possibility of this limitless, eternal defeat on the same footing as risks that we run in the ordinary conduct of our affairs in our particular transient moment of human history. To employ a mathematical analogy, we can say that although the risk of extinction may be fractional, the stake is, humanly speaking, infinite, and a fraction of infinity is still infinity. In other words, once we learn that a holocaust *might* lead to extinction we have no right to gamble, because if we lose, the game will be over, and neither we nor anyone else will ever get another chance. Therefore, although, scientifically speaking, there is all the difference in the world between the mere possibility that a holocaust will bring about extinction and the certainty of it, morally they are the same, and we have no choice but to address the issue of nuclear weapons as though we knew for a certainty that their use would put an end to our species. In weighing the fate of the earth and, with it, our own fate, we stand before a mystery, and in tampering with the earth we tamper with a mystery. We are in deep ignorance. Our ignorance should dispose us to wonder, our wonder should make us humble, our humility should inspire us to reverence and caution, and our reverence and caution should lead us to act without delay to withdraw the threat we now pose to the earth and to ourselves.

In trying to describe possible consequences of a nuclear holocaust, I have mentioned the limitless complexity of its effects on human society and on the ecosphere—a complexity that sometimes seems to be as great as that of life itself. But if these effects should lead to human extinction, then all the complexity will give way to the utmost simplicity—the simplicity of nothingness. We—the human race—shall cease to be.

Regarded objectively, as an episode in the development of life on earth, a nuclear holocaust that brought about the extinction of mankind and other species by mutilating the ecosphere would constitute an evolutionary setback of possibly limited extent—the first to result from a deliberate action taken by the creature extinguished but perhaps no greater than any of several evolutionary setbacks, such as the extinction of the dinosaurs, of which the geological record offers evidence. (It is, of course, impossible to judge what course evolution would take after human extinction, but the past record strongly suggests that the reappearance of man is not one of the possibilities. Evolution has brought forth an amazing variety of creatures, but there is no evidence that any species, once extinguished, has ever evolved again. Whether or not nature, obeying some law of evolutionary progress, would bring forth another creature equipped with reason and will, and capable of building, and perhaps then destroying, a world, is one more unanswerable question, but it is barely conceivable that some gifted new animal will pore over the traces of our self-destruction, trying to figure out what went wrong and to learn from our mistakes. If this should be possible, then it might justify the remark once made by Kafka: "There is infinite hope, but not for us." If, on the other hand, as the record of life so far suggests, terrestrial evolution is able to produce only once the miracle of the qualities that we now associate with human beings, then all hope rides with human beings.) However, regarded subjectively, from within human life, where we are all actually situated, and as something that would happen to us, human extinction assumes awesome, inapprehensible proportions. It is of the essence of the human condition that we are born, live for a while, and then die. Through mishaps of all kinds, we may also suffer untimely death, and in extinction by nuclear arms the number of untimely deaths would reach the limit for any one catastrophe: everyone in the world would die. But although the untimely death of everyone in the world would in itself constitute an unimaginably huge loss, it would bring with it a separate, distinct loss that would be in a sense even huger—the cancellation of all future generations of human beings. According to the Bible, when Adam and Eve ate the fruit of the tree of knowledge God punished them by withdrawing from them the privilege of immortality and dooming them and their kind to die. Now our species has eaten more deeply of the fruit of the tree of knowledge, and has brought itself face to face with a second death—the death of mankind. In doing so, we have caused a basic change in the circumstances in which life was given to us, which is to say that we have altered the human condition. The distinctness of this second death from the deaths of all the people on earth can be illustrated by picturing two different global catastrophes. In the first, let us suppose that most of the people on earth were killed in a nuclear holocaust but that a few million survived and the earth happened to remain habitable by human beings. In this catastrophe, billions of people would perish, but the species would survive, and perhaps one day would even repopulate the earth in its former numbers. But now let us suppose that a substance was released into the environment which had the effect of sterilizing all the people in the world but otherwise leaving them unharmed. Then, as the existing population died off, the world would empty of people, until no one was left. Not one life would have been shortened by a single day, but the species would die. In extinction by nuclear arms, the death of the species and the death of all the people in the world would happen together, but it is important to make a clear distinction between the two losses; otherwise, the mind, overwhelmed by the thought of the deaths of the billions of living people, might stagger back without realizing that behind this already ungraspable loss there lies the separate loss of the future generations.

The possibility that the living can stop the future generations from entering into life compels us to ask basic new questions about our existence, the most sweeping of which is what these unborn ones, most of whom we will never meet even if they are born, mean to us. No one has ever thought to ask this question before our time, because no generation before ours has ever held the life and death of the species in its hands. But if we hardly know how to comprehend the possible deaths in a holocaust of the billions of people who are already in life how are we to comprehend the life or death of the infinite number of possible people who do not yet exist at all? How are we, who are a part of human life, to step back from life and see it whole, in order to assess the meaning of its disappearance? To kill a human being is murder, and there are those who believe that to abort a fetus is also murder, but what crime is it to cancel the numberless multitude of unconceived people? In what court is such a crime to be judged? Against whom is it committed? And what law does it violate? If we find the nuclear peril to be somehow abstract, and tend to consign this whole elemental issue to "defense experts" and other dubiously qualified people, part of the reason, certainly, is that the future generations really are abstract— that is to say, without the tangible existence and the unique particularities that help to make the living real to us. And if we find the subject strangely "impersonal" it may be in part because the unborn, who are the ones directly imperilled by extinction, are not yet persons. What are they, then? They lack the individuality that we often associate with the sacredness of life, and may at first thought seem to have only a shadowy, mass existence. *Where* are they? Are they to be pictured lined up in a sort of fore-life, waiting to get into life? Or should we regard them as nothing more than a pinch of chemicals in our reproductive organs, toward which we need feel no special obligations? What standing should they have among us? How much should their needs count in competition with ours? How far should the living go in trying to secure their advantage, their happiness, their existence?

The individual person, faced with the metaphysical-seeming perplexities involved in pondering the possible cancellation of people who do not yet exist—an apparently extreme effort of the imagination, which seems to require one first to summon before the mind's eye the countless possible people of the future generations and then to consign these incorporeal multitudes to a more profound nothingness —might well wonder why, when he already has his own death to worry about, he should occupy himself with this other death. Since our own individual death promises to inflict a loss that is total and final, we may find the idea of a second death merely redundant. After all, can everything be taken away from us twice? Moreover, a person might reason that even if mankind did perish he wouldn't have to know anything about it, since in that event he himself would perish. There might actually be something consoling in the idea of having so much company in death. In the midst of universal death, it somehow seems out of order to want to go on living oneself. As Randall Jarrell wrote in his poem "Losses," thinking back to his experience in the Second World War, "it was not dying: everybody died."

However, the individual would misconceive the nuclear peril if he tried to understand it primarily in terms of personal danger, or even in terms of danger to the people immediately known to him, for the nuclear peril threatens life, above all, not at the level of individuals, who already live under the sway of death, but at the level of everything that individuals hold in common. Death cuts off life; extinction cuts off birth. Death dispatches into the nothingness after life each person who has been born; extinction in one stroke locks up in the nothingness before life all the people who have not yet been born. For we are finite beings at both ends of our existence—natal as well as mortal—and it is the natality of our kind that extinction threatens. We have always been able to send people to their death, but only now has it become possible to prevent all birth and so doom all future human beings to un-creation. The threat of the loss of birth—a beginning that is over and done with for every living person—cannot be a source of immediate, selfish concern; rather, this threat assails everything that people hold in common, for it is the ability of our species to produce new generations which assures the continuation of the world in which all our common enterprises occur and have their meaning. Each death belongs inalienably to the individual who must suffer it, but birth is our common possession. And the meaning of extinction is therefore to be sought first not in what each person's own life means to him but in what the world and the people in it mean to him.

In its nature, the human world is, in Hannah Arendt's words, a "common world," which she distinguishes from the "private realm" that belongs to each person individually. (Somewhat surprisingly, Arendt, who devoted so much of her attention to the unprecedented evils that have appeared in our century, never addressed the issue of nuclear arms; yet I have discovered her thinking to be an indispensable foundation for reflection on this question.) The private realm, she writes in *The Human Condition*, a book published in 1958, is made up of "the passions of the heart, the thoughts of the mind, the delights of the senses," and terminates with each person's death, which is the most solitary of all human experiences. The common world, on the other hand, is made up of all institutions, all cities, nations, and other communities, and all works of fabrication, art, thought, and science, and it survives the death of every individual. It is basic to the common world that it encompasses not only the present but all past and future generations. "The common world is what we enter when we are born and what we leave behind when we die," Arendt writes. "It transcends our life-span into past and future alike; it was there before we came and will outlast our brief sojourn in it. It is what we have in common not only with those who live with us, but also with those who were here before and with those who will come after us." And she adds, "Without this transcendence into a potential earthly immortality, no politics, strictly speaking, no common world, and no public realm is possible." The creation of a common world is the use that we human beings, and we alone among the earth's creatures, have made of the biological circumstance that while each of us is mortal, our species is biologically immortal. If mankind had not established a common world, the species would still outlast its individual members and be immortal, but this immortality would be unknown to us and would go for nothing, as it does in the animal kingdom, and the generations, unaware of one another's existence, would come and go like waves on the beach, leaving everything just as it was before. In fact, it is only because humanity has built up a common world that we can fear our destruction as a species. It may even be that man, who has been described as the sole creature that knows that it must die, can know this only because he lives in a common world, which permits him to imagine a future beyond his own life. This common world, which is unharmed by individual death but depends on the survival of the species, has now been placed in jeopardy by nuclear arms. Death and extinction are thus complementary, dividing between them the work of undoing, or threatening to undo, everything that human beings are or can ever become, with death terminating the life of each individual and extinction imperilling the common world shared by all. In one sense, extinction is less terrible than death, since extinction can be avoided, while death is inevitable; but in another sense extinction is more terrible—is the more radical nothingness—because extinction ends death just as surely as it ends birth and life. Death is only death; extinction is the death of death.

The world is made a common one by what Arendt calls "publicity," which insures that "everything that appears in public can be seen and heard by everybody." She writes, "A common world can survive the coming and going of the generations only to the extent that it appears in public. It is the publicity of the public realm which can absorb and make shine through the centuries whatever men may want to save from the natural ruin of time." But this publicity does not only shine on human works; it also brings to light the natural foundations of life, enabling us to perceive what our origins are. It thereby permits us not only to endow things of our own making with a degree of immortality but to see and appreciate the preexisting, biological immortality of our species and of life on the planet, which forms the basis for any earthly immortality whatever. The chief medium of the publicity of the common world is, of course, language, whose possession by man is believed by many to be what separates him from the other animals; but there are also the other "languages" of the arts and sciences. And standing behind language is that of which language is expressive— our reason, our psyche, our will, and our spirit. Through these, we are capable of entering into the lives of others, and of becoming aware that we belong to a community of others that is as wide as our species. The foundation of a common world is an exclusively human achievement, and to live in a common world—to speak and listen to one another, to read, to write, to know about the past and look ahead to the future, to receive the achievements of past generations, and to pass them on, together with achievements of our own, to future generations, and otherwise to participate in human enterprises that outlast any individual life—is part of what it means to be human, and by threatening all this nuclear weapons threaten a part of our humanity. The common world is not something that can be separated from the life we now live; it is intrinsic to our existence—something as close to us as the words we speak and the thoughts we think using those words. Descartes's famous axiom "I think, therefore I am" has perhaps been more extensively rebutted than any other single philosophical proposition. The rebuttal by Lewis Mumford happens to amount to a description of each person's indebtedness to the common world and to the common biological inheritance that the common world has brought to light. "Descartes forgot that before he uttered these words 'I think' . . . he needed the cooperation of countless fellow-beings, extending back to his own knowledge as far as the thousands of years that Biblical history recorded," Mumford writes in *The Pentagon of Power*, a book published in 1970. "Beyond that, we know now he needed the aid of an even remoter past that mankind too long remained ignorant of: the millions of years required to transform his dumb animal ancestors into conscious human beings." In our long and arduous ascent out of biological darkness, it seems, we forgot our indebtedness to the natural world of our origins, and now, in consequence, threaten to plunge ourselves into an even deeper darkness. The nuclear predicament is thus in every sense a crisis of life in the common world. Only because there is a common world, in which knowledge of the physical world accumulates over the generations, can there be a threat to the common world and to its natural foundations. Only because there is a common world, which permits us knowledge of other generations and of the terrestrial nature of which human life is a part, can we worry about, or even know of, that threat. And only because there is a common world can we hope, by concerting our actions, to save ourselves and the earth.

The common world has been the work of every generation that has lived in it, back to the remotest ages. Much as poets begin by using language as they find it but, usually as an unselfconscious consequence of their work, leave usage slightly altered behind them, people in general pursue their various ends in the yielding medium of the world and shape its character by their actions. But although the world receives the imprint of the lives of those who pass through it, it has never been given to any single generation to dictate the character of the world. Not even the most thoroughgoing totalitarian regimes have succeeded in wholly shaping the lives of their peoples. One has only to think of Alexander Solzhenitsyn growing up in the Soviet Union but drawing so much of his spiritual sustenance from earlier centuries of Russian life, or to think of China, where so many of the customs and qualities of the people have outlasted what was probably the longest and most concentrated assault in history by a government on the national tradition of its own country, to realize how deeply a people's past is woven into its present.

The links binding the living, the dead, and the unborn were described by Edmund Burke, the great eighteenth-century English conservative, as a "partnership" of the generations. He wrote, "Society is indeed a contract. . . . It is a partnership in all science; a partnership in all art; a partnership in every virtue, and in all perfection. As the ends of such a partnership cannot be obtained except in many generations, it becomes a partnership not only between those who are living, but between those who are living, those who are dead, and those who are to be born." Pericles offered a similar, though not identical, vision of the common life of the generations in his funeral oration, in which he said that all Athens was a "sepulchre" for the remembrance of the soldiers who had died fighting for their city. Thus, whereas Burke spoke of common tasks that needed many generations for their achievement, Pericles spoke of the immortality that the living confer on the dead by remembering their sacrifices. In the United States, Abraham Lincoln seemed to combine these two thoughts when he said in his Gettysburg address that the sacrifices of the soldiers who had died at Gettysburg laid an obligation on the living to devote themselves to the cause for which the battle had been fought. And, indeed, every political observer or political actor of vision has recognized that if life is to be fully human it must take cognizance of the dead and the unborn.

But now our responsibilities as citizens in the common world have been immeasurably enlarged. In the pre-nuclear common world, we were partners in the protection of the arts, the institutions, the customs, and all "perfection" of life; now we are also partners in the protection of life itself. Burke described as a common inheritance the achievements that one generation passed along to the next. "By a constitutional policy, working after the pattern of nature, we receive, we hold, we transmit our government and our privileges, in the same manner in which we enjoy and transmit our property and our lives," he wrote. "The institutions of policy, the goods of fortune, the gifts of Providence, are handed down, to us and from us, in the same course and order." These words appear in Burke's *Reflections on the Revolution in France*—the revolution being an event that filled him with horror, for in it he believed he saw a single generation violently destroying in a few years the national legacy of hundreds of years. But, whether or not he was right in thinking that the inheritance of France was being squandered by its recipients, the inheriting generations and their successors were at least biologically intact. In our time, however, among the items in the endangered inheritance the inheritors find themselves. Each generation of mankind still receives, holds, and transmits the inheritance from the past, but, being now a part of that inheritance, each generation *is received, is held, and is transmitted,* so that receiver and received, holder and held, transmitter and transmitted are one. Yet our jeopardy is only a part of the jeopardy of all life, and the largest item in the inheritance that we receive, hold, and must transmit is the entire ecosphere. So deep is the change in the structure of human life brought about by this new peril that in retrospect the Burkean concern about the "perfection" of life, indispensable as this concern is to the quality of our existence, seems like only the barest hint or suggestion of the incomparably more commanding obligation that is laid on us by the nuclear predicament. It strikes modern ears as prophetic that when Burke sought to describe the permanence in human affairs which he so valued he often resorted to metaphors drawn from the natural world—speaking, for example, of a "pattern of nature" that human society should imitate—as though he had had a premonition that an almost habitually revolutionary mankind would one day proceed from tearing society apart to tearing the natural world apart. Speaking of the society into which each of us is born, Burke angrily asked whether it could be right to "hack that aged parent in pieces." His words have acquired a deeper meaning than he could ever have foretold for them now that the parent in question is not merely human society but the earth itself.

* * *

Implicit in everything that I have said so far about the nuclear predicament there has been a perplexity that I would now like to take up explicitly, for it leads, I believe, into the very heart of our response—or, rather, our lack of response—to the predicament. I have pointed out that our species is the most important of all the things that, as inhabitants of a common world, we inherit from the past generations, but it does not go far enough to point out this superior importance, as though in making our decision about extinction we were being asked to choose between, say, liberty, on the one hand, and the survival of the species, on the other. For the species not only overarches but contains all the benefits of life in the common world, and to speak of sacrificing the species for the sake of one of these benefits involves one in the absurdity of wanting to destroy something in order to preserve one of its parts, as if one were to burn down a house in an attempt to redecorate the living room, or to kill someone to improve his character. But even to point out this absurdity fails to take the full measure of the peril of extinction, for mankind is not some invaluable object that lies outside us and that we must protect so that we can go on benefitting from it; rather, it is we ourselves, without whom everything there is loses its value. To say this is another way of saying that extinction is unique not because it destroys mankind as an object but because it destroys mankind as the source of all possible human subjects, and this, in turn, is another way of saying that extinction is a second death, for one's own individual death is the end not of any object in life but of the subject that experiences all objects. Death, however, places the mind in a quandary. One of the confounding characteristics of death—"tomorrow's zero," in Dostoevski's phrase—is that, precisely because it removes the person himself rather than something in his life, it seems to offer the mind nothing to take hold of. One even feels it inappropriate, in a way, to try to speak "about" death at all, as though death were a thing situated somewhere outside us and available for objective inspection, when the fact is that it is within us—is, indeed, an essential part of what we are. It would be more appropriate, perhaps, to say that death, as a fundamental element of our being, "thinks" in us and through us about whatever we think about, coloring our thoughts and moods with its presence throughout our lives.

Extinction is another such intangible, incomprehensible, yet all-important presence, surrounding and pervading life without ever showing its face directly. Extinction is, in truth, even less tangibly present than death, because while death continually strikes down those around us, thereby at least reminding us of what death is, and reminding us that we, too, must die, extinction can, by definition, strike only once, and is, therefore, entirely hidden from our direct view; no one has ever seen extinction and no one ever will. Extinction is thus *a human future that can never become a human present.* For who will suffer this loss, which we somehow regard as supreme? We, the living, will not suffer it; we will be dead. Nor will the unborn shed any tears over their lost chance to exist; to do so they would have to exist already. The perplexity underlying the whole question of extinction, then, is that although extinction might appear to be the largest misfortune that mankind could ever suffer, it doesn't seem to happen to anybody, and one is left wondering where its impact is to be registered, and by whom.

Lucretius wrote, "Do you not know that when death comes, there will be no other you to mourn your memory, and stand above you prostrate?" And Freud wrote, "It is indeed impossible to imagine our own death: and whenever we attempt to do so, we can perceive that we are in fact still present as spectators." Thought and feeling try to peer ahead and catch a glimpse of death, but they encounter their own demise along the way, for their death is what death is. In the same way, when we try to picture extinction we come up against the fact that the human faculties with which someone might see, hear, feel, or understand this event are obliterated in it, and we are left facing a blankness, or emptiness. But even the words "blankness" and "emptiness" are too expressive—too laden with human response—because, inevitably, they connote the *experience* of blankness and emptiness, whereas extinction is the end of human experience. It thus seems to be in the nature of extinction to repel emotion and starve thought, and if the mind, brought face to face with extinction, descends into a kind of exhaustion and dejection it is surely in large part because we know that mankind cannot be a "spectator" at its own funeral any more than any individual person can.

It might be well to consider for a moment the novel shape of the mental and emotional predicament that the nuclear peril places us in—a predicament that exists not because of a psychological failing or the inadequacy of the human mind but because of the actual nature of the thing that we are trying to think about. Strange as it may seem, we may have to teach ourselves to think about extinction in a meaningful way. (This seems less strange when we recall that whereas people may have a natural aversion to death no similar instinct moves them to ward off extinction—although most people's spontaneous reaction to the idea is hardly favorable, either. Like the peril of extinction itself, recognition of the peril and understanding of it can come only as a product of our life together in the common world—as a product, that is, not of instinct but of civilization. Other species not only do not resist extinction but are completely unaware that it is happening; the last passenger pigeon had no way of knowing that it *was* the last passenger pigeon, much less of doing anything about it.) On first looking into the consequences of a nuclear holocaust, one is struck by the odd fact that, beyond a certain point, the larger the imagined attack is, the less there is to say about it. At "low" levels of attack—the tens or hundreds of megatons—there is the complexity of the countless varieties of suffering and social and ecological breakdown to reflect on. But at higher levels—the thousands of megatons—the complexity steadily gives way to the simplicity and nothingness of death. Step by step, the "spectators" at the "funeral"—the sufferers of the calamity, in whose eyes it retains a human reality, and in whose lives it remains a human experience—dwindle away, until at last, when extinction is reached, all the "spectators" have themselves gone to the grave, and only the stones and stars, and whatever algae and mosses may have made it through, are present to witness the end.

Yet no matter how poor and thin a thing for imagination to grasp extinction may be, it seems to be in imagination alone that it can be grasped at all. Lacking the possibility of experience, all we have left is thought, since for us extinction is locked away forever in a future that can never arrive. Like the thought "I do not exist," the thought "Humanity is now extinct" is an impossible one for a rational person, because as soon as it is, *we* are not. In imagining any other event, we look ahead to a moment that is still within the stream of human time, which is to say within a time in which other human beings will exist, and will be responding to whatever they see, looking back to our present time and looking forward to future times that will themselves be within the sequence of human time. But in imagining extinction we gaze past everything human to a dead time that falls outside the human tenses of past, present, and future. By adopting a coldly scientific frame of mind, we can imagine that inert scene, but the exercise is oddly fruitless, and seems to hold no clue to the meaning of extinction. Instead, we find that almost everything that might engage our attention or stir our interest—even if only to repel us—has passed away. Struggling in this way to grasp the meaning of extinction, we may be led to wonder whether it can be grasped at all, and begin to suspect that nature provided an instinctual drive for the perpetuation of the species because it knew that our consciousness and will were so poorly equipped to deal with this task.

Given the special role of our mental faculties in any attempt to come to terms with extinction, it is not very surprising that a great deal of the writing that has been done about nuclear strategy is characterized by a highly abstract tone. The atmosphere in which this work goes forward is perfectly suggested by the nickname for the sort of institution in which much of it takes place: "the think tank." This term, evoking a hermetic world of thought, exactly reflects the intellectual circumstances of those thinkers whose job it is to deduce from pure theory, without the lessons of experience, what might happen if nuclear hostilities broke out. But, as Herman Kahn, the director of one of these think tanks (the Hudson Institute), and the author of *Thinking About the Unthinkable*, among other works on nuclear strategy, has rightly said, "it will do no good to inveigh against theorists; in this field, everyone is a theorist." Hence, while in one sense Kahn is right to call a nuclear holocaust "unthinkable," it is also true, as his remark suggests, that when it comes to grasping the nature of this peril thinking about it is all that we *can* do.

The intellectual and affective difficulties involved in trying to understand the nuclear predicament have no precedent (unless one is to count individual death as a precedent), but they were foreshadowed in at least some respects by certain barriers that have impeded understanding of other sudden revolutionary developments of the modern age. In *Democracy in America*, Tocqueville, speaking of the democratic revolution of his times, wrote, "Although the revolution that is taking place in the social condition, the laws, the opinions, and the feelings of men is still very far from being terminated, yet its results already admit of no comparison with anything that the world has ever before witnessed. I go back from age to age up to the remotest antiquity, but I find no parallel to what is occurring before my eyes; as the past has ceased to cast its light upon the future, the mind of man wanders in obscurity." But if in Tocqueville's day the past had ceased to cast its light upon the future, the present—what was occurring before his eyes-could still do so. Although the democratic revolution had not "terminated," it was nevertheless in full swing, and democratic America provided Tocqueville with enough factual material to fill the two thick volumes of his book. Drawing on this material, he was able to cast so much light on the future that we still see by it today.

The radical novelty of events became an even more troubling

impediment to the understanding of totalitarian revolutions of our century. Arendt, who, more than anyone else, performed the offices of a Tocqueville in casting light on totalitarianism, wrote, "The gap between past and future ceased to be a condition peculiar only to the activity of thought and restricted as an experience to those few who made thinking their primary business. It became a tangible reality and perplexity for all; that is, it became a fact of political relevance." The totalitarian regimes, of course, made active attempts to revise or erase the factual record of both the past and the present. Yet these attempts have not been successful, and, in spite of the sense of unreality we feel when we confront the acts of the totalitarian regimes, totalitarianism is for us today something that has left its bloody marks on history, and these events, when we are told of them by credible witnesses, fill us with active revulsion. In Hitler's Germany and Stalin's Russia, horrifying events of dreamlike incredibility occurred, and pure, everyday common sense might reject their very possibility if the historical record were not there. In Arendt's *Eichmann in Jerusalem*, we read the following description of the gassing to death by the Nazis of Jews in Poland:

This is what Eichmann saw: The Jews were in a large room; they were told to strip; then a truck arrived, stopping directly before the entrance to the room, and the naked Jews were told to enter it. The doors were closed and the truck started off. "I cannot tell [how many Jews entered, Eichmann said later], I hardly looked. I could not; I could not; I had had enough. The shrieking, and . . . I was much too upset, and so on, as I later told Müller when I reported to him; he did not get much profit out of my report. I then drove along after the van, and then I saw the most horrible sight I had thus far seen in my life. The truck was making for an open ditch, the doors were opened, and the corpses were thrown out, as though they were still alive, so smooth were their limbs. They were hurled into the ditch, and I can still see a civilian extracting the teeth with tooth plyers."

We don't want to believe this; we find it all but impossible to believe this. But our wishful disbelief is stopped cold by the brute historical fact that it *happened:* we are therefore forced to believe. But extinction *has not happened*, and hides behind the veil of a future time which human eyes can never pierce. It is true that the testimony of those who survived the bombings of Hiroshima and Nagasaki offers us a vivid record of devastation by nuclear arms, but this record, which already seems to exhaust our powers of emotional response, illumines only a tiny corner of a nuclear holocaust, and, in any case, does not reach the question of extinction, which, instead of presenting us with scenes of horror, puts an end to them, just as it puts an end to all other scenes that are enacted by human beings. After several centuries of bringing a variety of nightmarish futures into existence, we have now invented one so unbelievable and overwhelming that it cannot come to pass at all. ("Come to pass" is a perfect phrase to describe what extinction cannot do. It can "come," but not "to pass," for with its arrival the creature that divides time into past, present, and future—the creature before whose eyes it would "pass"—is annihilated.) Deprived of both past and present experience to guide us as we try to face the nuclear predicament, we are left in the unpromising position of asking the future to shed light on itself.

As we look ahead to the possibility of extinction, our secret thought, which is well-founded in the facts of the case, may be that since everyone will then be dead no one will have to worry about it, so why should we worry about it now? Following this unacknowledged but logical line of thinking, we may be led to the shrug of indifference that seems to have characterized most people's conscious reaction to the nuclear peril for the last thirty-six years. If extinction is nothing, we may unconsciously ask ourselves, may not no reaction be the right one? By contrast, our thoughts and feelings experience no such defeat when we consider a privation of future generations which falls short of denying them their existence—when we imagine, for example, that their supply of oil will run out, or that their supply of food will grow short, or that their civilization will go into decline. Then, through the widest possible extension of our respect for individual life, we can picture their plight, sympathize with their suffering, and perhaps take some action to forestall the evil. In effect, we are still following the ethical precept of doing unto others as we would have them do unto us, now expanding our understanding of who the others are to include the unborn, as Burke did. This comes naturally to us, as Burke pointed out, because a moment's reflection reveals to us the debt of gratitude that we owe past generations. However, in extending our sympathetic concern in this way, of course, we make the tacit assumption that there will *be* future generations, taking it for granted that nature, acting in and through us, will bring them forth, as it always has done. And in the pre-nuclear world, before it was in our power to extinguish the species, this confidence was warranted. But now the creation of new human beings is just the thing that is in question; and, in our attempt to grasp not the suffering and death of future generations but their failure to come into existence in the first place, a sympathetic response is inappropriate, for sympathy can extend only to living beings, and extinction is the foreclosure of life. The shuddering anticipation that we may feel on behalf of others when we realize that they are threatened with harm is out of place, because the lack of any others is the defining feature of extinction.

In removing the sufferer and his suffering with one blow, extinction again shows its resemblance to death. Montaigne writes, "Death can put an end, and deny access, to all our other woes," and adds, "What stupidity to torment ourselves about passing into exemption from all torment!" Extinction likewise brings not suffering but the end of suffering. Among feelings, suffering and joy are opposites, but both, like all feelings, are manifestations of life, and, as such, are together opposites of either death or extinction. Never having faced the end of human life before, we are led by mental habit to try to respond to it as though it were a disaster of one kind or another, in which people were going to be harmed or bereaved. But in doing so we strain for a reaction that, to our puzzlement, perhaps, does not come, for the excellent reason that in extinction there is no disaster: no falling buildings, no killed or injured people, no shattered lives, no mourning survivors. All of that is dissolved in extinction, along with everything else that goes on in life. We are left only with the ghostlike cancelled future generations, who, metaphorically speaking, have been waiting through all past time to enter into life but have now been turned back by us.

The distinction between harm to people in the world and the end of the world—or even the end of a world, such as occurred to European Jewry under Hitler—may give us some clue to the nature of what Arendt, borrowing a phrase of Kant's in order to describe the unparalleled crimes of Hitler's Germany and Stalin's Soviet Union, has called "radical evil." The "true hallmark" of radical evil, "about whose nature so little is known," she says, is that we do not know either how to punish these offenses or how to forgive them, and they therefore "transcend the realm of human affairs and the potentialities of human power, both of which they radically destroy wherever they make their appearance." By crimes that "transcend the realm of human affairs and the potentialities of human power," she means, I believe, crimes so great that they overwhelm the capacity of every existing system of jurisprudence, or other organized human response, to deal with them adequately. She goes on to say, "Here, where the deed itself dispossesses us of all power, we can indeed only repeat with Jesus: 'It were better for him that a millstone were hanged about his neck, and he cast into the sea.' " I would like to suggest that evil becomes radical whenever it goes beyond destroying individual victims (in whatever numbers) and, in addition, mutilates or destroys the *world* that can in some way respond to—and thus in some measure redeem—the deaths suffered. This capacity of evil was demonstrated on a large scale in modern times by the totalitarian regimes, which, in a manner of speaking, attempted to tear gaping, unmendable holes in the fabric of the world—holes into which entire peoples or classes would sink without a trace—but now it has fully emerged in the capacity of the species for self-extinction, which, by ending the world altogether, would "dispossess us of all power" forever. When crimes are of a certain magnitude and character, they nullify our power to respond to them adequately because they smash the human context in which human losses normally acquire their meaning for us. When an entire community or an entire people is destroyed, most of those who would mourn the victims, or bring the perpetrators to justice, or forgive them, or simply remember what occurred, are themselves destroyed. When that community is all mankind, the loss of the human context is total, and no one is left to respond. In facing this deed, we will either respond to it before it is done, and thus avoid doing it, or lose any chance to respond, and pass into oblivion.

If this interpretation is correct, every episode of radical evil is already a small extinction, and should be seen in that light. Between individual death and biological extinction, then, there are other possible levels of obliteration, which have some of the characteristics of extinction. The "end of civilization"—the total disorganization and disruption of human life, breaking the links between mankind's past and its future—is one. Genocide—the destruction of a people— which can be seen as an extinction *within* mankind, since it eliminates an element in the interior diversity of the species is another; in fact, genocide, including, above all, Hitler's attempt to extinguish the Jewish people, is the closest thing to a precursor of the extinction of the species that history contains. What the end of civilization, geno- cide, and extinction all have in common is that they are attacks not merely on existing people and things but on either the biological or the cultural heritage that human beings transmit from one generation to the next; that is, they are crimes against the future. The connection between genocide and extinction is further suggested by the fact that what the superpowers *intend* to do if a holocaust breaks out (leaving aside the unintended "collateral effects" for the moment) is to commit genocide against one another—to erase the other side as a culture and as a people from the face of the earth. In its nature, human extinction is and always will be without precedent, but the episodes of radical evil that the world has already witnessed are warnings to us that gigantic, insane crimes are not prevented from occurring merely because they are "unthinkable." On the contrary, they may be all the more likely to occur for that reason. Heinrich Himmler, a leading figure in the carrying out of the destruction of the Jews, assured his subordinates from time to time that their efforts were especially noble because by assuming the painful burden of making Europe "Jew-free" they were fighting "battles which future generations will not have to fight again." His remark applies equally well to a nuclear holocaust, which might render the earth "human-free." This is another "battle" (and the word is as inappropriate for a nuclear holocaust as it was for the murder of millions of Jews) that "future generations will not have to fight again."

If our usual responses to disasters and misfortunes are mismatched to the peril of extinction, then we have to look in some other quarter of our being to find its significance. Individual death once more offers a point of departure. We draw closer to death throughout our lives, but we never arrive there, for just as we are about to arrive we are gone. Yet although death thus always stands outside life, it nevertheless powerfully conditions life. Montaigne writes, "You are in death while you are in life; for you are after death when you are no longer in life. Or, if you prefer it this way, you are dead after life; but during life you are dying; and death affects the dying much more roughly than the dead, and more keenly and essentially." We are similarly "in extinction" while we are in life, and are after extinction when we are extinct. Extinction, too, thus affects the living "more roughly" and "more keenly and essentially" than it does the nonliving, who in its case are not the dead but the unborn. Like death, extinction is felt not when it has arrived but beforehand, as a deep shadow cast back across the whole of life. The answer to the question of who experiences extinction and when, therefore, is that we the living experience it, now and in all the moments of our lives. Hence, while it is in one sense true that extinction lies outside human life and never happens to anybody, in another sense extinction saturates our existence and never stops happening. If we want to find the meaning of extinction, accordingly, we should start by looking with new eyes at ourselves and the world we live in, and at the lives we live. The question to be asked then is no longer what the features and characteristics of extinction are but what it says about us and what it does to us that we are preparing our own extermination.

Because the peril is rooted in basic scientific knowledge, which is likely to last as long as mankind does, it is apparently a permanent one. But in the presence of that peril opposite poles of response, both in feeling and, above all, in action, are possible, and the quality of the lives we live together is conditioned in opposite ways according to which response we choose. The choice is really between two entire ways of life. One response is to decline to face the peril, and thus to go on piling up the instruments of doom year after year until, by accident or design, they go off. The other response is to recognize the peril, dismantle the weapons, and arrange the political affairs of the earth so that the weapons will not be built again. I remarked that we do not have two earths at our disposal—one for experimental holocausts and the other to live on. Neither do any of us have two souls—one for responding to the nuclear predicament and the other for living the rest of our lives. In the long run, if we are dull and cold toward life in its entirety we will become dull and cold toward life in its particulars— toward the events of our own daily lives—but if we are alert and passionate about life in its entirety we will also be alert and passionate about it in its dailiness.

It is a matter of record that in our thirty-six years of life in a nuclear-armed world we have been largely dead to the nuclear peril, and I would like to consider more closely what this failure of response seems to have been doing to our world. Pascal, taking note of the cerebral character of the condition of mortality, once observed that "it is easier to endure death without thinking about it than to endure the thought of death without dying." His observation perfectly describes our response so far to the peril of extinction: we have found it much easier to dig our own grave than to think about the fact that we are doing so. Almost everyone has acknowledged on some level that the peril exists, but the knowledge has been without consequences in our feelings and our actions, and the superpowers have proceeded with their nuclear buildups, in the recent words of George Kennan, "like the victims of some sort of hypnotism, like men in a dream, like lemmings heading for the sea."

For a very short while before and after the first bomb was produced, a few men at and near the top of the American government seemed prepared to deal with the nuclear predicament at its proper depth. One of them was Secretary of War Henry Stimson, who knew of the Manhattan Project and, in March of 1945—four months before the Trinity test, at Alamogordo—confided to his diary an account of a discussion he had had about the new weapon with Harvey Bundy, his closest personal assistant. "Our thoughts," he wrote, "went right down to the bottom facts of human nature, morals, and governments, and it is by far the most searching and important thing that I have had to do since I have been here in the Office of the Secretary of War because it touches matters which are deeper even than the principles of present government." Yet those deep thoughts somehow did not take root firmly enough in the hearts of the American leaders or of the world at large, and the old ways of thinking returned, in the teeth of the new facts. The true dimensions of the nuclear peril, and of its significance for mankind, had been glimpsed, but then the awareness faded and the usual exigencies of international political life—including, shortly, the Cold War between the United States and the Soviet Union—laid claim to people's passions and energies. The nuclear buildup that has continued to this day began, and the nuclear question, having emerged abruptly from the twofold obscurity of scientific theory and governmental secrecy, was almost immediately thrust into the new obscurity of the arcane, abstract, denatured world of the theorists in the think tanks, who were, in effect, deputized to think the "unthinkable" thoughts that the rest of us lacked the will to think.

Thus began the strange double life of the world which has continued up to the present. On the one hand, we returned to business as usual, as though everything remained as it always had been. On the other hand, we began to assemble the stockpiles that could blow this supposedly unaltered existence sky-high at any second. When the scientists working on the Manhattan Project wanted to send word to President Truman, who was at the Potsdam Conference, that the detonation near Alamogordo had been successful, they chose the horrible but apt code phrase "Babies satisfactorily born." Since then, these "babies"—which are indeed like the offspring of a new species, except that it is a species not of life but of anti-life, threatening to end life—have "proliferated" steadily under our faithful care, bringing forth "generation" after "generation" of weapons, each more numerous and more robust than the last, until they now threaten to do away with their creators altogether. Yet while we did all this we somehow kept the left hand from knowing—or from dwelling on—what the right hand was doing; and the separation of our lives from awareness of the doom that was being prepared under us and around us was largely preserved.

It is probably crucial psychologically in maintaining this divorce that, once Hiroshima and Nagasaki had been pushed out of mind, the nuclear peril grew in such a way that while it relentlessly came to threaten the existence of everything, it physically touched nothing, and thus left people free not to think about it if they so chose. Like a kindhearted executioner, the bomb permitted its prospective victims to go on living seemingly ordinary lives up to the day that the execution should suddenly and without warning be carried out. (If one nuclear bomb had gone off each year in one of the world's cities, we can well imagine that public attitudes toward the nuclear peril would now be quite different.) The continuity, however illusory, between the pre-nuclear world and the nuclear world which was made possible by these years of not using nuclear weapons was important in preserving the world's denial of the peril because it permitted a spurious normality to be maintained—although "normality" was at times embraced with a fervor that betrayed an edge of hysterical insecurity. The spectacle of life going on as usual carried with it a strong presumption that nothing much was wrong. When we observed that no one seemed to be worried, that no one was showing any signs of alarm or doing anything to save himself, it was hard to resist the conclusion that everything was all right. After all, if we were reasonable people and we were doing nothing how could there be anything the matter? The totality of the peril, in particular, helped to disguise it, for, with everyone and everything in the world similarly imperilled, there was no flight from imperilled things to safe things—no flow of capital from country to country, or migration of people from one place to another. Thoughts of the nuclear peril were largely banned from waking life, and relegated to dreams or to certain fringes of society, and open, active concern about it was restricted to certain "far-out" people, whose ideas were on the whole not so much rejected by the supposedly sober, "realistic" people in the mainstream as simply ignored. In this atmosphere, discussion of the nuclear peril even took on a faintly embarrassing aura, as though dwelling on it were somehow melodramatic, or were a sophomoric excess that serious people outgrew with maturity.

It was not unless one lifted one's gaze from all the allegedly normal events occurring before one's eyes and looked at the executioner's sword hanging over everyone's head that the normality was revealed as a sort of mass insanity. This was an insanity that consisted not in screaming and making a commotion but precisely in *not* doing these things in the face of overwhelming danger, as though everyone had been sedated. Passengers on a ship who are eating, sunning themselves, playing shuffleboard, and engaging in all the usual shipboard activities appear perfectly normal as long as their ship is sailing safely in quiet seas, but these same passengers doing these same things appear deranged if in full view of them all their ship is caught in a vortex that may shortly drag it and them to destruction. Then their placidity has the appearance of an unnatural loss of normal human responses—of a pathetic and sickening acquiescence in their own slaughter. T. S. Eliot's well-known lines "This is the way the world ends/Not with a bang but a whimper" may not be literally correct—there will decidedly be a very big bang—but in a deeper sense it is certainly right; if we do end the world, the sequence is likely to be not a burst of strong-willed activity leading to a final explosion but enervation, dulled senses, enfeebled will, stupor, and paralysis. Then death.

Since we have not made a positive decision to exterminate ourselves but instead have chosen to live on the edge of extinction, periodically lunging toward the abyss only to draw back at the last second, our situation is one of uncertainty and nervous insecurity rather than of absolute hopelessness. We know that we may fall into the abyss at any moment, but we also know that we may not. So life proceeds—what else should it do?—but with a faltering and hesitant step, like one who gropes in darkness at the top of a tall precipice. Intellectually, we recognize that we have prepared ourselves for self-extermination and are improving the preparations every day, but emotionally and politically we have failed to respond. Accordingly, we have begun to live *as if* life were safe, but living *as if* is very different from just living. A split opens up between what we know and what we feel. We place our daily doings in one compartment of our lives and the threat to all life in another compartment. However, this split concerns too fundamental a matter to remain restricted to that matter alone, and it begins to influence the rest of life. Before long, denial of reality becomes a habit—a dominant mode in the life of society—and unresponsiveness becomes a way of life. The society that has accepted the threat of its utter destruction soon finds it hard to react to lesser ills, for a society cannot be at the same time asleep and awake, insane and sane, against life and for life.

To say that we and all future generations are threatened with extinction by the nuclear peril, however, is to describe only half of our situation. The other half is that we are the authors of that extinction. (For the populations of the superpowers, this is true in a positive sense, since we pay for extinction and support the governments that pose the threat of it, while for the peoples of the non-nuclear-armed world it is true only in the negative sense that they fail to try to do anything about the danger.) Like all those who are inclined to suicide, we approach the action in two capacities: the capacity of the one who would kill and that of the one who would be killed. As when we dream, we are both the authors and the sufferers of our fate. Therefore, when we hide from ourselves the immense preparations that we have made for our self-extermination we do so for two compelling reasons. First, we don't want to recognize that at any moment our lives may be taken away from us and our world blasted to dust, and, second, we don't want to face the fact that we are potential mass killers. The moral cost of nuclear armament is that it makes of all of us underwriters of the slaughter of hundreds of millions of people and of the cancellation of the future generations—an action whose utter indefensibility is not altered in the slightest degree by the fact that each side contemplates performing it only in "retaliation." In fact, as we shall see, this retaliation is one of the least justified actions ever contemplated, being wholly pointless. It is another nonsensical feature of the nuclear predicament that while each side regards the population of the other side as the innocent victims of unjust government, each proposes to punish the other government by annihilating that already suffering and oppressed population. Nor is there any exoneration from complicity in this slaughter in the theoretical justification that we possess nuclear arms not in order to use them but in order to prevent their use, for the fact is that even in theory prevention works only to the degree that it is backed up by the plausible threat of use in certain circumstances. Strategy thus commits us all to actions that we cannot justify by any moral standard. It introduces into our lives a vast, morally incomprehensible—or simply immoral—realm, in which every scruple or standard that we otherwise claim to observe or uphold is suspended. To be targeted from the cradle to the grave as a victim of indiscriminate mass murder is degrading in one way, but to target others for similar mass murder is degrading in another and, in a sense, a worse way. We endeavor to hold life sacred, but in accepting our roles as the victims and the perpetrators of nuclear mass slaughter we convey the steady message—and it is engraved more and more deeply on our souls as the years roll by—that life not only is not sacred but is worthless; that, somehow, according to a "strategic" logic that we cannot understand, it has been judged acceptable for everybody to be killed.

As it happens, our two roles in the nuclear predicament have been given visual representation in the photographs of the earth that we have taken with the aid of another technical device of our time, the spaceship. These pictures illustrate, on the one hand, our mastery over nature, which has enabled us to take up a position in the heavens and look back on the earth as though it were just one more celestial body, and, on the other, our weakness and frailty in the face of that mastery, which we cannot help feeling when we see the smallness, solitude, and delicate beauty of our planetary home. Looking at the earth as it is caught in the lens of the camera, reduced to the size of a golf ball, we gain a new sense of scale, and are made aware of a new relation between ourselves and the earth: we can almost imagine that we might hold this earth between the giant thumb and forefinger of one hand. Similarly, as the possessors of nuclear arms we stand outside nature, holding instruments of cosmic power with which we can blot life out, while at the same time we remain embedded in nature and depend on it for our survival.

Yet although the view from space is invaluable, in the last analysis the view that counts is the one from earth, from within life—the view, let us say, from a bedroom window in some city, in the evening, overlooking a river, perhaps, and with the whole colored by some regret or some hope or some other human sentiment. Whatever particular scene might come to mind, and whatever view and mood might be immediately present, from this earthly vantage point another view—one even longer than the one from space—opens up. It is the view of our children and grandchildren, and of all the future generations of mankind, stretching ahead of us in time—a view not just of one earth but of innumerable earths in succession, standing out brightly against the endless darkness of space, of oblivion. The thought of cutting off life's flow, of amputating this future, is so shocking, so alien to nature, and so contradictory to life's impulse that we can scarcely entertain it before turning away in revulsion and disbelief. The very incredibility of the action protects it from our gaze; our very love of life seems to rush forward to deny that we could do this. But although we block out the awareness of this self-posed threat as best we can, engrossing ourselves in life's richness to blind ourselves to the jeopardy to life, ultimately there is no way that we can remain unaffected by it. For finally we know and deeply feel that the ever-shifting, ever-dissolving moments of our mortal lives are sustained and given meaning by the broad stream of life, which bears us along like a force at our backs. Being human, we have, through the establishment of a common world, taken up residence in the enlarged space of past, present, and future, and if we threaten to destroy the future generations we harm ourselves, for the threat we pose to them is carried back to us through the channels of the common world that we all inhabit together. Indeed, "they" are we ourselves, and if their existence is in doubt our present becomes a sadly incomplete affair, like only one word of a poem, or one note of a song. Ultimately, it is subhuman.

Because the weight of extinction, like the weight of mortality, bears down on life through the mind and spirit but otherwise, until the event occurs, leaves us physically undisturbed, no one can prove that it alters the way we live. We can only say that it hardly stands to reason that the largest peril that history has ever produced—a peril in which, indeed, history would swallow itself up—should leave the activities of life, every one of which is threatened with dissolution, unaffected; and that we actually do seem to find life changing in ways that might be expected. Since the future generations are specifically what is at stake, all human activities that assume the future are undermined directly. To begin with, desire, love, childbirth, and everything else that has to do with the biological renewal of the species have been administered a powerful shock by the nuclear peril. The timeless, largely unspoken confidence of the species that although each person had to die, life itself would go on—the faith that on earth life was somehow favored, which found one of its most beautiful expressions in Christ's admonition "Consider the lilies of the field, how they grow; they toil not, neither do they spin: And yet I say unto you, That even Solomon in all his glory was not arrayed like one of these"—has been shaken, and with it the also largely unspoken confidence that people had in their own instinctual natures has been upset. It seems significant that Freud, who pioneered our century's self-consciousness in sexual matters, should have been one of the first observers to warn that humanity was headed down a path of self-destruction. In the last paragraph of *Civilization and Its Discontents*, published in 1930, he wrote:

> The fateful question for the human species seems to me to be whether and to what extent their cultural development will succeed in mastering the disturbance of their communal life by the human instinct of aggression and self-destruction. It may be that in this respect precisely the present time deserves a special interest. Men have gained control over the forces of nature to such an extent that with their help they would have no difficulty in exterminating one another to the last man. They know this, and hence comes a large part of their current unrest, their unhappiness and their mood of anxiety. And now it is to be expected that the other of the two "Heavenly Powers," eternal Eros, will make an effort to assert himself in the struggle with his equally immortal adversary [death]. But who can foresee with what success and with what result?

It is as though Freud perceived that the balance between man's "lower," animal, and instinctual nature, which had historically been so much feared and despised by religious men and philosophers as a disruptive force in man's spiritual development, and his "higher," rational nature had tipped in favor of the latter—so that now the greater danger to man came not from rampant, uncontrolled instinct breaking down the restraining bonds of reason and self-control but from rampant reason oppressing and destroying instinct and nature. And rampant reason, man found, was, if anything, more to be feared than rampant instinct. Bestiality had been the cause of many horrors, but it had never threatened the species with extinction; some instinct for self-preservation was still at work. Only "selfless" reason could ever entertain the thought of self-extinction. Freud's merciful, solicitous attitude toward the animal in our nature foreshadowed the solicitude that we now need to show toward the animals and plants in our earthly environment. Now reason must sit at the knee of instinct and learn reverence for the miraculous instinctual capacity for creation.

It may be a symptom of our disordered instinctual life that, increasingly, sexuality has lost its hiding place in the privacy of the bedroom and been drawn into the spotlight of public attention, where it becomes the subject of debate, advice, and technical instruction, just like any other fully public matter. In Freud's day, open discussion of sexual questions helped to free people from a harshly restrictive Victorian morality, but in our day it appears that sex, which no longer suffers from that traditional suppression, is drawn into the open because something has gone wrong with it and people want to repair it. By making it a public issue, they seem to acknowledge indirectly that our instincts have run up against an obstacle, as indeed they have, and are in need of public assistance, as indeed they are. Odd as it may seem, the disorder of our private, or once private, lives may require a political solution, for it may not be until the human future has been restored to us that desire can again find a natural place in human life.

The biological continuity of the species is made into a fully human, worldly continuity by, above all, the institution of marriage. Marriage lends permanence and a public shape to love. Marriage vows are made by a man and a woman to one another, but they are also made before the world, which is formally present at the ceremony in the role of witness. Marriage *solemnizes* love, giving this most inward of feelings an outward form that is acknowledged by everyone and commands everyone's respect. In swearing their love in public, the lovers also let it be known that their union will be a fit one for bringing children into the world—for receiving what the Bible calls "the grace of life." And the world, by insisting on a ceremony, and by attending in the role of witness, announces its stake in its own continuity. Thus, while in one sense marriage is the most personal of actions, in another sense it belongs to everybody. In a world that is perpetually being overturned and plowed under by birth and death, marriage—which for this reason is rightly called an "institution"—lays the foundation for the stability of a human world that is built to house all the generations. In this sense as well as in the strictly biological sense and the emotional sense, love creates the world.

The peril of extinction surrounds such love with doubt. A trembling world, poised on the edge of self-destruction, offers poor soil for enduring love to grow in. Everything that this love would build up, extinction would tear down. "Eros, builder of cities" (in Auden's phrase, in his poem eulogizing Freud on the occasion of his death) is thwarted. Or, to put it brutally but truthfully, every generation that holds the earth hostage to nuclear destruction holds a gun to the head of its own children. In laying this trap for the species, we show our children no regard, and treat them with indifference and neglect. As for love itself, love lives in the moment, but the moment is dying, as we are, and love also reaches beyond its moment to dwell in a kind of permanence. For

Love's not Time's fool, though rosy lips and cheeks
Within his bending sickle's compass come
Love alters not with his brief hours and weeks,
But bears it out even to the edge of doom.

But if doom's edge draws close, love's vast scope is narrowed and its resolve may be shaken. The approach of extinction drives love back into its perishable moment, and, in doing so, tends to break up love's longer attachments, which now, on top of all the usual vicissitudes, have the weight of the whole world's jeopardy to bear.

There is, in fact, an odd resemblance between the plight of love and the plight of war in the nuclear world. Military hostilities, having been stopped by dread of extinction from occurring on the field of battle, are relegated to a mental plane—to the world of strategic theory and war games, where the generals of our day sit at their computer terminals waging shadow wars with the ostensible aim of making sure that no real hostilities ever happen. Love, too, although it has not been prevented altogether, has in a way lost its full field of action—the world that included the future generations—and so has tended to withdraw to a mental plane peculiarly its own, where it becomes an ever more solitary affair: impersonal, detached, pornographic. It means something that we call both pornography and nuclear destruction "obscene." In the first, we find desire stripped of any further human sentiment or attachment—of any "redeeming social value," in the legal phrase. In the second, we find violence detached from any human goals, all of which would be engulfed in a holocaust—detached, that is, from all redeeming social value.

The Japanese used to call the pleasure quarters of their cities "floating worlds." Now our entire world, cut adrift from its future and its past, has become a floating world. The cohesion of the social realm—the dense and elaborate fabric of life that is portrayed for us in the novels of the nineteenth century, among other places, inspiring "nostalgic" longing in us—is disintegrating, and people seem to be drifting apart and into a weird isolation. The compensation that is offered is the license to enjoy life in the moment with fewer restrictions;

but the present moment and its pleasures provide only a poor refuge from the emptiness and loneliness of our shaky, dreamlike, twilit world. The moment itself, unable to withstand the abnormal pressure of expectation, becomes distorted and corrupted. People turn to it for rewards that it cannot offer—certainly not when it is ordered to do so. Plucked out of life's stream, the moment—whether a moment of love or of spiritual peace, or even of simple pleasure in a meal—is no longer permitted to quietly unfold and be itself but is strenuously tracked down, manipulated, harried by instruction and advice, bought and sold, and, in general, so roughly manhandled that the freshness and joy that it can yield up when it is left alone are corrupted or destroyed.

It is fully understandable that in the face of the distortion and disintegration of human relationships in a doom-ridden world a "conservative" longing for a richer, more stable, and more satisfying social existence should spring up. Unfortunately, however, this longing, instead of inspiring us to take political measures that would remove the world from jeopardy, and thus put life on a solid footing again, all too often takes the form of a simple *wish* that the world would stop being the way it is now and return to its former state, with what are often called "the old values" intact. Rather than take cognizance of the radical causes of the world's decline, with a view to doing something about them, these would-be upholders of the past tend to deny the existence of our new situation. It is only one more part of this denial—the most dangerous part—to imagine that war, too, still exists in its traditional form, in which one's enemies can be defeated on the field of battle without bringing an end to everything. Conservatism in personal and social questions has often gone together with militarism in the past, but now the combination is far more perilous than ever before. It represents a denial of what the world has now become which could lead to the end of the world. If a nation indulges itself in the illusion that, even with nuclear arms, war is possible, and that "victory" can be won with them, it risks bringing about its own and the world's extinction by mistake. Alert and realistic conservatives, by contrast, would see that everything that anyone might wish to conserve is threatened by nuclear weapons, and would recognize in them a threat not only to "the old values" but to any values whatever. And instead of dreaming of the vanished wars of past times they would place themselves in the forefront of a movement for disarmament.

Politics, as it now exists, is even more thoroughly compromised than personal and social life by the peril of extinction. Marriage lays down its map of hereditary lines across the unmarked territory of generational succession, shaping the rudiments of a common world out of biological reproduction, which without marriage would continue anyway, as it did before civilization was born, and does still among animals. Marriage is thus half submerged in the unconscious, instinctual, biological life of the species, and only half emergent into the "daylight" (in Hegel's term) of history and the common world. Politics, on the other hand, is wholly the creature of the common world, and could have no existence without it. (If people did not have reason and language, they could still reproduce but they could not set up a government among themselves.) There is no political "moment," as there is a sensual moment, to fall back on in an attempted retreat from the futility of a jeopardized common world. Politics, accordingly, is fully stuck with the glaring absurdity that with one hand it builds for a future that with the other hand it prepares to destroy. Each time a politician raises his voice to speak of making a better world for our children and grandchildren (and this is an intrinsic part of what politics is about, whether or not it happens to be explicitly stated), the peril of extinction is there to gainsay him with the crushing rebuttal:

But there may *be* no children or grandchildren. And when, far more ridiculously, politicians let us know of their desire for a "place in history," it is not only their swollen vanity that invites anger but their presumption in trying to reserve a place in a history whose continued existence their own actions place in doubt.

Since Aristotle, it has often been said that the two basic aims of political association are, first, to assure the survival of members of society (that is, to protect life) and, second, to give them a chance to fulfill themselves as social beings (that is, to enable them to lead a noble or a good life). The threat of self-extermination annuls both of these objectives, and leaves the politics of our day in the ludicrous position of failing even to aim at the basic goals that have traditionally justified its existence. If our economy were to produce a wonderful abundance of silverware, glasses, and table napkins but no food, people would quickly rebel and insist on a different system. The world's political arrangements, which now aim at providing some accoutrements of life but fail to lift a finger to save life itself, are in no less drastic need of replacement. People cannot for long place confidence in institutions that fail even to recognize the most urgent requirement of the whole species, and it is therefore not surprising that, more and more, people do actually look on politicians with contempt, though perhaps without having quite figured out why.

As long as politics fails to take up the nuclear issue in a determined way, it lives closer than any other activity to the lie that we have all come to live—the pretense that life lived on top of a nuclear stockpile can last. Meanwhile, we are encouraged not to tackle our predicament but to inure ourselves to it: to develop a special, enfeebled vision, which is capable of overlooking the hugely obvious; a special, sluggish nervous system, which is conditioned not to react even to the most extreme and urgent peril; and a special, constricted mode of political thinking, which is permitted to creep around the edges of the mortal crisis in the life of our species but never to meet it head on. In this timid, crippled thinking, "realism" is the title given to beliefs whose most notable characteristic is their failure to recognize the chief reality of the age, the pit into which our species threatens to jump; "utopian" is the term of scorn for any plan that shows serious promise of enabling the species to keep from killing itself (if it is "utopian" to want to survive, then it must be "realistic" to be dead); and the political arrangements that keep us on the edge of annihilation are deemed "moderate," and are found to be "respectable," whereas new arrangements, which might enable us to draw a few steps back from the brink, are called "extreme" or "radical." With such fear-filled, thought-stopping epithets as these, the upholders of the status quo defend the anachronistic structure of their thinking, and seek to block the revolution in thought and in action which is necessary if mankind is to go on living.

Works of art, history, and thought, which provide what Arendt calls the "publicity" that makes an intergenerational common world possible, are undermined at their foundations by the threat of self-extermination. Each such work is a vessel that bears the distillation of some thought, feeling, or experience from one generation to another. In his 1970 Nobel Prize acceptance speech, Solzhenitsyn said, "Woe to that nation whose literature is disturbed by the intervention of power. Because that is not just a violation against 'freedom of print,' it is the closing down of the heart of the nation, a slashing to pieces of its memory." In reminding us that totalitarian governments seek to break the connections between generations, which are so inconvenient to all monomaniacal campaigns, Solzhenitsyn might well have been demonstrating that totalitarianism is indeed one of the precursors of the peril of extinction, which puts an end to all the generations. (The difference is that whereas totalitarianism destroys the memories, extinction destroys all the rememberers.) A work of art will often celebrate the most evanescent thing—a glance, a vague longing, the look of a certain shadow—but as soon as the artist picks up his brush or his pen he takes up residence in the immortal common world inhabited by all generations together. As the poets have always told us, art rescues love and other mortal things from time's destruction. And it is not only the artists who reach beyond their own lifetimes with art; it is also the readers, listeners, and viewers, who while they are in the presence of a work of art are made contemporary with it and, in a way, with all other readers, listeners, and viewers, in all ages. Through art, we "are able to break bread with the dead, and without communion with the dead a fully human life is impossible" (Auden). The timeless appeal of the greatest works of art, in fact, testifies to our common humanity as few other things do, and is one of the strongest grounds we have for supposing that a political community that would embrace the whole earth and all generations is also possible.

The other side of art's communion with the dead (which is the basis for Camus's lovely remark "As an artist . . . I began by admiring others, which in a way is heaven on earth") is its communion with the unborn. In nothing that we do are the unborn more strongly present than in artistic creation. It is the very business of artists to speak to future audiences, and therefore it is perhaps not surprising that they— probably more than any other observers, at least in the modern age— have been gifted with prophetic powers. (In our century, the name of Kafka, who seemed to foresee in so many particulars the history of our time, inevitably comes to mind.) Indeed, great works of art are often so closely attuned to the future that it takes the world a few decades to understand them. There is no doubt that art, which breaks into the crusted and hardened patterns of thought and feeling in the present as though it were the very prow of the future, is in radically altered circumstances if the future is placed in doubt. The ground on which the artist stands when he turns to his work has grown unsteady beneath his feet. In the pre-nuclear world, an artist who hoped to enable future generations to commune with his time might be worried that his work would be found wanting by posterity and so would pass into oblivion, but in the nuclear world the artist, whose work is still subject to this danger, must also fear that even if he produces nothing but timeless masterpieces they will fall into oblivion anyway, because there will be no posterity. The masterpieces cannot be timeless if time itself stops. The new uncertainty is not that one's work will be buried and forgotten in the tumult of history but that history, which alone offers the hope of saving anything from time's destruction, will itself be buried in the indifference of the nonhuman universe, dragging all human achievements down with it. The two fates, which now constitute a double jeopardy for artistic creation, are utterly different. In the first, it is life—the "onslaught of the generations," in Arendt's phrase—that undoes the work while itself surviving. In the second, it is death that swallows up both life and the work. The first peril makes us feel our individual mortality more keenly, but, for that very reason, makes us feel the common life of the species more strongly, and both feelings may inspire us to increase our efforts to accomplish whatever it is that we hope to offer the world before we die. The second peril threatens not each individual work but the world to which all works are offered, and makes us feel that even if we did accomplish our individual aims it would be pointless, thus undercutting our will to accomplish anything at all.

It would be futile to try to prescribe to art what it "can" and "cannot" do, as though we in the present had a visionary capacity to foresee art's future forms and, like an omniscient critic, accept some while ruling out others; but it is possible to reflect on what has already occurred, and to wonder what role political and other events in the world may have played in this or that development. Bearing in mind the irreducible mysteriousness of artistic creativity, we may note that some of the developments in art in recent decades have the look of logical, if unconscious, adjustments to the newly imperilled condition of the species. The art critic and social and political observer Harold Rosenberg has spoken of a "de-definition" of art, by which he meant a blurring of the boundary lines that have traditionally separated artistic creation from other human activities. Among the distinctions that have been lost—or deliberately breached—are the ones between the artist and his work of art and between the work of art and its audience. Rosenberg found the first breach in Action painting, in which the meaning of the work came to reside in the act of painting rather than in the finished canvas, and he found the second in all those artistic events that are called "happenings," in which the audience is more or less dispensed with and the "aesthetic effects are given by the event itself, without intervention on the part of the spectator-participant." In trying to do away with the enduring, independently existing art product and its audience, and concentrating on the act of creation, these artists, who "left art behind," seemed to be working toward an art that would fulfill itself—like the sexual act that is isolated from the past and the future—in the moment, thus giving up on communion with the dead and with the unborn: doing away, in fact, with art's whole dependence on the common world, which assumes the existence of the human future. If art could manage this, of course, it would escape the futility of trying to communicate with generations that now may never arrive. Politics is simply powerless to cut itself off from the future and compress itself into a highly charged present (although some of the radical students of the nineteen-sixties seemed at times to be making the attempt), but art may have more leeway for experimentation, perhaps because, as the traditional rescuer of fleeting things from oblivion, it starts off being closer to life in the moment. Whether these experiments can produce much that is worthwhile is another question. Rosenberg spoke of "all those ruses of scrutinizing itself and defiantly denying its own existence" by which art has survived in recent decades, but he held out little hope that these devices could sustain art much longer. Looked at in terms of the predicament of the species as a whole, art appears to be in a quandary. Art attempts both to reflect the period in which it was produced and to be timeless. But today, if it wishes to truthfully reflect the reality of its period, whose leading feature is the jeopardy of the human future, art will have to go out of existence, while if it insists on trying to be timeless it has to ignore this reality—which is nothing other than the jeopardy of human time—and so, in a sense, tell a lie. Art by itself is powerless to solve its predicament, and artists, like lovers, are in need of assistance from statesmen and ordinary citizens.

By threatening to cancel the future generations, the nuclear peril not only throws all our activities that count on their existence into disorder but also disturbs our relationship with the past generations. We need the assurance that there will be a future if we are to take on the burden of mastering the past—a past that really does become the proverbial "dead past," an unbearable weight of millennia of corpses and dust, if there is no promise of a future. Without confidence that we will be followed by future generations, to whom we can hand on what we have received from the past, it becomes intolerably depressing to enter the tombs of the dead to gather what they have left behind; yet without that treasure our life is impoverished. The present is a fulcrum on which the future and the past lie balanced, and if the future is lost to us, then the past must fall away, too.

Death lies at the core of each person's private existence, but part of death's meaning is to be found in the fact that it occurs in a biological and social world that survives. No one can be a spectator at his own funeral, but others can be there, and the anticipation of their presence, which betokens the continuity of life and all that that means for a mortal creature, is consolation to each person as he faces his death. Death suffered in the shadow of doom lacks this consolation. It is a gap that threatens soon to be lost in a larger gap—a death within a greater death. When human life itself is overhung with death, we cannot go peacefully to our individual deaths. The deaths of others, too, become more terrible: with the air so full of death, every death becomes harder to face. When a person dies, we often turn our thoughts to the good he did while he was alive—to that which he gave to the world, and which therefore outlasts him in the world's affection. (When someone who did great harm to the world dies, we feel that death has had a more thorough victory, since there is so little of his that the world wishes to preserve. Rather, it may wish to bury him even more thoroughly than any grave can.) But when the whole world, in which the dead in a sense live on, is imperilled, this effort at remembrance and preservation seems to lose its point, and all lives and deaths are threatened with a common meaninglessness.

There have been many deaths in our century that in certain respects resembled those that would be suffered in a nuclear holocaust: the deaths of the millions of people who died in the concentration camps of the totalitarian regimes, which sought not only to kill their victims but to extirpate their memory from the historical record. Because the camps threatened people not only with death but with oblivion, remembrance has become for some survivors a passion and a sacred obligation. When Solzhenitsyn accepted the Nobel Prize, he was at pains to remind the world that he spoke on behalf of millions who had not survived, and his whole historical reconstruction of the Soviet camp system is pitted against totalitarian forgetfulness. Likewise, the command "Never forget," so often heard in connection with the Nazis' genocidal attack on the Jews, is important not only because it may help the world to prevent any repetition but because remembering is in itself an act that helps to defeat the Nazis' attempt to send a whole people into oblivion. Just because genocide, by trying to prevent the future generations of people from being born, commits a crime against the future, it lays a special obligation on the people of the future to deal with the crime, even long after its perpetrators are themselves dead. The need to bear witness and then to remember was felt first by the inmates of the camps and only later by the world at large. The French journalist David Rousset, a survivor of several camps, including Buchenwald, has written of his experiences in those camps:

How many people here still believe that a protest has even historic importance? This skepticism is the real masterpiece of the S.S. Their great accomplishment. They have corrupted all human solidarity. Here the night has fallen on the future. When no witnesses are left, there can be no testimony. To demonstrate when death can no longer be postponed is an attempt to give death a meaning, to act beyond one's own death. In order to be successful, a gesture must have social meaning. There are hundreds of thousands of us here, all living in absolute solitude.

Thanks to a few heroic witnesses, and to the existence outside the totalitarian world of a nontotalitarian world, which could find out about what happened and then remember it, the connections between the camp victims and the rest of humanity were never altogether severed. There *was* testimony, the "historic importance" of the events in the camps *was* preserved, "human solidarity" *was* partly maintained, however tragically late, and the "masterpiece" of the S.S. was spoiled. Indeed, if we read the testimony of those in the camps deeply enough it may help us in our effort to avoid our extinction. Arendt, writing in her classic study *The Origins of Totalitarianism*, made the connection:

> Here [in the camps], there are neither political nor historical nor simply moral standards but, at the most, the realization that something seems to be involved in modern politics that actually should never be involved in politics as we used to understand it, namely all or nothing—all, and that is an undetermined infinity of forms of human living-together, or nothing, for a victory of the concentration-camp system would mean the same inexorable doom for human beings as the use of the hydrogen bomb would mean the doom of the human race.

Yet we must insist, I think, that in fact extinction by nuclear arms would be the more profound oblivion, since then the very possibility of remembrance or renewal—of the existence of a Solzhenitsyn or Rousset to bear witness, or of an Arendt to reflect on their testimony, or of readers to ponder what happened and take it to heart—would be gone. In extinction, and only in extinction, the connections between the victims and the rest of humanity would really be severed forever, and the "masterpiece" of the mass murderers would be perfected, for the night would have "fallen on the future" once and for all. Of all the crimes against the future, extinction is the greatest. It is the murder of the future. And because this murder cancels all those who might recollect it even as it destroys its immediate victims the obligation to "never forget" is displaced back onto us, the living. It is we—the ones who will either commit this crime or prevent it—who must bear witness, must remember, and must arrive at the judgment.

A nuclear holocaust would destroy the living and cancel the unborn in the same blow, but it is possible, as I mentioned earlier, at least to imagine that, through sterilization of the species, the future generations could be cancelled while the living were left unharmed. Although the condition of being extinct is by definition beyond experience this remnant—the living cells of the dead body of mankind—would, like a prisoner who knows that he is condemned to die on a certain day, be forced to look extinction in the face in a way that we, who can always tell ourselves that we may yet escape extinction, are not. To them, the futility of all the activities of the common world—of marriage, of politics, of the arts, of learning, and, for that matter, of war—would be driven home inexorably. They would experience in their own lives the breakdown of the ties that bind individual human beings together into a community and a species, and they would feel the current of our common life grow cold within them. And as their number was steadily reduced by death they would witness the final victory of death over life. One wonders whether in these circumstances people would want to go on living at all—or whether they might not choose to end their own lives. By killing off the living quickly, extinction by nuclear arms would spare us those barren, bitter decades of watching and feeling the end close in. As things are, we will never experience the approach of extinction in that pure form, and are left in an irremediable uncertainty. Nevertheless, the spectre of extinction hovers over our world and shapes our lives with its invisible but terrible pressure. It now accompanies us through life, from birth to death. Wherever we go, it goes, too; in whatever we do, it is present. It gets up with us in the morning, it stays at our side throughout the day, and it gets into bed with us at night. It is with us in the delivery room, at the marriage ceremony, and on our deathbeds. It is the truth about the way we now live. But such a life cannot go on for long.

Because the unborn generations will never experience their cancellation by us, we have to look for the consequences of extinction before it occurs, in our own lives, where it takes the form of a spiritual sickness that corrupts life at the invisible, innermost starting points of our thoughts, moods, and actions. This emphasis on us, however, does not mean that our only reason for restraining ourselves from elimination of the future generations is to preserve them as auxiliaries to *our* needs—as the audience for our works of art, as the outstretched hands to receive our benefactions (and so to bring our otherwise frustrated charitable impulses to fulfillment), as the minds that will provide us with immortality by remembering our words and deeds, and as the successors who will justify us by carrying on with the tasks that we have started or advanced. To adopt such an expedient view of the future generations would be to repeat on a monumental scale the error of the philanthropist who looks on the needy only as a convenient prop with which he can develop and demonstrate his moral superiority, or the more familiar and more dangerous figure of the politician who looks on the public only as a ladder on which he can climb to power. It would also put us in the company of those who, in pursuit, very often, of visionary social goals, make the opposite but closely related error of regarding the *present* generations only as auxiliaries—as the expendable bricks and mortar to be used in the construction of a glorious palace in which the future generations will take up residence. (We have merely to remember how many people have been murdered so that "history" might "go forward" to be reminded how great the costs of this mistake have been.) Whether we were subordinating the living or the unborn generations, this reduction of human beings to a supporting role in the completion of cross-generational tasks would suggest that we had come to place a higher value on the achievements of life than we did on life itself, as though we were so dazzled by the house man lives in that we had forgotten who lives there. But no human being, living or unborn, should be regarded as an auxiliary. Although human beings have their obligations to fulfill, they are not to be seen as beasts of burden whose purpose in existing is to carry on with enterprises that are supposedly grander and more splendid than they are. For in the last analysis these enterprises, which together make up the common world, are meant to serve life, not to be served by it. Life does not exist for the sake of the governments, the buildings, the books, and the paintings; all these exist for the sake of life. The works of man are great, but man himself is greater.

The reason that so much emphasis must be laid on the living generations is not that they are more important than the unborn but only that at any given moment they, by virtue of happening to be the ones who exist, are the ones who pose the peril, who can feel the consequences of the peril in their lives, and who can respond to the peril on behalf of all other generations. To cherish life—whether one's own or someone else's, a present life or an unborn life—one must already be in life, and only the living have this privilege. The question that the peril of extinction puts before the living, however, is: Who would miss human life if they extinguished it? To which the only honest answer is: Nobody. That being so, we have to admit that extinction is no loss, since there cannot be loss when there is no loser: and we are thus driven to seek the meaning of extinction in the mere anticipation of it by the living, whose lives this anticipation corrupts and degrades. However, there is another side to the entire question. For while it is true that extinction cannot be felt by those whose fate it is—the unborn, who would stay unborn—the same cannot be said, of course, for extinction's alternative, survival. If we shut the unborn out of life, they will never have a chance to lament their fate, but if we let them into life they will have abundant opportunity to be glad that they were born instead of having been prenatally severed from existence by us. The idea of escaping extinction before one was born is a strange one for us, since it is so new, but to generations that live deep in nuclear time, and who know that their existence has depended on the wisdom and restraint of a long succession of generations before them, we can be sure that the idea will be familiar.

Of every other bequest that the present makes to the future it can be said that that which would be gratefully received if it was given would also be sorely missed if it was withheld. Of life alone is it the case that while its receipt can be welcomed, its denial cannot be mourned. The peril of extinction, by bringing us up against this reality, concentrates our attention in a new way on the simple and basic fact that before there can be good or evil, service or harm, lamenting or rejoicing there *must be life.* (Even those who wish to exploit and harm other human beings must first want human beings to exist.) In coming to terms with the peril of extinction, therefore, what we must desire first of all is that people be born, for their own sakes, and not for any other reason. Everything else—our wish to serve the future generations by preparing a decent world for them to live in, and our wish to lead a decent life ourselves in a common world made secure by the safety of the future generations—flows from this commitment. Life comes first. The rest is secondary.

To recapitulate: In a nuclear holocaust great enough to extinguish the species, every person on earth would die; but in addition to that, and distinct from it, is the fact that the unborn generations would be prevented from ever existing. However, precisely because the unborn are not born, they cannot experience their plight, and its meaning has to be sought among the living, who share a common world with the unborn as well as with the dead, and who find that if they turn their backs on the unborn, and deny them life, then their own lives become progressively more twisted, empty, and despairing. On the other hand, if instead of asking what the act of extinction means we ask what the act of survival means—and in the nuclear world survival has, for the first time, become an act—we find that the relationship between the generations is reconstituted, and we can once again ask what the meaning of our actions will be for the people directly affected by them, who now, because they are presumed to exist, can be presumed to have a response. By acting to save the species, and repopulating the future, we break out of the cramped, claustrophobic isolation of a doomed present, and open a path to the greater space—the only space fit for human habitation—of past, present, and future. Suddenly, we can think and feel again. Even by merely imagining for a moment that the nuclear peril has been lifted and human life has a sure foothold on the earth again, we can feel the beginnings of a boundless relief and calm—a boundless peace. But we can open this path only if it is our desire that the unborn exist for their own sake. We trace the effects of extinction in our own world because that is the only place where they can ever appear, yet those sad effects, important as they are, are only the side effects of our shameful failure to fulfill our main obligation of valuing the future human beings themselves. And if at first we find these future people to be somewhat abstract we have only to remind ourselves that we, too, were once "the future generation," and that every unborn person will be as vivid and important to himself as each of us is to himself. We gain the right perspective on extinction not by trying to peer into the inhuman emptiness of a post-human universe but by putting ourselves in the shoes of someone in the future, who, precisely because he has been allowed to be born, can rejoice in the fact of being alive.

The Abolition
THE NEW YORKER, JANUARY 2, 1984

THE CONCENSUS, AMONG so many of those who have thought deeply about the nuclear predicament, that nuclear weapons cannot be abolished unless world government is established seems to find support in traditional political theory: in the distinction between the so-called state of nature, in which men live in anarchy and resolve their disputes among themselves, with war serving as the final arbiter, and the so-called civil state, in which men live under a government and submit their disputes to its final arbitration. In reflecting on the formation of states out of warring tribes or principalities, political thinkers have often observed that the transition from the state of nature to the civil state is usually radical and abrupt, frequently involving some act of conquest or other form of violence, and admits of no partial or halfway solutions, in which, say, a central authority is given the legislative power to "decide" the outcome of disputes but not the executive power to enforce its decisions. We seem to be faced with the same radical, either-or choice in the world as a whole, in which nations, although each constitutes a civil state within its own borders, have, according to the traditional view, always lived in an anarchic state of nature in their relations with each other. The United Nations, which has been helpful in moderating hostilities in our tense and warlike world but has not been empowered to resolve basic disputes among nations, appears to exemplify what halfway measures toward entry into the civil state lead to in the global arena.

The reason that halfway measures toward the civil state never seem to amount to very much is straightforward and basic. Human beings, existing on earth in large numbers and possessed of separate and independent wills, inevitably get into disputes, and government and war are the two immemorial means by which the disputes have been bindingly resolved. Nations do not dare to give up war and disarm until world government, or some equivalent, is in place, because if they did they would be left without any final arbiter for settling disputes. This situation would be inherently unstable, because as soon as a serious dispute arose—concerning, for example, who was to control a certain piece of territory—nations would reach for the instruments of war, and the impotent, halfway civil measures would be ignored or swept aside (as happened, for example, to the League of Nations in the 1930s). That is why the political thinkers of our time have, with rare unanimity, declared that either total disarmament or full nuclear disarmament is impossible without the simultaneous establishment of world government—and we are left with the unfortunate choice between living with a full balance of nuclear terror, which we would like to get away from, and instituting a full global state, which we would like to avoid. (Mere nuclear disarmament is seen as impossible without world government because among the instruments of war nuclear arms overrule all the others. They have the final word.)

The key event in the transition from the state of nature to the civil state is the centralization of power, in which the individual nations (or people) renounce their right to resort to force at their own discretion, yielding it to the central authority, which is then empowered to make and enforce final decisions. Unfortunately, the centralization of power does not necessarily require a shift from "lawlessness" to "law," as advocates of world government sometimes seem to suggest. The central authority can be, in a moral sense, as "lawless" as any individual. When the central authority in question is a world government, this possibility assumes terrifying proportions, which have no precedent in the annals of politics. Moreover, the establishment of a central authority does not necessarily entail a reduction in the levels of violence, as the record of the totalitarian regimes in the first half of our century makes clear (and as the record of the Pol Pot government in Kampuchea has made clear more recently). Governments, we are forced to acknowledge, are fully as capable of slaughtering huge numbers of people as war is. And if a lawless government were to assume control of the world and such slaughter were to be carried out in the global darkness of the oppression of all mankind the horror of the situation would be beyond all imagining.

What the world's entry into the civil state would accomplish, however, is, as everyone acknowledges, an end to war—or, in our time, an end to the possibility of "mutual assured destruction" and human extinction. In war, the level of force used is bid up to the maximum, because victory (if any) goes to the side that keeps on fighting longer. War is, in Clausewitz's words, a form of "reciprocal action" that "must lead to an extreme" in order to reach a conclusion. And for that reason nuclear weapons spoil war as a final arbiter of international disputes: the extreme they run to is total annihilation. Central governments, on the other hand, don't need to run to any extremes of force to carry out even the most extensive slaughter. One bullet for each "subversive," fired into the back of the head, will suffice. In fact, strictly speaking, no active violence at all is necessary. Vast populations can be killed off by simple deprivation. If you place a multitude of people in a camp, force them to work hard, and cut back their rations, you can kill as many of them as you want to. Certainly no nuclear bombs will be necessary to kill them. In that limited, tragic sense, world government, even at its worst, would be a way out of the nuclear predicament. (Of course, if world government were to break down, and civil war were to arise, the nuclear peril might re-arise with it; but just at the moment the peril of a nuclear holocaust resulting from a breakdown of world government is, I should say, the least of our worries.) Even if one regards these worst-case nightmares of world government run amok as unlikely, the prospect of a supreme political power ruling over the whole earth remains chilling. Anarchy is not liberty, yet it could be that in anarchy, with all its violence, the human spirit has greater latitude to live and grow than it would have in the uniform shadow of a global state.

To be sure, for a number of people it is not the attractions of world government that lead them to favor that particular resolution of the nuclear predicament. It is their dismay at what they see as the alternative: an indeterminate period of life on the edge of the abyss, terminated by extinction. The real choice, they say, is not between world government and anarchy but between world government and nothing—"one world or none," as people used to put it. Nevertheless, most people are agreed that the immediate political choice before us is between an anarchic state of nature, in which nations possess nuclear weapons, and the civil state, or world government, in which they would not. (Some people, it is true, have suggested that the world government itself might have to possess nuclear weapons—a prospect that can only increase one's misgivings about this institution.) This definition of the actions open to us is at the heart of an impasse in which the world has been stuck throughout the nuclear age.

In *The Nuclear Revolution: International Politics Before and After Hiroshima,* of 1981, the political scientist Michael Mandelbaum, reflecting the opinion of the consensus—which includes both the advocates of world government and the advocates of our present-day policy of nuclear deterrence—writes, "Relations among sovereign states are still governed by the principle of anarchy. War is still possible." And he goes on:

A logical way to do away with war among nation-states is to abolish national armaments altogether. This, in turn, requires abolishing the incentives for states to have armaments. They have them because of the insecurity that arises from the anarchical structure of the international system. So the requirement for disarmament is the disappearance of anarchy, in favor of an international system organized along the lines of the state in domestic politics. States must give up sovereignty. This is the political revolution that some anticipated in 1945 but that has not come to pass.

In this view, evidently, our world of nuclear-armed deterrence remains in the traditional anarchic state of nature. I should like to argue, however, that inasmuch as nuclear weapons have spoiled war—the final arbiter in the state of nature—we are mistaken about this, having been misled by the habits of pre-nuclear political thought, which so often lead us astray in the new and strange nuclear world. A deterred world, I believe, is no longer in anarchy—in the traditional state of nature. Nor, of course, is it in the civil state. It is not even quite in between the two but, rather, is in a new state altogether—the deterred state—which has been brought into being by the all-pervasive, deeply rooted, manmade reality of a nuclear-capable world. It was, I believe, an unacknowledged change of this kind that Einstein was referring to when he made his famous remark, "The unleashed power of the atom has changed everything save our modes of thinking, and thus we drift toward unparalleled catastrophe." But if our world, because of the invention of nuclear weapons, has already departed from the traditional state of nature, then the possibility seems to open up that our choices may not be restricted to the either-or one between nuclear-armed anarchy and world government. New and more promising alternatives may be available. I believe that they are. In particular, I believe that within the framework of deterrence itself it may be possible to abolish nuclear weapons. But to understand how this might be so we need to examine deterrence more deeply—its mechanisms, its scientific and technical foundations, and its political goals.

A simple analogy may help to clarify the full novelty of the deterred state. Let us suppose that one day my neighbor comes into my house and starts to carry off my furniture. If he and I live in the civil state, I will call the police, and some organ of government will eventually decide what is to be done. If he and I live in a state of nature, there are no police or organs of government, and it is for me alone to try to stop him—by persuasion, if possible, or, if that fails, by force. Force is my last resort, the final arbiter of my dispute with my neighbor, and what then ultimately decides our dispute is whether it is he or I who lies dead on the ground. It's worth noting, though, that there is nothing inherently violent in the fact of a dispute. My neighbor may have quietly carried off my furniture while I was out. It is as a solution to the dispute that violence—or some alternative—enters the picture. In the civil state, my dispute with my neighbor is arbitrated by government, and in the state of nature it is arbitrated by the fight between him and me (if it comes to that). But when one turns to deterrence one finds that neither of these things is happening. Deterrence arbitrates nothing. Underlying the traditional belief that my neighbor and I must resolve our dispute either by violence or by government was the unstated assumption that the dispute must *be* resolved. Deterrence, however, discovers another possibility—that disputes can be suspended, can be kept in abeyance, without any resolution. It uses terror to prevent disputes from ever coming into being. Under deterrence, I neither call the police nor shoot my neighbor—or even lay hands on him—because he doesn't enter my house to begin with. For under deterrence I have, in anticipation of my neighbor's depredations, filled my house with explosives, wired them to go off the moment any unauthorized person crosses my threshold, and (an essential step) informed my neighbor of what I have done—hoping, of course, that he will then have the good sense to give up any plans he might have for stealing my furniture. Deterrence intervenes at a point in the action quite different from that at which either force or an organ of government intervenes. Force or an organ of government steps in after the dispute has arisen and has reached an impasse, to settle it, whereas deterrence steps in before anyone has made a move, to keep the dispute from taking place.

The mechanism of deterrence is as different from the mechanism of war as its end result is from the end result of war. Deterrence is essentially psychological in its action. It uses terror to produce a mental result—the decision not to act. In the international sphere, its aim is to make government leaders *reflect* before they engage in aggression. When its action is effective, no one lies dead on the ground (although if it fails all do). It relies for its success not on the corpse of the fallen soldier but on the prudence of the live, thinking statesman. War, by contrast, while it has its psychological elements, including an element of deterrence, is in essence physical in its action: it blasts the opponent out of the way, as though he were a thing rather

than a person, and his soon to be darkened psyche is of purely secondary interest.

In making deterrence possible, nuclear weapons have thus offered
a new answer to the question (which lies at the heart of the nuclear
predicament) of how disputes among nations are to be handled—an
answer in which the disputes, instead of being arbitrated either by
government or by war (or by anything else, for that matter), are kept
out of "court" altogether. Because both government and war were
ways of settling disputes, the civil state and the state of nature were
both states of change. The deterred state, by contrast, is a stalemate.
In the sphere of international politics, all is held stationary, in a sort of
global-political version of "the freeze"—a version in which it is not
arms that are frozen in place but national boundaries—and change is
relegated to other spheres, such as the economic, the cultural, and the
spiritual, and to domestic turmoil, including revolution. (Revolutionary war escapes incapacitation by nuclear weapons because the
enemies—often belonging to the same families—are too closely
intertwined to be able to kill one another by such indiscriminate
means. Furthermore, while people have shown themselves willing to
consider precipitating the annihilation of their own countries by
antagonizing another nuclear power, they have yet to show themselves
willing to threaten their own countries with nuclear weapons.)

Whatever may be the advantages or disadvantages of the state of
deterrence, its foundations are solid. They are deeply lodged in the
nature of things. They lie, in the last analysis, in the structure of
matter, which we are powerless to return to its former, Newtonian
state—a feat that would require us to forget twentieth-century
physics. We are used to thinking of deterrence as a policy, but before
it is a policy it is a simple fact of life for nuclear-armed nations. Hand

two nations the wherewithal to dip their buckets into the bottomless pools of energy that lie in the heart of matter and a state of deterrence springs up between them, whatever their policies may be. For their leaders, if they are rational, will grasp without the help of theory that if they drop nuclear bombs on their nuclear-armed foe, the foe may drop nuclear bombs on them in return. In the last analysis, victory is ruled out in the nuclear world because the adversaries are matched not against reserves of power that belong in any basic way to either of them individually but against the unlimited, universal power of nuclear energy, which is now more or less available to all. And what human power can hope to defeat the universe? The role of deterrence *policy* is to acknowledge, codify, and shore up this situation, and then seek certain advantages from it.

It would be a mistake, however, to suggest that the deterred state has been added to the two traditional ones, as though we were now free to choose among three states. Rather, the foundations of the traditional state of nature have themselves been altered, so that now we must distinguish between two states of nature—the pre-nuclear one and the nuclear one. The idea of an alteration in nature comes as something of a shock to us, as the very word "nature" suggests that it might. The word suggests the *given*—all that exists, has always existed, and always will exist, independent of human power to alter it. It was not in this realm that we expected alteration. We looked for alteration, on the whole, in the civil state, where our efforts and our will were supposed to make a difference. Whatever else might change, "anarchy" appeared to be a constant—stable, if you will. But we failed to reckon with modern physics (one of the "natural" sciences), which proved capable of transforming nature. Anarchy rested on a shaky base. When the atom was cracked open and its vast energy was spilled into our human world, anarchy's underpinnings were washed away. Thanks to physics, the supposedly changeless physical world was unexpectedly changed, and nations were simply obliged to adjust as best they could. (One of the ironies of our situation is that the natural world has proved to be more changeable than the supposedly flexible political world.)

Of course, the phrase "altering nature" is not literally accurate. In literal fact, nature remains just as it was before we pried into its secrets (as far as we know, neither the detonation of a few tens of thousands of nuclear weapons on our planet nor our disappearance as a species would have the slightest effect on any of the hundred billion or so galaxies in the universe), and what we really mean by the expression is that the physical world in which human beings live and conduct their affairs has been altered. We are not the inventors but only the discoverers of the energy in matter. The universe has always been built this way, and human beings, belonging to a rational and inquiring species, were bound to discover the fact. And then we were bound to try to figure out—as we are now doing—how to survive in such a universe. Nothing now seems more "unnatural" to us than the nuclear peril, and yet in reality nothing is more "natural," inasmuch as the peril is rooted in the basic structure of nature itself.

Whether or not one subscribes to the policy of nuclear deterrence —the threat to strike back with nuclear weapons if one's country is attacked with them or if it starts to lose a conventional war—one has to recognize as an objective fact that the equations of war and peace have had to be rewritten in our nuclear world, and that in those rewritten equations war comes out a suicidal proposition. Not only has war been taken away from us by physics—been "spoiled"—but we can't get it back. Some have tried. Among them are the devotees of "nuclear-war-fighting," who believe that it is possible to fight and survive, and even prevail in, a nuclear war, and who are now in the ascendancy in Washington. But their efforts inevitably founder in the boundless destruction of the more than a million Hiroshimas that are waiting to happen in the world's fifty-thousand-odd nuclear weapons. What these strategists can never explain is how anyone can "prevail" in a "war" after which no one would be left. Their "victories," or restorations of the peace "on terms favorable to the United States," are apparently of an extra-human sort—"victories" in which, after all the people have been killed, our bombs triumph over the other side's bombs. And the strategists' sometimes intricate and ingenious scenarios of nuclear-war-fighting are testimony only to the ability of the human mind, transported by pure abstract theory, to take leave of reality altogether.

In short, under deterrence the passage to a world in which the use of force is given up as the means of settling international differences *has already begun.* In a way, it has been accomplished. In the first days of the nuclear age, it seemed to some "idealists" that the task facing mankind was to abolish war, but "realists" replied that this was impossible—at least, in the short run—because it required the establishment of world government; instead, they proposed the policy of deterrence. However, when one looks at deterrence closely it turns out that war has not been preserved by it. Isn't this what the political scientist Bernard Brodie was getting at when he said, in 1946, in *The Absolute Weapon,* that in the nuclear world the only purpose of military preparations was to avert wars, not to win them? And isn't this what countless statesmen of our time have been telling us in saying that the purpose of their nuclear policies is only to prevent the use of nuclear and other weapons? The statement "War has been spoiled," which stands in such sharp contrast to Mandelbaum's "War is still possible," thus refers not to an idealistic aspiration but to a fait accompli. We cannot abolish war, because nuclear weapons have already done the job for us. What we can and must abolish is mutual assured destruction and the possibility of human extinction, the threat of which we now trade on to keep the peace. Our ambivalence toward this threat, which we try simultaneously to renounce and to exploit for our political ends, defines our new predicament. Just by thinking a little harder, and by looking a little bit more closely at both theory and practice in our nuclear world, we seemingly have already accomplished this "impossible" thing of abolishing war (among nuclear powers, anyway). This is not a mere phrase but a bedrock reality of our time, on which we may rely as we seek elements with which to build the edifice of our future safety. All the debates, carried over from the pre-nuclear age, about whether or not war is moral, and whether or not world government might be preferable, are no doubt extremely interesting, but they are anachronistic, for the world to which they have reference has gone out of existence.

Nuclear weapons, we see, have knocked the sword of war from our hands. Now it is up to us to decide what we will pick up in its place. The question before us shifts from how to abolish war to how to get along in a world from which war has been abolished. And we can start by seeing the first alternative that we have hit on—deterrence—in a new light: not as a continuation of international "anarchy," in which "war is still possible," but as *one* possible system for getting along in a world without war. Without quite recognizing it, we have taken the first steps toward global agreement. It is true that force, while it is no longer the final arbiter, or any sort of arbiter, still plays the central role, as it did in the pre-nuclear state of nature, for a by-product of force, terror, is what holds everybody immobile. Yet it is also true that, as in the civil state, each individual's force, in a kind of tacit agreement, is supposed never to be used. And, as in the civil state, the whole system depends on the recognition by each individual actor of a common interest—survival—that must take precedence over individual interests. Since everybody knows and acknowledges that the use of force by any party may push everybody toward a common doom, all make efforts together to ensure that the "first use" never occurs—although at the same time each side, paradoxically, must constantly bristle with resolve to use force to repel any aggression, should it somehow occur. Moreover, right at the heart of deterrence there is an element of cooperation and consent—a crucial ingredient of every civil state, no matter how oppressive. This is the "psychological" element in deterrence, on which all else depends. For while it is true that sheer terror is the operative force in deterrence it is also true that the statesman on whom it operates must give his consent if it is to work. To be sure, his freedom of action is no greater than that of someone who is being told to do something at gunpoint; nevertheless, he remains a free agent in extremely important ways. His state of mind— his self-interest, his sanity, his prudence, his self-control, his clear-sightedness—is the real foundation of his country's and everyone else's survival. In short, he must *decide* that the world he lives in is not one in which aggression pays off. In all these respects, a deterred world is not a state of anarchy awaiting the imposition of a world order but, rather, already a sort of world order, albeit one that is in many ways contradictory and absurd.

In a deep sense, unless the species does destroy itself our world will remain a deterred world. By this I do not mean that we shall forever maintain nuclear weapons and threaten one another with mutual assured destruction. I mean that whether we possess nuclear weapons or abolish them the terror they inspire will dominate our affairs and dictate the character of our political decisions. Even if mankind were now to enter formally into the civil state, and found a world government to replace war, deterrence would, in a way, still be in effect. In the pre-nuclear world, entry into the civil state would have been a free act, arising out of an abundant faith in humanity and confidence in its betterment. For us, however, who live surrounded by doom, like people in a town at the foot of a rumbling volcano (it is our peculiar distinction not to have built our town next to Vesuvius but to have built Vesuvius next to our town), entry into the civil state would be a compelled act: a measure taken not so much to better life as only to hold on to it—not to bring heaven to earth but only to preserve the earth. Being inspired by terror, entry into the civil state would be a variant of the balance of terror under deterrence—a variant in which nations, instead of deterring each other from starting a nuclear holocaust, would all join together to deter the species as a whole from extinguishing itself. While the shift from multiplicity to unity would require a global political revolution—it would be some equivalent of what Einstein called for—even that revolution would not suspend the underlying transformation of human existence which was brought about by the development of nuclear weapons. We can never recover war. We will always be at risk, somewhere down the road, of extinguishing ourselves. We will always live in a state of deterrence. These changes mark a transformation of our world. And it is this transformed world, not the vanished, pre-nuclear one, that is our true starting point as we face the nuclear peril.

Such are the means and ends of the doctrine of deterrence, on which we rely today for the safety of the nuclear world. They present us with a striking disparity. The over-all end—the military stalemate— is modest and conservative. The means, however—two nations' threats to annihilate one another and, perhaps, all mankind—are extreme in a way that gives new meaning to that word. The problem with deterrence is not that it doesn't "work"—it is, I am sure, a very effective (though far from infallible) way of restraining the super-powers from attacking one another, should they be inclined to do so—but that we must pay an inconceivable price if it fails. Regarded as a sort of world order, deterrence is a regime in which every crime is punished by the severest possible penalty, as though the ruler of a state had decreed that if just one of the citizens commits a burglary all the citizens must be put to death. This radical disproportion between ends and means invites us to inquire whether we might not be able to achieve our modest ends by less extreme means—a means by which we did not threaten ourselves with doom. This definition of our task is, of course, quite different from the one in which we were invited to found world government in the midst of "anarchy" or else accept a life lived perpetually on the edge of extinction. Now we would be working within deterrence defined in its broadest sense—as the new "state of nature," brought into being by the very peril that we wish to alleviate. This could come about because deterrence offers us ele-ments to work with that were not available in the pre-nuclear age. Two stand out. The first is the stalemate itself, which was made pos-sible only because of the fearsome destructive power of the military invention that backs it up. The second is the unlosable nature of the knowledge that underlies the invention, and prevents us from ever wholly expunging the possibility of nuclear destruction from our affairs.

Our first step would be to accept the political verdict that has been delivered by deterrence, and formalize the stalemate. The achieve-ment of the stalemate was, in the broadest sense, accidental: conceived as a makeshift for coping in the short term with a sudden peril that the world lacked either the imagination or the will (or both) to tackle head-on, it gradually took shape, over a period of decades, through trial and error. Its creation was the principal work of a generation. The question for that generation (once world government and full nuclear disarmament were jointly ruled out) was whether, given the presence of nuclear weapons in the world, stability could be achieved. It could be. It was. But now, with the answer to that question in hand, we can start with the stability—the stalemate—and invert the question, asking whether, within the new context of our transformed world, there might not be a better means of preserving that same stability: a means with less extreme risk attached. What for the people of the earlier generation was the end point of their efforts can for us be the starting point. For even as we see that deterrence is possible we know, and have felt in our hearts, that the bargain now struck by it is unworthy of human life, because it turns us into potential mass slayers of our species. This lesson, too, is a fruit of our experience in the nuclear age, and it drives us to seek to dismantle the doomsday machine at the earliest possible moment. A deepening awareness of the full meaning of that bargain—frequently and rightly described as "Faustian"—for strategy, for the state of our civilization, and for the state of our souls is what now inspires the world's gathering protest against nuclear arms.

Our method can be to convert into a settlement in principle the settlement of political differences which we have achieved in fact under the pressure of the nuclear threat. We can, in a manner of speaking, adopt our present world, with all its injustices and other imperfections, as our ideal, and then seek the most sensible and moderate means of preserving it. This effort is consistent with the spiritual task that nuclear weapons have put before us, which is at bottom to awaken ourselves to a new appreciation and gratitude for the world that is given to each of us at birth. For the time being, instead of asking ourselves how, in the light of the peril to all life, we must transform all life, we ask what the best way is to keep everything just the same. Not improvement but mere continuation is our dream. This, of course, is a deeply conservative aim, but then the nuclear peril seems to call on us to be conservative, inasmuch as *conserving* ourselves and our world is the challenge that we now face. To many peoples, the idea of freezing the status quo might seem discouraging, especially if for them the status quo includes intervention in their affairs by a great power. The peoples of Eastern Europe are a case in point. They cannot wish to formalize Soviet domination of their countries. The formalization of the status quo envisioned here, however, would not do that. It would permit those peoples every means to liberate themselves that they now have at their disposal, and would remove only means that they now already lack—Western military intervention in their struggles.

The next question is whether, after formalizing the status quo, we can reduce our reliance on the extreme means by which we now uphold it, and how far a reduction can go. The invaluable lesson of deterrence theory is that in the nuclear age the use of force is self-cancelling. This is the profound truth that the statesmen of our day are struggling to articulate when—expressing, no doubt, their fervent desire, though it is not the actual case—they tell us that they possess nuclear weapons only in order *not* to use them. At first, the simple and almost irresistible implication of that truth for policy seems to be that we can take the whole hateful machinery of force—conventional and nuclear—and clear it out of our lives. The moment we did that, all the paradoxes, contradictions, absurdities, and abominations that we live with under deterrence would evaporate. If the whole doomsday machine is intended only to paralyze itself—to do nothing—why do we need it? Can't we accomplish nothing without threatening suicide? But the very question reveals that after all—semi-covertly and somewhat shamefacedly—we actually rely on the doomsday machine to serve another end: the preservation of our sovereignty. We still exploit the peril of extinction for our political ends. And we don't know how to wean ourselves from that reliance without taking radical steps, such as unilateral disarmament or world government. But while some of us may be ready for radical steps the world as a whole, it is clear, is not, and demands that we preserve the sovereignty of states, even though it requires a risk to our survival. Given this political reality—which shows no sign of changing soon—it appears that, in one form or another, our reliance on the nuclear threat cannot be broken. Nevertheless, even under these terms we have far more flexibility than we have thought. It is a flexibility that, I believe, extends all the way to the abolition of nuclear arms.

On the face of it, there appears to be a contradiction between the two goals we have set for ourselves. It appears that we want to keep the stalemate but to abolish the weapons that make it possible. Yet this contradiction exists in present policy—taking the form of our threatening to use the weapons in order *not* to use them. Either way, paradox is our lot. We seek to preserve a stalemated, purely defensive world but must apparently make use of—or at least make provision for—purely offensive weapons to do it. Indeed, one way of looking at the nuclear predicament is to see it as the final outcome of a competition between offense and defense which has been going on throughout the history of war, in a sort of war within war. The invention of nuclear weapons gave the victory once and for all, it appears, to the offensive side. Although the unpredictability of science prevents a truly definitive judgment, the chances that the defense will ever catch up look vanishingly dim. The entire history of warfare supports this conclusion: although the balance between offense and defense has swung back and forth, the general trend has been unvaryingly toward the increasing destructiveness of offensive war. It is this rising general destructiveness, and not the recent success of one particular offensive weapon in eluding destruction by a defensive counterpart, that has now culminated in the whole planet's being placed in mortal peril. The ultimate vulnerability of human beings is the result of the frailty of nature itself, on which we depend utterly for life; as is now clearer to us than ever before, nature cannot stand up to much nuclear destruction. Given this flood tide of destructive power, which was rising steadily even before nuclear weapons were developed, and has continued since their development (in the fields of chemical and biological warfare, for example), the hopes for defense are not so much slight as beside the point. Most of these hopes rest on weapons that counter not the effects of nuclear weapons but, rather, the nuclear weapons' delivery vehicles. Yet a delivery vehicle is simply anything that gets from point A to point B on the face of the earth. A horse and cart is a delivery vehicle. An army battling its way into enemy territory is a delivery vehicle. A man with a suitcase is a delivery vehicle. There seems little chance that all existing vehicles—not to mention all the vehicles that science will dream up in the future—can be decisively countered. And it is even more unlikely that the devices designed to attack all the delivery vehicles would remain invulnerable to devices that scientists would soon be inventing to attack *them*. The superiority of the offense in a world of uninhibited production of nuclear weapons and their delivery vehicles therefore appears to be something that will last for the indefinite future.

The contradiction between the end we seek and the means of attaining it becomes even clearer when we try to imagine the situation we would have if in 1945 the scientists, instead of handing us the ultimate offensive weapon, had emerged from their laboratory with an ultimate defensive weapon—perhaps one of those impenetrable bubbles with which science-fiction writers like to surround cities. Then a thoroughgoing, consistent defensive world would be possible. Aggressively inclined nations might hurl their most lethal weapons at their neighbors, but the weapons would all bounce off harmlessly, and no one would be hurt. Peoples would then live safely within their own borders, suffering only the torments that they managed to invent for themselves. Under our present circumstances, by contrast, we have not perfect defense but perfect vulnerability.

It was in addressing this contradiction that the strategists came up with the doctrine of deterrence in the first place. Their chief discovery was that the threat of retaliation could substitute for the missing defenses. But while defense and deterrence have the same ends the way they work is nearly opposite. In a defensive system, you rely on your military forces actually to throw the enemy forces back: the swung sword falls on the raised shield without inflicting damage; the advancing foot soldier falls into the moat; the warhead is pulverized by the laser beam. But in a system of deterrence you have given up all hope of throwing the enemy back, and are hoping instead, by threatening a retaliatory attack that *he* cannot throw back, to dissuade him from attacking at all. Deterrence thus rests on the fear of a double offense, in which everyone would destroy everyone else and no one would be defended. The crucial element in deterrence is the foreknowledge by the potential aggressor that if he starts anything this is how it will end. Offensive means are made to serve defensive ends. But in the process the continuation of our species is put in jeopardy.

Inasmuch as the goal we have chosen is to shore up a stalemated, defensive world, one way of defining our task would be to ask whether, having agreed to live with the status quo, we might by further agreement accomplish what we are unable to accomplish through technical efforts; namely, to snatch the victory away from offensive arms and hand it, at least provisionally, back to defensive ones. The question is whether as political and diplomatic actors we could rush into the fray on the side of the defense and turn the tables. I think that, within certain all-important limits, we can. The key is to enter into an agreement abolishing nuclear arms. Nations would first agree, in effect, to drop their swords from their hands and lift their shields toward one another instead. They would agree to have not world government, in which all nations are fused into one nation, but its exact opposite—a multiplicity of inviolate nations pledged to leave each other alone. For nations that now possess nuclear weapons, the agreement would be a true abolition agreement. For those that do not now possess them, it would be a strengthened nonproliferation agreement. (A hundred and nineteen nations have already signed the nonproliferation treaty of 1968.) Obviously, an agreement among the superpowers on both the nature of the status quo and the precise terms of abolition would be the most difficult part of the negotiation. The agreement would be enforced not by any world police force or other organ of a global state but by each nation's knowledge that a breakdown of the agreement would be to no one's advantage, and would only push all nations back down the path to doom. In the widest sense, the agreement would represent the institutionalization of this knowledge. But if nuclear weapons are to be abolished by agreement, one might ask, why not go all the way? Why not abolish conventional weapons and defensive weapons as well? The answer, of course, is that even in the face of the threat of annihilation nations have as yet shown no willingness to surrender their sovereignty, and conventional arms would be one support for its preservation. While the abolition of nuclear arms would increase the margin of mankind's safety against

nuclear destruction and the peril of extinction, the retention of conventional arms would permit the world to hold on to the system of
nation-states. Therefore, a second provision of the agreement would
stipulate that the size of conventional forces be limited and balanced.
In keeping with the defensive aim of the agreement as a whole, these
forces would, to whatever extent this was technically possible, be
deployed and armed in a defensive mode.

There is also another reason for retaining defenses. One of the
most commonly cited and most substantial reasons for rejecting the
abolition of nuclear arms, even if the nuclear powers should develop
the will to abolish them, is that the verification of a nuclear-abolition
agreement could never be adequate. And, as far as I know, it is true
that no one has ever devised a system of verification that could, even
theoretically, preclude significant cheating. Like defense, it seems,
inspection is almost inherently imperfect. When arsenals are large, the
argument runs, a certain amount of cheating on arms-control agreements is unimportant, because the number of concealed weapons is
likely to be small in relation to the size of the arsenals as a whole. But
as the size of the arsenals shrinks, it is said, the importance of cheating
grows, and finally the point is reached at which the hidden arsenals tip
the strategic balance in favor of the cheater. According to this argument, the point of maximum—indeed, total—imbalance is reached
when, after an abolition agreement has been signed, one side cheats
while the other does not. Then the cheater, it is said, has an insuperable advantage, and holds its innocent and trusting cosigner at its
mercy. But if anti-nuclear defenses are retained the advantage in
cheating is sharply reduced, or actually eliminated. Arrayed against
today's gigantic nuclear forces, defenses are helpless. Worse, one
side's defenses serve as a goad to further offensive production by the
other side, which doesn't want the offensive capacity it has decided on

to be weakened. But if defenses were arrayed against the kind of force that could be put together in violation of an abolition agreement they could be crucial. On the one side would be a sharply restricted, untested, and clandestinely produced and maintained offensive force, while on the other side would be a large, fully tested, openly deployed, and technically advanced defensive force. Such a force might not completely nullify the danger of cheating (there is always the man with a suitcase), but no one can doubt that it would drastically reduce it. At the very least, it would throw the plans of an aggressor into a condition of total uncertainty. Moreover, as the years passed after the signing of the agreement the superiority of the defense would be likely to increase, because defensive weapons would continue to be openly developed, tested, and deployed, while offensive weapons could not be. Therefore—probably as a separate, third provision of the agreement—anti-nuclear defensive forces would be permitted.

President Reagan recently offered a vision of a world protected from nuclear destruction by defensive weapons, many of which would be based in space. The United States, he said, should develop these weapons and then share them with the Soviet Union. With both countries protected from nuclear attack, he went on, both would be able to scrap their now useless nuclear arsenals and achieve full nuclear disarmament. Only the order of events in his proposal was wrong. If we seek first to defend ourselves, and not to abolish nuclear weapons until after we have made that effort, we will never abolish them, because of the underlying, technically irreversible superiority of the offensive in the nuclear world. But if we abolish nuclear weapons first and then build the defenses, as a hedge against cheating, we can succeed. Abolition prepares the way for defense.

However, none of these defensive arrangements would offer much protection if the agreement failed to accompany them with one more provision. The worst case—which must be taken into account if nations are to have confidence in the military preparations for thwarting aggressors—is not mere cheating but blatant, open violation of the agreement by a powerful and ruthless nation that is determined to intimidate or subjugate other nations, or the whole world, by suddenly and swiftly building up, and perhaps actually using, an overwhelming nuclear arsenal. This possibility creates the all-important limits mentioned earlier. As soon as it happened, the underlying military superiority of the offensive in the nuclear world would again hold sway, and the conventional and anti-nuclear defenses permitted under the abolition agreement would become useless, (Just how soon in this buildup the offensive weapons would eclipse the defensive ones would depend on the effectiveness of the defenses that had been built up.) The only significant military response to this threat would be a response in kind: a similar nuclear buildup by the threatened nations, returning the world to something like the balance of terror as we know it today. But in order to achieve that buildup the threatened nations would probably have to have already in existence considerable preparations for the manufacture of nuclear arms. Therefore, a fourth provision of the abolition agreement would permit nations to hold themselves in a particular, defined state of readiness for nuclear rearmament. This provision would, in fact, be the very core of the military side of the agreement. It would be the definition, in technical terms, of what "abolition" was to be. And it would be the final guarantor of the safety of nations against attack. However, this guarantor would not defend. It would deter. The most important element in this readiness would simply be the knowledge of how to make the weapons—knowledge that nations are powerless to get rid of even if they want to. This unlosable knowledge is, as we have seen, the root fact of life in the nuclear world, from which the entire predicament proceeds. But, just as the potential for nuclear aggression flows from the knowledge, menacing the stability of the agreement, so does the potential for retaliation, restoring the stability of the agreement. Its persistence is the reason that deterrence doesn't dissolve when the weapons are abolished. In other words, in the nuclear world the threat to use force is as self-cancelling at zero nuclear weapons as it is at fifty thousand nuclear weapons. Thus, both in its political ends—preservation of a stalemate—and in its means—using the threat of nuclear destruction itself to prevent the use of nuclear weapons—the abolition agreement would represent an extension of the doctrine of deterrence: an extension in which the most terrifying features of the doctrine would be greatly mitigated, although not finally removed.

The agreed-upon preparations would be based on the knowledge. In all likelihood, they would consist both of inspectable controls on nuclear reactors and on other facilities producing weapons-grade materials and of rules regarding the construction of delivery vehicles. One question that the policymakers would put to the scientists would be what precise level of technical arrangements would permit some particular, defined level of armament to be achieved in a fixed lead time to nuclear rearmament—say, six weeks. Possible lead times would be defined in such terms as the following: an eight-week lead time to the production of two hundred warheads mounted on cruise missiles, or a six-week lead time to a hundred warheads mounted in military aircraft. The lead time would have to be short enough so that the would-be aggressor, seeking to make use of the interval as a head start, would not be able to establish a decisive lead. "Decisive" in this, or any, nuclear context refers to the ability to destroy the victim's retaliatory capacity in a preemptive first strike. Preemption is the spectre that haunts the deterrence strategists, for if one side can destroy the retaliatory capacity of the other side in a preemptive strike, then deterrence dissolves. This is the point at which victory looms up again as a possibility, and force stops being self-cancelling. (At least, it does in the short run. It's much more difficult to see how a nuclear aggressor could escape retaliation over a longer run.) So it is today, and so it would be in a world of zero nuclear weapons.

The task for strategy in a nuclear-weapon-free world would be to design a capacity for nuclear rearmament which could not be destroyed in a first strike by a nation that took the lead in rearmament by abrogating the abolition agreement, secretly or openly. Retaliatory capacity would have to be able to keep pace with aggressive capacity—to the extent that a disarming first strike would be excluded. If that requirement was satisfied, possession in a nuclear-weapon-free world of the capacity for rebuilding nuclear weapons would deter nations from rebuilding them and then using them, just as in our present, nuclear-armed world possession of the weapons themselves deters nations from using them. Today, missile deters missile, bomber deters bomber, submarine deters submarine. Under what we might call weaponless deterrence, factory would deter factory, blueprint would deter blueprint, equation would deter equation. In today's world, when the strategists assess one another's arsenals they see that every possible escalation in attack can be matched by an escalation on the other side, until the arsenals of both sides are depleted and both nations are annihilated. So the two sides are deterred from attacking one another. With weaponless deterrence in effect, the strategists would see that any possible escalation in rearmament by one side could be matched by an escalation on the other side, until both were again fully armed and ready to embark on mutual assured destruction. So they would be deterred from rearming.

It has often been said that the impossibility of uninventing nuclear weapons makes their abolition impossible. But under the agreement described here the opposite would be the case. The knowledge of how to rebuild the weapons is just the thing that would make abolition *possible,* because it would keep deterrence in force. Indeed, the everlastingness of the knowledge is the key to the abolition of nuclear arms within the framework of deterrence. Once we accept the fact that the acquisition of the knowledge was the essential preparation for nuclear armament, and that it can never be reversed, we can see that every state of disarmament is also a state of armament. And, being a state of armament, it has deterrent value. In pointing out the deterrent value of preparations for nuclear rearmament, and even of the mere knowledge of how to rebuild the weapons, we make the reply to the present opponents of abolition which Bernard Brodie made to Robert Oppenheimer. Oppenheimer, rightly observing that nuclear weapons could not be defended against, called them inherently "aggressive" weapons and predicted that they would inevitably be used in lightning-swift aggressive war. In such a world, of course, there would have been no stability whatever. But to this Brodie responded that the would-be aggressor would not be the only one possessing nuclear weapons, and that when the aggressor saw that its foe possessed them—and was ready to retaliate with them—its aggressive fever would be cooled down. Now we are told that aggressors will take advantage of the abolition of nuclear weapons to rebuild and use nuclear weapons, and to this the answer again is that the intended victims will have the same capacities, and these will act as a deterrent, saving the world's stability.

The notion that abolition is impossible because uninvention is impossible appears to stem from a failure to distinguish clearly between these two things. The confusion is exemplified in *Living with Nuclear Weapons,* in which, in support of their conclusion that a world without nuclear weapons is "a fictional Utopia," the Harvard authors write, "The discovery of nuclear weapons, like the discovery of fire itself, lies behind us on the trajectory of history: it cannot be undone. Even if all nuclear arsenals were destroyed, the knowledge of how to reinvent them would remain and could be put to use in any of a dozen or more nations. The atomic fire cannot be extinguished." The authors fear that "the knowledge of how to reinvent" the weapons will upset any abolition agreement. But if one has "the knowledge," there is no need to "reinvent" anything, because one can go ahead and rebuild the weapons right away by using that knowledge. If, on the other hand, reinvention is really required, then one must have somehow lost the knowledge, but this is impossible. Of course, if one speaks of the knowledge of how to rebuild the weapons rather than "the knowledge of how to reinvent" them, the inconsistency disappears; but then one is speaking of rearming after abolition rather than after uninvention. By inadvertently blurring the distinction between the two, the Harvard authors, like many other proponents of deterrence, make abolition appear to be, like uninvention, impossible, and confer upon the world's nuclear arsenals a durability and irremovability that in fact only the knowledge of how to make them possesses. Though uninvention is impossible, abolition is not. Or if it were true that both were impossible it would have to be for completely different reasons—in the case of uninvention because we don't know how to rid the world of basic scientific knowledge, and in the case of abolition because we lack the necessary political will. If the distinction is kept clear, then the hope opens up that the impossibility of uninvention, which is the fundamental fact of life in the nuclear world, makes abolition, which is just one of the conceivable ways of organizing that world, possible. For it was the invention, not the buildup, of nuclear arms that irreversibly placed mankind within reach of its own self-slaughtering hand, ruined war as the final arbiter in global affairs, and set mankind adrift in a new and unfamiliar political world.

The stages of nuclear escalation are often pictured as a ladder reaching from a peaceful but nuclear-armed world up through various levels of nuclear attack and retaliation to the end of the world. Deterrence calls for the ability of each potential adversary to match the others at each rung of the ladder. The levels of nuclear armament, from zero up to a full-scale doomsday machine, can be pictured as lower rungs on that same ladder, and the levels of technical and industrial preparation for the production of nuclear arms as still lower rungs. On this extended ladder, the bottom rung is not zero nuclear weapons but the bare knowledge of how to make them, unaccompanied by any preparations to rebuild them. In actuality, however, this lowest rung can never be reached, because every general level of technical proficiency, whether geared to weapons production or not, is a state of readiness for nuclear armament at one level or another. That is why there can be no such thing as a return to the pre-nuclear world but only increases in the lead time to nuclear armament and from there to a holocaust. At present, the lead time is virtually the shortest possible: we might say that it is seven minutes—approximately the time that it would take for forward-based strategic missiles on each side to reach targets in the opposing country. If world government, or some equivalent political solution, were in place, the lead time might arguably be centuries, but there would still *be* a lead time, because the knowledge of how to build nuclear weapons would remain in the world. Under the abolition agreement described here, our modest but invaluable achievement would be in increasing this lead time from its present seven minutes to weeks or months.

The technical choice available to us, then, is not whether to possess or to eradicate nuclear weapons but what should be the state of readiness—or, if you want to look at it that way, of unreadiness—for nuclear hostilities in which, by international agreement, we would hold the world. The either-or character of the choice between deterrence with full-scale nuclear arsenals and world government without them no longer has to paralyze the world, for we find that within deterrence itself there are endless gradations, leading all the way down to zero and beyond, as the state of readiness is reduced and diplomatic and political arrangements are improved. Deterrence has more extensive possibilities than we have yet acknowledged. It is our curse—a kind of second fall from grace—that the knowledge of how to extinguish ourselves as a species will never leave us. And it is perhaps only modest compensation that that same knowledge, by ruining war—a lesser but more ancient curse under which our species has labored—has laid the foundations for a world at peace. Nevertheless, to throw this advantage away would be a monumental mistake, since it is one of the few elements that work in our favor as we seek to avoid extinction. The durability of the invention and the collapse of war which has come with it provide a strong foundation on which to begin to build our safety. But on this strong foundation we have so far built only a rickety, improvised shelter. We suffer the danger that flows from the fact that the fateful knowledge is inexpungible from our world, but we have so far turned down the advantages that flow from that fact. We arrange to terrorize one another with annihilation, but we have so far failed to achieve the full measure of safety obtainable from the terror. It is a paradox fully worthy of this elaborate doctrine that if we were to permit ourselves to recognize clearly the breadth and depth of the peril—to assure ourselves once and for all of its boundlessness and durability—we might thereby clear a path to our salvation.

The Unfinished Twentieth Century
HARPER'S, JANUARY 2000

A TALE OF THREE AUGUSTS

AN AGE ENDED, we know, when the Berlin Wall fell, auguring, soon after, the dissolution of the Soviet Union. But which age was it? The Cold War was over—that much was clear. Yet many felt and understood that some longer historical period, or perhaps several, had also come to a close. One clear candidate is the age of totalitarianism—a period coextensive with the life of the Soviet Union, which bracketed the rise and fall of Nazi Germany. (China's current government which has evolved into a strange hybrid that some are calling "market communism," is the only one of the great totalitarian states of the twentieth century that has not actually been overthrown.) Another candidate is the age of world wars, which, as suggested by the war that remained cold, have been rendered unwinnable and therefore unlikely by the invention of nuclear weapons. And when the histories of the two world wars and the two great totalitarian regimes are considered together, they form a third candidate—an age that many historians are now calling the "short twentieth century." The calendar's divisions of the years, they've observed, match up inexactly with history's turning points. According to this way of reckoning, the nineteenth century began not in 1800 but in 1789, with the French Revolution, and came to its close not in 1900 but in 1914, when the First World War broke out, putting an end to the so-called long nineteenth century. The twentieth century, having begun in August of 1914, lasted only until the failed hard-line Communist coup in Moscow in 1991, which, in another pivotal August of the twentieth century, set in motion the Soviet collapse. Some years before, the Russian poet Akhmatova had expressed a similar idea:

> *Snowdrifts covered the Nevskii Prospect* . . .
> *And along the legendary quay,*
> *There advanced, not the calendar,*
> *But the real Twentieth Century.*

It is this real twentieth century—the twentieth century of the Somme, of the Gulag, of the Holocaust —that in 1991 startled the world, the historians are now saying, by turning out to be short. On either side of it were the calmer seas of a predominantly liberal civilization. A bolder assertion of this notion was Francis Fukuyama's renowned claim that the liberal restoration of 1991 marked the "end of history"—by which he meant not that the end of days had arrived but, only a little more modestly, that humanity's long search for the best form of government had reached its destination in a nearly global embrace of liberal democracy.

The distinction between the real twentieth century and the cal-endrical one is based on the convincing idea that the century's bouts of unprecedented violence, both within nations and between them, possess a definite historical coherence—that they constitute, to put it simply, a single story. The proposed periodization is clearly optimistic, suggesting that the tide of bloodshed has reached its high-water mark and is now receding. The failure of the Cold War to become hot and the liquidation in 1991 of the world's last thoroughly totalitarian regime lend substance to the hope. I wish to suggest, however, that this appraisal remains starkly incomplete if it fails to take into account one more age that reached a turning point in 1991. I mean the nuclear age, which opened in another epochal August of the twentieth century, August of 1945, (Somehow in this century August was the month in which history chose to produce a disproportionately large number of its most important events.) No narrative of the extraordinary violence of the twentieth century can possibly be told without taking into account the greatest means of violence ever created.

The Greeks used to say that no man should be called happy before he died. They meant not only that even the most contented life could be undone by misfortune at the last minute but also that the meaning of an entire life might depend on its ending. For a life's fast chapter was not merely an event, with its freight of suffering or joy; it was a disclosure, in whose light the story's beginning and middle might need to be drastically rewritten. Or, to vary the metaphor, stories, including the stories of historical epochs, are like pictures of heavenly constellations drawn by connecting dots—in this case, historical facts. The addition of new dots may merely add detail to the picture that has already taken shape, but it may also alter the entire image. The swan will turn out to be a crab; what looked like a whale turns into a dragon. Such was the case, certainly, with the end of the Soviet Union and the Cold War. The Soviet Union's infirmities, we now must suppose, were eating away at its power long before, one fine day in 1991, the empire evaporated. It is understandable that contemporaries are usually startled by events, but historians have no right to present surprise endings to the tales they tell. Their new job will be to retell the story of the Soviet Union in such a way that the sudden collapse at the end makes sense.

So it must eventually be with the nuclear age. The story of a Cold War that was the scene of history's only nuclear arms race will be very different from the story of a Cold War that turned out to be only the first of many interlocking nuclear arms races in many parts of the world. The nuclear dilemma, in sum, hangs like a giant question mark over our waning century. To 1914 and 1991 two dates therefore need to be added. The first is 1945 and the second is the as yet unknown future date on which the end of the nuclear age will be disclosed. Whether this conclusion will be the elimination of nuclear weapons (either before or after their further use) or, conceivably, the elimination of the species that built them is the deepest of the questions that need answering when we consider the still-open book of the real twentieth century.

In the United States, the historians' oversight is only one symptom of a wider inattention to the nuclear question. In the first years of the post-Cold War period, the nuclear peril seemed to all but disappear from public awareness. Some of the reasons were understandable. As long as the Cold War lasted, it had seemed almost indistinguishable from nuclear danger—the more so since both looked as if they were going to last indefinitely. One half of this assumption was of course negated by the Soviet collapse. For a while, the public seemed to imagine that nuclear danger, too, had unexpectedly proven ephemeral. The political antagonism that had produced the only nuclear terror Americans had ever known had, after all, really ended with the Cold War. The prospect of a second Cuban Missile Crisis became remote. It was reasonable for a while to imagine that the end of the struggle in whose name nuclear weapons had been built would lead to their end. Perhaps it would happen quietly and smoothly. The Comprehensive Test Ban Treaty would be accepted and succeeded by arms reductions. START II would be ratified and followed by START III, START III by START IV (at some point the lesser nuclear powers would be drawn into the negotiations), and so on, until the last warhead was gone. American presidents encouraged the public complacency. "I saw the chance to rid our children's dreams of the nuclear nightmare, and I did," President George Bush said at the Republican convention in 1992; and in 1997, President Bill Clinton boasted that "our children are growing up free from the shadows of the Cold War and the threat of nuclear holocaust."

The news media took their cue from this official fantasy. Nuclear weapons all but dropped out of the news and opinion pages. In the decade since the Berlin Wall was torn down, newspaper readers and television viewers were given little indication that some 31,000 nuclear weapons remained in the world, or that 6,000 of them were targeted at the United States. A whole generation came of age lacking even rudimentary information regarding nuclear arms and nuclear peril. On the tenth anniversary of the end of the wall, few commentators taking stock of the decade bothered to mention the persistence of nuclear danger.

A frightening new landscape was coming into view. To begin with, the presidents who said that they had ended nuclear danger had not acted that way. Clinton's repeated though little-reported "bottom up" reviews of defense policy left the strategy of nuclear deterrence—and the arsenals it justified—untouched. His spokesmen let it be known that nuclear weapons were to remain the foundation of American security for the indefinite future. Russia followed suit—abandoning a willingness expressed by Gorbachev to eliminate nuclear weapons and stalling on the ratification of the START II Treaty. And so the nuclear arsenals of the Cold War, instead of withering away with the disappearance of that conflict, were delivered intact, like a package from a deceased sender, into the new age, though now lacking the benefit of new justification—or, for that matter, of new opposition.

Meanwhile, newcomers to the nuclear game moved to acquire the weapons. If nuclear powers such as Russia and the United States, which no longer had a quarrel, were entitled to maintain nuclear arsenals, why not countries that, like India and Pakistan, were chronically at war? To insist otherwise would, in the words of India's foreign minister Jaswant Singh, be to shut the Third World out of the "nuclear paradigm" established by the First and Second Worlds, and so to accept "nuclear apartheid." In May of 1998, India and Pakistan, accordingly, fired off their rival salvos of nuclear tests. The antagonism between the Soviet Union and the United States had been "cold," but this conflict was hot. The three wars that the two countries had fought since the late 1940s were in short order followed by a fourth in the summer of 1999. The world's multiplying nuclear arsenals were meanwhile supplemented by a new prominence of their repellent siblings in the family of weapons of mass destruction—chemical and biological weapons, which may become the instrument of choice of nations or terrorist groups worried about the expense and difficulty of making nuclear weapons.

By the century's end, the web of arms-control agreements that had been painstakingly woven during the last half century of the Cold War was tearing apart. The United States Senate voted down the Comprehensive Test Ban Treaty—an act that cut away the foundation of several decades of effort by the United States to halt the spread of nuclear weapons. The Senate also persuaded the Clinton administration to develop a national missile defense, which would violate the Antiballistic Missile Treaty of 1972, thereby threatening to turn Russia's stalling on the START negotiations into outright opposition.

The combined resolve of the five senior nuclear powers (the United States, Russia, England, France, and China) to keep their arsenals and of other countries to obtain them likewise threatened the breakdown of the Nuclear Nonproliferation Treaty, under which 180 countries have agreed to forgo nuclear weapons in exchange for promises by the nuclear powers to abolish theirs.

From the very first moments of the nuclear age, scientists have warned the world that it is in the nature of nuclear technology—as of all technology—to become universally available and therefore that, in the absence of political will, the world would tend to become nuclear-armed. In a world boiling with local (and not so local) hatreds, the retrogression of arms control raises the question of whether the Cold War, instead of being the high point of danger in a waning nuclear age, will prove to have been a mere bipolar rehearsal for a multipolar second nuclear age.

A number of voices challenged this status quo by calling for the abolition of nuclear weapons, but their views went largely unreported by the news media that had ignored the dangers of which they warned. Among these voices were leaders of the traditional antinuclear peace movement; the seven governments of the New Agenda coalition, composed of Brazil, Egypt, Ireland, Mexico, New Zealand, Sweden, and South Africa; and an impressive array of retired military officers and civilian leaders, including President Jimmy Carter, Senator Alan Cranston, former commander of the Strategic Air Command General George Lee Butler, and the commander of the allied air forces in the Gulf War, General Charles Horner. In a series of reports and statements, these people have argued that the end of the Cold War has provided a historically unique but perishable opportunity to remove nuclear danger by eliminating nuclear arsenals everywhere. (Since only eight nations possess nuclear weapons, and of

these only India, Pakistan, and Israel have not signed the Nonproliferation Treaty, abolition means persuading just three nations to live as
would the 185 signatories.) Notable among the new abolitionists were
some of the most hawkish figures of the Cold War, including Paul
Nitze, drafter in 1950 of National Security Council Memorandum-68,
regarded by many as the charter of American Cold War policy. He
recently argued that the United States' huge lead in the development
of high-precision weaponry created a new military context in which
the United States simply did not need nuclear weapons. Considering
this advantage, Nitze could "think of no circumstances under which it
would be wise for the United States to use nuclear weapons," and
therefore recommended that the nation "unilaterally get rid" of them.
The emergence of this hawkish strain of abolitionism, in which precision, highly-explosive conventional bombing would give the United
States a usable military superiority that nuclear weapons could never
confer, assured that, should the idea of abolition ever take hold, a
debate within the ranks of the abolitionists themselves would be
robust. But Nitze's dramatic proposal fell into the media silence that
had swallowed up all other proposals for abolition.

PREFACE TO A CENTURY

It seems timely, then, to take a fresh look at the nuclear question in the
context of the century that has just ended. The exercise, we can hope,
will shed light on both the nuclear dilemma and the story of the century, short or otherwise, in which nuclear weapons have played, and
unfortunately go on playing, so important a part. One place to begin
is with a work that, as it happens, was first published in *Blackwood's
Edinburgh Magazine*, in London, at the turn of the last century, in
1899: Joseph Conrad's *Heart of Darkness*. Conrad wrote in the

heyday of a liberal civilization that had seemed to spread steadily and grow stronger for most of the nineteenth century. Its articles of faith were that science and technology were the sources of a prosperity without limits; that the free market would spread the new abundance across the boundaries of both classes and nations; that liberty and democracy, already established in several of the most powerful and advanced nations, were gaining ground almost everywhere; and that all of these forces were welling an unstoppable tide of overall human progress. It is, of course, a revival of these ideas—minus, notably, the idea of progress—that has inspired the belief that the twentieth century, or even history itself, ended in 1991. Conrad was not an acolyte of this faith. He was perhaps the most acute among a number of observers who, having witnessed firsthand what the "civilized" countries were doing in the "backward" parts of the world, where colonialism was at its zenith, discerned the shape of a radically different future. *Heart of Darkness* was many things. It was a tale of travel to an exotic place. It was a glimpse, through the eyes of the seaman Marlow, of the atrocities committed by King Leopold's International Association of the Congo. It was an investigation by literary means of the extremes of evil. And it was, as we today are in a position to appreciate, a topographic map, clairvoyant in its specificity, of the moral landscape of the twentieth century.

"It was like a weary pilgrimage amongst hints for nightmares," Marlow says of his sea journey to the Congo along the African coast. The hinted nightmares turned out to be the waking experience of the century ahead. That century, Conrad apparently understood, was about to open up new possibilities for evil. In *Heart of Darkness*, he seems to thumb through them prospectively, as if through a deck of horrific tarot cards. The concentration camps are there. The black men "dying slowly," "in all the attitudes of pain, abandonment, and despair," whom Marlow wimesses in a grove of trees immediately upon arriving at an outer station, are unmistakable precursors of the millions of men and women who were to die in the concentration camps soon to be built in Europe. The monster Kurtz, the charismatic station chief who murders in the name of progress, and who, although "hollow at the core," was gifted with magnificent eloquence and "electrified large meetings," is a sort of prefiguration of Hitler. Conrad even has a Belgian journalist comment that Kurtz would have made a "splendid leader of an extreme party." Which one? "Any party," is the answer. For, the journalist stammers, "he was an—an—extremist." But Kurtz is not to be understood as a fringe character. "All Europe contributed to the making of Kurtz," Marlow says, in a rare moment of editorializing.

Consider, by way of inexplicably refined forecasting, the likeness of some of Marlow's comments about Kurtz to some comments Hitler makes about himself in 1936. The power of Hitler's voice, carried to the German public over the radio, was a basic element of his power. Conrad notes something similar in Kurtz. Marlow:

> Kurtz discoursed. A voice! a voice! It rang deep to the very last. Yet beneath the rich and resonant voice lay an emptiness: The voice was gone. What else had been there?

And, for comparison, Hitler speaking at a rally in 1936 about his appeal to the German people:

> At this hour do we not again feel the miracle that has brought us together! Long ago you heard the voice of a man, and it struck to your hearts, it awakened you, and you followed this voice. You followed it for years, without so much as having

seen him whose voice it was; you heard only a voice, and you followed.

To give just one more example, anyone who witnessed the monotonous, ceaseless American artillery fire into "free-fire zones" in Vietnam will experience a shock of recognition in the following description of a French naval vessel firing into the African jungle:

> In the empty immensity of earth, sky, and water, there she was, incomprehensible, firing into a continent. Pop, would go one of the six-inch guns; a small flame would dart and vanish, a little white smoke would disappear, a tiny projectile would give a feeble screech—and nothing happened. Nothing could happen. There was a touch of insanity in the proceeding, a sense of lugubrious drollery in the sight.

Nor did Conrad fail to take note of those indispensable props of the gigantic, insane, state-sponsored crimes of our time: the obedient functionaries. The "banality" of their evil, famously described after the fact by Hannah Arendt in *Eichmann in Jerusalem*, is foreshadowed in Conrad's description of a minor bureaucrat in the ivory-gathering operation at the Central Station. This man, mistaking Marlow for an influential figure, curries favor with him, prompting Marlow to observe, "I let him run on, this papier-mache Mephistopheles." He adds, "It seemed to me that if I tried I could poke my forefinger through him, and would find nothing inside but a little loose dirt, maybe." Conrad described well the humiliation that so many decent people were to experience in having to take ridiculous personages seriously solely because of the immense suffering they were causing. Face to face with Kurtz in the jungle at night, Marlow comments, "I resented bitterly the absurd danger of our situation, as if to be at the mercy of that atrocious phantom had been a dishonoring necessity." The inspired anti-Nazi diarist Friedrich Reck-Malleczewen, who was executed by the Nazis in 1944, experienced a similar feeling of humiliation when he thought back to an accidental encounter he had once had with another atrocious phantom—Hitler. "If I had had an inkling of the role this piece of filth was to play, and of the years of suffering he was to make us endure," he wrote, "I would have done it [shot him] without a second thought. But I took him for a character out of a comic strip, and did not shoot."

The most remarkable and telling augury of *Heart of Darkness*, however, was the glimpse that Conrad, vaulting ahead in prophecy to 1945, provided of the destination toward which all these preposterous and terrifying tendencies somehow were heading: namely, the threat that, with the help of the Kurtzes of this world, the human species might one day get ready to wipe itself off the face of the earth. After his climactic meeting with Kurtz in the jungle, Marlow further comments, "There was nothing either above or below him, and I knew it. He had kicked himself loose of the earth. Confound the man! he had kicked the very earth to pieces." This foreboding of annihilation was no incidental feature of the work; it returns several times, always at critical moments in the story. The most renowned passage in which it occurs is the legendary addendum "Exterminate all the brutes" that Kurtz pinned to the bottom of the dithyramb to nineteenth-century progress that he left as his legacy. The foreboding recurs even more explicitly when, after Kurtz has died and Marlow is on his way to inform Kurtz's betrothed of the fact, he reports, "I had a vision of him on the stretcher, opening his mouth voraciously, as if to devour all the earth with all its mankind." The technical means for destroying the species lay far in the future, but the psychological and moral preparations, it appears, were well under way in 1899.

THE FIRST AUGUST: THE BEGINNINGOF THE REAL TWENTIETH CENTURY

As the scholar Jessica Reifer has pointed out, Conrad's intimations in a single text of virtually all the unprecedented evils, including the threat of self-extinction, that Western humanity was about to visit upon itself and the world in the twentieth century are evidence before the fact of their common roots and essential unity. These "hints for nightmares," however, did not materialize into real historical events in Europe until, during the first of the century's fateful Augusts, the First World War broke out. Then the nightmares followed, one after another, in a chain whose unusually clear linkage points to the underlying continuity.

The judgment that the outbreak of the First World War was the starting point in the twentieth century's plunge into horror did not originate with the inventors of the idea of the short twentieth century; it has been the belief of a remarkably wide consensus of historians. George Kennan spoke for this consensus in his diplomatic history *The Decline of Bismarck's European Order*:

> With the phenomenon of the Second World War before me, it was borne in upon me to what overwhelming extent the determining phenomena of the interwar period, Russian Communism and German Nazism and indeed then the Second World War itself, were the products of that first great holocaust of 1914-18. . . . And thus I came to see the First World War . . . as the great seminal catastrophe of the century. . . .

As Kennan suggests, the stories of the two world wars on the one hand and of the two great totalitarian regimes on the other were as tightly intertwined at every crucial juncture as the proteins on the strands of a double helix. Total war and totalitarianism were kin in more than name. From 1914 onward, each fed the other in a vicious spiral of violence. To begin with, the shock of the First World War is widely understood to have created the social conditions essential to the success of the Bolshevik revolution in Russia. In the words of the historian Martin Malia, "This war disorganized Russia's still immature political structures to the point where the Bolshevik Party, a throwback to the violent and conspiratorial politics of the 1870s, was able to seize power. . . . " Many understood even at the time that the brutality of the war had been carried over to the system of rule that followed. As the contemporary socialist Victor Chernov put it, "The moral nature of the Bolshevik Revolution was inherited from the war in which it was born."

That the Nazis' rise to power in Germany was made possible by the war is also accepted widely. It will be enough here—without trying to recount the story of the destabilization of German politics and society by her defeat and the harsh terms of the peace settlement—to recall two comments made by Hitler. The first is his remark that "if at the beginning of the war twelve or fifteen thousand of these Hebrew corrupters of the people had been held under poison gas, as happened to hundreds of thousands of our very best German workers in the field, the sacrifice of millions at the front would not have been in vain." The idea of killing Jews by gas was not one that Hitler, who had been a victim of an English gas attack, was to forget. The second comment is his description of his reaction to the declaration of the First World War. "Even today," he wrote in *Mein Kampf*, "I am not ashamed to say that, overpowered by stormy enthusiasm, I fell down on my knees and thanked Heaven from an overflowing heart."

If in the century's teens and twenties total war prepared the way for totalitarianism, in the thirties, when Hitler carried out the series of aggressions that brought on the Second World War, the process worked the other way around. Hitler's biographers tell us that while at the front in the First World War he felt so much at home in the trenches and so ill at ease in civilian society that he canceled all his leaves. For him, it seems, not war but peace was hell, and there is a sense in which the interwar period was just one more leave that was canceled by a peace-weary Hitler.

The plainest of these links, finally, is that between the war against Hitler and the decision by the United States and England to build atomic weapons. In October of 1939 (more than two years before the United States went to war with Germany and Japan), when the businessman Alexander Sachs visited President Franklin Roosevelt to recommend an atomic-weapons program, Roosevelt commented, "Alex, what you are after is to see that the Nazis don't blow us up." Sachs replied, "Precisely." Throughout the war, the scientists at Los Alamos—many of them refugees from Europe—held before their eyes the prospect that Hitler would succeed in building the bomb first.

Evil, even when opposed, has a way of preparing the ground for more evil, and Hitler by this route became a progenitor of the bomb. His extraordinary malevolence induced his adversaries to embrace an evil that otherwise they conceivably might have forgone. Through this indirect paternity were reborn key aspects of the policies that he, more than anyone else, had pioneered. As in a magic trick— appropriately accompanied by a gigantic world-blinding flash and (mushroom-shaped) puff of smoke—the politics of mass annihilation, even as they were going down to defeat in Hitler's bunker, were in 1945 transferred to the care of Washington.

EXTERMINATION

What was the nature of the new possibilities for evil that Conrad had discerned in the Congo and that the series of calamities inaugurated by the war in 1914 brought, as if through the action of a pendulum swinging in an ever-widening arc, to fuller and fuller realization, until the human species created weapons whereby it could destroy itself? Violence on a previously unimaginable scale was the obvious common denominator. This violence was the basis for the increasing use of that lingua franca of twentieth-century politics, terror—terror as an instrument of rule, which is to say totalitarian rule; terror as a strategy of war, and especially of "strategic" bombing, aimed at breaking the morale of civilian populations; and, finally, nuclear terror, rather optimistically referred to as a "balance of terror." (Terror in nuclear strategy, let us note, is terror in not only its most extensive but also its purest form, inasmuch as its practitioners sometimes imagine that it can be projected forever without actual use of the instruments that produce it.) But something more than a colossal increase in violence and terror was involved. In Kurtz's phrase "Exterminate all the brutes," Conrad gives us the concept we need: extermination. The capacity and will to destroy not just large numbers of people but entire classes of people was the new invention. Policies of extermination, of course, require slaughter on a mass scale, but they aim at more than slaughter. By seeking to eradicate defined human collectivities, extermination aims not only at those groups but at their progeny, who are shut out of existence when the policy succeeds. The distinction is basic. Mass slaughter is a crime against the living; extermination is, in addition, a crime against the future. When Hitler launched the Final Solution, his target was not just the living Jews but all future Jews together with the culture they had created and, if they were permitted to live, would go on creating. Murder is a crime that, by destroying individual lives, violates the legal and moral order of a community; extermination is a crime that, by destroying an entire community, is a crime against the family of communities that make up humankind—a crime, as international law has come to recognize, "against humanity."

Genocide—the destruction of a people, whether defined as a race or a tribe or a nation—is the quintessential act of extermination, but it is not the only one. Another is the extermination of social classes, practiced by Stalin and Mao Zedong and Pol Pot, among others. In the Bolsheviks' very first year in power, they discovered a category of crime that they called "objective." A crime was "subjective" when you had done something wrong; it was "objective" when, through no deed of your own, you belonged to a social class that the government wanted to liquidate. As early as 1918, Latvian Latsis, one of the chiefs of the Cheka, the precursor of the KGB, announced the goal in plain language: "We are engaged in annihilating the bourgeoisie as a class." Thus there was no need, Latsis explained, to "prove that this or that man acted against the interests of Soviet power." It was enough to ask, "To what class does he belong, Where does he come from, what kind of education did he have, what is his occupation?" The answers to these questions "decide the fate of the accused." "That," he said, "is the quintessence of the Red Terror"—terror that was to cost the Soviet people an estimated 50 or 60 million lives in the coming half-century.

A third target of policies of extermination was cities and their populations. Let us consider two examples. The first is, the bombing of Hamburg by the British air force in 1943. As early as July 1940, Churchill, while commanding the Battle of Britain, had called for "exterminating" air attacks on Germany. From then until 1942, the Bomber Command, afflicted by high loss rates and fearful of losing out in interservice rivalry with the Navy and the Army, drifted away from "precision" bombing, which had to be carried out in daylight, into "area bombing," which could be carried out at night. The aim was to destroy the morale of the German people by killing German civilians and destroying their homes. By the end of 1942, giant raids on Lubeck and Cologne had made it clear that the annihilation of entire cities in one or a few raids was feasible. Accordingly, Most Secret Operation Order No. 173, of May 27, 1943, stated, under the heading "Intention," that the aim of the raid was "to destroy Hamburg." The order estimated that 10,000 tons of bombs would have to be dropped to "complete the process of elimination." And thus it was done, producing a firestorm in the city and killing some 45,000 people in a single night.

The second example is Hitler's plan, formed even before his attack on Russia, in June of 1941, for the annihilation of Moscow and Leningrad. Moscow was to be razed because it was "the center of [Bolshevik] doctrine"—for Hitler's larger goal was an "ethnic catastrophe." He intended to dig a reservoir where Moscow had once been. At first, he planned to spare Leningrad, because it was "incomparably more beautiful" than Moscow; but soon he put Leningrad, too, on the list of cities to be destroyed. His explanation sheds light on the mentality of those who are preparing to exterminate entire human communities:

> I suppose that some people are clutching their heads with both hands to find an answer to the question, "How can the Fuhrer destroy a city like St. Petersburg?". . . I would prefer not to see anyone suffer, not to do harm to anyone. But when I realize the species is in danger, then in my case sentiment gives way to the coldest reason.

The Nazi general Franz Halder concurred with this supposedly cold reasoning: annihilating the two cities, he wrote, would be a "national catastrophe which [would] deprive not only Bolshevism but also Muscovite nationalism of their centers."

A plan was drawn up. Leningrad would be sealed off, to weaken it "by terror and growing starvation"; then the Germans would "remove the survivors in captivity in the interior of Russia, level Leningrad to the ground with high explosives, and leave the area to the north of the Neva to the Finns."

Of course, we know that the two cities survived, owing not to any thaw in Hitler's cold reasoning but to the almost superhuman resistance mounted by the Russian people.

EXTERMINATION AS A SYSTEMATIC EVIL

Just as the twentieth century's policies of extermination—whether of peoples, classes, or cities—enveloped entire human communities, so also they were carried out by entire communities—or, at any rate, by the state authorities that putatively represented those communities. Extermination, a species of crime requiring extensive social resources, is—can only be—a systemic evil. To the extent that popular support was present, the policies amounted to attempted murders of one society by another. Although there can be debate over just how extensive popular support was for Stalin's and Hitler's policies of extermination, there can be no doubt that, through the states that ruled over these peoples, the resources of entire societies were placed at the disposal of those carrying out the policies.

Those resources were not just the obvious ones—the secret police, the transportation systems, the concentration-camp administrations, the armies, the bomber forces. They had to include mass cooperation of the kind that control of the state alone provides. When the state becomes an exterminator, and the law, instead of enjoining evil, supports and enforces it—as does the whole tremendous weight of custom, habit, bureaucratic inertia, and social pressure—the individual who might seek to oppose the policies is left in an extremity of moral solitude. Even the voice of conscience, in these circumstances, can become an enlistee in the ranks of the evildoers. People find themselves in the dilemma defined by Mark Twain when he presented Huck Finn's inner deliberations whether to turn in his friend the runaway black slave, Jim. Huck's "conscience," he believes, is telling him that it is wrong not to turn Jim in. Nevertheless, Huck decides to do what is "wrong" and hides Jim. Adolf Eichmann, too, heard the voice of an inverted conscience, but he, unlike Huck, obeyed it. At the end of the war, with the defeat of Germany in sight, he had an opportunity to slow down or even halt the transports of the Jews to the killing centers, but instead he redoubled his efforts. "The sad and very uncomfortable truth," Arendt writes, "probably was that it was not his fanaticism but his very conscience that prompted Eichmann to adopt his uncompromising attitude during the last year of the war. . . ." For "he remembered perfectly well that he would have had a bad conscience only if he had not done what he had been ordered to do—to ship millions of men, women, and children to their death with great zeal and the most meticulous care."

EXTERMINATION AS PSEUDOSCIENCE

As if to leave individual judgment in even greater perplexity, science— or, be precise, pseudoscience (otherwise known as ideology)—was summoned to lend its pseudoauthority to the policies of extermination. In the late nineteenth century, in a wholesale resort to the persuasive power of sheer metaphor, social Darwinists had taught that nations in history, like species in evolution, were subject to the law of survival of the fittest. As early as 1848, Friedrich Engels had distinguished between "historical nations" (they included Germany, England, and France), which were destined to flourish, and "ahistorical nations" (they included most of the Balkan peoples), which were destined for history's scrap heap. His interest in these ideas is one illustration of the intellectual roots that the Marxist theory of classes shared with racial theories of evolution. In Stalin's Russia, classes—some doomed, some destined to rule—played the role that races played in Hitler's Germany.

Hitler's Final Solution of the Jewish "problem" was in his mind only one part of a vast scheme of ethnic expulsion, resettlement, extermination, and racial engineering, in which he planned to eradicate Poland and Ukraine, among other nations. For example, of forty-five million inhabitants in Western Russia, according to a memo prepared by the Ministry for Occupied Eastern Territories, thirty-one million were to be expatriated or killed. "Drop a few bombs on their cities, and the job will be done," Hitler suggested.

The extent to which Hitler, caught up in the grandiose theories of racial pseudoscience, had transcended mere nationalism is shown by his often-stated readiness to sacrifice even the German people if they showed themselves cowardly or weak. No nationalist could have said, as Hitler did in 1941, when still at the height of his power, that if the Germans were "no longer so strong and ready for sacrifice that they will stake their own blood on their existence, they deserve to be annihilated by another, stronger power." In that event, he added, "I would not shed a tear for the German people." He made good his promise when, facing defeat in 1945, he ordered the destruction of the entire infrastructure of German society, including its industry, buildings, and food stocks. But then had he not warned the world, as if in fulfillment of Conrad's vision of Kurtz devouring all the earth with all its mankind, that "we may perish, perhaps. But we shall take the world with us. Muspili, universal conflagration"? Hitler's willingness to accept—and even to carry out—the destruction of Germany (and the whole world into the bargain) was an early warning of the ease, later illustrated on a much greater scale in the nuclear policy of "mutual assured destruction" during the Cold War, with which those who adopt policies of annihilation can overshoot the mark and wind up involving themselves in suicidal plans. Unfortunately, once the scruples that inhibit the extermination of millions of "others" have been discarded, there are very few left with which to protect "ourselves."

EXTERMINATION AS A RADICAL EVIL

The new policies—of which the extermination of human populations was the objective, states or whole societies were the authors, the instruments of modern science were the means, and for which the concepts of pseudoscience were the rationalization—prompted new thinking about the nature of evil. They precipitated what might be called a crisis in the meaning of evil, by which I mean a crisis in all of the human capacities whereby, once evils have occurred, the world tries, as best it can, to respond to them—to incorporate them into memory and the historical record, to understand them, to take appropriate action against their recurrence. The crimes of the twentieth century seemed to make a mockery of these powers. In *The Origins of Totalitarianism*, Arendt, making use of a phrase of Immanuel Kant's, named the new phenomenon "radical evil." According to Kant, ordinary evil occurred when the will, driven by some fear or lured by some temptation away from the principals of equity and justice, committed a selfish act. Radical evil occurred when the will, even when unafraid or unswayed by temptation, somehow inspired itself to commit evil. Whereas ordinary evil, being dependent on the happenstance of external threats or temptations, was by its nature occasional, radical evil, being ever-present in the will, might infect any or all of a person's actions. If we extend this idea from the individual to the state, we arrive at the distinction between a state that commits a crime in violation of its own good laws and a state whose laws ordain and enforce evil. Obviously, the latter is more dangerous, for it has corrupted one of the main defenses we sometimes have against evil—the state and its laws. This nullification of the human power of response brings a new feeling of bafflement and helplessness. For outbreaks of radical evil, Arendt explained, do not only destroy their victims, often in stupefying numbers, but "dispossess us of all power" (italics mine), for they "transcend the realm of human affairs," and "we can neither punish nor forgive such offenses."

The problem for the most elementary of responses, memory—a problem deliberately created by totalitarian regimes, which have sought to erase their crimes from the historical record—was simply to rescue the facts from their intended oblivion. Against these efforts were eventually pitted heroic acts of witness—by an Aleksandr Solzhenitsyn, a Nadezhda Mandelstam, a Primo Levi. The problem for feeling was the exhaustion that empathy must encounter in the face of suffering on such a scale. And the problem for thought was nothingness—the sheer absence created by the extinction of communities. The problem for law, in addition to the corruption of the perpetrators' own laws, was the likely destruction of the victims' legal system, if one ever existed. What remained were third parties who might seek to judge the wrongdoers by newly created laws, as was done in the Nuremberg trials. (This problem was solved after the fact for the Jews by the foundation of the state of Israel, which put Eichmann on trial.)

The twentieth century's policies of extermination were radical in one more sense. "Radical" evil, as the Latin origins of the word suggest, is evil that goes to the root. The root, though, of what? The answer must be: that which extermination afflicts and destroys; namely, life. The root of life, the spring from which life arises—as distinct from life itself—is birth, which is the power that enables communities composed of mortal beings to regenerate and preserve themselves in history. And it is this power, precisely, that acts of extermination annul.

After witnessing the trial of Eichmann, a "papier-mache Mephistopheles" if there ever was one, Arendt backed away from the phrase "radical evil." "Only the good has depth and can be radical," she wrote in a letter to her friend Gershom Scholem. Evil, she now believed, "is never 'radical,' only extreme." It was this very shallowness, she concluded, that produced the frustration of the mind faced with the new crimes. "It is 'thought-defying,'" she explained, "because thought tries to reach some depth, to go to the roots, and the moment it concerns itself with evil, it is frustrated because there is nothing." (This relationship between evil and nothingness, though it has been most clearly manifested in history only in this century, was signposted in Christian theology, in which, as St. Augustine maintains, being, taken as a whole, is good, and its absence is called evil.)

In truth, though, "there is nothing" in two senses where radical evil is concerned. First, there is nothing (perhaps just "a little loose dirt") in the souls of bureaucrats such as Eichmann, for when the state of which they are a part goes berserk, they can, merely by thoughtlessly doing their jobs (quitting would take some imagination), participate in gargantuan evils. Second, as Arendt had pointed out earlier, the erasure of a community from the face of the earth leaves a kind of "nothing" behind; namely, the "hole of oblivion" in the human order where that community had once existed. Perhaps banal evildoers, as Conrad knew, are capable of committing evil that is radical (or "extreme," if you prefer), as if the emptiness of their minds and souls prefigures the emptiness in the world that they and the policies they serve leave behind. What is "thought-defying" after the fact is, appropriately done thoughtlessly to begin with.

THE SECOND AUGUST: NUCLEAR EXTERMINATION

In her reflections on radical evil, Arendt was addressing policies of extermination that had been adopted before the advent of nuclear weapons, but it is plain that what she had to say applies in almost every particular to nuclear policies and nuclear danger. In other words, although Hiroshima came as a great surprise and shock to the world, it did not arrive without a historical context and historical precedents. On the contrary, it was the supreme expression of forces that had been developing ever since Conrad had Kurtz write, "Exterminate all the brutes." Behind Hiroshima stood not only the obvious precedent of area bombing but all of the twentieth century's policies of extermination. These amounted, by the end of the Second World War, to what might be called a legacy of extermination, and in August of 1945 the United States fell heir to it. The hallmarks of the legacy were all present. The nuclear threat was a threat of extermination—extermination, this time, not only of nations find peoples but of the human species. The root of life that now would be severed would be the root of all human life, birth itself, and would shut all future human beings out of existence: The evil was a systemic evil: The system posing the threat, once the "balance of terror" was established, went beyond any single state to incorporate the greatest powers of the world, which, in the system of mutual assured destruction, became jointly complicit in the project. The threat was supported by pseudoscience, spun this time from game theory and other forms of futurology manufactured in think tanks and academic institutions that subserved power. Nuclear "strategy"— regarded by many as a contradiction in terms—became the very epicenter of banality. Nuclear arms increased the capacity of human beings to destroy one another to its absolute limit, beyond which any further improvements would merely be "overkill." The arsenals threatened radical evil, in the fullest and most exact sense of that term: they brought radical evil to perfection. The powers of human response to evil would be entirely destroyed by the evil deed itself. Policies of extermination again spilled over into suicidal policies. The "coldest reason" again was invoked to rationalize genocide. The conscience of the individual was again thrown into crisis by the policies of the state. The deeds in question again were, as Arendt had said, "thought-defying." The "nothingness" that now awaited was absolute, the crisis of meaning full-blown. The atomic bomb that burst over Hiroshima burned for a moment as bright as the sun, but at its heart was a darkness that was eternal. The twentieth century had, so to speak, arrived at the heart of the heart of darkness.

The advent of the nuclear age, however, brought with it another major change in the development of the century's policies of extermination. At a stroke, it removed them from their totalitarian residence and planted them at the core of liberal civilization, which is to say at the core of the national security policy of the powerful democratic nation about to assume leadership of the non-Communist world—the United States. The new location brought with it a new moral and practical riddle of the first order. Instruments of the most radical evil imaginable—the extinction of the human species—had appeared, but they were first placed in the hands of a liberal republic. The fact that, more or less by an accident of history, the bomb was born in New Mexico, U.S.A., in 1945, rather than, say, Heidelberg, Germany, in 1944 (no sheer impossibility of science or history rules out our imagining the latter possibility), lent it a triple warrant of virtue that it otherwise would have lacked.

In the first place, the bomb gained luster from its new residence. Without becoming jingoistic about the United States or overlooking the dark passages in its history, including slavery and the near-extinction of Native Americans, it must be said that the United States was no Nazi Germany or Stalinist Russia. History had in a sense played a trick on the world, as it so often does. If history had been logical, it would have given the bomb to Hitler, whose policies (including his suicidal inclinations) so clearly pointed in the direction of extermination on the new scale. It's easy to imagine what civilized people would have said if Hitler had been the first to use nuclear weapons—perhaps against Moscow or London. They very likely would have said that nuclear war was a natural culmination of *Vernichtungskrieg* and an ideology that sanctioned the extermination of peoples, and that with nuclear weapons Hitler was enabled to do quickly and efficiently what he had already been doing slowly and clumsily with gas chambers. The United States, on the other hand, had shown no recent inclination for policies of extermination, as was demonstrated shortly by its mild, liberal, extremely successful occupation policies in Germany and Japan. In the second place, the bomb arrived just in time to hurry along the end of the most destructive war in history. It made its appearance as a war-ending, war-winning device. The totalitarian and the liberal regimes had arrived at their policies of extermination along very different historical paths. Whereas Hitler and Stalin destroyed peoples, classes, and cities for reasons that even today defy rational explanation, the United States destroyed Hiroshima and Nagasaki for the perfectly clear and comprehensible purposes of ending the war quickly and getting the upper hand over the Soviet Union in the embryonic Cold War. (To point this out is not to justify these acts; it is only to observe that the goals of policy were conventional and rational.) In the third place, the almost immediate outbreak of the Cold War with the totalitarian Soviet Union created a justification for continuing to build nuclear arsenals, lending the bomb still another warrant of virtue. It assumed the role of guardian of the free world.

To this triple validation of policies of nuclear extermination, accorded by the accident of timing and place, a fourth, of later origin, must be added. Although it was true that with the growth of the arsenals the depth and range of terror were soon increased to their earthly maximum, it also happened that none was ever used after Nagasaki. Instead, they were held suspended, like the sword of Damocles cited by President John Kennedy, over a completely jeopardized yet undevastated world. It was as if, in the nuclear arsenals of the Cold War, the destruction and mass killing of the entire first half of the twentieth century had been distilled into a poison of fantastic potency but then this poison, instead of being administered to a doomed world, had been held in reserve, being employed only to produce terror. To the question whether Western Civilization had put behind it the legacy of extermination that it had been developing for half a century, the nuclear policy makers of the Cold War in effect gave an equivocal answer. Their answer was, No, for we have plans for extermination that beggar Hitler's and Stalin's, but our sincere wish is never to be provoked into actually committing the deed. Certainly, the legacy of extermination had not been renounced. Rather, it had been hugely developed and assigned a more important role in world affairs than ever before. Now the world's greatest power as well as its adversary relied upon it for basic security.

On the other hand, the very fearsomeness of the new threat was invoked to prevent its being carried out. And not only did the bomb prevent its own nuclear war, the theorists said; it prevented the worst of the conventional wars: no conventional third world war broke out. In the meantime, however, an estimated 40 million people, most of them civilians, were killed in local wars—a fact suggesting that major war was as much displaced as deterred.

Whether a third world war was headed off because of nuclear deterrence or for some other reason is a question not easily resolved. It is a historical fact, however, that in the minds of most policy makers as well as millions of citizens nuclear deterrence worked. The bomb, already seen, as a war-winner and a freedom-defender, now was granted the additional title of peacemaker. (The MX missile was given this very name, and the Strategic Air Command adopted the motto "Peace Is Our Profession.") Here was a bargain with the devil to make Faust green with envy. Victory, freedom, peace: was there anything else for which the world might petition an openhanded Lucifer?

And yet none of these benefits altered in the slightest particular the irreducible facts of what nuclear weapons were, what they could do, and what they were meant to do "if deterrence failed." One bomb of the appropriate megatonnage would still obliterate any city; ten bombs, ten cities. Hitler had killed an estimated 6 million Jews; Stalin had sent an estimated 20 million of his fellow Soviet citizens to their deaths. A few dozen well-placed nuclear bombs could outdo these totals by an order of magnitude. But at the height of the Cold War, there were not a few dozen nuclear bombs; there were almost 70,000, with thousands poised on hair-trigger alert. A policy of extermination did not cease being that because the goals it supported were laudable. Described soberly and without the slightest hyperbole, it was a policy of retaliatory genocide.

For most people most of the time, these perils remained all but unimaginable. But every now and then the reality of the policy was borne in on someone. That happened, for instance, to Robert McNamara shortly after he became secretary of defense in 1961, when he received a briefing on the Single Integrated Operational Plan at the headquarters of the Strategic Air Command. In the event of a Soviet conventional attack on Europe—or merely the plausible likelihood of such an attack—the United States' Plan 1-A, which was its only true option for major nuclear war, McNamara learned, was to annihilate every Communist country from Poland to China. There was no operational means, he further learned, by which, if the president desired, he could spare one or more of these countries. Albania, then engaged in bitter polemics with Moscow, was to be obliterated merely because a Soviet radar facility was stationed on its soil. The plan was for obligatory multiple acts of genocide. In *The Wizards of Armageddon*, Fred Kaplan reports that "McNamara was horrified." He set about trying to create other options. Today McNamara favors the abolition of nuclear weapons because, in his carefully chosen words, they threaten "the destruction of nations."

Hiroshima, in sum, had created a gulf between ends and means. Never had evil been more radical; never had the good that was hoped from it been greater. The means were an evil that exceeded the capacity of the human being to imagine them; the ends were all the splendors of liberal civilization and peace.

Thus, through the invention, production, and deployment of nuclear arsenals, was the tradition of extermination glimpsed in prospect by Conrad in colonized Africa, pioneered and developed under totalitarian government and in total war, conjoined to the liberal tradition that had been knocked off course at the beginning of the real twentieth century by the First World War. In a political as well as a moral sense, however, the union was tentative. During the Cold War years, the Western nuclear powers (the United States, England, and France) did indeed learn the art of *Living with Nuclear Weapons*, in the title of the Harvard-sponsored book of 1983, but they had not taken the marriage vows. Reliance on nuclear arms was widely considered an extraordinary, provisional response to an extraordinary, provisional emergency: the threat, as many people in the West believed, to the freedom of the entire world by the Soviet Union, which, of course, soon developed nuclear arsenals of its own.

The Soviet threat shaped the West's embrace of nuclear terror in two fundamental ways. First, it was placed in the moral scales opposite the nuclear threat, rendering the latter acceptable. The mere physical existence of humankind, many people believed, was worth risking for the sake of its moral and spiritual existence, represented by the survival of freedom. Second, most people were persuaded that the secretive nature of the Soviet regime ruled out effective inspection of radical nuclear-arms-control agreements, thus making full nuclear disarmament impossible. In 1946, when the United States put forward the Baruch Plan, which proposed the abolition of nuclear arms, the Soviet Union, now working at full tilt to develop its own bomb, turned it down. Historians still argue whether it was reasonable for the United States, already in possession of the bomb, to expect the Soviet Union, which did not yet possess the bomb, to close down its nuclear program as part of a global agreement to abolish nuclear weapons. However that may be, there is no doubt that the Soviet rejection of the Baruch Plan played an important role in the United States' understanding of its own moral and historical responsibility for the nuclear arms race that followed. The United States, Americans believed from 1946 on, had proved itself ready to eliminate nuclear weapons, but the Soviet Union stood in the way. The Soviet threat, in American eyes, thus both justified nuclear arms and placed an insuperable practical obstacle in the way of their abolition. As long as this appeared to be the case, the United States could regard itself as a reluctant threatener of nuclear destruction, merely forced into this unwelcome role by the character of the regimes it felt obliged to oppose.

THE FUTURE OF EXTERMINATION:
THE THIRD AND FOURTH AUGUSTS

The third of our Augusts, in which the failed coup in Moscow brought on the collapse of the Soviet Union, dissolved this equation. The age of totalitarianism, which had opened in October of 1917, was over. The balancing factor in the moral equation that for almost fifty years had justified nuclear arsenals had fallen away. Would total war survive the loss of its linguistic and historical brother? Could the one exist without the good of the other? Should nuclear weapons survive the end of the "short twentieth century," not to speak of the "end of history"? And if they did, had the century (the "real" one) or history really "ended"? This question, which has hung over the decade between the end of the proposed short twentieth century and its calendrical end, has acquired even greater urgency as we move into the next century and millennium.

At the beginning of this essay, I recalled the old Greek idea that because the end of a story can force us to rewrite its earlier chapters, we cannot know what the story is until it is over. No single narrative can or should attempt to encompass the history of an epoch, which contains a limitless variety of entwined tales; yet, as the concept of a real twentieth century suggests, the very choice of the dates that mark off one era from another means that certain stories lay special claim to our attention. It's already clear that it will be impossible to write the political history of the twentieth century without reference to the many-chaptered story of the century's policies of extermination, some of whose main chapter headings will surely be the three Augusts we have mentioned. The final shape of that story, however, will not be known until the arrival of that future date—some future August day, perhaps—on which the ultimate fortunes of the arms that were born in 1945 are decided. Interpretations of the real twentieth century now require not so much smarter interpreters as the world's decision whether, in the wake of the Cold War, it will reject nuclear weapons or once again embrace them.

Let us, then, perform a thought experiment in which we try to imagine how the twentieth century will appear in retrospect, in light of two possible next chapters of the nuclear story. In the first, we will imagine that the next chapter is the last—that the world decides to eliminate nuclear weapons. In the second, we will imagine that the Cold War legacy of nuclear arms has been accepted and has led to their proliferation. Our glance, in the two cases, is not chiefly forward, to the world that lies ahead, but backward upon the century that has just ended.

In the event that abolition is embraced, we will find, I suggest, that what the American government said and the American public believed from 1946, when the. Soviet Union rejected the Baruch Plan, until 1991, when the Soviet Union collapsed, was essentially true: that the policymakers were as dismayed by nuclear danger as ordinary people were; that in their minds the reason for enduring the risk of human extinction really had been the threat to freedom around the world posed by the Soviet Union; that the government would indeed have preferred to abolish nuclear weapons in 1946 but had been prevented by the Soviet Union; and that this was truly why, when the Soviet Union collapsed, the United States seized the opportunity to lead the world to nuclear abolition. We will, further, take seriously the often-repeated argument that "arms control" was an invaluable temporary holding action for reducing nuclear danger until political conditions were ripe for full nuclear disarmament. We will take even more seriously the arguments of those who held that it was not nuclear arms that fueled the political differences of the Cold War but the political differences of the Cold War that fueled the nuclear-arms race, and who therefore argued against arms control. And then we will show how, precisely because the anti-Communism of the time had been authentic, Communism's end naturally opened the way to abolition of the arms that had protected us against Communism. We will be unsurprised to record that many of the Cold War's fiercest hawks had become abolitionists. And we will note with satisfaction how the example of these former hawks was emulated by hawks in other nations, including India, Pakistan, and Israel, who therefore agreed to relinquish their countries' nuclear weapons as part of the general settlement.

Even the evolution of high nuclear strategy, historians may go on to relate, will then seem to have been a slow education in the realities of the nuclear age, especially after the shock of the Cuban Missile Crisis in 1962, which left such a deep impression of the horror of nuclear war in the minds of later abolitionists, such as Robert McNamara. It will be the gratifying task of analysts to record how, even on the political right, the most militant believers in armed force slowly came around to an understanding that, in the words of Ronald Reagan, the most conservative president of the era, "nuclear war can never be won and must never be fought," and they will trace the path from that understanding to his discussion of nuclear abolition at the Reykjavik summit meeting of 1986 with the Soviet leader Mikhail Gorbachev.

Paralleling this slow evolution in thought, we will see, was the equally slow development in practice of the so-called tradition of nonuse, which gradually taught statesmen that even when they possessed a nuclear monopoly they could extract no military or political benefit from it and so did not use nuclear weapons after Nagasaki. In this story, acts of nuclear restraint—by the United States in Vietnam, by the Soviet Union in Afghanistan, by China in its border war with Vietnam in 1979—will have the place that battles have in bloodier narratives. The Cold War thus will be partially redeemed in our eyes as a vast laboratory in which, at the price of a few hair-raising close calls, the world learned through patient reflection and oblique experience that nuclear weapons were as futile as they were abhorrent and that they could and should be eliminated.

The lessons will go deeper still. When the last nuclear plutonium pit has been liquidated (or, more likely, adulterated and buried away in some deep cavern), we will see that the ground for nuclear disarmament had been prepared, on the one hand, by the peace movement in the United States, and, on the other, by the movement against Soviet power by dissidents in the Soviet empire (two movements that at the time failed, on the whole, to grasp the common drift of their activity). The astounding success of the resistance movement in the East will emerge as the first stage in a global movement against not only Soviet terror but all terror—against not only totalitarianism but its close relative, total war—whose last stage will be the elimination of nuclear arms, thereby truly ending the spiral of violence that began in 1914.

The rise and fall of totalitarianism from start to finish will wear an altered aspect. It will turn out to have been a ghastly, protracted detour from the progress (the word itself might even gain new credit) and enlightenment offered by liberal civilization, which, although capsized in 1914 by the First World War, will have righted itself in 1991, bringing on an era of prosperity and peace. Then liberal civilization itself, freed of its complicity in the policies of extermination it adopted in 1945, will rest at last on a sure foundation. The political history of the twentieth century will thus be the story not only of the rise of policies of extermination in all their variety but also of the human recoil against them, leading, first, to the renewed rejection of totalitarianism and embrace of democracy in the 1990s and then, in the years following, to the abolition of nuclear weapons along with other weapons of mass destruction.

In the second thought experiment—in which we suppose that the nuclear powers have renewed their embrace of their nuclear arsenals in the post-Cold War period, setting the example for several other powers, and so installing nuclear weapons as a deep- and many-rooted structural feature of life in the twenty-first century—the political and military history of the twentieth century will have to be written very differently. To begin with, we will not be able to take so seriously the West's stated justifications for building nuclear arsenals. How will we continue to believe that the democratic nations endured the risk of human annihilation for the sake of human freedom when, with the threat to freedom gone, the threat of annihilation is preserved? How will we continue to say that the totalitarianism of the Soviet Union was the great obstacle to full disarmament when, with the Soviet Union collapsed and Russia (under Gorbachev) inviting full inspection and proposing full disarmament, the United States refused? Having discovered that the end of Communism left our will to possess nuclear arms intact, the old claim that in the Cold War we chose to risk being "dead" rather than going "Red" will ring hollow. The entire, fifty-year confrontation between totalitarianism and democracy will shrink in importance as an explanatory factor. Our attention will be drawn instead to the ease with which the United States shifted its nuclear planning in 1945 from Germany to Japan, and then from

Japan to the Soviet Union, and we will see this flexibility as a precedent for the much more drastic and shocking shift of targeting at the end of the Cold War from the Soviet Union to . . . well, what? A few feeble "rogue" states, the mere possibility that Russia will again become an enemy of the United States?

We'll hardly be surprised to see that several nations outside the original nuclear "club" have followed the "nuclear paradigm." As for arms control, it will be understood as just one of the means by which public anxiety about the nuclear danger was put to sleep. Our policy of nonproliferation will seem to have been halfhearted, since it will have been shown that we preferred to permit the whole world to acquire nuclear arms than to give up our own.

The process of education that occurred during the Cold War will seem to be the opposite of what it would have seemed had we abolished nuclear weapons: one not of deepening understanding of the horror and futility of the arsenals but of simply getting used to them in preparation for accepting them fully and without reservation as a normal instrument of national policy, of learning to "stop worrying and love the bomb," in the words of the subtitle to the movie *Dr. Strangelove*, which will have lost their ironic connotations.

A graver suspicion will be confirmed: that the United States and its nuclear allies did not build nuclear weapons chiefly in order to face extraordinary danger, whether from Germany, Japan, or the Soviet Union, but for more deep-seated, unarticulated reasons growing out of its own, freely chosen conceptions of national security. Nuclear arsenals will seem to have been less a response to any particular external threat, totalitarian or otherwise, than an intrinsic element of the dominant liberal civilization itelf—an evil that first grew and still grows from within that civilization rather than being imposed from without. And then we will have to remember that the seminal event of

the real twentieth century, the First World War, sprang in all its pointless slaughter and destructive fury from the midst of that same liberal
civilization, and we will have to ask what it is in the makeup of liberalism that pushes it again and again, even at the moment of its greatest
triumphs, into an abyss of its own making.

Our understanding of the historical place of totalitarianism will
likewise change. Instead of seeming a protracted bloody hiatus
between the eclipse of liberal civilization of 1914 and its restoration in
1991, totalitarianism will appear to have been a harsh and effective
tutor to liberalism, which was its apt pupil. The degree of moral separation from the tradition of extermination that was maintained
during the Cold War will have disappeared. If we look at nuclear arms
as a lethal virus that spreads by contagion around the world, then
totalitarianism in this picture of events becomes a sort of filthy
syringe with which the dominant liberal civilization managed to inject
the illness into its bloodstream, where it remained even after, in 1991,
the syringe was thrown away. Liberalism will itself have unequivo-
cally embraced extermination.

At stake is the very character of the victorious civilization that in
the twentieth century buried its two greatest totalitarian antagonists
and now bids to set the tone and direction of international life in
the century ahead. Will it shake off the twentieth century's legacy
of terror or, by embracing nuclear weapons even in the absence of
totalitarian threat, incorporate that legacy into itself? Will we find
that protecting civilization is unimaginable without threatening extermination? If so, a critical watershed will have been crossed, and we
will have passed, by default, from a period in which an extraordinary justification, such as the Soviet threat, seemed needed to justify
the extraordinary peril of nuclear arms to a period in which the quo-
tidian fears, jealousies, ambitions, and hatreds that are always with

us are found to be justification enough. At that moment, a nuclear arsenal will cease to be felt as Conrad's "dishonoring necessity" and become a fully legitimized voluntary component of the state: a permanent subbasement, or catacomb, on which the fairer upper floors of civilization—the freedom, the democracy, the prosperity—rest. But if this happens, can liberalism itself survive, or will it in the long run find itself sucked, as in 1914, into a vortex of destruction that it cannot stop?

Nuclear arsenals do not exist in isolation from the rest of politics, and no single policy, whether regarding these arms or anything else, can decide the character of the century that is about to begin. Nor will a decision to abolish nuclear weapons even put an end to the legacy of extermination that disfigured the century now ending. The deeds of Pol Pot in Cambodia and of the former Hutu government in Rwanda have made it clear that genocide remains attractive and achievable for many governments in many parts of the world. No nuclear weapons or other weapons of mass destruction are needed to bring it off; Kalashnikovs, or even machetes or hoes, will do. What seems clear, however, is that if the triumphantly restored liberal order of the 1990s cannot renounce the threat of extermination of peoples as a condition for its own survival, then it will forfeit any chance that it can successfully oppose a resurgence of barbarism anywhere else in the twenty-first century. We will be unable to say that any year—whether 1991 or 2000 or 2050—has undone 1914 until we have also undone 1945. More than any other decision before us, this one will decide who we are, who we are to be, and who, when the last line of the story of the real twentieth century is truly written, we will have been.

THE REPUBLIC IN CRISIS || III

"Notes and Comment" from *The New Yorker*

December 6, 1969

Some events of the last few weeks indicate that the Nixon administration may have come to view the issue of the war in Vietnam as a problem more of ending dissent against the war than of ending the war itself. When, near the end of his November 3rd address to the nation on Vietnam—at the point where presidents, in their speeches, often make an appeal to all the citizens of the country to support administration policies—President Nixon said, "So tonight, to you, the great silent majority of my fellow-Americans, I ask for your support," we felt that although the administration's policy toward the war seemed to be unchanged, a new tone had been set in its policy toward the American people. Never before in our democracy has silence had such a high reputation. This administration's praise and encouragement of the "silent majority," together with its campaign to silence the "vocal minority," suggest a new vision of America—as the Silent Nation. But we found the presidential appeal to one segment of the population disturbing, in part because it seemed to add authority to an idea that had been expressed in much more intemperate and frightening language by the vice president shortly before. The vice president had referred to protest against the war as "sick and rancid" and to the protesters—millions of American citizens—as "vultures," "ideological eunuchs," and "parasites," and had said that "we can afford to separate them from our society with no more regret than we should feel over discarding rotten apples from a barrel." He had given no explanation of what he meant by "separate them from our society," and, with our imagination left free to wander, we could not help thinking of the prisons and concentration camps employed by other men in our century who have spoken of separating parasites from society. The president has himself remained silent since his Vietnam address, except to give public approval to speeches made by the vice president, but a number of administration officials have made moves and stated opinions that, taken together, constitute a trend that poses the gravest threat in our memory to the rights guaranteed by the Constitution to all citizens.

One of the most telling signs of this danger was the position that the Justice Department took toward the New Mobilization march in Washington on November 15th. Before the march, Justice Department officials attempted to discourage citizens from attending it by spreading alarms of violence, troops were called into the city on the basis of Justice Department "intelligence reports" stating that the march was organized by Communists. After the march, a number of administration officials made baseless and inflammatory allegations about the people who had marched. Transportation Secretary John Volpe declared that most of the organizers of the march were "Communist or Communist-inspired," and Postmaster General Winton M. Blount said that dissent in America was "killing American boys." And—most significant of all—Attorney General Mitchell claimed that the march had been characterized by violence and that the Mobilization leaders had wanted violence to occur. Anyone who saw the march or has read reports of it knows that there were only two infinitesimal incidents of violence in a vast peaceful event and that the attorney general's statements are not just distortions of the truth but are simply false. Nonetheless, Deputy Attorney General Richard G. Kleindienst announced shortly after he made them that the Justice Department had embarked on investigations that could lead to indictments against a number of the Mobilization leaders. If the organizers of this peaceful march, who, whatever their other political beliefs may be, are nearly all fervent advocates of non-violence, and who attempted, through the deployment of their marshals, to prevent violence wherever it threatened, can be brought to trial on the basis of Mitchell's charges, then the right of free assembly in this country is seriously imperilled. And while the Justice Department was threatening the leaders of the march with indictments, Vice President Agnew gave two speeches, one attacking television and the other attacking the nation's newspapers, which, in combination with several moves made by other administration officials, pose a parallel threat to the freedom of the press.

Of course, there is no reason a vice president, or even a president, should not defend his administration and his policies against criticism by the press. Government officials are as free as any newspaper or any television commentator to enter into press debates on government policies. It is when the government sets out not only to disagree with the press but to threaten or coerce it that the danger line is crossed. Several officials of the present administration have crossed that line. Federal Communications Commission Chairman Dean Burch crossed the line when—in a gesture that, in its timing and in its context, was intimidating—he called up several television stations after Nixon's Vietnam speech and asked for transcripts of their editorial comments on it. The vice president crossed the line when he pointedly asserted, in his attack on television news coverage, that commentators enjoy a "monopoly sanctioned and licensed by government." (It is precisely *because* television stations are federally licensed that officials of the federal government, when they choose to engage in political debate with television commentators, have a special duty to debate the issues, and not to brandish the government's power to revoke licenses.) Communications Director Herbert G. Klein crossed the line in a particularly threatening way when he said, "If you [people in the television industry] look at the problems you have today and you fail to continue to examine them, you do invite the government to come in. I would not like to see that happen." The vice president crossed it again when he took it upon himself, in his speech attacking television, to inaugurate a public write-in campaign against the networks. Indeed, the burden of Agnew's two speeches was not the defense of administration policies against criticism—in fact, he hardly mentioned any questions of administration policy in either of his speeches about the news media—but the setting in motion of forces that would bring about concrete changes in the news media, in the form of greater support for the president's policies. Although the vice president certainly sees himself as a defender of our system of government and no doubt believes that the actions of the administration he belongs to pose no threat to it, the content of his two speeches—and also his decision, as vice president, to give them—rests on several fundamental misunderstandings of democracy and of the Constitution, and these same misunderstandings may underlie the administration's entire ill-advised campaign.

The Bill of Rights was added to the Constitution in order to protect the people against the government, because of the government's great power. After Thomas Jefferson had seen a draft of the Constitution which did not contain a bill of rights, he wrote in a letter to a friend, "What I disapproved from the first moment also, was the want of a bill of rights, to guard liberty against the legislative as well as the executive branches of the government." In a letter to James Madison, again urging the inclusion of a bill of rights, he wrote, "The tyranny of the legislatures is the most formidable dread at present, and will be for many years," and then he added, "That of the executive will come in its turn, but it will be at a remote period." The freedom of the press was not intended for the benefit of the press. Like the rest of the Bill of Rights, it was intended as a protection for the people against the enormous power of the government. As for protecting the people against the press, we have libel laws to do that. In Vice President Agnew's speeches, the relationships between the people, the press, and the government are muddled and reversed. He does seem to have had some idea that his thinking represented a departure from the Constitution, for, in one of the more ominous passages in his first speech, he said of the influence exercised by the networks, "We cannot measure this power and influence by the traditional democratic standards." What, then, are the new standards? At several points, he spoke as though the right of free speech had been established to protect the government against censorship by the press or by the people. In his speech attacking the press, he said, "My political and journalistic adversaries seem to be asking that I circumscribe my rhetorical freedom while they place no restriction on theirs," and at the beginning of that speech he had referred to his speech attacking the networks as an exercise of "my right to dissent." But his "right to dissent" (if one can even speak of the government as having a "right to dissent," since in our democracy the term "dissent" refers to the citizens' right to criticize their government) is not a *right* at all but simply *a fact,* since there is no power great enough to threaten its exercise. In both his speeches, the vice president consistently portrayed the press and the government as foes that were equally powerful, except that one of them—the government—had been unfairly shackled until the moment when he decided to speak out. In an article in the *Times*, he was quoted as carrying this idea to an absurd extreme by saying, "The vice president has a right to dissent, too. If anybody is intimidated, it should be me. I don't have the resources the networks have." But, as the framers of the Constitution well knew, the press and the government are not two adversaries with equal powers and equal rights. There is no comparison between the power of the government and the power of the press. Whereas the government has virtually unchallengeable power in the form of, among other things, the Army, the Air Force, the Navy, the Marines, and the various police forces, the press has only its rights, and can survive only as long as the government continues to honor them.

The vice president's concept of censorship is like his concept of rights. In a democracy, the word "censorship" refers specifically to official government interference with the press. When the vice president told us in his speech attacking television that he opposed censorship, he said that he was "not asking for government censorship" but was "asking whether a form of censorship already exists when the news that forty million Americans receive each night is determined by a handful of men responsible only to their corporate employers." But, like his idea of his rights and the Constitution's idea of the people's rights, the two kinds of "censorship" are not comparable, one, by definition, is censorship and the other is not. The presentation of a consistently biassed interpretation of the news by the networks, if that were possible, would result in an extremely regrettable state of public misinformation, but government censorship would interfere with the public's right to know and would mean the loss of liberty. Because of the inescapability of federal licensing, what must be devised is a set of guarantees that protects the public against any political misuse of the air and also—what is far more important—protects the stations and networks, and thus, again, the public, against such political intervention as Vice President Agnew's. The vice president's statements seemed to show contempt for any kind of criticism of any government by its citizens. In an article in *Life*, he said, "Consider the idea of protest purely, removing it from any issue. . . . It does not offer constructive alternatives and it is not conducive to creating the thoughtful atmosphere where positive answers may be formulated." In his speech about television, he said that "when Winston Churchill rallied public opinion to stay the course against Hitler's Germany, he didn't have to contend with a gaggle of commentators raising doubts about whether he was reading the public right." This, of course, is not true. Churchill had many vocal opponents, both in the press and among politicians. A more nearly correct statement is that Hitler didn't have to contend with any commentators when he was rallying his people against Churchill's England.

As for the vice president's idea of the role of the press in a democracy, it is as strange as his concepts of rights and of censorship. In his speech on newspapers, he said that "the time for naïve belief in their neutrality is gone." But are publications obliged to be neutral? There is nothing in the Constitution that says the press has to be neutral. Nor, for that matter, is there anything that says it has to be objective, or fair, or even accurate or truthful, desirable though these qualities are. For who is to be the judge? The press is simply *free*, and its freedom, like any other freedom, has to be absolute in order to be freedom. It is free to print any information it wants to print and to write from any point of view whatever. The framers of the Constitution wisely left it up to the individual citizen, not the government, to decide which publications to read and which to believe, and to find his own way, in an atmosphere of freedom, to the truth. In a democracy, the people are free only as long as the press is free, and, in the long run, the majority is only as free as the most unpopular minority. Once this or any other administration gets the machinery in place that can control the press or deny the rights of a dissenting minority, then the rights of all the people, even of those who support the government, are lost. Although this administration may have intended only to produce greater support for the president's policies, in the belief that this would help him withdraw in an orderly way from Vietnam, the campaign of intimidation it has launched against the protesters and against the press has set this nation on a dangerous course that will be hard to reverse—a course that could lead us to a day when we put an end not to the war in Vietnam but to democracy in America.

OCTOBER 14, 1972

Alexander Solzhenitsyn recently wrote, in his speech accepting the Nobel Prize for literature, "Violence, less and less embarrassed by the limits imposed by centuries of lawfulness, is brazenly and victoriously striding across the whole world." In 1972, the primary representatives of victorious violence on the world scene have been the terrorist and the bombardier, each of whom has been having extraordinary success in extending the domain of political violence into new regions. Yet these eminently contemporary figures are the agents of seemingly opposite contemporary trends. The terrorist is an agent of the trend toward politicizing every aspect of life. He wants to bring war into the living room and the bedroom—not to mention the airport, the airplane, the ocean liner, the university, the office building, and the public square. He is so obsessed by politics that distinctions—between political life and private life, between the soldier and the civilian, between the adult and the child—have vanished from his mind. Daily life becomes his enemy. The family picnicking on the grass, the schoolchild at his desk, the elderly couple out for an evening stroll—all are his foes and his potential victims. His program is to charge all innocent, ordinary things with uncertainty and fear, so that people everywhere must live with the possibility that any sports event may turn into a massacre and the morning mail may blow up in their faces. The bombardier, on the other hand, has become the chief representative of a trend toward depoliticizing. Whereas the terrorist is white-hot, the bombardier is cool. The Arab guerrilla is wholly possessed by his cause, but the B-52 crewman may hardly give a thought to what ends he serves. He may hardly consider himself at war. And the people at home who send him on his missions can also remain unconcerned. His way of fighting takes the sting and the passion out of war, both for himself and for his country. Yet the bombardier, like the terrorist, is an eraser of boundaries, both legal and national. Women and children are massacred by the bombs of both of them. So the terrorist, agent of hysteria, and the bombardier, agent of apathy, arrive, in the end, at the same point. Some people today are more inclined to inveigh against hysteria and the brutal, face-to-face murders that it makes possible, others prefer to inveigh against apathy and the "impersonal" killing that it makes possible. The truth is that both states of mind are murderous.

Of course, the extension of violence into all departments of life was largely accomplished decades ago. The terrorist achieved his masterpiece in the universal, undiscriminating terror of the Hitler and Stalin regimes, and the bombardier achieved universal scope for his variety of terror with the invention of nuclear weapons. And yet, as Solzhenitsyn notes, in recent years there have been new breakdowns of the boundaries that protected us from violence. There once was a time when violence was seen as a means of last resort. Men employed it to get what they wanted after talking had failed. Violence then was usually directed toward some particular, concrete end, such as crushing the resistance of an enemy. Now we employ violence in a different way: we begin with violence, and we use it not so much to accomplish a particular end directly as to prove a point to a third party. Violence has become our method of communication. The terrorist calls his violence "symbolic." Its aim is not to bring the oppressor to his knees, or even to weaken him directly, but, rather, to "educate," or to politicize, the world by making headlines with spectacular explosions and murders. Almost any explosions and murders will do. Consider the recent killings at Lod Airport, in Israel. In that episode, Japanese gunmen killed, among others, a number of Puerto Rican Protestants on a pilgrimage to the Holy Land. This was meant to aid the cause of Palestinian refugees. But how could the deaths of Puerto Ricans at the hands of Japanese help the Palestinians? According to the logic of the terrorists, it taught the world some sort of "lesson" about the desperate, insane resolve of the Arabs not to stop at anything, no matter how unrelated to their cause, until their demands were met. It was as though, in their frustration at not being able to strike effectively at their real foe, Israel herself, they had taken the innocent people of the world hostage. These victims, at least, were easily accessible to them. And the lack of discrimination in the choice of victims has gone even further—to the point where the connection between "revolutionary acts" and the particular revolutions they are meant to advance is often so tenuous that the act affords no clue to the identity of the revolutionary group or the nature of its cause. For instance, a while back a bomb went off at the New School for Social Research here, yet the people at the New School were simply at a loss to know who their foe had been. Had it been anti-Castro Cubans? Or pro-Castro Cubans? Had it been Puerto Rican nationalists? Or a group opposing the war? Or a group favoring the war? In instances like this, the survivors of the attack must wait for the scrawled note in the mail letting them know who is claiming "credit" for the bloodshed. And even then they are sometimes left in the dark, for a number of groups may vie in claiming credit for crimes they did not commit.

In the case of the bombardier and those who dispatch him on his missions, a similar logic has come into play. They, too, are not out to accomplish anything directly so much as they are out to prove a point. The bombardier's violence, too, is symbolic, that is, it is carried out more for the sake of appearances than to accomplish concrete ends. His bombing is undertaken as a demonstration to third parties of our "toughness" and our "resolve." A memo in the Pentagon Papers, for instance, describes our aim in Vietnam this way: "However badly SEA [Southeast Asia] may go over the next 1–3 years . . . we must have . . . been tough . . . gotten bloodied, and hurt the enemy very badly. We must avoid harmful appearances which will affect judgments by, and provide pretexts to, other nations . . . regarding U.S. policy, power, resolve, and competence to deal with [its] problems." Interestingly, among the nations most often mentioned as those we are trying to impress with our toughness is Egypt—a nation we tend to hold accountable for the activities of the Palestinian terrorists. So it emerges that we are engaged in a global shadow war in which all the victims are proxies. The guerrillas kill scores of innocent people at airports in the Middle East, and we retaliate by killing scores of innocent people in Indo-China. Just as the Palestinian guerrillas, who are unable to get at the source of their difficulties, the nation of Israel, kill Puerto Ricans instead, we, who are unable to strike at our presumed real adversaries, China and Russia, must content ourselves with killing Vietnamese to show our power and resolve. And the victims of our bombing, including the villagers of Vietnam, Laos, and Cambodia, are as bewildered about our purposes as the people at the New School were about the purposes of the presumed revolutionaries who bombed them. What do the villagers of Indo-China know of the arcane geopolitical reasoning of our experts? To explain ourselves, we, too, must resort to little notes delivered after the fact—in this case, the millions of propaganda leaflets we drop over Indo-China explaining why the bombs have fallen. For Vietnam in itself is no more a threat to the United States than the Puerto Rican pilgrims were to the Palestinians. As for our direct dealings with the Chinese and the Russians, we find it more expedient to stick to friendly, televised summit conferences and grain deals.

The violence of the terrorist and the bombardier has broken the final restraint—the limits and the direction imposed on violence by its own purpose. This kind of violence does not single out a particular foe but treats us all as foes. And whether we are threatened by the bombs that fall from overhead or by the bombs that come from the underground, we are all held hostage by every determined fanatic who has some point to prove. What is the real message of all this symbolic killing? When the connections between violent acts and the causes they are meant to promote are as tenuous as the connection between the massacre of Puerto Rican pilgrims and the plight of Palestinian refugees, and as tenuous as the connection between the bombing of Indo-China and our competition with the Russians and the Chinese, then it may be said that the acts are without specific content. What is left is only the willingness to kill—it no longer matters whom or for what reason. Perhaps that is the real message, sent out over and over, in so many forms. To take human life is undoubtably a fearsome thing. The political powers in the world wish to be feared and taken seriously. They prove their seriousness by killing. By killing, they show that, whatever it is they mean—and this becomes harder to discern with every day that passes—*they really mean it.*

So the messages fly back and forth—every one with a bomb enclosed.

APRIL 8, 1974

A couple of months ago, when we read that four leaders of the radical movement of the nineteen-sixties—Jerry Rubin, Abbie Hoffman, Tom Hayden, and Rennie Davis—were going to be interviewed on the *Dick Cavett Show*, we tuned in at the appointed hour. We had been watching a lot of television lately—particularly anything to do with the impeachment proceedings in Washington. Much of what we had been seeing was bewildering to us. Sometimes the events in Washington seemed like the rites of an alien civilization. By our reckoning, for example, a leader whose administration is in disgrace might be showing some public signs of regret or contrition, whereas others in the public realm might be showing some signs of anger and disgust. But just the opposite was happening. The president and his men were in a towering rage at their investigators in the Congress, and the congressmen, by comparison, were meek and silent. We wondered what Cavett's radical—or ex-radical, for all we knew—guests might be thinking about it all. We settled into our chair. The show was announced. Then came the familiar theme song. Then the list of Cavett's guests. Sally Struthers, Anthony Quinn, Ike and Tina Turner. Cavett came on. No word from him about what had happened to the radicals. Soon, an out-of-date reference made us realize that we were watching canned material. Cavett couldn't explain anything, because at the moment he was speaking there was nothing to explain. We felt annoyed, puzzled, and a little frightened. What was more disturbing than the fact that we weren't being allowed to see the show was the fact that it had disappeared without any explanation. We tried calling ABC, but the line was busy for several hours. Somebody, somewhere, didn't want us to see that show, and we had no way of finding out who it was.

Later, we read that the management at ABC had decided that the show wasn't "balanced" enough for its viewers. Our thoughts went back to a memo that came out during the Watergate investigation and that had to do with "balance" on television programs. We got hold of a copy and read it with new interest. Charles W. Colson had been reporting to H. R. Haldeman on a meeting he had had in September of 1970 with the top executives of all three of the big networks. At the time, of course, the public had no idea that network executives were having meetings with political advisers to the president. Colson had been pleased with the meeting. He wrote, "They were startled by how thoroughly we were doing our homework—both from the standpoint of knowledge of the law, as I discussed it, but, more importantly, from the way in which we have so thoroughly monitored their coverage and our analysis of it. . . . They are terribly concerned with being able to work out their own policies with respect to balanced coverage and not to have policies imposed on them by either the Commission [the Federal Communications Commission] or the Congress. . . . In short, they are very much afraid of us and are trying hard to prove they are 'good guys.' "

Not long after our unpleasant experience with ABC, we picked up an issue of *TV Guide* and got another jolt. There, in the pages of that previously unpolitical publication, was an article by Patrick Buchanan attacking television news. Later, we learned that *TV Guide* had just hired five regular contributors to comment on the news in a column called "News Watch." One is Buchanan, who is one of the president's chief speechwriters, and who was one of the drafters of ex-Vice President

Agnew's attacks on the press in 1969. We had seen Buchanan on TV recently, too. He had been interviewed by Bill Moyers on the Public Broadcasting Service, and we had been surprised to hear him say that even if the president were guilty of "a technical obstruction of justice," he should be allowed to remain as president, because of his achievements in foreign policy. Did we want to throw out a great president merely because he might have "sat on it [the evidence] too long," he asked. Buchanan had been on during what had turned out to be a wild period in our television-watching. The president had recently been in Nashville playing with a yoyo, and shortly afterward, in another public appearance, he had said, "I am suggesting that the House follow the Constitution. If they do, I will." It was the first time we had ever heard a president paraphrase his oath of office on a conditional basis. And since he had already said that the House Judiciary Committee had gone outside the bounds of the Constitution in asking for too much evidence, he seemed, in fact, to be making a declaration of independence from the Constitution. His audience, as it happened, was made up partly of the owners of the television stations on which the networks depend for their survival. The audience applauded the president's remarks. Another of the columnists that *TV Guide* had just hired is John D. Lofton, Jr., the former editor of *Monday*, which is a propaganda organ published by the Republican National Committee. Lofton had worked with Buchanan in bringing the administration line to the public. In a memo to Haldeman, Buchanan had recommended Lofton as a member of a committee that would work on the "Assault Strategy" against McGovern during the election. Another of the columnists is Edith Efron, the author of *The News Twisters*, which attacks network news from a right-wing point of view. In *The News Twisters*, Miss Efron adds up the number of words she considers anti-Nixon in a given news program and then adds up the words she considers pro-Nixon, and compares the results. Usually, she arrives at the conclusion that there were more anti-Nixon words. Another of the columnists is Kevin P. Phillips, the author of *The Emerging Republican Majority* and a onetime aide to former Attorney General Mitchell. Phillips is now getting out a publication called *Media Report*, which purports to have discovered the "beginnings of public interest in breaking up the television networks." The fifth of the *TV Guide* columnists is John P. Roche, a Democrat who describes himself as a liberal but whom some liberals describe as a conservative. He had been added, the editors of *TV Guide* said, to provide "balance." This lineup of columnists recalled to our mind another memo we heard about a few months ago—a memo from Mr. Buchanan to the president. In it Mr. Buchanan had proposed setting up a foundation that would seem to be independent but would actually be run by and for the administration. Describing the foundation as "a countervailing power outside the federal government," Buchanan suggested that one of its aims would be to "bring together experts—on the networks, for example—to discuss and produce a book of papers on their lack of objectivity and need for reform." Of how it would be run, Buchanan wrote, "We would have to lock it into the White House with probably two individuals at the top level—who had the ear of the president at all times. . . . The board of directors would run from right to center of the political spectrum, no kooks but unquestioned pro-Nixon people would have to have a complete lock on it, we would have to have people there who knew what was up and agreed to it; and then let the handpicked staff run the thing." *TV Guide* happens to be owned by Triangle Publications, the president of which is Walter H. Annenberg, President Nixon's Ambassador to England. *TV Guide* has the largest circulation of any weekly in the country and reaches a third of the adult population of the United States each week.

A couple of weeks ago, ABC decided to let us see the four radical leaders after all, but in a changed format. After their hour-and-a-half show, two conservatives would come on for half an hour, presumably to right the "balance" of any minds that had been tipped too far to the left during the first part of the show. We tuned in again, interested now to see what it was we had been protected against on the first occasion. Jerry Rubin said that he and many others were getting in touch with their bodies. There was a "revolution" of getting in touch with one's body, he said. When enough people got in touch with their bodies, capitalism would collapse. Asked what it meant to be out of touch with your body, Rubin said that President Nixon was a good example of someone who was out of touch with his body. Abbie Hoffman said that he had been doing "quiet things" recently. Hayden said that he had been lobbying in Congress against continued American support for the South Vietnamese government. Rennie Davis displayed the nonstop, glowing smile and the glazed eyes of one who is "blissed out." He is now a follower of Guru Maharaj Ji, the sixteen-year-old spiritual leader from India, and he described his belief that the guru was God. (This was enough "balance" for us.) Toward the end of the show, Cavett asked what any of them would do if someone came up to them and announced his intention of throwing a bomb at a munitions plant. Hayden dodged the question, and said it was more important now to "blow up what's in people's heads." Hoffman suggested that it might be more productive now to bomb an oil-refinery office than a munitions plant, but we were not allowed to hear this. (We learned it later.) His voice was momentarily silenced, and we were allowed only to see his lips move. Suddenly, we lost our appetite for the show, and we turned it off. It seemed to us that the screen was radiating fear into our living room and into other living rooms across the country. The show had become a public display of fear: of the networks' fear of the government, of the government's fear of the left wing, and of the fear all of us now seem to have—the *embarrassment* we feel—when *any* political views are expressed without inhibition by anyone but the president. We remembered the staggering power that, Watergate or no Watergate, lies coiled in the White House—power that is veiled for the moment but can be used any day by the incumbent or by a successor to lash out at those who he decides are his foes. Our thoughts went back to the men in Washington—the leaders of the Judiciary Committee (Representative Pete Rodino and Representative Edward Hutchinson); their counsel (John Doar and Albert Jenner); Special Prosecutor Leon Jaworski, and their colleagues on the Judiciary Committee and in the Special Prosecutor's office—who are approaching, in their gingerly way, the wrathful presence in the White House, and we wished them whatever strength and courage they can find for the time of danger that lies ahead.

AUGUST 5, 1974

Last week, in the days leading up to the House Judiciary Committee's votes on impeachment, there seemed to be a change in the American air. It was not that—as the thought is often expressed—"the tide was moving against the president." Another tide appeared to be running in our affairs, and that tide had remarkably little to do with the president. Indeed, it was a part of the new atmosphere that suddenly the president seemed almost a peripheral figure in the proceedings. The fusillades of charges coming out of the White House—that the Judiciary Committee was a "lynch mob," that it was a "kangaroo court"—were not so much opposed as ignored. A shift in the country's attention seemed to have occurred. The nation's gaze was moving away from the one, omnipresent man whose angry statements and restless travels about the country and the world had held us spellbound for so long—as though it were he, and not we, who held the key to our future—and was focussing on scores of other men, justices and congressmen, who now occupied the center of the stage for the first time. Suddenly our affairs seemed to be in the hands of "reasonable men, acting reasonably" —in the phrase of John Doar, special counsel of the Committee. The shift in attention was a sign of recuperation in the body politic. Observers had been on the lookout for one more "firestorm" to resolve the issue, instead, they found themselves in the midst of this quiet mending. The fortunes of Richard Nixon were never the main issue of the impeachment proceedings. "Our judgment is not concerned with an individual but with a system of Constitutional government" is how House Judiciary Committee Chairman Peter Rodino put it in his statement opening the impeachment debate. In fact, it had been the president's blurring of his own interests with the nation's interests, and his use of government power to "get" his own political opponents, that had led to some of the offenses under examination by the Committee. The change in atmosphere was anticipated by the moving words of counsellor Doar, when, in recommending the president's impeachment, he said, "As an individual, I have not the slightest bias against President Nixon. I would hope that I would not do him the smallest, slightest injury." Doar's words were a signal that the president would be judged by new standards. This was not a case of the "enemies" taking revenge. The new judges, perhaps bearing in mind that the way we now handle a president may set the standard for the way future presidents will handle all of us, were steering clear of vengeance. The intemperate accusations levelled by the president's aides seemed to invite a response in kind. But the Committee left all that aside. They were not hitting back. They were starting over.

AUGUST 12, 1974

In Greece, a military dictatorship has yielded in favor of a democratic civilian regime. Performing an act that we think is without precedent, a general who was serving on the military junta put through a call to a civilian in exile and invited him to come home and form a government. There was jubilation throughout the country. Thousands of people poured into the streets of Athens, holding candles aloft and shouting "Democracy!" Immediately, newspapers began to publish uncensored news. Political prisoners were released, to joyous welcomes. A composer and an actress returning from exile were mobbed by well-wishers at the airport. In Portugal, meanwhile, military leaders have deposed a civilian dictatorship and are apparently moving the country in the direction of democratic government. In Thailand, a military junta has been replaced by a civilian government In France, where Valéry Giscard D'Estaing, a conservative, has recently been elected president, one of the new government's first acts was to ban wiretapping. In Spain, Generalissimo Franco has handed power over to Juan Carlos de Borbón, a man of more moderate persuasion, and an ad hoc coalition of civilian leaders is reported to have announced its willingness to form a new government and restore full democratic freedom. The unbroken succession of coups of recent years has now been interrupted, in a manner of speaking, by a series of reverse coups, in which power reverts to the people. For reasons unknown, a shift in the political climate of the world has occurred, and it seems to favor liberty. Here in the United States, of course, the House Judiciary Committee has met and cast its votes. No regime fell, no one was out in the streets with candles. But some invisible equivalent of these celebrations was quietly taking place. And when it was all over, everything was changed. Here, too, freedom had somehow won the day.

AUGUST 19, 1974

On Thursday night, when President Nixon announced his resignation, his demeanor was hardly different from the demeanor we had grown accustomed to in the last five years. His face was a mask; his words were cold and unreal. But on Friday morning, when he appeared before his Cabinet and staff to bid them farewell, everything was changed. The mask was gone, and the man was before us. Human feeling played across his face: grief, regret, humor, anger, affection. He spoke of his parents. His father, he said, had failed at many things he had undertaken, but he "did his job" and had been "a great man." His mother "was a saint," he said simply. However, no books would be written about her, he said, weeping now. All at once, he was reading what Theodore Roosevelt had written when his first wife had died: "She was beautiful in face and form, and lovelier still in spirit. . . . Her life had always been in the sunshine. There had never come to her a single great sorrow . . . Then, by a strange and terrible fate, death came to her." We hardly knew why President Nixon was telling us these things, and it seemed to us that he hardly knew, either. Yet there was more warmth and feeling in these chaotic, uncontrolled words than in all the other words of his presidency put together. A few hours later, President Ford addressed the nation. He, too, spoke movingly and with feeling. Three times in his remarks he spoke of love. Hearing the word gave us a small start. Love was something we had not looked for in any of its shapes or forms in the public sphere for a very long time. The America of the last ten or twelve years was a loveless place. "Nobody is a friend of ours," Richard Nixon had told his young legal counsel John Dean. Of the 1972 election, he had said, "This is a war." For lawbreakers, his world had been one, as he put it, "without pity." The wretched of the earth had been out of luck in his scheme of things, whether they were the peasants of Vietnam and Bangladesh or the poor at home. His had been a cold universe. Listening to President Ford speak of love, we thought back to President Nixon's incoherent remarks shortly before. For the first time in several years, he had been talking like a free man. Something in the new atmosphere had dissolved the walls of reserve and released a torrent of emotion. Richard Nixon, freed, like the rest of us, from the oppression of his rule, was pouring his heart out to the whole nation.

April 14, 1975

The victory of the revolutionary forces in Vietnam has been something like a certainty for years now, indeed, to speak the awful whole truth about this matter, it has been something like a certainty for more than a quarter of a century, and all the efforts that the French and we ourselves have made to prevent it—the thirty years of forced evacuation, massacre, and carpet-bombing—have been a waste and a crime of measureless proportions. If this endeavor has had any redeeming features, they have yet to be discovered. Certainly none have appeared in recent days, as the war has moved toward its end. Events have unfolded more swiftly than thought could follow. At the heart of the South Vietnamese collapse there seems to have been a vacuum: the Saigon government. One moment, it was there, with its 1,100,000 men under arms and its gigantic Air Force—the third largest in the world—and the next moment it was gone. Reporters used words like "juggernaut" and "blitzkrieg," but observers on the scene had a different story to tell. "There is no war," one American eyewitness said. Speaking of the fall of Danang, a French eyewitness said, "There never was a last battle for Danang." And an American intelligence official said, "There's a complete lack of communication, a breakdown in the chain of command. Colonels aren't following orders. No one cares. It's become every man for himself. There's paralysis in the government [brought on] by worry and panic. And there's silence at the top." City after city was falling without a battle. The North Vietnamese invasion, swift as it was, could not keep pace with the South Vietnamese collapse. Cities fell, days later, the foe approached. So rapidly did the territory of South Vietnam change hands that many Vietnamese were convinced that President Thieu had made a deal with the Communists. Others maintained that the deal was between the Americans and the Russians. Few seemed to doubt that their fate had been bartered in one manner or another. If at the top there was silence, at the bottom there was something for which there is no adequate word—something described in news reports as "breakdown of law and order," "chaos," and "panic." The South Vietnamese troops were not only fleeing the enemy but attacking the civilian population and each other. As the Army disintegrated, directionless rage burst out on all sides. In Danang, a mob sacked the deserted United States Consulate. Lieutenant General Ngo Quang Truong, the commander of the troops in the area, removed himself to a "command post" on a boat offshore, and his soldiers proceeded to go on a rampage. They fired randomly and for no reason at passers-by, including children. The bodies of their victims littered the streets. An American reporter on the scene wrote, "People are jogging crazily and pointlessly down the streets. Others are taking houses apart, piece by piece. A young man walks outside carrying a wooden door, wrenched from its hinges, atop his head. Another is carrying bits of broken glass in his hands." At the end, the soldiers went down to the beach, where some threw away their weapons and their uniforms and dived into the sea to swim out to waiting American ships, while others commandeered boats and then began firing at one another on the open water. Americans had long spoken a great deal about bloodbaths in Vietnam. Those who favored the war effort had spoken of a bloodbath that might be per-petrated by the Communists if they should take control of the South. Those who opposed the war effort had spoken of the bloodbath of war itself. But no one had foreseen this bloodbath: the massacre of civilians by the disintegrating South Vietnamese Army. Soon the scenes in Danang were repeated in cities through most of South Vietnam. In one city, the renegade soldiers were shooting at the owners of the restaurants where they ate. Something deeper than the collapse of an army's discipline—deeper, even, than the collapse of a body politic—was taking place. It was the disintegration of a society that had been pulverized by war and corrupted by foreign invaders for thirty years. A society that had lost all sense of self-respect and that despised itself for its subservience to one foreign master after another—a society that had been turned into a literal brothel for mil-lions of soldiers from foreign countries—was tearing itself apart in a frenzy of self-destruction. Naturally, the soldiers' anger, insofar as it was not directed at themselves, was directed at the American oppressor/protector, rather than at the foe. On several occasions, South Vietnamese troops fired on American aircraft. And President Thieu summed up the general feeling when, as a visitor has reported, he said, "Many Vietnamese now have the feeling that they actually have been lured into all this and then abandoned." And so they had. For more than a decade, the United States had imposed an American fantasy on Vietnamese reality. Then we had left, and now the South Vietnamese government was fading like the mirage it had in fact always been.

Faced with the disappearance of the world that America had built up over the years, the American authorities had two ideas. One was to send in "spare parts" and similar supplies, and the other was to "rescue" South Vietnamese refugees from the North Vietnamese by transporting them to "safe" parts of the south. The spare-parts debate in the United States was attended by a great deal of military analysis of the kind that crops up whenever war is being waged anywhere. There was discussion of the strategic strengths and weaknesses of the South Vietnamese Army and the North Vietnamese Army. Command structures were compared. The decentralized structure of the South Vietnamese Air Force command was noted and deplored. The unified structure of the North Vietnamese Army command was noted and admired. The merits of a Russian anti-aircraft rocket—the SA-7— were weighed. The performance of both armies, and even of individual units, was predicted. But in the event there was "no war." The SA-7s never had to be fired. The units never met in combat. Instead, there was the sudden dissolution of the South Vietnamese side. It was not spare parts that had been missing. Even when all the parts are available, weapons cannot fire themselves. And no number of troops is of any use if the troops attack civilians and each other instead of attacking the foe. Rarely has there been a clearer illustration of the lesson, never grasped by the United States in Vietnam, that the foundations of power are political, not military. With the fall of Danang, the full irony of the spare-parts debate was driven home. In their flight southward, the South Vietnamese abandoned some three hundred aircraft and other American-made military equipment, altogether worth as much as a billion dollars. At a glance, it appeared that the North Vietnamese would be greatly aided by their capture of so many planes. But then it appeared that they might not. They would lack spare parts.

The rescue mission was announced in the early days of the collapse. Army Colonel Robert Burke, a Pentagon spokesman, said, "We have all kinds of contingency plans." In the minds of the Americans, the aim of the mission was to bring people to "safety." But, as has so often been true of American ideas for Vietnam, noble intentions led to horrific results. There were the boats. Thousands of refugees crowded onto barges that were to take them out to ships that, in turn, were to take them to points south. But the ships were slow in coming, and hundreds perished of thirst, starvation, and exposure. Often, children would fall overboard and their mothers would dive in after them, and both would drown. On the American ship *Pioneer Commander,* renegade South Vietnamese Marines murdered twenty-five refugees for no apparent reason. The rapings, robbings, and random brutality that had begun in Danang continued on the ships. Many civilians were thrown overboard by soldiers. By the time the boats arrived at Nha Trang and Cam Ranh Bay, down the coast, with their cargo of the suffering, the dying, and the dead, these cities, too, had come under attack by renegade South Vietnamese soldiers. Meanwhile, it was reported, the revolutionary authorities had restored order in Danang. The trip to "safety," as it was usually put in the newscasts, turned out to be a trip to danger, or to death.

A few planes were made available, too. An airlift from Danang that would carry as many as three hundred and fifty thousand people to "safety" had been announced, but the collapse proceeded too swiftly, and the airlift was abandoned. At the last minute, the president of an outfit called World Airways, Edward Daly, shortly to be known to newsmen as Ed, took it upon himself to fly into Danang in a Boeing 727 to evacuate refugees. But when he arrived his plane was mobbed—not by the expected "widows and children," as it was sometimes put, but by the Black Panthers, the remnants of a disintegrated unit of the South Vietnamese Army. Daly, the would-be savior of the Vietnamese, was soon throwing punches at soldiers and firing a pistol into the air. It was reported that as the plane took off, it ran over several people, and it was fired upon by berserk soldiers on the ground.

Other soldiers clung to the jammed landing gear of the plane. Once the plane was aloft, several fell off. A reporter described the flight as "a flight out of hell," and it was, but it was also a flight into hell. And the flight itself was hell. A completely senseless movement of millions of people, encouraged and abetted by the United States, had started up all over South Vietnam. Some people were said to be fleeing the Communists, and others were said to be fleeing war. But wherever they went they found both. The United States was busy transferring people from one end of a sinking ship to the other, and it always seemed to choose the end where the danger was greater. These unfortunates were not the first Vietnamese to be doomed by American efforts to "save" them. But they may have been some of the last.

If the unreal world that had been created by the Americans was collapsing last week in South Vietnam, it was still standing in America. In the momentous days when the northernmost two-thirds of South Vietnam was falling to the Communists, Americans were mechanically continuing to do the things that Americans had done throughout the war. Some were opposing the war, some were supporting the war. The debate over spare parts raged. A debate over "phase-out" aid intensified. Secretary of State Henry Kissinger, speaking as though America were still able to influence the situation, said we could not afford to "destroy an ally." To this, one was tempted to answer that it was the North Vietnamese, not the Americans, who were destroying our ally. But the truth was stranger still. Our ally was destroying itself. Many Americans were blaming one another for the fall of South Vietnam. But the one thing in South Vietnam that the United States was not responsible for was its fall. What the United States was responsible for was the death and devastation brought about by the futile prolongation of the war for some fifteen years.

At the White House, too, Americans were going on doing what

they had been doing for years. They were sending ships; they were sending military observers; they were installing new telephone lines; they were sending military supplies. (A day or so after it became known that the South Vietnamese had abandoned hundreds of aircraft in their flight southward, an American C-5A arrived in Saigon and unloaded fourteen howitzers.) The South Vietnamese military machine had broken down, but the American support machine was grinding on, even though its reason for existing had disappeared. Where could the ships land? To whom could the telephone calls be made? Who would take delivery of the spare parts? The lines of communication and control stretched out from Washington as always, but now they connected with nothing. At times, the ships bobbed helplessly on the high seas, unable to find safe ports at which to land; the phones in Hué, Danang, and Cam Ranh Bay had gone dead, the supplies were being delivered to the North Vietnamese. The administration policymakers were confronted with a situation that they could not fathom: there were no more "contingencies" for the United States in Vietnam. One project after another was stillborn, or recoiled upon itself. Ronald Nessen, the president's press secretary, announced that "diplomatic initiatives" were under way, and then he withdrew the announcement. The airlift was announced, and then it was abandoned. Even in their public statements, officials went on mouthing the old words, as though they were unaware that the world to which the words referred had dissolved. "I believe that if we support the people of South Vietnam, in the way that they deserve, that no enemy can ever defeat them," Army Chief of Staff Frederick Weyand said after the inspection tour he made for the White House.

In the United States, as in Saigon, there was silence at the top. The president was playing golf in Palm Springs. Correctly anticipating a question about Vietnam at an airport, he laughed playfully and broke into a run. When his press secretary was asked if it was proper for the president to play golf at a time of such great suffering for the Vietnamese, he answered, "Would it prevent anything from happening in Vietnam if he didn't play golf?" Meanwhile, the nation, seeing that its military efforts were futile, turned its attention to the projects for shifting civilians about, which now came to be known everywhere as "humanitarian" projects. A large part of the nation, including the administration, repaired to this cause as though to safe high ground. At the close of the most inhuman war in our history, American officialdom was suddenly turning sentimental. In the midst of moral confusion, the "humanitarian" projects seemed to offer moral simplicity. In the midst of boundless shame, they seemed to offer reasons for pride. Could anyone fail to be moved by the plight of the refugees? But this was Vietnam. This was the war where the "good" intentions had consistently led to the grotesque consequences. Already corpses were piling up on the "rescue" ships, and soldiers were falling to their death off Ed Daly's plane. But Daly had one more idea. He would rescue orphans. Soon the government took up the idea. As one reporter observed, many children had lost their parents in the war or "had been separated" from their parents. Now Ed Daly and the government would fly those children to America. Suddenly, the news was filled with babies. These were not, at first, wounded babies or dead babies or babies falling into the South China Sea, like the ones we had been seeing all week, they were live, happy, well babies. Smiling prospective American parents were interviewed. "It's fantastic," one delighted American mother said. (As it happens, there is a shortage of children up for adoption in the United States at the moment.) Unable to do anything else in Vietnam, the United States was now making off with planeloads of Vietnamese babies. Somehow, a conviction seemed to have grown up that their lives were being saved. If the Vietnamese authorities did not allow them to go to America, one correspondent reported, then they would have a difficult time growing up in South Vietnam, "and perhaps will never grow up at all." Similarly, a reporter on Daly's flight from Danang who had seen an old woman try to get on the plane and fail had written that "life itself" had slipped out of her hands. However, there was no reason to think that orphans or old women would be endangered by a North Vietnamese takeover. Yet there were many Vietnamese—perhaps tens of thousands—who from having worked with us might well be in danger. We were "saving" people who didn't need saving, and we were leaving behind people who did. And then, in an accident that no one could have foreseen, an American Air Force plane carrying orphans crashed, and the "baby-lift," ill-conceived from the start, also turned to tragedy.

The Vietnam War was coming to a close, and at the end, by chance, there was only Ed Daly—compassionate millionaire, adventurer, and, according to a friend, "an outgoing good party guy who will gather up a planeload of friends and fly off to Europe for a weekend." On our television screens, there was Ed Daly in Danang waving his pistol and socking a South Vietnamese soldier in the jaw; there was Ed Daly getting fired at as his plane took off; there was Ed Daly in Saigon giving news conferences; there was Ed Daly stopping over in Tokyo with his babies. Despised by those on whom his compassion had fastened, attacked by the people he wanted to help, Ed Daly was rushing all over South Vietnam, as though he really were what to all of us at home he seemed to have become; the last American in Vietnam.

FEBRUARY 3, 1986

NEWS IN OUR day is supposed to flash around the world at the speed of light, "shrinking" our planet and making of it the famed global village, but from some regions, it turns out, information comes slowly, as if still traveling by clipper ship, or by desert caravan into a global village, sometimes seem to have dropped off the edge of the earth. For them, the planet, rather than shrinking, it is expanding. The reason is not that the regions are technologically backward but that in them the powers that be don't want anyone—but the whole globe, and not the local population, either—to know what they are doing. One such place is Afghanistan, where the Soviet Union has been waging a full-fledged war, mostly out of sight, for six years. Just recently, though, several whole caravan loads of news have arrived from that country, in the form of an excellent series of articles in the *Washington Post*— information that permits all of us to begin to try to answer questions about the war that have been on our minds. One of these questions is how much the Soviet war in Afghanistan resembles the American war in Vietnam. To judge from the *Post* articles, the answer at first glance must be: A lot. In an amazing number of particulars, the similarities are present. There is the rebel force nourished by popular support which is battling a central government propped up by the funds and military forces of a superpower. There is the division between a countryside largely under the control of the rebels and cities largely under the control of the government. There are the in-between areas that are under the control of the rebels by night and of the government by day. There is the indiscriminate—or perhaps discriminate and systematic, depending on your interpretation—aerial bombardment of the countryside. There is the de-facto policy of trying to deprive the rebels of their support by depopulating rural areas, through the bombing and other brutal measures. (In Vietnam, American military officers, proud to have studied up on their Mao Zedong, would often announce that they were familiar with his dictum and the rebel guerrillas are the fish and the people the sea, and would say that the United States was seeking to strand the fish by drying up the sea. In Afghanistan, one rebel described Soviet policy in identical terms to the *Post*.) There are the millions of refugees. (The largest refugee population in the world today is Afghan.) There are the massacres and other atrocities in the villages. There is the protracted stalemate that apparently often arises when opposing forces are not so much equal in strength as completely different in the varieties and sources of their strength—with the strength of one side being mainly political, and consisting of popular support, and the strength of the other side being mainly military, and consisting of effectively limitless firepower.

Differences between the two wars also emerge, however. One of the most important is suggested by the Soviet practice of sending Afghan children—sometimes without their parents' consent—to the Soviet Union for education and political indoctrination. This practice is part of a policy of seeking to do nothing less than shape the whole of Afghan culture, including, above all, its Islamic religion, to suit Soviet purposes, and suggests an implacable patience and resolve on the part of the Soviets which were lacking in American policy in Vietnam. The force that disrupted American policy was, of course, the American public, which, after much turmoil, rejected continuation of the war. At the time, some officials publicly ruminated and fretted about the difficulty of maintaining "steadiness" in the foreign policy of a democracy, and others complained that the hands of the military had been needlessly "tied behind their backs" by timid civilian officials, but what actually tied the military's hands, and forced the eventual withdrawal from Vietnam, was not any official; it was the people of the United States, engaging in an immense exercise of their political powers under the Constitution. The thongs tying the military's hands were the fundamental laws on which the nation was founded. The Soviet leaders need fear no such hindrance, as they well know.

Barring revolutionary change in their country, they can remain in Afghanistan for the next hundred yours without encountering serious domestic opposition. For them, a policy of permanent—or, at least, decades-long—occupation, like the one they have carried out in Eastern Europe, is quite possible. No similar plans formed in the minds of even the most hawkish American officials in their thinking about Vietnam. Their persistent—and persistently disappointed— hope was to win the war in Vietnam and then leave. Knowing of the public's distaste for endless war and endless occupation, they kept trying to convince the country, and even to convince themselves, that the United States was on the verge of victory—that they could see the light at the end of the tunnel, as they used to say. And it was for their failure, over more than a decade, to fulfill this promise which turned the public as a while against the war. The plain fact is that when it comes to forcing its will on a foreign people—or on its own people— the Soviet government has incomparably more latitude than the United States government. No one ties its hands. No one shakes the steadiness of its policy. The deeper question, though, is whether this latitude constitutes an advantage. Steadiness in pursuit of a mistake is not beneficial. In Eastern Europe, where the Soviet policy of domination has been tried for about forty years now, its success is anything but clear. In the aftermath of the establishment of the Solidarity movement in Poland, it is even open to question whether complete Soviet domination of the Eastern European countries can be long sustained—whether those countries, like the colonial nations of the Third World before them, may not in some way break free. It could be that, just as the independence movements against the European colonial powers occupied the political stage in the beginning and middle of our century, independence movements against Soviet domination will occupy the political stage for the rest of the century and beyond. However that may be, the occupation of other countries is something that was best left to the Soviet Union. The very nature of our political system unfits us for such work. If that is a disadvantage, it is one that we accepted when we decided, more than two hundred years ago, to constitute ourselves as free people.

The Time of Illusion

The New Yorker, JULY 7, 1975

CREDIBILITY

IN THE YEARS of the Vietnam War, the United States experienced a systemic crisis, which reached its final stage when, under the Nixon administration, the American Constitutional democracy was almost destroyed by its president. Then, as the Nixon administration was forced from office, the nation seemed—for the time being, at least—to reaffirm its allegiance to its Constitutional traditions. After a period in which almost any situation called an emergency was considered reason enough for the executive branch to suspend the rights of citizens, to arrogate power to itself, and otherwise to distort or simply break the law, the nation seemed to rediscover its forgotten political principles. It was reminded, for example, that great power can easily be abused; that if one powerful man is allowed to rise above the law, the law as a whole is placed in jeopardy; and that a heavy reliance on secrecy is incompatible with democracy. All these principles were dealt with in millions of words in the press and in hundreds of hours of television, and I will not be further concerned with them here. Instead, I will offer some thoughts on the particular conditions that made our time the one in which the most serious threat to liberty in American history could take place.

One school of thought has it that the nature of the various stages of the Vietnam period was determined largely by the background and character of the various men who occupied the White House in those years. According to this way of thinking, the great accumulation of powers in the presidency served to expand the character flaws of the officeholders and their staffs into national disasters. In the Kennedy and Johnson years, it is said, government policy came to be dominated by a group of brilliant, overconfident, privileged men of an East Coast "Establishment," whose character flaws were soon writ large in the war in Vietnam. And in the Nixon years, it is said, government policy came to be dominated by a ruthless, unprincipled group of men, many of them from southern California, whose character flaws were soon writ large in "Watergate" (as President Nixon's attempt to seize power came to be called). And certainly the variations in the character of the men in the White House were reflected in the events of the time. However, what stands out much more sharply than any variations is the astonishing degree of continuity which binds the stages of the mounting systemic crisis together—the marked differences in character of the officeholders notwithstanding. The distortions in the conduct of the presidency which deformed national politics in the Vietnam years—the isolation from reality, the rage against political opposition, the hunger for un-Constitutional power, the conspiratorial-mindedness, the bent for repressive action—knew no party lines. They were all as clearly evident on a small scale at the Democratic Convention in Chicago in 1968 as they were on a national scale in the Nixon presidency. The Kennedy and Johnson men supposedly belonged to "the Establishment," and the Nixon men regarded themselves as enemies of "the Establishment" and wished to destroy it forever; yet in handling the policies that had the most direct bearing on the Constitutional crisis the men of the three administrations made decisions that were strikingly alike. In fact, when it came to making contributions to the Constitutional crisis President Nixon seemed to pick up precisely where President Johnson had left off, as though there had been no change of party in the White House.

The most telling decisions were, by and large, in the area of "foreign affairs"—our anachronistic euphemism for the unlimited sphere of action which now encompasses the life and death of every soul on earth. For in the Vietnam years the exigencies of foreign policy, and particularly the exigencies of the nuclear dilemma, began to dominate the course of the nation's politics. In those years, presidents consistently sacrificed the welfare of the nation at home to what they saw as the demands of foreign affairs; and in the domestic record of the period one finds only discontinuity and neglect. The Johnson presidency embodied the dominance of foreign affairs in a tragic form. President Johnson was more interested in domestic affairs than in foreign affairs, yet it was foreign affairs that, in the shape of the Vietnam war, determined the fate of his presidency, leaving his dreams of reform at home in ruins. Under President Nixon, the role of foreign affairs was even larger. Foreign affairs were his chief interest to begin with, and he looked on domestic politics almost entirely as a cheering section for his foreign policy and—what amounted in practice to the same thing—as an arena for his reelection. His indifference to the substance of the most important issues facing the country at home was, apparently, complete. He came closer to destroying the American Constitutional system than any man or group of men had come before, yet he had no clear conception of a system to put in its place. In the domestic record of the Nixon administration one finds, instead of rigid adherence to a system of ideas, a deliberate separation of the image of government policy from the substance of government policy, and also a chaotic veering from one policy to another under the pressure of political expediency. In fact, more often than not the promises that the Nixon administration made to the public turned out to have been signals that exactly the opposite of what was promised was about to occur. At the beginning of his first term, President Nixon promised to work for national unity, but then he launched a drive to polarize national politics. In economic affairs, he portrayed himself as a champion of the system of free enterprise, but then he became the first president to impose wage and price controls for any reason other than war, and also set about transforming the Cabinet departments and the agencies of the federal government into instruments for the coercion and political control of businessmen. (The fact that some sixty million dollars was raised by his reelection campaign committee, much of it from corporations and wealthy individuals, provides eloquent testimony to the success of his efforts.) In the field of social programs, he championed a major expansion of spending for social needs, in the form of his Family Assistance Plan—which never came to fruition—but then he initiated a highly organized drive to cut back even the existing programs. As for the question of a political philosophy, he preached the decentralization of federal power, but then he attempted to gather the whole power of the federal government into his own hands. From the moment of taking office, when he promised, in his first Inaugural Address, to build a "great cathedral of the spirit" and unify the nation, to the spring of 1973, when he had Senate Minority Leader Hugh Scott announce on his behalf, "We have nothing to hide," he filled the air with empty and intentionally misleading phrases—phrases that in both tone and content were without relation either to each other or to the actions of his administration. In the domestic sphere, far from being guided by an unwavering vision of how he wanted things to be, he had no guiding purposes at all. At times, his statements were merely ridiculous, as when he promised "the lift of a driving dream," or promised a "New American Revolution," which would be "as exciting as that first revolution almost two hundred years ago," and then forgot about it immediately. But often the consequences were grave, as they were when, in the words of his political planning group for the 1972 campaign, he set out to "exacerbate" national problems solely in order to "divide the Democrats" in the 1972 presidential primaries and then win "far the larger half" of the electorate in the general election—and so became the first president on record to establish a program consciously aimed at worsening the torments afflicting the nation. No issue was above exploitation—not the issue of race, not the issue of Supreme Court nominations, not the issue of social spending. All were to be exacerbated. It is true that themes emerged from time to time. President Nixon's feelings were closely attuned to certain deep-running resentments in American politics—resentments against the press, against the television networks, against black people, against the rebellious young, and against the ill-defined entity known as "the Establishment"—and in late 1969 and for most of 1970 he sought to make a partisan drive against these supposed menaces the central theme of national politics. But even this theme, so congenial to the president's temperament, was suddenly dropped from his public statements after the congressional elections of 1970, in which its political usefulness had been tested and found wanting.

In foreign affairs, the gap between image and substance was no less wide, and the sudden, unexplained reversals of policy were no less startling: as a candidate, in 1968, Richard Nixon promised an early end to the war, but then, as president, he continued the war effort for four more years; in 1969, he spoke of "great powers who have not yet abandoned their goals of world conquest," clearly referring to China and Russia, but then in 1972 he went to China and Russia and drank toasts of friendship with the leaders of those powers, while promising the world a "generation of peace." In foreign affairs, however, if one looks behind the surface of shifting images, the more constant concerns can be made out. If one examines the covert record, as it appears in the Pentagon Papers and in other secret memoranda, and ignores the public justifications that were put forward only for reasons of propaganda, a remarkable consistency of purpose emerges; and if guiding principles in government policy are to be found in the years in which the American democracy experienced its crisis, they are buried here, in the realm of strategic theory. For from January of 1961, when John Kennedy took office, until August of 1974, when Richard Nixon was forced to leave office, the unvarying dominant goal of the foreign policy of the United States was the preservation of what policymakers throughout the period called the credibility of American power. (And, indeed, since President Nixon's fall the preservation of American credibility has remained the dominant goal of United States foreign policy.) The various policymakers phrased the aim in many ways. To have a formidable "psychological impact . . . on the countries of the world" is how the Joint Chiefs of Staff put it in a memo to Secretary of Defense Robert McNamara in January of 1962. To prevent a situation from arising in which "no nation can ever again have the same confidence in American promise or in American protection" is how President Johnson put it at a news conference in July of 1965. To "avoid humiliation" is how Assistant Secretary of Defense John McNaughton put it in a memo in January of 1966. To shore up "the confidence factor" is how Assistant Secretary of State William Bundy put it in a speech in January of 1967. To prevent "defeat and humiliation" is how President Nixon put it in a speech in November of 1969. To demonstrate America's "will and character" is how President Nixon put it in a speech in April of 1970. To prevent the United States from appearing before the world as a "pitiful, helpless giant" is another way that President Nixon put it in that speech. To maintain "respect for the office of President of the United States" is how President Nixon put it in a speech in April of 1972. To win an "honorable" peace or a "peace with honor" is how President Nixon put it from time to time. But, whatever words it was couched in, the aim was always the same: to establish in the minds of peoples and their leaders throughout the world an image of the United States as a nation that possessed great power and had the will and determination to use it in foreign affairs. In the name of this objective, President Kennedy sent "advisers" to Vietnam in the early nineteen-sixties, and President Johnson escalated the Vietnam War in secrecy and persisted in carrying on the war in the face of growing public opposition. In the name of this objective, also, President Nixon sent planes and troops into Cambodia, sent an aircraft carrier into the Indian Ocean at the time of the India-Pakistan war, mined North Vietnamese ports in the spring of 1972, and carpet-bombed North Vietnam during the Christmas season of 1972. In the pursuit of this objective, massacres were condoned, hundreds of thousands of lives were lost, dictatorial governments were propped up, nations friendly to the United States were turned into adversaries, the domestic scene was thrown into turmoil, two presidents were forced from office, the Constitution was imperilled, and the entire world was repeatedly brought to the verge of war.

The doctrine of credibility, far from being a fanatical ideology, was a coldly reasoned strategic theory that was designed to supply the United States with effective instruments of influence in an age dominated by nuclear weapons. The doctrine did not take shape all at once but evolved gradually as the full sweep of American military policy, including, especially, nuclear policy, was subjected to a reexamination, which got under way outside the government in the late nineteen-fifties and was carried forward within the government in the early nineteen-sixties, after President Kennedy took office. When Kennedy entered the White House, the nation's nuclear policy had remained all but unchanged since the end of the Korean War, in 1953. In fact, although the conditions under which men lived and conducted their politics were altered more drastically by the invention of nuclear weapons than by any previous single invention, nuclear weapons had never become the subject of intensive public debate. In the aftermath of the Second World War, the United States had made a brief effort at the United Nations to bring the new weapons under some form of international control, but the atmosphere of the Cold War had soon settled in and the effort had been abandoned. Then, in the nineteen-fifties, the nation's attention had been further distracted from the new peril by rising levels of consumption, which quickly climbed beyond the highest expectations. In the United States, unprecedented wealth and ease came to coexist with unprecedented danger, and a sumptuous feast of consumable goods was spread out in the shadow of universal death. Americans began to live as though on a luxuriously appointed death row, where one was free to enjoy every comfort but was uncertain from moment to moment when or if the death sentence might be carried out. The abundance was very much in the forefront of people's attention, however, and the uncertainty very much in the background; and in the government as well as in the country at large the measureless questions posed by the new weapons were evaded. As far as any attempt to find a way out of the nuclear dilemma was concerned, the time was one of sleep. But in the late nineteen-fifties, as the reexamination of the American military position gathered momentum, a few men began to think through the whole subject of nuclear strategy anew. Among them were two men whose writings proved to be of special importance, not only because the ideas expressed were influential in themselves but because each man was to take a high post in government in the years ahead. One was Henry Kissinger, who was a professor at Harvard during the nineteen-fifties and nineteen-sixties, and whose book *Nuclear Weapons and Foreign Policy* appeared in 1957. The other was General Maxwell Taylor, who was the Army chief of staff under President Eisenhower, and whose book *The Uncertain Trumpet* appeared in 1960.

Both men were disturbed by a paradox that seemed to lie near the heart of the nuclear question. It was that nuclear weapons, the most powerful instruments of violence ever invented, tended to immobilize rather than strengthen their possessors. This paradox was rooted in the central fact of the weapons' unprecedented destructive force, which made mankind, for the first time in its history, capable of annihilating itself. Nuclear weapons, Kissinger and Taylor realized, were bound to have a chilling effect on any warlike plans that their possessors, including the United States, might entertain. Wars were supposedly fought for ends, but a war fought with nuclear arms might well obliterate any end for which a war could be fought. Not only that but it might obliterate all means as well, and, for that matter, obliterate the only earthly creature capable of thinking in terms of means and ends. As Kissinger put it in his book, "the destructiveness of modern weapons deprives victory in an all-out war of its historical meaning." He decided that "all-out war has therefore ceased to be a meaningful instrument of policy." Thenceforward, the United States would be in the position of having to fear its own power almost as much as it feared the power of its foes. Taylor, in his book, described his doubts about the usefulness of nuclear weapons in somewhat different language. The notion that "the use or the threatened use of atomic weapons of mass destruction would be sufficient to assure the security of the United States and its friends," he wrote, was "The Great Fallacy" in the prevailing strategic thinking of the day. The new strategists were saying that nuclear weapons, instead of making the nuclear powers more formidable, appeared to be casting a pall of doubt over their military policies. The doubt did not concern the amount of military power at their disposal; it concerned their willingness in the face of the dread of extinction, to unleash that power. Kissinger wrote, "Both the horror and the power of modern [nuclear] weapons tend to paralyze action: the former because it will make few issues seem worth contending for; the latter because it causes many disputes to seem irrelevant to the over-all strategic equation"—which had to do with the victory of one side or the other. In strength, it had turned out, lurked weakness; in omnipotence, impotence.

Kissinger and Taylor, working separately, set out to a frame foreign policy that would take into account the implications of nuclear weapons. Each of them began to think through a policy that would accommodate two broad aims. One aim was to prevent the extinction of the world in a nuclear war, and the other aim was to prevent the domination of the world—naturally, including the domination of the United States—by Communist totalitarian forces. It was clear to the two men that these aims conflicted at many points. The aim of preventing human extinction, which was peculiar to the nuclear age, seemed to call for unprecedented restraint in military matters, but the aim of preventing global Communist totalitarian rule seemed to call for unceasing military efforts on an unprecedented scale. On the one hand, nuclear dread inhibited the United States from using its military power aggressively; on the other hand, the ambitions, ideals, and fears that have traditionally impelled powerful nations onto the world stage impelled the United States to use its military power aggressively. Kissinger wrote: "The dilemma of the nuclear period can, therefore, be defined as follows: the enormity of modern weapons makes the thought of war repugnant, but the refusal to run any risks would amount to giving the Soviet rulers a blank check." The aim of standing firm in the face of Soviet power, which, of course, corresponded to the broad aim of preventing world domination by Communist totalitarian forces, struck a responsive chord in the thinking of American politicians of the late nineteen-fifties. American political life had been dominated at least since the decade began by a conviction that the freedom and independence of nations all over the world was threatened by a unified, global Communist conspiracy that was under the control of the Soviet Union. Since then, "anti-Communism" not only had been the mainspring of American foreign policy but for a time—when Senator Joseph McCarthy hunted for Communists in the United States—had also been the central preoccupation of domestic politics. In this atmosphere, a reluctance to give Soviet leaders "a blank check" was quickly understood. However, the second aim recognized by Kissinger and Taylor—the avoidance of a nuclear catastrophe—was harder for the politicians of that time to grasp; and it was in championing this aim that the two men had to do the greater part of their explaining. (Something that helped them greatly in getting a hearing on the nuclear question was the fact that the anti-Communism of each of them was so strong as to be above suspicion.) The military, in particular, was difficult to persuade. The notion that an increase in military strength might, in effect, enfeeble the nation was a paradox not to the liking of the military mind. It was therefore difficult at first for the military to agree that, as Kissinger put it, in the nuclear age "the more powerful the weapons . . . the greater becomes the reluctance to use them"—in other words, the greater the power, the greater the paralysis.

Kissinger and Taylor, however, had an answer to those who were afraid that a recognition of the paralyzing influence of nuclear weapons might weaken the nation. While the two men were prepared to point out that reliance upon nuclear weapons might lead to a sort of impotence, they were far from willing to accept the condition. In fact, they were convinced that by failing to take cognizance of the danger the government was actually making the United States weaker in world affairs than it need be. In the late nineteen-fifties, the Eisenhower administration was relying almost exclusively on the threat of nuclear attack to cope with military challenges around the world. As Kissinger observed, American military policy was governed by the belief that "the chief deterrent to Soviet aggression resides in United States nuclear superiority." The policy was deliberate, and had been framed in response to the nation's experience in the early nineteen-fifties, during the Korean War. At that time, the public had shown that it reacted unenthusiastically to the sacrifice of American ground troops in inconclusive small wars fought far from the United States for goals that were difficult to grasp; and in 1954, after the war was brought to an end, Secretary of State John Foster Dulles had established a policy of using the threat of nuclear retaliation to achieve the sort of limited, local objective for which ground troops had been used in Korea. In a speech in January of that year, he said that in responding to a Communist challenge in any part of the world the United States would "depend primarily upon a great capacity to retaliate instantly by means and at places of our choosing," and he pointed out that a policy of reliance upon the nuclear threat not only would keep the troops at home but would be less expensive than ground operations. The Dulles policy became known as the policy of "massive retaliation," and also as "brinksmanship." It required the United States to rush toward the brink of nuclear war each time a crisis broke out somewhere in the world, and then to draw back at the last moment, having, it was hoped, frightened the foe into complying with American wishes. The strategy assumed, of course, that the Communist movement was a single force, controlled by the Soviet Union, and that a threat of nuclear retaliation against the Soviet Union would serve to stop Communist moves in, say, the Far East. Kissinger and Taylor were no less firm believers than Dulles in the unity of World Communism, and they did not oppose the Dulles policy on this point. Their charge was that his policy ignored the implications of the all-encompassing destructive force of nuclear weapons. Kissinger, employing a word that was just beginning to come into vogue, observed that a threat to use nuclear weapons in each minor crisis around the world would lack "credibility." What worried him was not only that the United States might make a misstep at the brink, it was also that the Communists might not be adequately deterred by a threat of massive nuclear retaliation. He was afraid that the Communists would find it implausible that the United States should be willing to risk nuclear annihilation merely to serve some minor purpose thousands of miles from home, and that they would therefore be unafraid to oppose the United States. For in the strategy of massive retaliation the government seemed to take the use of nuclear force almost lightly, as though nuclear weapons were ordinary, readily usable instruments of policy rather than engines of doom. The danger was, as Kissinger saw it, that "every move on [the Soviet bloc's] part will . . . pose the appalling dilemma of whether we are willing to commit suicide to prevent encroachments, which do not, each in itself, seem to threaten our existence directly but which may be steps on the road to our ultimate destruction." Kissinger was attempting to work out the implications of the distressing fact that once both adversaries were armed with nuclear weapons, a decision to use nuclear weapons was as dangerous to oneself as it was to the foe, for the result might be "suicide." And a threat to commit suicide was not a very convincing way of deterring a foe. Kissinger was suggesting that the policy of brinksmanship menaced the world with both great dangers of the period: global totalitarianism *and* human extinction. On the one hand, that policy threatened to transform every small crisis into a major nuclear crisis, and, on the other hand, it left the United States without "credible" instruments of force in situations where the stakes were too small to justify any risk of "suicide." The need was for a policy that would steer a middle course between the two dangers—for a policy that would, in Kissinger's words, "provide a means to escape from the sterility of the quest for absolute peace, which paralyzes by the vagueness of its hopes, and of the search for absolute victory, which paralyzes by the vastness of its consequences."

A middle course was available, both Kissinger and Taylor believed, in a strategy of limited war. "A strategy of limited war," Kissinger wrote, "would seek to escape the inconsistency of relying on a policy of deterrence [that is, massive retaliation], whose major sanction involves national catastrophe." And Taylor wrote, "The new strategy would recognize that it is just as necessary to deter or win quickly a limited war as to deter general war." Kissinger, for his part, believed that even in the nuclear age the freedom actually to use force rather than merely to threaten the use of force was indispensable to the maintenance of international order. He derided "the national psychology which considers peace as the 'normal' pattern of relations among states," and, while granting that "the contemporary revolution cannot be managed by force alone," he maintained that "when there is no penalty for irresponsibility, the pent-up frustrations of centuries may seek an outlet in the international field." Therefore, "to the extent that recourse to force has become impossible the restraints of the international order may disappear as well." In his view, dangerous as the use

of force was in the nuclear age, the United States would have to overcome its uneasiness and thus "face up to the risks of Armageddon."
And limited war, he believed, was both a more acceptable and a more
effective way of facing up to these risks than was massive retaliation.
For a strategy of limited war would rescue the use of force from
nuclear paralysis. It would provide "credible" means of threatening
the foe. It would make the world safe again for war.

More specifically, there were, in Kissinger's view, "three reasons
. . . for developing a strategy of limited war." He listed them as follows: "First, limited war represents the only means for preventing the
Soviet bloc, at an acceptable cost, from overrunning the peripheral
areas of Eurasia. Second, a wide range of military capabilities may
spell the difference between defeat and victory even in an all-out war.
Finally, intermediate applications of our power offer the best chance
to bring about strategic changes favorable to our side." (By "victory
even in an all-out war" Kissinger meant the survival after nuclear war
of enough conventional forces in the United States to impose
America's will on the surviving remnant of the Soviet population.)
His reference to "the best chance to bring about strategic changes
favorable to our side" had to do with what he saw as the possibility
that on occasion limited war might be used offensively as well as
defensively, and would place the United States in a position to reduce
"the Soviet sphere." These aims—the defense of a perimeter, the
attainment of "victory" in all-out hostilities, and the attainment of
improved strategic positions that would reduce "the Soviet sphere"—
were straightforward military aims of a traditional kind. They can be
called the tangible objectives of limited war.

One aim of the strategy of limited war, then, was to free the use of
military force from nuclear paralysis, so that the United States might
still avail itself of its arms to stop Communism from spreading

around the globe. But there was also a second aim. It was to help in preventing a nuclear war. It was Kissinger's hope that the new policy could "rescue mankind from the horrors of a thermonuclear holocaust by devising a framework of war limitation." Or, in Taylor's words, the new policy "is not blind to the awful dangers of general atomic war; indeed, it takes as its primary purpose the avoidance of that catastrophe." By assigning largely to limited war the achievement of the tangible objectives in the fight against Communist enemies, the policy opened the way to a crucial shift in the mission of the American nuclear force. Secretary of State Dulles had sought to use the threat of nuclear war to work America's will in small crises around the world, but if limited-war forces could take over this job, the nuclear force, relieved of its provocative, belligerent role, could be retired into the purely passive one of deterring nuclear attack. Thereafter, the role of the nuclear force would simply be that of threatening retaliation in order to dissuade the Soviet Union from using its nuclear force in a first strike. Neither Taylor nor Kissinger spelled out the possibility of this shift, but it was implicit in their writings, and was later adopted as policy, under the name of deterrence. The strategy of limited war was thus a necessary companion to the policy of deterrence. In fact, it had been designed, in part, to wean the United States from its perilous sole reliance on the threat of massive nuclear retaliation. The policies of nuclear deterrence and limited war represented a division of labor, in which nuclear weapons would take on the defensive role in military policy and the limited-war forces would take on the offensive role. Taylor, describing a proposal along these lines he had made to the National Security Council in 1958, wrote, "Our atomic deterrent forces would be the shield under which we must live from day to day with the Soviet threat. This shield would provide us protection, but not a means of maneuver. It was rather to the so-called limited-war forces that we henceforth must look for the active elements of our military strategy."

The limited-war strategy would dovetail with nuclear strategy in another way, too. It would give the United States a new opportunity to make demonstrations of its "will" or "resolve" to use force in the world. It would, that is, give the nation a chance to demonstrate its credibility. This objective of limited war can be called the psychological objective. In a passage setting forth some of the fundamental reasoning behind the policy of limited war, Kissinger described the importance of the psychological objective to the whole of American strategic policy:

Deterrence is brought about not only by a physical but also by a psychological relationship: deterrence is greatest when military strength is coupled with the willingness to employ it. It is achieved when one side's readiness to run risks in relation to the other is high; it is least effective when the willingness to run risks is low, however powerful the military capability. It is, therefore, no longer possible to speak of military superiority in the abstract. What does "being ahead" in the nuclear race mean if each side can already destroy the other's national substance? ... It is the task of strategic doctrine to strike a balance between the physical and the psychological aspects of deterrence, between the desire to pose a maximum threat and the reality that no threat is stronger than the belief of the opponent that it will in fact be used. ... The reliance on all-out war as the chief deterrent inhibits the establishment of this balance. By identifying deterrence with maximum power it tends to paralyze the will. Its concern with the physical basis of deterrence neglects the psychological aspect. Given the

power of modern weapons, a nation that relies on all-out war
as its chief deterrent imposes a fearful psychological handicap
on itself. The most agonizing decision a statesman can face is
whether or not to unleash all-out war; all pressures will make
for hesitation, short of a direct attack threatening the national
existence. In any other situation he will be inhibited by the
incommensurability between the cost of the war and the
objective in dispute. And he will be confirmed in his hesita-
tions by the conviction that, so long as his retaliatory force
remains intact, no shift in the territorial balance is of decisive
significance. . . . The psychological equation, therefore, will
almost inevitably operate against the side which can extricate
itself from a situation *only* by the threat of all-out war. Who
can be certain that, faced with the catastrophe of all-out war,
even Europe, long the keystone of our security, will seem
worth the price? As the power of modern weapons grows, the
threat of all-out war loses its credibility.

A strategy of limited war would help overcome the deficiency in the
psychological equation and restore credibility. By advertising
America's strength to the world at levels below the brink, it would hold
the world a few steps back from nuclear extinction and at the same time
would deter the Communists from aggressive moves. New room for
military maneuvering would open up. Whereas under the strategy of
massive retaliation there was only one step on the ladder between peace
and the holocaust, under the strategy of limited war there would be
many steps, and at each step the superpowers would have the opportunity to take stock of each other's intentions, to send each other clear signals of their "resolve," and, perhaps, to draw back before things got out
of hand. In a passage that compared the opportunities for demonstrating

credibility which were offered by the strategy of massive retaliation (in which only threats were possible) with the opportunities offered by a strategy of limited war (in which actual military efforts were possible), Kissinger wrote, "It is a strange doctrine which asserts that we can convey our determination to our opponent by reducing our overseas commitments, that, in effect, our words will be a more effective deterrent than our deeds." Under the policy he was proposing, America's deeds—its actions in limited wars—would "convey our determination." Taylor similarly underscored the psychological importance of limited war, writing, "There is also an important psychological factor which must be present to make this retaliatory weapon [the nuclear deterrent force] effective. It must be clear to the aggressor that we have the will and determination to use our retaliatory power without compunction if we are attacked. Any suggestion of weakness or indecision may encourage the enemy to gamble on surprise. And the best way to prevent "any suggestion of weakness or indecision" from appearing, he thought, was to prepare for limited war. The strategy would, in his words, guard against the danger that "repeated [Communist] success in creeping aggression may encourage a Communist miscalculation that could lead to general war."

The psychological objective was to be sharply distinguished from the tangible objectives. The tangible objectives grew out of an effort to escape the paralyzing influence of nuclear strategy, but the psychological objective was part and parcel of the nuclear strategy. In the new scheme, the attainment of the tangible objectives would belong wholly to the limited-war forces, but the attainment of the psychological objective of maintaining credibility though it was also an important aim of limited war, would still be long primarily to the nuclear retaliatory force. For it was the inherent futility of ever using the nuclear retaliatory force—a futility that threatened military paralysis—that had driven the policymakers to rely so heavily on credibility in the first place. It was dread of extinction in a nuclear war that had placed in doubt the "will" of the United States to use its undeniably tremendous nuclear arsenal. Of course, there were additional factors that might paralyze America's will to use its military forces. One was the element of isolationism that had long existed in American political life, and another was the natural revulsion of any peaceful people against warfare. Yet these obstacles had been overcome in times of danger in the past. The dread of nuclear war was a paralyzing influence of new dimensions. Now, even if the public should develop a will to victory, a clear upper limit had been placed on the usefulness of violence as an instrument in foreign affairs. The strategists were preoccupied with the question of how to demonstrate America's will—or "resolve," or "determination," or "toughness," as it was variously put. How to make demonstrations of credibility was, above all, a problem of public relations, since what counted was not the substance of America's strength or the actual state of its willingness but the image of strength and willingness. To put it more precisely, the substance of the nation's strength was useful only insofar as it enhanced the image of strength. In Kissinger's words, "Soviet reactions to what we do will depend not on what we intend but on what the Soviet leaders think we intend." Or, as he also wrote, "until power is used, it is . . . what people think it is." The strategy of massive retaliation had been one way of maintaining credibility—the technique in that case being to attest to America's will to go to war by *almost* going to war—but it was in the doctrine of nuclear deterrence that the doctrine of credibility found its purest expression. The deterrent force was real, but its entire purpose was to *appear* so formidable that the Soviet Union would hesitate to take aggressive actions that might provoke the United States into retaliating. The deterrent was not meant for use, because its use would lead to the utter futility of mutual extinction. Appearances, therefore, were not merely important to deterrence—they were everything. If the deterrent was used, deterrence would have failed. If the image did not do its preventive work and there was a resort to action, the whole purpose of the policy would have been defeated, and the human race, with all its policies and purposes, might be lost. In the strategy of nuclear deterrence, the "psychological relationship" was the whole relationship. If power, until it was used, was what people thought it was, then nuclear power could never be anything more than what people thought it was, for its use was forever ruled out, except in retaliation. The strategy of nuclear deterrence presented the nuclear dilemma in the form of pure paradox. It provided for weapons of limitless power whose whole purpose was to prevent their ever having to be used. It called for ceaseless preparations for a war whose prevention was the preparations' whole aim.

This arrangement was what opened up the fissure dividing image and substance which characterized American policy in the Vietnam years. The United States, blocked by nuclear dread from using its military forces on a scale commensurate with its global aims, began to use its power to strike poses and manufacture images. In the strategy of deterrence, the very survival of mankind was made to depend upon an image. An image, however, was a distressingly undependable thing on which to rest the species' hope of escaping extinction. And the image that was required in this case was even more undependable than most. In the first place, the system of deterrence was aimed at producing an impression of certainty in the minds of America's foes about the mental state of the American people; and mental states are inherently obscure. In the second place, the mental state involved was a future one, concerning what the United States *would* do *if* such-and-such a train of events chanced to occur; and therefore it was highly change-able. And, in the third place, the future mental state to be depicted in the image was a willingness to risk destroying the human race, and this willingness was in its very nature open to question. The policy-makers might declare their willingness to "face up to the risks of Armageddon," but the meaning of such a declaration was far from transparent. After all, what *did* it mean to "face up" to the extinction of the race? And what did their willingness say about the men who declared it? Clearly, this intention was one of the least "credible" ones imaginable. The doubts became especially keen as soon as one tried to imagine what a president really would do once the Soviet Union had launched a first strike—once deterrence had failed. Would he retal-iate, out of pure revenge, and risk completing the annihilation of the human race for no reason? And if he would not, then what became of the doctrine of credibility, which rested on the assumption that the president would do just that? Since the whole system was so shaky, with its cross-currents of belligerence and dread of annihilation, it was perhaps not surprising that the strategists turned in any direction they could, including the direction of limited war, to find theatres where the crucial but elusive quantity of "credibility" might be demonstrated. Certainly limited wars were among the last places where the appearance of "weakness or indecision," which Taylor feared so much could be tolerated. For, in this system, if the credi-bility of American power should be destroyed in a limited war, then the middle ground between global extinction and global totalitari-anism would be lost, and the government would be forced once again to choose between the risk of giving the Soviet leaders "a blank check" and the risk of committing suicide.

———

In considering the origins and the character of the war in Vietnam, the extent of the theoretical preparations for limited war in general must be kept in mind. Today, the notion that the war was a "quagmire" into which successive administrations were sucked, against their will, has won wide acceptance. The metaphor is apt insofar as it refers to the policymakers' undoubted surprise, year after year, at the way their policies were turning out in Vietnam, and to the evident reluctance of both President Kennedy and President Johnson to get involved there; but it is misleading insofar as it suggests that the United States merely stumbled into the war, without forethought or planning. In 1960, Taylor recommended the establishment of a "Limited War Headquarters"— and this was before the nation began fighting in Vietnam. Rarely has such a large body of military theory been developed in advance of an outbreak of hostilities. The war in Vietnam was, in a sense, a theorists' war *par excellence*. The strategists of the late nineteen-fifties were only slightly interested in the question of which country or countries might be the scene of a limited war. When they turned their attention to questions of geography—which they did only rarely—they tended to speak blurrily of "peripheral areas" around the Soviet Union and China which stretched from Japan, in the east, through India and the Middle East, in the south, to Europe, in the west. A reader in the nineteen-seventies of Kissinger's and Taylor's books is struck by how seldom Vietnam is mentioned. Today, the very word "Vietnam" is so rich in association and so heavily laden with historical significance that an atmosphere of inevitability—almost of fate—hangs over it, and it is difficult to imagine oneself back in a time when few Americans even knew of that nation's existence. Instead of speaking in terms of particular wars, whether in Vietnam or elsewhere, the theorists tended to speak in terms of types of wars. One type that came under discussion was limited nuclear war. The strategists drew a sharp distinction between limited nuclear war and all-out nuclear war. Kissinger devoted a chapter of *Nuclear Weapons and Foreign Policy* to limited nuclear war. What might be called the fear of the fear of nuclear weapons was one of the keystones of the policy he was proposing, and he wrote, "The greater the horror of our destructive capabilities, the less certain has it become that they will in fact be used"—a situation that he evidently contemplated with alarm, for he saw it as undermining American credibility. The use of nuclear weapons in limited war, he thought, would help to overcome this dangerous uncertainty. As he put it, "in this task of posing the maximum *credible* threat, limited nuclear war seems a more suitable deterrent than conventional war." Another way he suggested of combatting the paralyzing effect of the fear of nuclear arms was to fashion "a diplomacy which seeks to break down the atmosphere of special horror which now surrounds the use of nuclear weapons, an atmosphere which has been created in part by skillful Soviet 'ban-the-bomb' propaganda." Kissinger, however, was not strictly consistent on this point, for it had been precisely the "special horror" of nuclear weapons which had inspired him in the first place to recommend the shift from the policy of massive retaliation to the policy of limited war, and in another passage in *Nuclear Weapons and Foreign Policy* he wrote that "a thermonuclear attack may . . . become the symbol of the vanity of all human strivings"—a statement that might be thought to add to the atmosphere of "special horror" surrounding nuclear weapons. Another type of limited war that the new strategists recommended would rely on conventional forces that could be flown to troubled areas around the globe at a moment's notice in a fleet of special transport planes, whose construction the strategists counselled. In virtually all the planning for limited war, the speed of the American reaction was seen as crucial. The strategists of the time apparently believed that limited war would be not only limited but short.

Once one has worked out the strategy and the goals of a war, and has gone as far as to contemplate setting up a "headquarters" from which to fight it, the step to actual hostilities is not necessarily a very large one; in the early nineteen-sixties the abstractions in Kissinger's and Taylor's books came to life in the hostilities in Vietnam. John Kennedy found the arguments of the limited-war strategists persuasive, and in February of 1960, while he was still a senator, he stated, "Both before and after 1953 events have demonstrated that our nuclear retaliatory power is not enough. It cannot deter Communist aggression which is too limited to justify atomic war. It cannot protect uncommitted nations against a Communist takeover using local or guerrilla forces. It cannot be used in so-called brushfire peripheral wars. In short, it cannot prevent the Communists from gradually nibbling at the fringe of the free world's territory and strength, until our security has been steadily eroded in piecemeal fashion—each Red advance being too small to justify massive retaliation, with all its risks. . . . In short, we need forces of an entirely different kind to keep the peace against limited aggression, and to fight it, if deterrence fails, without raising the conflict to a disastrous pitch." Kennedy was saying that the limited-war forces would accomplish the two great objectives of policy that Kissinger and Taylor had set forth in their books: the prevention of global totalitarianism and the prevention of human extinction. By using limited forces to push back "limited aggression," the United States would be able to oppose the spread of Communism, and at the same time avoid confrontation at the brink. Kennedy, moreover, had become persuaded that the outcome of a limited war would be important not only for tangible objectives that might be attained but for the psychological objective of demonstrating America's "will" to oppose Communism, and after he became president he often referred to the hostilities in Vietnam as a "test case" of America's determination to protect its allies.

The spirit of the Kennedy administration was activist, and the policymakers set about their tasks in a mood of high excitement. In April of 1961, three months after his inauguration, Kennedy made a speech to the American Society of Newspaper Editors in which he defined the nature of the challenge that lay ahead:

> We face a relentless struggle in every corner of the globe that goes far beyond the clash of armies or even nuclear armaments. The armies are there, and in large number. The nuclear armaments are there. But they serve primarily as the shield behind which subversion, infiltration, and a host of other tactics steadily advance, picking off vulnerable areas one by one. . . . We dare not fail to see the insidious nature of this new and deeper struggle. We dare not fail to grasp the new concepts, the new tools, the new sense of urgency we will need to combat it—whether in Cuba or South Vietnam. . . . The message of Cuba, of Laos, of the rising din of Communist voices in Asia and Latin America—these messages are all the same. The complacent, the self-indulgent, the soft societies are about to be swept away with the debris of history. Only the strong, only the industrious, only the determined, only the courageous, only the visionary who determine the real nature of our struggle can possibly survive. No greater task faces this country or this administration. No other challenge is more deserving of our every effort and energy. . . . We intend to reexamine and reorient our forces of all kinds—our tactics and our institutions here in this community. . . . For I am convinced that we in this country and in the free world possess the necessary resources, and the skill, and the added strength that comes from a belief in the freedom of man. And I am equally

convinced that history will record the fact that this bitter struggle reached its climax in the late nineteen-fifties and the early nineteen-sixties. Let me then make clear as the President of the United States that I am determined upon our system's survival and success, regardless of the cost and regardless of the peril.

One of the members of President Kennedy's staff was Maxwell Taylor, who had been appointed military representative of the president, and in the fall of 1961 he was sent to Vietnam to take stock of the situation there. In Vietnam, the strategists of limited war, who had been thinking mainly in global terms, found themselves face to face with the challenge of guerrilla warfare. They quickly set about devising techniques to meet the challenge. Turning to the manuals of the Communist foe for guidance, they came up with the concept of "counterinsurgency" war. Men in the Pentagon began to regard themselves as potential guerrilla soldiers, and soon they were repeating such Maoist phrases as "The soldiers are the fish and the people are the sea." And in the early nineteen-sixties it was not only in the military area that the theories of professors were being translated into governmental policy in the struggle against Communism. During that period, a new breed of professor, trained in the social sciences and eager to test theories in the laboratory of real societies, came forward to offer "models" of economic and social development with which the government could rival the Communist "model."

In spite of all the expertise that was being brought to bear on the war, however, the reports from the field in Vietnam, when they began to come in, were discouraging. The long, sad tale of optimistic predictions followed by military reverses, to be followed, in turn, by increasingly drastic military measures, began to unfold, and by the mid-nineteen-sixties it was plain that the war would be far longer and far more difficult to end than any of the professors or policymakers had foreseen. The theory of limited war had been abstract and general, but Vietnam was a particular country, with a particular history and a particular society, and these particularities turned out to be more important than the strategists had ever dreamed they could be. Awed, perhaps, by the magnitude of America's global power and global responsibilities, the strategists had overlooked the possibility that purely local events, not controlled by a centralized, global conspiracy, might pose serious obstacles to their plans. Yet it was on the local events, and not on the balance of nuclear forces, that the outcome in Vietnam was proving to depend. For Vietnamese life had its own tendencies, which not even the power of the United States could alter. Moreover, the strategic theory had it that human beings behaved according to certain laws—that if people were punished sufficiently, they could be deflected from their goals, even if they had not been defeated outright. Accordingly, the strategists had fashioned a policy known as escalation, in which the level of violence would be raised, notch by notch, until the foe, realizing that America's instruments of pain were limitless and its will to inflict pain unshakable, would reach the breaking point and desist. The Vietnamese revolutionaries, however, did not behave in this way at all. Their will stiffened under punishment. And many Americans at home, too, behaved in an unexpected way. Their will to inflict the punishment began to falter. The material resources for inflicting punishment were indeed nearly limitless, but the capacity of the American spirit for inflicting punishment, although great, did have limits. The stubborn uniqueness of the situation in Vietnam was perhaps even more devastating to the plans of the theorists than the unexpected stiffness of the opposition. It meant not only that the war was going to be difficult to win but that it was not the war they had thought it was—that the United States might have sent its troops into the wrong country altogether. For if the Vietnam War was primarily a local affair, rather than a rebellion under the control of World Communism, then it was not a test case of anything. Then, instead of being one of those limited wars between global forces of freedom and global forces of totalitarianism which the theorists had foreseen in their books, it was just a civil war in a small country.

If the war had been planned only to achieve the tangible objectives that Kissinger assigned to limited war in 1957, the unexpected intractability of Vietnamese affairs and the revelation that the Vietnamese forces were not under the control of World Communism might well have inspired a reappraisal of the American effort, and perhaps a withdrawal. After all, even if Vietnam *had* been the right place to oppose World Communism, only a limited tangible advantage could have been gained there: at best, the freedom of one-half of one small country could be protected. And when the situation had deteriorated to the point where the possible strategic gains were outweighed by the manifold costs of the war effort, a strict accounting logic would have dictated that the United States should cut its losses and leave. In the mid-nineteen-sixties, that point was apparently reached. However, the war was not being fought only for the tangible objectives. It was being fought also for the psychological objective of maintaining American credibility—an aim that was bound up in the strategists' thinking with the prevention of nuclear war and the prevention of global totalitarianism. The war had a symbolic importance that was entirely separate from any tangible objective that might or might not be achieved. The policymakers were divided on many points, but they were united on this one. In both their private and their public statements, they unwaveringly affirmed the absolute necessity of preserving the integrity of America's image in the fighting in Vietnam. For the Joint Chiefs of Staff, the importance of the war lay in "the psychological impact that a firm position by the United States will have on the countries of the world—both free and Communist," according to the memo they sent Secretary of Defense McNamara in 1962. For Assistant Secretary of Defense John McNaughton, writing a memo in 1965, the aim of the war was to "avoid harmful appearances which will affect judgments by, and provide pretexts to, other nations regarding how the U.S. will behave in future cases of particular interest to those nations—regarding U.S. policy, power, resolve, and competence." For President Johnson, in a speech in April of 1965, the United States was in Vietnam because it had "a promise to keep." He went on, "We are also there to strengthen world order. Around the globe, from Berlin to Thailand, are people whose well-being rests in part on the belief that they can count on us if they are attacked. To leave Vietnam to its fate would shake the confidence of all these people in the value of an American commitment and in the value of America's word. The result would be increased unrest and instability, and even wider war." By 1966, the aim of upholding credibility had become virtually the sole aim of the war. In January of that year, McNaughton wrote the memo in which he said, "*The present U.S. objective in Vietnam is to avoid humiliation.* The reasons why we *went into* Vietnam to the present depth are varied; but they are now largely academic. Why we have *not withdrawn* is, by all odds, *one* reason. (1) To preserve our reputation as a guarantor, and thus to preserve our effectiveness in the rest of the world. We have not hung on (2) to save a friend, or (3) to deny the Communists the added acres and heads (because the dominoes don't fall for that reason in this case), or even (4) to prove that 'wars of national liberation' won't work (except as our reputation is involved)." In this memo, McNaughton affirmed the aim of upholding credibility ("to preserve our reputation as guarantor") and specifically dismissed the tangible aims ("to deny the Communists the added acres and heads"). The aim of upholding American credibility superseded any conclusions drawn from a simple accounting of tangible gains and tangible losses, and it dictated that the war must go on, for it was on American credibility, the strategists thought, that the safety of the whole world depended. Secretary of State Dean Rusk wrote in a letter to a hundred student leaders in January of 1967, "We are involved in Vietnam because we know from painful experience that the minimum condition for order on our planet is that aggression must not be permitted to succeed. For when it does succeed, the consequence is not peace, it is the further expansion of aggression. And those who have borne responsibility in our country since 1945 have not for one moment forgotten that a third world war would be a nuclear war." Nor did the question of whether or not Vietnam was the wrong country to be fighting in matter much in this thinking. The fact that the United States was fighting there made it the right country; America's presence in Vietnam invested the war with the global significance that it lacked intrinsically, for if the United States involved itself in a war, its credibility was by that very action placed at stake. An analyst representing the Joint Chiefs of Staff wrote in commenting upon a draft paper of a Project Outline on Courses of Action in Southeast Asia, which had been prepared by a National Security Council "working group," "It is *our* judgment, skill, capability, prestige, and national honor which are at stake, and we put them there." And Secretary Rusk wrote in his letter to the student leaders, "We are involved because the nation's word has been given that we would be involved."

Limited war had been conceived in part as a way for the United States to do bold things in an age when nuclear dread made the doing of bold things—particularly if they were violent things—especially dangerous. But now all hope of *doing* anything was abandoned. That aim was now considered to be, in McNaughton's phrase, "largely academic." What remained was proving something, to friends and foes alike: America's will and determination. The tangible objectives of limited war had been completely eclipsed by the psychological objective. The war had become an effort directed entirely toward building up a certain image by force of arms. It had become a piece of pure theatre. The purpose of the enterprise now was to put on a performance for what John McNaughton called "audiences." In the memo in which he mentioned the need to avoid harmful appearances, he went on to say, "In this connection, the relevant audiences are the Communists (who must feel strong pressures), the South Vietnamese (whose morale must be buoyed), our allies (who must trust us as 'underwriters'), and the U.S. public (which must support our risk-taking with U.S. lives and prestige)." The triumph of the doctrine of credibility had introduced into the actual conduct of the war the gap between image and substance which characterized the doctrine of nuclear deterrence. The whole aim of having a nuclear retaliatory force for deterrence was to create an image of the United States as a nation not to be trifled with, and so to forestall challenges that could lead to a nuclear holocaust. Now a real and bloody war was being fought for precisely the same end. As the paper of the National Security Council "working group" put it, the loss of South Vietnam could lead to "the progressive loss of other areas or to taking a stand at some point where there would almost certainly be major conflict and perhaps the great risk of nuclear war." Those who were opposed to the war tirelessly pointed out the disparity between the Johnson administration's depiction of South Vietnam as a free country battling international Communist aggression and their own impression that the South

Vietnamese government was a corrupt dictatorship that, supported by foreign arms and foreign money, was fighting a civil war against indigenous Communist forces. What those opposed to the war did not know was that the Johnson administration had largely lost interest in Vietnam *per se*. What primarily interested the Johnson administration from the mid-sixties on was not what was going on in Vietnam but how what was going on in Vietnam was perceived by what the Joint Chiefs referred to as the "countries of the world." In fact, so important were appearances in the official thinking that as things went from bad to worse on the battlefield the policymakers began to dream of completely separating the nation's image from what happened in the war, in order that even in the face of failure the desired image of American "will" might be preserved. The effort to rescue the national image from the debacle conditioned the tactics of the war from the mid-nineteen-sixties on. On one occasion in 1965, McGeorge Bundy, a special assistant to the president for national-security affairs, discussing a plan for "*sustained reprisal* against North Vietnam," wrote, "It may fail. . . . What we can say is that even if it fails, the policy will be worth it. At a minimum, it will damp down the charge that we did not do all that we could have done, and this charge will be important in many countries, including our own. Beyond that, a reprisal policy—to the extent that it demonstrates U.S. willingness to employ this new norm in counterinsurgency—will set a higher price for the future upon all adventures of guerrilla warfare." To Bundy, a disastrous war effort was better than no war effort, because even a disastrous war effort would "demonstrate" the crucial "willingness" to use force in the nuclear age, and so would enhance American credibility. John McNaughton, writing in the same vein in a draft of a memo to Secretary of Defense McNamara in March of 1965, advised, "It is essential—however badly SEA [Southeast Asia] may go over the next

1-3 years—that U.S. emerge as a 'good doctor.' We must have kept promises, been tough, taken risks, gotten bloodied, and hurt the enemy very badly." McNaughton may have been one of the first military advisers ever to suggest that getting bloodied should in itself be an objective of an army in the field. (He was telling men that they must get wounded or killed even though they knew they could not win.) Only in a war fought for credibility could the question of victory or defeat ever seem so immaterial.

The men in charge of the government were struggling to work out what the uses of military force might be in the age of nuclear weapons. The dilemma in which they found themselves was expressed in a memo that Walt Rostow, chairman of the State Department Policy Planning Council, wrote to Secretary of State Rusk in November of 1964, in which he mentioned "the real margin of influence . . . which flows from the simple fact that at this stage of history, we are the greatest power in the world—if we behave like it." Rostow's qualifying phrase "if we behave like it" summed up the maddening predicament of the great power in the nuclear age. For in reality "the fact" that the United States was "the greatest power in the world" was not "simple" at all. It was endlessly complicated, and contained deep, and perhaps irreconcilable, ambiguities. The reality was that the United States could by no means "behave like" the greatest power in the world if that meant acting the way great powers had acted on the world stage in the past. And it was not only idealism or moral scruple that stood in the way (although one can hope that these factors, too, did have a restraining influence) but also the unprecedented destructiveness, and self-destructiveness, of nuclear war. In October of 1964, in a paper titled "Aims and Options in Southeast Asia," McNaughton wrote that the United States must create an appearance of success in its operations in Vietnam in order to show that the nation was not "hobbled by restraints." But, whatever appearance the United States might create in Vietnam, or anywhere else, the fact was that the United States *was* hobbled by restraints—the very restraints inherent in the possession of nuclear weapons which Kissinger and Taylor had tried to come to grips with in their books in the late nineteen-fifties. Indeed, it was these restraints that had given rise to the doctrine of credibility, which now dominated government policy. It is true that before the development of nuclear weapons powerful nations had sought to cultivate aspects of their power which were similar to what the American policymakers meant when they spoke of credibility. In military affairs, a nation would often make a show of force in the hope of having its way without resorting to arms. The appearance of a gunboat in a harbor might be used to bring a rebellious colony back into line, or a troop movement on a border might be used to deter an attack. But in any matter of the first importance the show of force would give way to the use of force. The situation of a great power in the nuclear age was altogether different. A nuclear power was stuck on the level of show. When nuclear powers confronted one another over an important issue, major use of force was ruled out, since the unrestrained use of force could lead to national "suicide," and even to human extinction. Nuclear powers were in the situation—unprecedented in military history—of always having more power in their possession than they were free to use. The question of "will," which in former times was a question of a nation's capacity for making great sacrifices in order to protect itself, now became a question of a nation's willingness to approach the point of suicide. For the closer a nation was willing to come to that point, the more force it could permit itself to unleash. According to the doctrine of credibility, a nation that wished to have its way in international affairs was obliged, in a sense, to make demonstrations of indifference to its own survival, for it was obliged constantly to show its willingness not just to unleash force on others but to put the gun to its own bead and pull the trigger—its willingness, that is, to "face up to the risks of Armageddon." Perhaps for this reason, policymakers of the time often announced that it was an aim of American policy to cultivate a reputation for "unpredictability." The ultimate in unpredictability, of course, would be to blow up the world, oneself included. Leaving the question of unpredictability aside, the will to victory in the nuclear age was tempered by the realization that victory could be a worse disaster than defeat. This new circumstance had a shaping influence on every phase of the warfare in Vietnam—on the limits of the war effort, on the justifications for the war, and on the atmosphere engendered in the home country by the war. The nuclear predicament forced the great powers to take military action only within a narrowed sphere, and always to behave with extreme caution and trepidation, not because they were weak but because they were too strong, and it taught them to rely more on the reputation of power—on show—than on the use of power. Still, the level of show was not without its possibilities. It provided the military strategists with what they regarded as an entire new sphere of action—the image world, in which battles were fought not to achieve concrete ends but to create appearances. Through actions taken to buttress the image of the United States, the strategists believed, the nation might still lay claim to the "margin of influence" that flowed from being the greatest power in the world. The United States might still have its way in international affairs, they thought, by fighting the admittedly militarily useless but presumably psychologically effective war in Vietnam. The image world was not the world of borders defended, of strategic positions won or lost, of foes defeated in great and bloody battles; it was the world of "reputations," of "psychological impact," of "audiences." It was, in a word, the world of credibility.

———

In the late nineteen-sixties, the war began to come home. The very nature of the war aims made a political struggle in the United States inevitable. Any long war, and particularly one that is poorly understood and is a failure besides, is likely to stir up opposition in the home country. But when the war, in addition, is being fought to uphold the nation's image, the strife at home takes on a deeper significance. When a government has founded the national defense on the national image, as the United States did under the doctrine of credibility, it follows that any internal dissension will be interpreted as an attack on the safety of the nation. The strain of such a situation on a democratic system is necessarily great. An authoritarian government has the means to project a single, self-consistent image of itself to its own people and the world, unchallenged by any disruption from within, but the image of the government of a free country is vulnerable to assault from every side on the home front. In a democracy, where anyone can say whatever he wants to say, and can frequently get on television saying it, the national image is the composite impression made by countless voices and countless deeds, all of them open to inspection by the whole world. It is not only the president and his men who form the image but anyone who wants to get out on the street with a sign. If the Vietnam War was one aspect of the nation's image, then the political process at home was the very essence of the nation's image. After all, in the United States the public, and not the government, *was* the nation. If the standing of the United States as the greatest power in the world was conditional upon its behaving like the greatest power in the world, then the way the public, in its scores of millions, was seen to behave at home was far more important to the national defense than the way a few hundred thousand soldiers were seen to behave nine thousand miles away. The soldiers in Vietnam could hardly demonstrate that America possessed the "will" to use force freely in the world while America itself denied it. When a war is being fought as a demonstration of the nation's "will and character," as President Nixon put it, what better way is there to oppose the war than to mount a demonstration of one's own—a demonstration, for instance, in which thousands of people march through the streets of the nation's capital in protest against the war? What better way is there to oppose a public-relations war than with a public-relations insurrection? The anti-war movement was often taken to task for its "theatricality." The fact is that it was precisely in its theatricality that its special genius lay. The war had been conceived as theatre—as a production for multiple "audiences"—and the anti-war movement was counter-theatre, and very effective counter-theatre. The demonstrations at home, if they were large enough, said as much about the nation's will and character as the demonstrations that the government was staging in Vietnam with B-52s. And the "psychological impact" of the demonstrations at home was probably greater around the world than that of the demonstrations in Vietnam, because the ones at home were voluntary, whereas the ones in Vietnam were backed by the coercive power of the government. Officials of the government often objected that the demonstrations at home undermined the war effort by giving encouragement to the enemy and by spreading demoralization among the troops. The opposition denied the charges, but here the government was probably right. Yet even the government never fully articulated why domestic dissent had such a devastating effect on the war cause. The fact is that the demonstrations at home struck at the very foundation of the larger aims for which the war was being fought. They struck a crippling blow at the credibility on which the whole strategy was based. In considering the shattering impact of the anti-war movement on the government, and the drastic responses of both the Johnson administration and the Nixon administration, it is important to recall that the nation's credibility was not an afterthought of the strategists of national defense but, rather, the linchpin of the deterrence strategy on which the government rested its hopes for avoiding the alternatives of global totalitarianism and nuclear extinction. A blow to the image of "toughness" was not just a blow to the pride of the men in government, or a political setback for them, or a blow to the war policy; it was a blow to the heart of the national defense. The aim of the war was to say something to the "countries of the world" about America's willingness to use force in the world, but the demonstrations at home tended to show the countries of the world that Americans were unwilling to use it. The war was meant to show that America was "tough," but the anti-war movement tended to show that it was "soft." The purpose of the war to say one thing; the anti-war movement said the opposite thing. Some of the demonstrators took to wearing old Army uniforms, as though to parody the real Army; and they *were* a counter-army, which undid at home the work that the Army was doing in the field. (Certainly part of the special bitterness engendered by the war grew out of the fact that while people died in the field for the sake of an image, people at home who were not risking death could effectively undermine the image merely by talking on television programs or by marching in the streets a few times a year.) Under these circumstances, even if the war could somehow be won militarily, the whole purpose of the war would be destroyed: in the process of fighting the war abroad the all-important appearance of a willingness to fight many more wars of this kind would have been lost at home. On the other hand, if the public were to suffer the war in silence, or were to make some show of supporting the war, then even if the war should be lost militarily, the image of a "tough" nation, unafraid to use its power in the nuclear age, might still be salvaged from the debacle, and McGeorge Bundy's "new norm" might yet be established. In fact, if the public were to go on supporting a disastrous policy indefinitely, that might be the most impressive display of will there could be. What could be tougher than a nation that, as it loses one war, is eager for the next? In this war, it was literally true that the battle at home for public opinion was more crucial to the war aims than the battle in the field against the foe.

The uproar at home over the war took the Johnson administration by surprise. None of the theorists or practioners of limited war had foreseen the domestic implications of their policy; their thinking had been restricted to the foreign sphere. President Johnson therefore attempted to cope with his domestic difficulties in a loose and improvisatory—and often a repressive—way, such as when he sent out the F.B.I., the C.I.A., and the military to spy on and harass the opposition. Yet, for all his rage at his opponents, when he saw that his war policy was threatening the fundamental health of the body politic he resisted the temptation to turn an election into a contest between the representatives of order in the White House and disloyal anarchists in the streets; instead, he made his decision to quit political life and offered to open negotiations on the war. Thus, Lyndon Johnson remained devoted to the domestic well-being of the nation, even to the extent of being willing to risk reverses in foreign policy. It was not until President Nixon came to power that the full impact of the war policy made itself felt at home, and put the democratic system in jeopardy. For when President Nixon saw the domestic opposition to the war policy taking shape again, he accepted the challenge: he made national division the principal theme of national politics, and sought to reorganize the national life around the issue of the war and around such issues subsidiary to the war as the news coverage of the war and the protesters' response to the war. And when he saw that the domestic strife was starting to quiet down, he took covert steps to whip it up again: he launched his secret program of "exacerbating" divisive issues. Here was the basic difference between the two presidents. President Johnson, a man of great cunning, vanity, and pride, who had no love for the rebels opposing him, and who was not above deceptions and manipulations of all kinds, and who remained convinced up to the end that his Vietnam policy was correct, nevertheless withdrew from politics and altered his course when he saw that, somehow, his policy was leading the nation toward a ruinous political crisis. President Nixon, when he saw the same crisis mounting, set about "exacerbating" it, and eventually had to be driven from office in mid-term.

The immediate question that the nation faced when President Nixon took office, was, at bottom, whether the president or the people would have the last word in the forum of public discourse. The Constitution required that it be the people, but strategic doctrine required that it be the president. For the doctrine of credibility, once it was challenged, could succeed only if the president was empowered to take sole charge of the nation's image. The democracy could survive, however, only if the people were allowed, in chaotic, uncontrolled democratic fashion, to demand what they pleased, and let the nation's image take care of itself. In fact, the impression that a democratic nation makes on the world can never, strictly speaking, be organized into an image. Image-making is by its very nature calculated and centralized, whereas the democratic process is by nature spontaneous and decentralized. By the time Richard Nixon assumed the presidency, the tension between the public-relations requirements of strategic doctrine and the Constitutional requirements of democratic practice had reached the point where the president had to choose either credibility or the Republic. At first, President Nixon seemed to choose the Republic, for he promised the openness, the decentralization of power, the easing of tempers, and, above all, the withdrawal from the war which a full recovery of the democracy required. But his commitment to the war, and to the doctrine of credibility that was the principle justification for the war, was deep, and before long he was speaking of "peace with honor," and the like, and the domestic strife was revived with a new fury. The president then embarked on his effort—which was to continue throughout his remaining years in office—to make himself the unchallenged scenarist of American political life. Vietnam was one stage on which the credibility of American power was being demonstrated, and American life, if he had his way, would be another. Under his administration, the separation of substance and image which characterized nuclear policy, and had come to characterize the war policy, now grew to characterize virtually all the policies of the administration, including its domestic policies. After all, what was the use of fighting a war abroad to establish credibility when that same credibility was under challenge at home? How could foreign governments be taught to have "respect for the office of President of the United States" when the Americans themselves had not learned to respect it?

President Nixon's anxiety that the powers of his office were inadequate was reinforced by another worry that grew directly out of the nuclear dilemma: his fear that the United States was threatened with impotence in world affairs. The fear of impotence was a recurrent one in his public statements. President Nixon dreaded that the country might "tie the hands" of the president, that it would "cut off the president's legs," that the nation would be turned into a "pitiful, helpless giant." If the separation of substance and image was the form that the doctrine of credibility took, the fear of impotence—of "softness"—was its content. Everywhere the president looked, at home as well as abroad, he saw "appeasement," "passive acquiescence," Americans inclined to "whine and whimper about our frustrations" and "turn inward." In the courts, in the schools, and in the home, no less than in foreign affairs, he saw signs that the will on which everything now depended was eroding. His uneasiness on this score led him to his belief that the Congress, the courts, the press, the television networks, the federal bureaucracies, and the demonstrators in the streets were usurping powers that were rightfully his, and it fed his apparently insatiable appetite for new powers—powers that would destroy the independence of the other branches of the government and cancel out the rights of the people. It also led him to try to attempt to compensate for the lack of will he found among the people with a fierce will of his own, which would operate independently of the people. Some observers tended to see the roots of President Nixon's fear of impotence in the psychological idiosyncrasies of his character, and certainly these abounded. He was, however, far from being the first occupant of the White House to fear that the presidency was in danger of becoming crippled. The fear of executive impotence in world affairs had been one of the deepest themes of nuclear politics for some fifteen years, having been powerfully augmented by the fear of nuclear paralysis which had worried Kissinger as far back as 1957. Indeed, the whole policy of limited war, which became the principal issue between the president and his opposition, had been designed as a means whereby the United States could continue to use military force in a world threatened with extinction—a means whereby "our power can give impetus to our policy rather than paralyze it," as Kissinger put it. Only in the nuclear age was there any question, if one was a giant, of being pitiful and helpless. The Kennedy and Johnson men, too, had argued that the president needed expanded powers if he was to discharge the global responsibilities that were now vested in the office. Moreover, President Kennedy, in his 1961 speech to the newspaper editors, had said that the international challenge facing the

United States would require that we abandon our "self-indulgent," "soft" ways and "reexamine and reorient . . . our institutions here in this community." If a whole succession of presidents seemed to attach virtually limitless importance to their continued ability to wage limited war, it was because in the prevailing scheme of national defense limited war had been assigned the burden of providing what Taylor called the "active" element in American military policy. In this scheme, to deprive the president of his power to wage limited war was to deprive him of the only instruments of force available to him, and so was to paralyze the presidency.

There was one more characteristic of the Nixon presidency which had its roots in the nuclear dilemma: President Nixon's apparent isolation from the world around him. Presidential isolation, like the presidential preoccupation with images and the presidential fear of impotence, had a history at least as long as the war in Vietnam. The fact that whoever was president was alone required to concern himself from day to day with the practical and moral problems of survival while his countrymen thought, for the most part, about pleasanter things was at the source of his isolation. The strategists in the White House regarded the war as one way of "facing up to the risks of Armageddon," but the public remained largely unaware of this function. The fundamental principles of the foreign policy of the time had grown out of an elaborate theoretical structure that was meant to accommodate the two broad aims of opposing the spread of Communism and coping with the risk of nuclear war, but the policymakers, in their public statements, tended to give the aim of opposing Communism far the greater emphasis. The aim of preventing nuclear war, when it was brought up at all, tended to be mentioned only in passing. This anomalous state of affairs, in which the government was cultivating a grim "resolve" to brave the risks of annihilation, and was preparing itself for terrible sacrifices and for getting "bloodied," while the public lacked any such sentiments, was partly of the government's own making. Kissinger had warned in his 1957 book that the policy he was proposing would require "a public opinion which has been educated to the realities of the nuclear age"—by which he meant a public that had been educated to accept the need for limited wars. But no such education ever took place. Instead, the executive branch sent American forces into the limited war in Vietnam by stealth while promising to stay out. One reason for the government's failure to apprise the public of the full importance of nuclear strategy in its war policy may have been simply the peculiar combination of abstractness and horror which made the subject so forbidding to think about. An aura almost of obscenity surrounded the calculations of how many millions might be killed and in what manner, and this may have helped cause public figures to shun the whole topic when they could. Another reason for their reticence, certainly, was the political vitality of the anti-Communist position, which made it very dangerous for any politician with national ambitions to suggest policies that smacked in any way of weakness or lack of resolve in the fight against Communism. It may have been that few politicians felt they could afford to maintain publicly that the dread of nuclear war should in any way be allowed to modify the nation's anti-Communist stand; as a result, a strategy such as the doctrine of credibility, which was in fact inspired in great measure by an enlarged respect for the dangers of nuclear war, had to be presented almost entirely as though it were only an improved method of opposing the Communists. But an even more important reason for the politicians' failure to give the public the necessary education in "the realities of the nuclear age" seems to have been intrinsic to the doctrine of credibility itself. For the doctrine included within it a ban of sorts on giving too much public emphasis to what Kissinger called the "special horror" surrounding nuclear weapons, the reason being that the efficacy of the doctrine depended upon maintaining an image of the United States as a nation that was unafraid to use its power—that would not shrink from "the risks of Armageddon." Too great an emphasis on the "special horror" could itself spoil the image. Therefore, although Kissinger's own appreciation of that horror was apparently great, he felt obliged to counsel a diplomacy that would seek to "break down" the atmosphere of horror. It was, after all, fear of a collapse of the image of strength and will that inspired the government to continue the war in Vietnam for so many years and to enter into protracted struggle with Americans who opposed the war. One might say that it was in the very nature of the doctrine of credibility that it had to be presented misleadingly to the public and the world. For to explain the policy fully would be to undermine it. As a result, in part, of these inhibitions, the government strategists and the public they were supposed to represent began to live in two different worlds, and to cease to understand each other.

In the second half of his first term, as President Nixon went on disengaging American ground troops from the fighting in Vietnam and inaugurated his policy of détente with the Soviet Union, hopes were raised that a spirit of disengagement and détente might come to prevail in the domestic wars, too. It had been these hopes, after all, that carried Mr. Nixon into office in 1968. But just the opposite occurred. The anger in the White House intensified, the president's isolation deepened, and the campaign to humble the Congress, the press, and the other powers in the society which rivalled the executive branch was stepped up. Once again, the public, never having been adequately informed about the imperatives of the doctrine of credibility, had failed to take them into account. For, according to the doctrine, if the president was going to risk American credibility by withdrawing from a war, it became all the more important to uphold credibility on the home front. A period of military retrenchment was no time to allow suggestions of "weakness or indecision" to crop up in domestic affairs. Instead, dramatic and unmistakable demonstrations of firmness were required. And the withdrawal itself could not be rushed or panicky. It would have to be stately and slow. It would have to be accompanied by many awesome displays of unimpaired resolve—displays such as the invasion of Cambodia, the invasion of Laos, the mining of the ports of North Vietnam, and the carpet-bombing of North Vietnam in the Christmas season of 1972. In an era in which the president was haunted by a fear of seeming impotent, a withdrawal was the most delicate of operations. Under no circumstances could it be allowed to appear an expression of weakness or loss of will. The Nixon administration's resolution of its dilemma was the one suggested by John McNaughton and McGeorge Bundy years earlier—that of trying to maintain an image of toughness in the face of failure by mounting futile but tough-seeming military campaigns. McNaughton had written in 1965 that it was important for the United States to get bloodied even as it failed in Vietnam, and this is exactly what happened. The United States did fail in Vietnam, and it did get bloodied, in Vietnam and at home as well.

If withdrawal from ground operations in Vietnam increased the pressures for militancy in other spheres of presidential action, the policy of détente increased them even more. The apparent contradiction between the militancy both in Vietnam and at home and the spirit of friendly cooperation at the summit conferences with the Russians and the Chinese baffled the public. For a moment, as President Nixon proclaimed that "America's flag flies high over the ancient Kremlin fortress" while Americans were dying in Southeast Asia in an attempt to counter the Kremlin's influence, the fighting in Vietnam came to look like something without precedent in military history: a war in which the generals on the opposing sides had combined into a joint command. But President Nixon's split policy was in keeping with the fundamental requirements of American strategy as they had been conceived by men in the White House at least since the time of President Kennedy. Throughout the sixties and the early seventies, White House strategists had sought to balance each move toward peace in the nuclear sphere with militancy in other spheres of competition with the Communists. In the early nineteen-sixties, the move toward peace in the nuclear sphere came in the shift from the provocative doctrine of massive retaliation to the passive doctrine of nuclear deterrence, and the balancing display of anti-Communism came in the adoption of the aggressive strategy of limited war. Now, in the early nineteen-seventies, an administration was once again taking a step away from the brink in the nuclear sphere—this time by its conclusion of agreements on the limitation of strategic arms at the Moscow summit meeting of May, 1972—and was once again seeking out other spheres in which to shore up the president's reputation as a fierce anti-Communist: to give him opportunities for the expression of his "ruthless" side, to quote the fourth, and final, draft of the speech by Kissinger to Soviet Communist Party Secretary Leonid Brezhnev a few weeks before the summit meeting. In the framework of Kissinger's thinking, it made perfect sense to move toward the summit, and so toward peace, in the sphere of direct relations with the Soviet Union while simultaneously moving toward confrontation, and so toward intensified war, in the sphere of Vietnam policy. As far back as 1957, Kissinger had noted and deplored "the notion that war and peace, military and political goals, were separate and opposite." Now, under his guidance, war and peace were being pursued simultaneously. At the summit, the president would work for a relaxation of nuclear tension (what he now called a "generation of peace"), and in the "peripheral areas" he would continue to make demonstrations of his credibility (what he now called "respect for the office of President of the United States").

There were political considerations to be weighed, too. Although the politics of nuclear strategy were nothing if not complex, one broad rule seemed to be that the political right tended to give greater weight to the fear of global Communist totalitarianism and the political left tended to give greater weight to the fear of human extinction. The right, therefore, tended to favor policies allowing for the free use of military force, and the left tended to favor policies calling for military restraint. The Kennedy policy, belligerent as it was, conformed to this political rule. His administration was slightly to the left of the Eisenhower administration, and, accordingly, his military strategy gave a larger place to the fear of nuclear weapons than Eisenhower's had. The same split appeared—though in a different political context—in the presidential contest of 1964, when President Johnson campaigned as a proponent of restraint in Vietnam and Senator Barry Goldwater campaigned as a proponent of a quick victory. For a man on the right, the political danger lay in seeming oblivious of the danger of nuclear war—as Goldwater then learned. For a man on the left, however, the political danger lay in appearing to have a "soft" attitude toward Communism. From a political point of view, therefore, the course followed by President Johnson in 1964 was probably the most advantageous that could have been devised at the time. By escalating the war somewhat during the campaign, he headed off the charge that he was soft on Communism, and by vowing that he would never take precipitate military action of the kind that Goldwater seemed to be recommending he signalled his determination to avoid a nuclear war. What the public did not know was that this apparently sensible middle course had dangers of its own—dangers that became clear soon after Johnson had been elected to office. President Nixon, too, saw himself as charting a middle course in his dealings with the Communist adversary. During his years in office, it became a cliché to point out that only a seemingly determined anti-Communist like President Nixon could afford the political risks of visiting China and of establishing a policy of détente with the Soviet Union. But even President Nixon, with his impeccable anti-Communist credentials, nevertheless felt obliged to reaffirm his militancy, and he and other members of his administration often hinted darkly to journalists that a "humiliating defeat" in Vietnam might lead to a dangerous right-wing backlash at home. Politically as well as strategically, therefore, the policy of detente created a pressure to find places where the credibility of American power could be affirmed, and in the early nineteen-seventies those places were Vietnam and the domestic politics of the United States.

It has not been the purpose of these remarks to blame theorists of the nineteen-fifties for the calamities of the nineteen-sixties and the nineteen-seventies, or to suggest that when they devised the strategies that would rule American politics in the years ahead they should have foreseen the bizarre events that unfolded. Many Americans found these events all but unbelievable even as they occurred. Moreover, the strategists' attention was concentrated on a dilemma that overarched all particular events. This dilemma—the dilemma of nuclear warfare —remains entirely unresolved to this day. And it can also be said that the combined strategies of limited war and nuclear deterrence still seem an improvement over the strategy of massive retaliation, which to the contemporary eye seems to have been an exceptionally reckless and shortsighted way of handling the question of human survival. On the other hand, it is not the purpose of these remarks to in any way excuse the political actors of the period—some of whom were also key strategists—from responsibility on the ground that they did what they did in the cause of human survival. All governments have their burdens to bear and their decisions to make, and if the heaviness of the responsibilities were to be considered justification for repressive action, no country would remain free. A free country does not place responsibilities in one of the scales and the liberties of the people in the other. It holds to the faith that only in an atmosphere of freedom can the responsibilities be squarely met. Moreover, precisely because the United States is a free country, choices were at all times open to the government in the Vietnam years. At each stage, alternative policies were offered—sometimes by men in high positions in the government. In the Kennedy and Johnson years, the names of George Kennan, William Fulbright, George Ball, John Kenneth Galbraith, and Clark Clifford are among those that come to mind. In the Nixon years, the name of Walter Hickel comes to mind. And, what was of greater importance, millions of ordinary citizens, making use of their freedom, raised their voices to insist that the war be brought to an end. In fact, their voices finally prevailed. And of still greater importance was the broad political coalition that forced president Nixon from office. There is every reason to believe that if this coalition had not been successful, the United States, by then a presidential dictatorship, would still be pursuing credibility in Vietnam. For nothing in the record suggests that President Nixon was anything but dead serious both when he promised President Thieu that the United States would "respond with full force" if the North Vietnamese attempted to take over the South and when he told John Dean, speaking of his struggle with his domestic "enemies," "This is war."

However, if the record of American statesmanship in the Vietnam years, with its sheer mendacity, fumbling, and brutality—not to mention the apparent dementia in the White House which first made its appearance in the Johnson years and emerged fully into public view in President Nixon's last days in office—has a tragic aspect as well, it lies in the fact that in those years the nation experienced the defeat of its first sustained, intellectually coherent attempt to incorporate the implications of nuclear weaponry into national policy. For today it is clear that the doctrine of credibility has failed. It has failed not only in the terms of those who opposed it but also in its own terms. The doctrine of credibility did not provide the United States with an effective means of promoting its interests and ideals at levels of violence below the brink of nuclear war; instead, it provided the notorious quagmire in Vietnam into which the United States poured its energy and power uselessly for more than a decade. The doctrine of credibility, though different from the doctrine of massive retaliation, did not spare mankind from confrontations at the brink between the nuclear powers; far from freezing hostilities at a low level of the escalatory ladder, it led the United States up the ladder, step by step, until, in May of 1972, President Nixon felt obliged to lay down a frontal challenge to the Soviet Union and China by mining North Vietnamese ports against their ships. Finally, the doctrine of credibility failed to enhance American credibility; instead of enabling the United States to "avoid harmful appearances" and to create "respect for the office of President of the United States," it engendered appearances that were supremely harmful to the United States—appearances not only of helplessness, irresolution, and incompetence but of duplicity and ruthlessness—and precipitated a wave of disrespect for a particular president which culminated in his forced resignation from office. Nor did the doctrine of credibility merely fail; it was a catastrophe in its own right, which led to the needless devastation of the Indo-Chinese peninsula and the assault on Constitutional government in the United States.

The only benefit to be salvaged from the experience, it appears, is whatever may have been learned from it, and particularly what may have been learned about the political implications of nuclear weapons—for the Vietnam years do provide the record of an attempt to come to grips with the nuclear question, and of the ways in which that attempt drove two presidents into states of something like madness and led to the near-ruin of our political system. Among the hazards that were translated into reality was one that had been foreseen almost from the start: the tendency for whoever was given custody of the new weapons to gather into his hands a dangerous array of other powers. Something that had been less clearly foreseen was that efforts to bring the weapons under some form of control and to prevent their use would favor the concentration of power even more than the original grant of unlimited authority over their use had done. During the Vietnam years, there were, broadly speaking, two such efforts. The first was the shift from the strategy of massive retaliation to the strategy of limited war, which was inspired, in part, by the "special horror" of nuclear weapons. At first, the shift seemed to mean a reversion to types of warfare which, unlike nuclear warfare, could be brought under the control of Constitutional processes. In practice, however, the war-declaring power did not devolve back upon Congress, for the limited-war power remained a part of the broader military strategy in which the atmosphere of extreme emergency surrounding nuclear weapons prevailed, and the result was that the president gained the sort of discretionary control over conventional forces which he had already been given over the nuclear forces. The potential for immediate abuses was greater in this new grant of authority than in the grant of nuclear authority, for nuclear weapons were all but unusable, whereas conventional forces could be used easily. The second effort to bring nuclear weapons under control was the policy of détente.

Détente, too, was inspired by the horror of nuclear weapons, and it, too, had the effect of extending presidential power. For one thing, it meant that the president was continually moving about on a world stage, and so could utterly dominate the news in an election year. What was more important, though, was that it tended to draw a wide variety of governmental activities into the orbit of nuclear strategy. In fact, there was virtually no governmental activity in America which did not touch in some way on what President Nixon called "the structure of peace." After all, the leadership could ask, did the nation, having given the president the power, at his sole discretion, to effect the extinction of the human race in war, wish to curtail his power to make peace? Having given him the responsibility for framing and executing a global policy that would guarantee national and human survival, did the nation now want a host of others—congressmen, judges, newsmen, even teen-agers marching in the streets—to disrupt the carrying out of its parts? Should we save the Bill of Rights but lose mankind? President Nixon put these questions to the country directly in the impeachment proceedings against him in the spring and summer of 1974. For as soon as he was threatened with removal from office, he repaired to the sanctuary of "national security" and informed the nation that an assault on "the presidency" could fatally undermine "the structure of peace," on which, he claimed, the survival of mankind depended. He wished the country to weigh the crimes of his administration and the dangers they posed for the Republic against the danger of human extinction. In that balance, he thought, the crimes would weigh lightly. He was offering the nation the spurious deal implicit in the conduct of his whole administration: American survival at the price of American liberty.

Another unexpected political danger of the nuclear period which was revealed in the Vietnam years was the tendency for the government to enclose itself in a private reality. To begin with, the subject of nuclear weapons is confined by its very nature to the realm of theory. Since the principal aim of nuclear strategy is to guarantee that the nuclear deterrent forces will never be used, no body of direct experience can ever grow up against which the prevailing theories can be tested. (And probably if the weapons *should* ever be used no lesson will be learned, for the reason that there will probably be no one about to do the learning.) Yet in the postwar period an elaborate body of theory necessarily developed, and it was on the basis of this body of theory that the leaders of the nuclear powers were obliged to determine the shape of world politics. Never before, it seems safe to say, has pure, untested theory played such a decisive role in world affairs. Ordinarily, political men prefer to consult practice rather than theory, and are inclined to seek out men of broad experience to advise them, but on this one matter—the most important matter of all—they have been obliged to depend on the theorists themselves.

In the Vietnam years, the inherent unreality of the nuclear question was reinforced by the particular theories that the strategists relied on in framing their policies. One of these theories was the doctrine of linkage. Two kinds of linkage must be distinguished. One kind was the linkage that was assumed to bind America's foes together into the single force of World Communism. It lost a great deal of its application to the postwar scene when the Russians and the Chinese turned against each other, with each becoming a more resolute foe of the other than either was of the United States, and lost even more of its application during the Vietnam war, when it became apparent that even in small nations the success or failure of a left-wing revolution depended far more on the strengths and weaknesses of local forces than on any "links" with the Russians or the Chinese. (If most of the nations of Eastern Europe were exceptions, that was because in their case the links were not hidden lines of influence but invading Russian armies.) The second land of linkage was the kind that bound all the United States efforts to oppose Communism—or, indeed, to oppose anything or anyone else it might choose to oppose—into a single force. It was here that the doctrine of credibility came to play its decisive role. According to the doctrine of credibility, the president himself was the universal link: he bound all parts of the world together, for wherever he involved himself he placed the credibility of the United States at stake. The reason that American presidents became convinced that a single setback anywhere in the world would jeopardize the whole structure of American power was not only that they believed World Communism to be indivisible but that they believed the credibility of American power to be indivisible as well. And what threatened the credibility of American power—the crucial image of will and determination on which the survival of man was now thought to depend—was not only the Communists but, even more important, the American people themselves. In this struggle, "only Americans" could "defeat or humiliate the United States," President Nixon said in 1969. For it was the *Americans'* "special horror" of nuclear weapons, the *Americans'* scruples about endangering the human race, and the *Americans'* revulsion against pitilessly unleasing the nation's force on a small country that were leaving America "hobbled by restraints," and were preventing it from behaving like the greatest power in the world, and were turning it into a "pitiful, helpless giant." A president determined to uphold American credibility at all costs would have to get free of the American people, and the only way he could do that was to destroy the democratic system that gave the people power over him.

The strategic doctrine of the day therefore drew the nation into a confrontation with itself which was quite distinct from any confrontation with World Communism. It made the country self-absorbed, and distracted its attention from the world—for this internal struggle had an integrity of its own, which did not depend on events elsewhere. Even while America fought a war in distant Vietnam, it was they themselves that Americans were interested in—their own "character," their own "reputation"—and the rest of the world, as far as they were concerned, was, in John McNaughton's words, "largely academic." And, finally, of course, the images on which the whole strategic system rested—the images that were meant to build American credibility—tended in themselves to draw the government into a world of fantasy, for the images, like the theories that had given rise to them, could not be tested against experience. The evidence of their efficacy lay in the impenetrable territory of people's minds. Ultimately, the reliance on images for the national defense drew the government into an interior world in which success arid failure were determined not by visible results but by pure guesswork. The nuclear question, which revolved around the most concrete peril that the world had ever faced, was proving to be an elusive, phantom thing—the province of professors, psychologists, public-relations men, and other mind-readers and dealers in the shadowy, the insubstantial, the half real.

The fact that the inception of nuclear weapons coincided with the launching of a worldwide crusade by the United States against the spread of Communist influence; the fact that the president's exclusive control over the nuclear arsenal tended to concentrate other kinds of power in his hands; and the fact that nuclear strategy enclosed the White House in a hermetic world of theories and images which was all but impervious to real events and which fostered an atmosphere of unreality in the White House—all these were circumstances that belonged to a distinct phase of the nuclear story. The boastfulness, the hypocrisy, the hardheartedness, the obsession with outward appearance and the neglect of inward substance, and the nervous insecurity in spite of matchless power which marred American policy in the

Vietnam years may all be seen as aspects of one contortion in the nation's writhing in the grip of the nuclear dilemma. With the fall of President Nixon and the end of the war in Vietnam, this particular episode in the story of the nuclear dilemma has apparently come to an end, and, with it, some of the special problems of that time may have come to an end as well. What will not come to an end is the nuclear dilemma itself. Nor does it seem likely that the decisive influence of the nuclear dilemma on the American presidency—whatever form that influence may take as time goes on—will come to an end. For the advent of nuclear weapons has done nothing less than place the president in a radically new relation to the whole of human reality. He, along with whoever is responsible in the Soviet Union, has become the hinge of human existence, the fulcrum of the world. He lives and works astride the boundary that divides the living world from universal death. Surveyed from where he stands, the living creation has no more permanence than a personal whim. He or his Soviet counterpart can snuff it out as one might blow out a candle. If presidents in recent years have lost touch with reality, bringing disaster to their administrations and to the nation, may it not be because their grip on what is literally human reality—on the continued existence of mankind—is so tenuous and shaky? When the whole of human existence is trembling in one's grasp, it may be difficult to train one's attention on each detail. And, measured against the extinction of the whole, almost anything that does not contribute directly to the current scheme for survival may seem to be a detail. If President Nixon, then, slipped into the habit of treating the world as though it were nothing but a dream, may it not have been because the world's continued existence did rest on the foundation of his thoughts, his moods, his dreams? And if a false atmosphere of emergency came to pervade White House thinking on every issue that arose, surely it was in part because the men there lived with a vast, perpetual, genuine emergency. And, finally, if the president tended to gather tremendous new power into his hands, to violate the rights of others, to break the law, and generally to ride roughshod over every obstacle, the reason, at bottom, may have been much the same. He had discovered a rationalization without limits in the altogether real aim of protecting mankind from extinction. For what right, what law, what fact, what truth, what aspiration could be allowed to stand in the way of the imperative of human survival, in which all rights, laws, facts, truths, and aspirations were grounded? The first question of the age was how to guarantee survival. Another question was the one that the strategists asked themselves in the nineteen-fifties—how a great power can exercise its influence in the face of the paralyzing effects of nuclear dread. And still other questions that were posed by the ruinous experience of the Vietnam years were how, in the face of the nuclear imperatives, other human aims and human qualities, including freedom and sanity, could be preserved. For thirty years, the burden of nuclear weapons has rested upon the nation with a crushing weight. Their presence has corrupted the atmosphere in which the nation lives, distorted its politics, and coarsened its spirit. The questions they raised have all outlasted the presidency of Richard Nixon and the nation's reaffirmation of its Constitution and its laws. They are questions on which the framers of the Constitution and all other counsellors from other centuries are silent. The questions are unprecedented, they are boundless, they are unanswered, and they are wholly and lastingly ours.

Columns from *Newsday*

MARCH 15, 1992

FINDING MYSELF BEWILDERED in some new way about my reaction to the presidential campaign, I turned introspective for a moment. In a presidential election, the civics books tell us, the voters choose the person they think will be the best president. Yet as the campaign proceeds I discover that I am doing something considerably more elaborate. I am looking at each candidate with two sets of eyes. One set is my own pair: I am asking myself who I think will make the best president, just as the civics books say I should. The other set belongs to all the other voters. Once I have looked at the candidates in these two ways, a process of dickering and horse-trading starts up within me, as if a miniature political convention has convened right within my own mind.

Let me give an example. Using my own eyes, I was drawn to Gov. Bill Clinton's call to "invest in people"—a principle he seems ready and well-qualified to back up with specific legislation. However, I deeply dislike the support he gave to the Persian Gulf war, which I regard as having been a gigantic folly and diversion. On the other hand—closing my own eyes now and starting to look at Clinton through others voters' eyes—I am aware that this support recommends him to most people as president. In the smoke-filled room of my mind, I note that I may be able to get the social legislation Clinton offers if I'm ready to stomach his support for the Gulf War. It seems that I—a simple voter, not a corrupt "politician"—am tempted to compromise my principles even before I get into the voting booth. What hope, then, is there for the principles of politicians, who face all the temptations of power in their quest for votes? We have a word—"pandering"—for the politician who abandons his principles to align himself with a majority of voters. But what is the word for the voter who does likewise?

There is a word for the quality that is supposed to inspire this derivative loyalty—electability. Electability, however, is more than popularity. It is an aura of success—almost a sort of charisma— attracting to the candidate's side all of those for whom success (success in no matter what) is the dominant consideration.

In earlier times, knowledge of what and whom voters might prefer was sharply restricted, for the most part, to hunches. But with the rise of public opinion research such calculations have become a light industry. What is more, by a process that no one has yet described, an apparent rule has developed that political commentators on television must restrict themselves almost entirely to analysis of how well the candidates are doing in the race—of whether candidate X met "expectations" that were set for him in Florida, whether candidate Y did better than before with voters who want politicians to "care for someone like me," whether candidate Z succeeded in "defining himself" or let his opponent define him. (In politics today, it's taken for granted that a "self" is something that can be manufactured by the person who wants one, or even by his advisers.) Rarely is anyone heard giving his own opinion on the merits of a candidate. For example, in this election year I have yet to hear a single discussion on television among supporters of candidates—unless, of course, those supporters were the candidates themselves.

It is this stream of analysis that the campaign propagandists called spin-doctors seek to direct when they offer their self-serving interpretations of political debates and other events. The spinning arts are substance-neutral. The spinners never say that their candidate has the best program for the economy, that he will help the poor, that he will bring world peace. They always say that his campaign is succeeding in making lots of voters think those things. They always say that he is on his way to being elected, not that he deserves to be.

Probably, some compromises by voters are inherent in elections— inherent, that is, in democracy. If a mandate to govern is to emerge out of the votes of tens of millions of people, it seems unavoidable that voters, even as they consult their own judgment and consciences, will cast a sidelong glance at what they think the rest of the electorate is likely to do. The danger, though—greater in our time than ever before—is that in the process an elementary datum of political life will be lost: each individual voter's preference for president. It would be strange indeed if, in our passionate curiosity to know what the will of the people is, we meddled with that will. An election then would produce a result never anticipated by our founding fathers: the choice not of the president the people wanted but of the president that each person thought all the others wanted.

MARCH 17, 1994

By now, any number of observers have demonstrated that the Whitewater affair is not "another Watergate"—much less "worse than Watergate," in the daft phrase of New York's Sen. Alfonse D'Amato. To summarize, there is no proof, or even evidence, that: The president orchestrated the payment of bribes to silence witnesses in court; the president ordered law-enforcement officers not to enforce but to obstruct the law; the president tried to use the CIA to obstruct the FBI; the president used other agencies of the government to punish his "enemies," including those who were investigating his many other crimes; the president presided over a campaign of illegal "dirty tricks" to win re-election; the president ordered the secret wiretapping of journalists and his own aides; White House staff organized a team to carry out numerous burglaries and other crimes. These acts and many more of like character were the basis for the charge, leveled against President Richard Nixon in articles of impeachment, that he had "acted in a manner contrary to his trust as president and subversive of constitutional government, to the great prejudice of the cause of law and justice, and to the manifest injury of the people of the United States." Finally, there is no protracted record of abuses of the sort that made Watergate only the final act in a drive for presidential power that, if it had been left unchecked, threatened to subvert democracy itself. Clinton has not, in other words, waged a secret military campaign (such as Nixon's secret bombing of Cambodia) or a campaign of spying on and disrupting domestic political dissent; nor has he usurped Congress's power of the purse by executive impoundment of funds. (If any constitution was subverted in the Whitewater "affair," it must have been the constitution of Arkansas, since the alleged wrongdoing occurred in that state, before Clinton arrived in the White House.)

The question remains why so much attention is being paid to Whitewater, even by people who have no political ax to grind. Two clichés of the hour suggest an answer. The first is the assertion, made repeatedly on news programs, that on such and such a day Clinton was "hounded" or "dogged" or "pursued" by questions about Whitewater. Characteristically, the story suggests that Clinton wished to draw attention to something else—his health plan, aid to Russia, job creation—but was prevented by the "questions." To give but one of any number of possible examples, Bob Schieffer remarked on *Face the Nation* that during Clinton's recent trip to Moscow he was "dogged by questions about this old real estate deal that he was involved in." But who, we may ask, was doing this dogging? It was, of course, chiefly the press itself. To the self-fulfilling prophecy, the press has added the self-created news story: It asks someone questions, then reports that the person was dogged by questions. (To this, one might add that the person in question was also dogged by reporters reporting that they had dogged him with questions.)

The second cliché is the advice that whatever the truth may be, Clinton now is bound to deal with the "perception" that he did something wrong. For example, Rep. Lee Hamilton (D-Ind.) recently stated that although he knew "of no evidence that the president or the first lady has done anything wrong," nevertheless Congressional hearings on their possible wrongdoings should be held so that the Clintons can "overcome this inaccurate perception." But if hearings must be held to inquire into "perceptions" unsupported by any evidence, who, we need to ask, is safe from investigation? In a world in which the press creates "perceptions" by reporting its own questions as news, and Congress then feels an obligation to hold hearings to test those perceptions, the path appears to open to infinite investigation of anyone and anything whatsoever. No resemblance to Watergate, or to any other misbehavior, for that matter, is required.

JUNE 23, 1994

The apparent surrender of the whole country, led by its gigantic, multiform, all-pervading journalistic apparatus, to the morbid pleasures of the O.J. Simpson story brings to full flower a peculiarly American sickness. The obsession has been characterized by, on the one hand, irresistible compulsion, and, on the other, an obscure but pervasive feeling of shame—even of sinfulness—as when an addict, after a long but futile struggle, finally capitulates once and for all to his addiction.

The remarkable power of the story was put on display immediately, when, even in sports-crazed New York, coverage of the car-chase leading to Simpson's arrest was permitted to knock almost three quarters of an hour of the Knicks' championship game off the air. Another dimension of the response—which itself quickly became a key part of the story—was the appearance on the Los Angeles free-ways of Simpson's fans—people who came out, certainly, as much to be seen by the half-a-dozen television news helicopters overhead as to see Simpson. The television audience, famously passive and faceless, had got up out of its chairs and couches and thrust itself in front of the camera. The loop of electronic coverage was closed: The audience was watching itself.

But what was the source of the undercurrent of moral nausea? Was it disgust at oneself for finding enjoyment in murder? Such enjoyment was certainly present (many people confessed their disappointment that the chase yielded no suicide or shoot-out at the end), but this is an ancient story—as ancient, at least, as the audiences that watched glad-iators at Roman circuses. Was the cause of shame the near-total eclipse of serious news—for example, the nuclear crisis in North Korea? But the eclipse of substance by sensation was scarcely new, either.

The radically new element, it seems to me, was the astonishing resemblance of these extraordinary events to millions of extremely ordinary television programs. Words like "bizarre," and "unreal" were on everyone's lips, but it would have been equally fitting to call the events trite, banal. What could be more commonplace than a car-chase on television? Every element in the tale—the handsome sports star, the beautiful blonde wife, the gruesome murders themselves, the flight from justice, the evidentiary puzzle, even the presence of a Serious Issue (male abuse of women) as a sop to conscience—was familiar and over-familiar to the television audience. Only the fact that the people were real was new.

In recent years, we've become acquainted with the concept of virtual reality. In the Simpson story we see the birth of virtual fiction. Virtual reality is a full substitute for reality (its sights, its sounds, its smells, its feel), composed of artificial elements. Virtual fiction is a full substitute for fiction (its plot, its characters, its spectacles), composed of real people and events. The United States has been perfecting the craft of virtual fiction for some time. The so-called New Journalists, starting with Tom Wolfe and Truman Capote, made their contribution when they decided to render as fact what no journalists could ever really know—the thoughts inside a person's brain. Television followed with docudramas, which add "realistic" (that is to say, false) detail to factual stories. In film, Oliver Stone, who wedded fact and fiction in his rendering of the Kennedy assassination, is the pioneer. The presidency of Ronald Reagan was a giant step forward in virtual fiction: His crew mastered the art of glossing over the political life of the country with pleasing images that had little correspondence with reality ("It's morning in America," and so forth). But the Simpson story is the first full, unconstrained work of virtual fiction. Box office has been tremendous. Indulgence in virtual reality is a kind of betrayal of the real world, inasmuch as it seems to offer the weird possibility of doing without that world. Indulgence in virtual fiction is a worse betrayal, for it surrenders all the machinery of journalism, on which we rely to keep us in touch with reality, to the service of entertainment. The sin is abandoning the attention and care we owe the world beyond our personal horizons. A country that turns to its newsmen for the stuff of fantasy is a country lost in a world of dream.

Land of Dreams

The Nation, JANUARY 11, 1999

ANYONE WHO DECIDES to add his drop to the tidal wave of commentary on the impeachment of President Clinton must acknowledge, at the outset, a built-in difficulty. The very act of writing or speaking about the crisis, irrespective of what is said, tends, by adding to its momentum, to make it worse. Faced with the snowball rolling downhill that is everyone's favorite metaphor (unless it is the runaway train) for impeachment, the writer who tries to stand athwart its path, waving his puny arms in protest, is in danger, as it rolls over him, of becoming an additional particle of its filthy mass. Thus does impeachment, like so many other obnoxious products of the information age, co-opt resistance against itself. Under these conditions, writing about the crisis seems of doubtful use, and one might prefer, if this were possible, to subtract an article about impeachment from the swelling mass than to add another. Editors, however, do not offer the option of unwriting someone else's work.

A similar anxiety accounts for a question that has become a motif of the impeachment debate: whether the crisis is "historic" or not. By threatening to remove the chief executive of the self-described "world's only superpower" (last seen in action cruise-missiling Iraq), impeachment certainly seemed to qualify as the stuff of history. On the other hand, the proceedings entirely lacked the gravity, or grandeur, that we still, for some reason, associate with the historic. On the contrary, they possessed all the grandeur of one of the seamier talk shows. The feeling that we were watching a tragedy kept getting undermined by the suspicion that the whole story belonged in the category of farce, and it was difficult a good deal of the time to know whether to weep or giggle.

There was, in truth, no need to choose. For the essential mechanism of the impeachment crisis has been the elevation of the trifling (sex and lies about sex) to the earth-shaking (impeachment of a president and damage to the constitutional system), and the question that most urgently needs answering is how and why this happened. The most obvious reason is that, for reasons not yet well understood, the Republican Party, which styled itself "revolutionary" when it won control of Congress in 1994, has turned out, to most people's surprise, to be exactly that. ("Conservative" is the last word that would apply.) What sounded like mere bombast in 1994 turned out to be a plan. The business of revolution, let's not forget, is to overthrow the existing government. In 1995 the party merely shut down the government as a tactic to force legislation upon the president. Owing in part to the public backlash, Bill Clinton was re-elected in 1996. This year, in a sort of quasi-legal insurrection, the party has proceeded from shutdown to decapitation, in an attempt to reverse the results of that election.

None of this, however, could have happened were it not for a development that transcends the Republican Party—the creation of the media machine of the information age: the satellite feeds, the hundreds of cable channels, the multiplying sources of "infotainment," and the Internet. These media have supplied the screen (or the millions of screens), unavailable in earlier times, on which the small-bore misdeeds of the Clinton scandal have been blown up to billboard-sized proportions. We have traveled far from the days when the press was symbolized by the underpaid, seedy, hard-bitten, ink-stained wretch with a heart of gold and a pencil in his hat depicted in Ben Hecht's *The Front Page*. A better symbol for today's media would be the six-figure-earning, deceptively ingratiating TV interviewer plying celebrities with invasive, intimate questions while wearing an expression of fake concern and trenchancy. And this is not to mention Montel Williams, Howard Stern or Larry Flynt, or any of the other assorted monsters of the "new media"—tails that now wag the dog of American political life.

The framers of the Constitution warned their posterity against standing armies. Better, they advised, to raise armies to fight wars than to find wars to busy armies. The framers did not worry too much about the news media, but in our day the media machine has become a standing army of a kind. This army's need, to be sure, is not for wars per se; it is for any dramatic story to cover. These stories satisfy both the natural craving of the journalistic profession for novelty and excitement and the financial interests of its conglomerate corporate masters, who depend for their profits on high ratings. Most of the time, this machine is underfed. Like many of the largest industries today, it suffers from overcapacity—too many cable channels, too many Web sites, too many talk shows, too many networks, too many mouths dinning into too few ears. Left to its own devices, the world simply doesn't produce enough blockbuster stories to feed this beast.

December 19—the day Clinton was impeached, the Speaker-designate of the House Robert Livingston resigned from his position and the bombing of Iraq entered its third day—was the exception that proves the rule. At last, the supply of stories equaled the demand. For a moment, the machine was able to run on all cylinders. You could feel, behind all the long faces and solemn television talk, the glow of satisfaction of a profession at full employment. The question that needed asking, though, was to what extent the media standing army had created the news it was now so contentedly masticating.

The rise of the new media machine may have fatally tipped a newly endangered balance of power: the balance between fantasy and reality. In totalitarian countries, of course, it has proved possible, through the combination of ideology and terror, to fabricate wholly fictitious realities. In free countries, where terror is unavailable, political manipulators must satisfy themselves with a subtler, more limited and, we trust, milder—but still highly dangerous—variant of this. Even under conditions of democracy, human beings have a well-known capacity to mistake a world of their own making for the real one. In dreaming, for example, we create, behind our own backs, so to speak, a "reality" that we then experience as objective—frightening or arousing or even surprising ourselves with the creations of our own mind. Is it possible that because of the rise of the new media, which have given us the ability to manufacture what we call virtual reality, we are now able, without quite knowing what we are doing, to secrete a secondary world that we are liable to mistake for the primary world given to our senses at birth? If so, the prime need it serves is probably not political at all but the one Freud identified as the chief motive for dreaming: wish fulfillment—a need catered to both by our luxuriously proliferating sources of entertainment and the means of their support, namely, advertisement of consumer products. In our variant of self-deception, pleasure plays the role that terror plays under totalitarianism.

If—supposing that these suggestions are sound—a history of this secondary reality is ever written, a pivotal chapter, I believe, will concern the trial of O.J. Simpson, in which the media, making use of materials offered by the real world, managed to construct a drama indistinguishable from a soap opera. The key moment was, of course, the pursuit of O.J. along the freeway in his Bronco—an episode in which reality furnished a live version of that archetypal scene in movies and television programs, the car chase. At that moment, virtual reality and plain old-fashioned reality were inextricably fused in some new way.

The many commentators who opined that the trial of Clinton in the Senate may be "even bigger than O.J." were speaking to the point. In both stories, highly diverting ascertainable facts mingling sex and crime were presented as, among other things, entertainment. However, there is, of course, a critical difference. The O.J. trial marked the apotheosis of infotainment—the use of factual material to amuse. (If virtual reality is the use of fictional material to simulate a factual world, then the O.J. story was virtual fiction, which we can define as the use of factual material to satisfy the need for a fictional world.)

The Monica and Bill story started that way, too. A factual story became a bigger and better blockbuster than anything any of the ratings-chasers at the networks could confabulate. The entertainment value of the story certainly was one reason the public, though engrossed in the tale, has never taken it very seriously. Only a minority, for instance, has ever thought that Clinton should—or would—actually be impeached. But then the story was given a fateful turn. The soap opera suddenly became serious and real. Against the public's wishes and its expectations, Clinton actually was impeached. The public, which thought it had been watching a mere program and now would have liked to switch channels (perhaps to a football game, which CBS actually offered on a split screen alongside the impeachment debate in the House), discovered not only that the program was going on but that they were doomed to play a supporting role. The whole country found itself trapped inside a television program.

What was now happening was no longer infotainment (the manufacture of dramas out of real events) but reification—the sudden mutation of what the public had taken to be soap opera into something terrifyingly actual. All at once, the fun was over, and the amusing characters in the drama—the rascally president, his hypocritically puritanical inquisitors, the empty-headed ingenue, her comic-book-wicked, treacherous "friend"—were capable of authentic, long-term harm to the United States and its people. O.J. went the way of *Jurassic Park* and *Seinfeld*. Not so Bill and Monica. This sudden inversion of the O.J. process accounts for the dual character, so vexatious to commentators, of the crisis, which now is indubitably real while remaining at the same time false to the core. Never has James Joyce's saying that history is a nightmare—or perhaps we should say a TV miniseries—from which we are trying to awaken been more true than it is today.

It's often said that no one—not the feckless president, not the vindictive Republicans, not the spineless Democrats, not the braying, news-famished media—has come out of the scandal looking good. This accusation, however, overlooks a notable actor in the crisis—the public. It's true that the public had made a modest contribution to the problem by falling victim to a bait-and-switch procedure. The bait was sex and power (the usual stuff), and the public gobbled it down eagerly; the switch, which came with remarkable speed in the wake of the fall's Congressional election (whose results had mistakenly seemed to bury impeachment), was the authentic, if gratuitous, crisis in which the country now finds itself caught.

Nevertheless, if there has been a hero in the crisis, it has been a majority of this same public, which, notwithstanding its pardonable appetite for a sensational story, has in what amounts to an information-age act of mass civil disobedience resolutely chosen reality over fantasy and resisted the stampede to judgment urged upon it by the establishment. (It's almost enough to give apathy a good name.) Here is a very important body of sane men and women whose unbroken ranks give heart—let us all praise the silent majority!—to one wavering, anti-impeachment commentator and can, we may hope, shatter the dirty snowball that is rushing toward us into a thousand pieces.

A Force to Reckon With

The Nation, JANUARY 1, 2001

TUESDAY'S SUPREME COURT decision giving the presidency to George W. Bush, delivered in the dead of night in an opaque, anonymous opinion rendered by Justices who gave no oral presentation from the bench (as they usually do) but instead appropriately snuck out of the Court building through the garage, leaves the country facing a worrisome political future. The damage done to the courts and to the rule of law by the Supreme Court's judicial overreaching into politics and the damage done to democracy by the sudden interruption of a vote count (will the distressing, unprecedented televised image of vote-counters physically putting down ballots they had been examining become the symbol of an era?) have been commented upon by many observers. The politics of the struggle have been harder to assess. From the start, the contest presented a puzzle. Why, when the nation as a whole was prosperous, at peace, and thoroughly unexcited by the candidates, each of whom belongs to the moderate wing of his party, did the two sides wage such ferocious political war? The easy answer is that the campaigns, their huge momentum unchecked by an election that had failed to produce a result, were simply propelled onward into the narrow confines of courtrooms, which therefore became the scene of a disproportionate sound and fury. It was comforting to reflect that the country at large, though entertained by the spectacle, was scarcely concerned about it—refusing, according to poll results, even to regard it as a "crisis." How dangerous could the quarreling be if it was the product of sheer statistical accident and reflected no deep, real division in the country?

As the struggle continued, this sanguine view became harder and harder to maintain. Each party, aided by its army of lawyers, of course was doing its partisan best to beat the other in court, but before long it became clear that something more serious and frightening was occurring. As noted previously in this space, one party, the Republican, was prepared to go to extraordinary lengths, both constitutionally and in the streets, to win. First, the Bush campaign began to accuse Gore of seeking to "steal" the election. Second, the Republicans launched a vitriolic campaign to discredit the Florida Supreme Court when it delivered a ruling unfavorable to the Bush campaign. Bush's Florida manager, former Secretary of State Jim Baker, called the court's ruling in favor of hand counts "unacceptable," and John Feehery, spokesman for Speaker of the House Dennis Hastert, called the judges "partisan hacks," while House majority whip Tom DeLay, speaking the language of war, announced, "This will not stand." Third, Republican Congressional staffers and Bush operatives, led by New York Congressman John Sweeney, mounted the riot in the Miami-Dade County building to stop a recount that looked as if it would favor Gore; the recount did, in fact, stop. Fourth, in an act of remarkable effrontery to democracy, the Republican-dominated Florida legislature organized itself to choose a slate of electors for Bush, whatever Florida courts might say. Fifth, DeLay and others in Congress began to threaten that if Florida did not go the way they liked, Congress might take the matter into its own hands. These latter two steps were the substance of the Republican warning that if the

Supreme Court didn't settle the matter, a constitutional crisis would follow. The Republican message, in other words, was that if they were not allowed to win, there would be a constitutional crisis because they would produce one.

While all this was going on, the promises of bipartisanship that had been such a prominent feature of the Bush campaign were melting away. Such acts as the Florida legislature's decision to substitute its will for the will of the voters and the baseless charge that Gore's legal maneuvering constituted theft of the election hardly showed a bipartisan spirit. In the meantime, the Republicans in the Senate, which is divided 50/50 with the Democrats, refused any institutional power-sharing arrangement and elected some of their most conservative members as leaders. DeLay said that with the Republicans in charge of all three branches of government they would "set the agenda," and Senator Phil Gramm of Texas announced, "I have been waiting all my life for a Republican president and a Republican Congress." Something of what this resolve meant on the practical level was revealed in a number of news stories. The *Los Angeles Times* reported that the Republican hard right was gearing up to staff the White House and the courts with its members. "Most people are focusing on fumigating the Justice Department," said Grover Norquist, president of Americans for Tax Reform. Meanwhile, the tide of money on which Bush floated to the White House was rising to the rafters in Republican Washington. For instance, the contest within the Republican Party for the chairmanship of the House Commerce Committee is, in the words of Lizette Alvarez of the *New York Times*, between Billy Tauzin of Louisiana, "who is more closely allied to the Baby Bells," and Michael Oxley of Ohio, who is allied "to the long distance carriers." The *Wall Street Journal* notes that "a veritable bidding war erupted last year, as several candidates for chairmanships . . . raised millions of dollars for

GOP Congressional candidates." Now Hastert, fearful of cutting short the bidding war, has, according to legislators, been staying "'mum' on how chairmanships will be decided."

It is true that the extreme actions of the Republicans during the postelection crisis did not find much active support among the people (a majority of whom consistently favored the Florida recount), just as the party's impeachment effort a year ago failed to find such support. As we can now see, however, it is a mistake to suppose that political extremism is dangerous only if backed by popular fervor. The Republicans' impeachment campaign failed. But their postelection campaign succeeded. The Republicans, though enjoying the slenderest of legislative margins, will, as DeLay triumphantly pointed out, be in charge of the presidency and both houses of Congress. To this, in view of the recent ruling, it's tempting to add the judiciary. Popular support is the currency of democracy, but it is not the only currency. History shows that militant, highly organized, tightly disciplined parties can have their way even in the midst of apathy—or, perhaps, especially in the midst of apathy. Power, as the founders of this country well knew, is a mighty temptation. Money is another. Put the two together, and you have a force to reckon with.

A Hole in the World

THE NATION, OCTOBER 1, 2001

ON TUESDAY MORNING, a piece was torn out of our world. A patch of blue sky that should not have been there opened up in the New York skyline. In my neighborhood—I live eight blocks from the World Trade Center—the heavens were raining human beings. Our city was changed forever. Our country was changed forever. Our world was changed forever.

It will take months merely to know what happened, far longer to feel so much grief, longer still to understand its meaning. It's already clear, however, that one aspect of the catastrophe is of supreme importance for the future: the danger of the use of weapons of mass destruction, and especially the use of nuclear weapons. This danger includes their use by a terrorist group but is by no means restricted to it. It is part of a larger danger that has been for the most part ignored since the end of the Cold War.

Among the small number who have been concerned with nuclear arms in recent years—they have pretty much all known one another by their first names—it was commonly heard that the world would not return its attention to this subject until a nuclear weapon was again set off somewhere in the world. *Then,* the tiny club said to itself, the world would awaken to its danger. Many of the ingredients of the catastrophe were obvious. The repeated suicide-homicides of the bombers in Israel made it obvious that there were people so possessed by their cause that, in an exaltation of hatred, they would do anything in its name. Many reports—most recently an article in the *New York Times* on the very morning of the attack—reminded the public that the world was awash in nuclear materials and the wherewithal for other weapons of mass destruction. Russia is bursting at the seams with these materials. The suicide bombers and the market in nuclear materials was that two-plus-two that points toward the proverbial necessary four. But history is a trickster. The fates came up with a horror that was unforeseen. No one had identified the civilian airliner as a weapon of mass destruction, but it occurred to the diabolical imagination of those who conceived Tuesday's attack that it could be one. The invention illumined the nature of terrorism in modern times. These terrorists carried no bombs—only knives, if initial reports are to be believed. In short, they turned the tremendous forces inherent in modern technical society—in this case, Boeing 767s brimming with jet fuel—against itself.

So it is also with the more commonly recognized weapons of mass destruction. Their materials can be built the hard way, from scratch, as Iraq came within an ace of doing until stopped by the Gulf War and as Pakistan and India have done, or they can be diverted from Russian, or for that matter American or English or French or Chinese, stockpiles. In the one case, it is nuclear know-how that is turned against its inventors, in the other it is their hardware. Either way, it is "blowback"—the use of a technical capacity against its creator—and, as such, represents the pronounced suicidal tendencies of modern society.

This suicidal bent—nicely captured in the name of the still current nuclear policy "mutual assured destruction"—of course exists in forms even more devastating than possible terrorist attacks. India and

Pakistan, which both possess nuclear weapons and have recently engaged in one of their many hot wars, are the likeliest candidates. Most important—and most forgotten—are the some 30,000 nuclear weapons that remain in the arsenals of Russia and the United States. The Bush administration has announced its intention of breaking out of the antiballistic missile treaty of 1972, which bans antinuclear defenses, and the Russians have answered that if this treaty is abandoned the whole framework of nuclear arms control built up over thirty years may collapse. There is no quarrel between the United States and Russia that suggests a nuclear exchange between them, but accidents are another matter, and, as Tuesday's attack has shown, the mood and even the structure of the international order can change overnight.

What should be done? Should the terrorists who carried out Tuesday's attacks be brought to justice and punished, as the president wants to do? Of course. Who should be punished if not people who would hurl a cargo of innocent human beings against a fixed target of other innocent human beings? (When weighing the efficiency—as distinct from the satisfaction—of punishment, however, it is well to remember that the immediate attackers have administered the supposed supreme punishment of death to themselves.) Should further steps be taken to protect the country and the world from terrorism, including nuclear terrorism? They should. And yet even as we do these things, we must hold, as if to life itself, to a fundamental truth that has been known to all thoughtful people since the destruction of Hiroshima: *There is no technical solution to the vulnerability of modern populations to weapons of mass destruction.* After the attack, Secretary of Defense Rumsfeld placed U.S. forces on the highest state of alert and ordered destroyers and aircraft carriers to take up positions up and down the coasts of the United States. But none of these measures can repeal the vulnerability of modern society to its own inventions, revealed by that heart-breaking gap in the New York skyline. This, obviously, holds equally true for that other Maginot line, the proposed system of national missile defense. Thirty billion dollars is being spent on intelligence annually. We can assume that some portion of that was devoted to protecting the World Trade Center after it was first bombed in 1993. There may have been mistakes—maybe we'll find out—but the truth is that no one on earth can demonstrate that the expenditure of even ten times that amount can prevent a terrorist attack on the United States or any other country. The combination of the extraordinary power of modern technology, the universal and instantaneous spread of information in the information age, and the mobility inherent in a globalized economy prevents it.

Man, however, is not merely a technical animal. Aristotle pointed out that we are also a political animal, and it is to politics that we must return for the solutions that hold promise. That means returning to the treaties that the United States has recently been discarding like so much old newspaper—the one dealing, for example, with an International Criminal Court (useful for tracking down terrorists and bringing them to justice), with global warming and, above all, of course, with nuclear arms and the other weapons of mass destruction, biological and chemical. The United States and seven other countries now rely for their national security on the retaliatory execution of destruction a millionfold greater than the Tuesday attacks. The exit from this folly, by which we endanger ourselves as much as others, must be found. Rediscovering ourselves as political animals also means understanding the sources of the hatred that the United States has incurred in a decade of neglect and, worse, neglect of international affairs—a task that is highly unwelcome to many in current circumstances but nevertheless is indispensable to the future safety of the United States and the world.

It would be disrespectful of the dead to in any way minimize the catastrophe that has overtaken New York. Yet at the same time we must keep room in our minds for the fact that it could have been worse. To lose two huge buildings and the people in them is one thing; to lose all of Manhattan—or much, much more—is another. The emptiness in the sky can spread. We have been warned.

Disarmament Wars

The Nation, FEBRUARY 25, 2002

LONG BEFORE THE atomic bomb turned night into day in the desert of Alamogordo in July 1945, it was an idea in the minds of scientists, who deeply pondered the political and moral dilemma they were about to impose on the world. With few exceptions, they arrived at a basic conclusion. The great physicist Niels Bohr articulated it well when he said, "We are in a completely new situation that cannot be resolved by war." The reasons were clear and inescapable. In the first place, thanks to the unlimited destructive power of nuclear weapons, nuclear war "cannot be won and must never be fought," as Ronald Reagan was to put it much later. In the second place, the knowledge on which the bomb was based was destined, like all knowledge, to spread. In the long run, there would be no "secret" of the bomb. The conclusion was equally clear: If nuclear danger was to be contained or lifted, the task had to be accomplished by political means—above all, by international agreements.

The first and most ambitious of these—the Baruch plan, which was put forward by President Truman and called for the abolition of nuclear weapons—was rejected by the Soviet Union, which then put forward a plan that was rejected by the United States. The arms race that the scientists had hoped to head off began. Nevertheless, for the rest of the century the world followed the scientists' advice: Except on one occasion, no nuclear power used force to stop another power from getting nuclear weapons. The pattern was set in the late 1940s, when the United States declined to launch a pre-emptive attack on the Soviet Union in the years before it got the bomb. In the early days of the Soviet nuclear buildup, President Eisenhower likewise rejected what he called "preventive war." "How could you have one," he said at a press conference, "if one of its features would be several cities lying in ruins, several cities where many, many thousands of people would be dead and injured and mangled?" The pattern held when China launched its nuclear weapons program: Neither the United States nor the Soviet Union launched a pre-emptive attack. The one exception was the Israeli attack in June 1981 on a reactor that Iraq was using in its nuclear-weapons program.

All other attempts to stop the spread of nuclear weapons or reduce existing arsenals have been diplomatic and political. They include the Nuclear Nonproliferation Treaty, which came into force in 1974, the SALT and START treaties, under which the nuclear arsenals of the United States and the Soviet Union, and then Russia, have been cut by half, the Comprehensive Test Ban Treaty and the Anti-Ballistic Missile Treaty of 1972.

In his State of the Union address on January 29, George W. Bush, in one of the sharpest and most significant policy shifts of the nuclear age, overthrew this consensus of more than a half-century. He announced his decision to do just the thing that Niels Bohr said was impossible: to try to solve the nuclear dilemma by waging war. His words left no room for doubt about his intentions. After lumping together Iraq, Iran, and North Korea with the odd locution "axis of evil," he said, "I will not wait on events while dangers gather. I will not stand by as peril draws closer and closer. The United States of America will not permit the world's most dangerous regimes to threaten us with the world's most destructive weapons."

The historic importance of the shift was concealed by the context in which Bush placed it, namely the "war on terrorism." A radically new policy was presented as a mere expansion of an existing one. The segue came when he said that the evil-axis nations "could provide these arms to terrorists, giving them the means to match their hatred." After the fall of the Taliban, much ink was spilled speculating on what "phase two" of the war on terrorism might be. Would the United States chase Al Qaeda into Indonesia, Pakistan, Somalia, Lebanon? Now it turns out that phase two is not a war on terrorism at all but a whole series of much larger wars to stop the spread of weapons of mass destruction—history's first disarmament wars.

The new nonproliferation strategy is in truth only the culminating move in a much broader shift in American policy from diplomacy to force—or to put it more plainly, from peace to war. An accompanying move has been the widely uncommented-upon U.S. exit from the entire structure of nuclear arms control treaties that were built over the past thirty years or so. In 1999 the Senate refused to ratify the test ban treaty. Late last year, the Bush administration gave notice that its continuing reduction of strategic nuclear arms would occur outside any treaty, putting an end to START. A few weeks later, the administration announced its withdrawal from the Anti-Ballistic Missile treaty, the better to build national missile defense. Only the Nuclear Nonproliferation Treaty, to which the United States belongs as a nuclear power, remains intact, and it has never managed to put any constraints on U.S. behavior. Its raison d'être in the eyes of the United States has always been to constrain not the United States but the 182 nations that have agreed to forgo nuclear weapons. In any case, the new Bush policy clearly announces that the true prevention of proliferation is not to be any treaty but American attack.

These policies form a unity: The United States, safe behind its missile shield, will, at its sole discretion and unconstrained by treaties or even consultation with allies (there was no real consultation with the NATO countries on the new policy and no mention of NATO in Bush's address), protect its territory and impose its will in the world by using its unmatched military power to coerce or destroy, if possible by pre-emptive attack, every challenger.

Nothing Bush proposes, however, has undone the elementary truths that led Niels Bohr to warn, years ago, against trying to solve the nuclear dilemma by war. The ABM treaty can be torn up, but the laws of physics cannot. Smart bombs can destroy armies, but not even the most brilliant of them can remove a thought from a person's mind, or stop its conveyance to the mind of another. These are lessons that the world learned, however imperfectly, at the dawn of the nuclear age and that have been confirmed by more than a half-century of experience since. How many wars will be fought and how many lives will be lost before we learn them again?

Imposing Our Will

The Nation, AUGUST 4, 2003

THE UNITED STATES seems to interpret the news these days through a prism of catchphrases borrowed from history. Once, the phrases of the Second World War—"Munich," "appeasement," and so forth—were applied to the Vietnam War, with calamitous results. Now, the catchphrases of the Vietnam War are being pressed into service to describe the war on Iraq: "search and destroy," "quagmire," "winning hearts and minds," "the Baghdad triangle." Because I began my life as a journalist in the latter's namesake—the "iron triangle," a center of resistance near Saigon—I'm perhaps more likely than most to see any American war as "another Vietnam"; but for the same reason I recognize a need to hold the Vietnam-Iraq comparison up to scrutiny. The differences between the two conflicts are large and obvious. In Vietnam, America's enemy had powerful rear-guard support—in the first place, uninvaded North Vietnam; in the second place, the People's Republic of China and the Soviet Union, an acknowledged superpower. Today, the Iraqi resistance has no proven state support, and the United States is the world's "sole superpower." (The rear-area support that is likely to appear over time is international Islamic terrorism—a very significant force but hardly equal to China or the Soviet Union.) In Vietnam, the resistance forces had a half-century of continuous experience fighting colonial occupiers—first the French then the Japanese, then the French again and only last the Americans. Iraq, on the other hand, was an independent country when attacked by the United States. In Vietnam, national consciousness has roots that extend back hundreds of years. Iraq was cobbled together by the British in 1920. The Vietnamese resistance was Communist, but the Iraqi resistance is of unknown political complexion and seems to combine many elements. The Vietnam War was fought to stop the spread of Communism; the war on Iraq was allegedly fought to stop the spread of weapons of mass destruction.

But the similarities are equally obvious, and becoming more so every day. As in Vietnam, conventional American forces in Iraq face guerrilla resistance. As in Vietnam, an end to the Iraq War—a successful "exit strategy," to use the post-Vietnam catchphrase—depends on setting up a regime that can stand on its own and be acceptable to the United States. As in Vietnam, military forces have thus been given an essentially political task. As in Vietnam, political events will be more important than military ones. The politics in question are American and Iraqi. In America, the question is how long the public will endure a steady stream of casualties and expenditures. (Already, polls are showing a sharp drop in public support for the war.) In Iraq, the fundamental question is whether the Iraqi people will accept or reject a U.S.-founded regime. The outcome of the war will depend above all on the wills of the two peoples and their interaction. The more Iraqis hate and resist the occupation, the more Americans are likely to grow tired and force an end to the war, as they did in Vietnam.

The outlook for success is doubtful, and the reasons go deep into history. They are ones that we Americans, of all people, should well understand. We have recently celebrated the Fourth of July, the day we announced our claim "to assume among the Powers of the Earth the separate and equal Station to which the laws of Nature and of Nature's God entitle them." Arguably, the modern principle of national self-determination was born at that moment. Since then, almost every nation in the world has pursued the same path, with the result that the great empires of the nineteenth and twentieth centuries, from the British to the Soviet, have been dispatched to history's ash heap. The passion for independence from colonial rule, which Leonard Woolf called "the world revolt," has proved universal and, what is more surprising, has been all but universally successful. Is Iraq destined to be an exception—a country that, having achieved its independence, now gives it up again to a foreign power?

Not all the differences between Vietnam and Iraq, moreover, are favorable to the United States. For one thing, the stated goal of the war—finding weapons of mass destruction—has melted away. The short war to save America from nuclear destruction has turned into a long war with no clear purpose. For another thing, whereas in Vietnam the United States intervened in support of an existing government, in Iraq it intervened to overthrow a government. True, the government in South Vietnam depended wholly on American money and military power for its survival and had almost no independent source of strength in its own society. Still, it did have the signal, underappreciated virtue of existing: It employed thousands of people, delivered the mail, picked up the garbage. In Iraq there is no such creature. It's not for nothing that conquerors set up quisling regimes. The administration that promised "regime change" delivered only regime smash. In a colossal omission, it forgot that Iraq would after all have to have some sort of government or other.

This is something new. The American combat forces, who had been told that the road home goes "through Baghdad" were hastily enlisted to fill the political deficit. They found themselves trying to repair electrical lines, govern towns, guard banks. But immediately Iraqis, who quickly proved not to be missing the self-determination gene, turned against them, and some began to attack them. A new American administrator, L. Paul Bremer, was brought in to impose a new, tough policy. In his words, "We dominate the scene and we will continue to impose our will on this country." When this strategy, so drastically at odds with any idea of democracy or self-determination, appeared to backfire, Bremer reversed course and decided to appoint the "Governing Council" of Iraq that has just come into existence. Now he seeks to perform a miracle even more remarkable than any that was required in Vietnam—to create out of thin air a regime that will do America's will without the presence of American forces. Today, people are asking how long the United States "will have to stay" until success is achieved, but this masks the more important question of whether the mission is possible at all. The real question may be how long the United States can bear to stay before failure is accepted. In Vietnam, it took more than a decade.

The Importance of Losing

The Nation, SEPTEMBER 23, 2003

THE BASIC MISTAKE of American policy in Iraq is not that the Pentagon—believing the fairy tales told it by Iraqi exile groups and overriding State Department advice—forgot, when planning "regime change," to bring along a spare government to replace the one it was smashing; not that, once embarked on running the place, the administration did not send enough troops to do the job; not that a civilian contingent to aid the soldiers was lacking; not that the Baghdad museum, the Jordanian Embassy, the United Nations, and Imam Ali mosque, among other places, were left unguarded; not that no adequate police force, whether American or Iraqi, was provided to keep order generally; not that the United States, seeking to make good that lack, then began to recruit men from the most hated and brutal of Saddam's agencies, the Mukhabarat; not that, in an unaccountable and unparalleled lapse in America's once sure-fire technical know-how, Iraq's electrical, water and fuel systems remain dysfunctional; not that the administration has erected a powerless shadow government composed in large measure of the same clueless exiles that misled the administration in the first place; not that the administration has decided to privatize substantial portions of the Iraqi economy before the will of the Iraqi people in this matter is known; not that the

343

occupation forces have launched search-and-destroy operations that estrange and embitter a population that increasingly despises the United States; not that, throughout, a bullying diplomacy has driven away America's traditional allies.

All these blunders and omissions are indeed mistakes of American policy, and grievous ones, but they are secondary mistakes. *The main mistake of American policy in Iraq was waging the war at all.* That is not a conclusion that anyone should have to labor to arrive at. Something like the whole world, including most of its governments and tens of millions of demonstrators, plus the UN Security Council, Representative Dennis Kucinich, Governor Howard Dean and this magazine, made the point most vocally before the fact. They variously pointed out that the Iraqi regime gave no support to Al Qaeda, predicted that the United States would be unable to establish democracy in Iraq by force—and that therefore no such democracy could serve as a splendid model for the rest of the Middle East— warned that "regime change" for purposes of disarmament was likely to encourage other countries to build weapons of mass destruction, and argued that the allegations that Iraq already had weapons of mass destruction and was ready to use them at any moment (within forty-five minutes after the order was delivered, it was said) were unproven. All these justifications for the war are now on history's ash heap, never to be retrieved—adding a few largish piles to the mountains of ideological claptrap (of the left, the right, and what have you) that were the habitual accompaniment of the assorted horrors of the twentieth century.

Recognition of this mistake—one that may prove as great as the decision to embark on the Vietnam War—is essential if the best (or at any rate the least disastrous) path out of the mess is to be charted. Otherwise, the mistake may be compounded, and such indeed is the direction in which a substantial new body of opinion now pushes the United States. In this company are Democrats in Congress who credulously accepted the Bush administration's arguments for the war or simply caved in to administration pressure, hawkish liberal commentators in the same position and a growing minority of right-wing critics.

They now recommend increasing American troop strength in Iraq. Some supported the war and still do. "We must win," says Democratic Senator Joseph Biden, who went on *Good Morning America* to recommend dispatching more troops. His colleague Republican John McCain agrees. The right-wing *Weekly Standard* is of like mind. Others were doubtful about the war at the beginning but think the United States must "win" now that the war has been launched. The *New York Times*, which opposed an invasion without UN Security Council support, has declared in an editorial that "establishing a free and peaceful Iraq as a linchpin for progress throughout the Middle East is a goal worth struggling for, even at great costs." And, voicing a view often now heard, it adds, "We are there now, and it is essential to stay the course." Joe Klein, of *Time*, states, "Retreat is not an option."

"Winning," evidently, now consists not in finding the weapons of mass destruction that once were the designated reason for fighting the war but in creating a democratic government in Iraq—the one that will serve as a model for the entire Middle East. Condoleezza Rice has called that task the "moral mission of our time." Stanford professor Michael McFaul has even proposed a new cabinet department whose job would be "the creation of new states." The Pentagon's job will be restricted to "regime destruction"; the job of the new outfit, pursuing a "grand strategy on democratic regime change," will be, Houdini-like, to pull new regimes out of its hat. On the other hand, the Center for Strategic and International Studies, which recently produced a report on the situation in Iraq, thinks a big part of the problem is bad public relations and counsels "an intense communications and marketing campaign to help facilitate a profound change in the Iraqi national frame of mind."

These plans to mass-produce democracies and transform the mentalities of whole peoples have the look of desperate attempts—as grandiose as they are unhinged from reality—to overlook the obvious: First, that people, not excluding Iraqis, do not like to be conquered and occupied by foreign powers and are ready and able to resist; and, second, that disarmament, which is indeed an essential goal for the new century, can only, except in the rarest of circumstances, be achieved not through war but through the common voluntary will of nations. It is not the character of the occupation, it is occupation itself that the Iraqis are, in a multitude of ways, rejecting.

The practical problem of Iraq's future remains. The Iraqi state has been forcibly removed. That state was a horrible one; yet a nation needs a state. The children must go to school; the trains must run; the museums must open; murderers must be put in jail. But the United States, precisely because it is a single foreign state, which like all states has a highly self-interested agenda of its own, is incapable of providing Iraq with a government that serves its own people. The United States therefore must, to begin with, surrender control of the operation to an international force. It will not suffice to provide "UN cover" for an American operation, as the administration now seems to propose. The United States should announce a staged withdrawal of its forces in favor of and in conjunction with whatever international forces can be cobbled together. It should also (but surely will not) provide that force with about a hundred billion or so dollars to do its work—a low estimate of what is needed to rebuild Iraq.

Biden says we must win the war. This is precisely wrong. The United States must learn to lose this war—a harder task, in many ways, than winning, for it requires admitting mistakes and relinquishing attractive fantasies. This is the true moral mission of our time (well, of the next few years, anyway). The cost of leaving will certainly be high, just not anywhere near as high as trying to "stay the course," which can only magnify and postpone the disaster.

And yet—regrettable to say—even if this difficult step is taken, no one should imagine that democracy will be achieved by this means. The great likelihood is something else—something worse: perhaps a recrudescence of dictatorship or civil war, or both. An interim period—probably very brief—of international trusteeship is the best solution, yet it is unlikely to be a good solution. It is merely better than any other recourse. The good options have probably passed us by. They may never have existed. If the people of Iraq are given back their country, there isn't the slightest guarantee that they will use the privilege to create a liberal democracy. The creation of democracy is an organic process that must proceed from the will of the local people. Sometimes that will is present, more often it is not. Vietnam provides an example. Vietnam today enjoys the self-determination it battled to achieve for so long; but it has not become a democracy.

On the other hand, just because Iraq's future remains to be decided by its talented people, it would also be wrong to categorically rule out the possibility that they will escape tyranny and create democratic government for themselves. The United States and other countries might even find ways of offering modest assistance in the project. It's just that it is beyond the power of the United States to create democracy for them.

The matter is not in our hands. It never was.

Learning the Obvious

The Nation, OCTOBER 6, 2003

SOMETIMES WHEN I feel I want to raise my voice against the American folly in Iraq, my zeal is infected with boredom. I get the urge to say that the war in Iraq is worsening the nuclear proliferation problem (Iran and North Korea are speeding up their nuclear programs in part in order to avoid regime change); that there is no proven alliance between Saddam Hussein and Al Qaeda; that we are inflaming the peoples of the Middle East against us; that we are driving away even our traditional European allies by our highhanded policies; that we are making ourselves less secure, not more. But then I realize that these things are by now obvious, and to state what is obvious is boring. I want to say them not because they are fresh and interesting but because they are not heeded. But if to state the obvious is boring, then to repeat it is the very definition of boredom. The point was impressed on me when I read a quotation in the indispensable website Tomdispatch (www.tomdispatch.com) from President George H.W. Bush's memoir, *A World Transformed,* which was written with Brent Scowcroft. Bush was talking about why he did not overthrow Saddam Hussein at the end of the first Gulf War:

Trying to eliminate Saddam . . . would have incurred incalculable human and political costs. Apprehending him was probably impossible. . . . We would have been forced to occupy Baghdad and, in effect, rule Iraq. . . . there was no viable "exit strategy" we could see, violating another of our principles. Furthermore, we had been self-consciously trying to set a pattern for handling aggression in the post-Cold War world. Going in and occupying Iraq, thus unilaterally exceeding the United Nations' mandate, would have destroyed the precedent of international response to aggression that we hoped to establish. Had we gone the invasion route, the United States could conceivably still be an occupying power in a bitterly hostile land.

I couldn't have said it better myself. And this was written five years ago, by the father of the current president. So much for feeling brilliant for insisting upon such things now.

I'm reminded of my experience as one of those who opposed the war in Vietnam. In the mid-to-late 1960s, we tirelessly pointed out that the war was mainly a nationalist rebellion against foreign occupation, not mainly an advance probe of world Communism; that the issue could only be solved politically, not militarily; that the war was weakening, not strengthening, the United States; that the only solution was to withdraw America troops—and so on and so forth. We considered ourselves brave for saying such things, all of which were rejected by mainstream opinion. And yet at that time, too, the antiwar arguments were obvious, or soon became so. Just how obvious is revealed by Kai Bird's excellent biography of William and McGeorge Bundy, *The Color of Truth*. Bird reveals that as assistant secretary of state, William Bundy—widely seen as a Vietnam hawk—confessed in a 1964 paper that "a bad colonial heritage of long standing, totally inadequate preparation for self-government by the colonial power, a colonialist war fought in half-baked fashion and lost, a nationalist movement taken over by Communism ruling in the other half of an ethnically and historically united country, the Communist side inheriting much the better military force and far more than its share of the talent— these are the facts that dog us today." Bird says that in this sentence Bundy prefigured "just about all the points that I.F. Stone, Bernard Fall or other early critics of the war would make within a year."

Even more striking is a conversation in 1964 between President Lyndon Johnson and Richard Russell, chairman of the Senate Armed Services committee. "I don't believe the American people ever want me to [abandon Vietnam]," Johnson told Russell. "If I lose it, I think they'll say I've lost it. . . . At the same time, I don't want to commit us to a war." Russell's answer was a prophecy that turned out to be exact. A full-scale effort would "take a half million men." he said. "They'd be bogged down in there ten years." In short, all the arguments against the war were privately well-known—obvious—to the administration. Yet it plunged deeper and deeper into the war.

Why? There appear to be two closely related answers. One is political. As Johnson's comment hints, ever since the United States had "lost" China to Communism in 1949, it was considered politically fatal to "lose" another country. As McGeorge Bundy wrote to Johnson, "The political damage to Truman and Acheson from the fall of China arose because most Americans came to believe that we could and should have done more than we did to prevent it. This is exactly what would happen now if we should seem to be the first to quit in Saigon." The second answer was strategic. Policy-makers of the day believed that nothing in the foreign policy of the United States was more important than American "credibility." If American power was defeated anywhere, they believed, it might crumble everywhere. The idea of a strategic retreat was ruled out. Both motives, then, had to do with power—in the first place, domestic political power, in the second, global power.

Today, too, the obvious is trumped by the argument of power. The need therefore is not just to produce more facts and better arguments (though those are always needed) but to challenge the powers that uphold illusion. The best antidote is the counterforce of public opinion, which means, in the last analysis, the force of voting. Today, as in Vietnam thirty years ago, it is possible to win this battle. In the Vietnam years, public opinion gradually changed. It drove a president—Lyndon Johnson—out of office. It forced another, Richard Nixon, to end the war, and then he was driven out of office, too. Today, public opinion is already shifting. A recent ABC-*Washington Post* poll records that 60 percent of the public opposes George W. Bush's request to Congress for $87 billion for the war. The antiwar candidate Howard Dean has become the acknowledged front-runner for the Democratic nomination. In some polls, Bush's overall approval ratings are in negative territory. This is the kind of argument that presidents understand.

The question is, How many more people, American and Iraqi, will have to lose their lives to teach our leaders the obvious?

TOWARD PEACE ‖ IV

Introduction to
Letters from Prison by Adam Michnik

Rarer by far than originality in science or art is originality in political action. And rarer still is original political action that enlarges, rather than blights or destroys, human possibilities. The opposition movement in Poland, which remains active four years after the military government of General Wojciech Jaruzelski declared a "state of war" and banned the independent trade-union federation Solidarity, has made, it seems to me, such a contribution to the world. Hitherto, probably the most original invention of our century in the field of politics was, unfortunately, the catastrophic one of totalitarianism, which so hugely expanded the human capacity for organized evil. Now, at last, many decades and tens of millions of lives later, out of the human spirit has been born what has every appearance of being the first entirely fitting response. This response, it is true, may be possible in part because the totalitarian system in question—the Soviet communist one in its Polish version—has moderated considerably since it reached its apogee of brutality, in the days of Joseph Stalin. It is also true, of course, that totalitarian governments have been effectively opposed from without, by other governments—most notably by the Allies in the Second World War, who defeated the Nazi regime militarily and then dissolved it. But now a totalitarian government has summoned forth a powerful antagonist from within its own body politic. The Polish self-limiting revolution, as it has been called—self-limiting because, although it enjoyed the overwhelming support of the Polish public, it held back from attempting to overthrow the government—has many novel features. There is the crucial full-scale and sustained participation of the working class. There is the alliance of the secular opposition and the Catholic Church. There is the dedication to liberty, and the movement's internal democracy. But more important, perhaps, than any of these features has been the discovery of a new style of action—one that contributed greatly to making them all possible. Though schooled in opposition to totalitarian rule, the Polish movement has not grown to resemble its opponent; its answer to totalitarian violence and deception has not been violence and deception with some new twist, some new political coloration. Instead, in a radical break, it has ceded those ageless instruments completely to its governmental foe, and sought its strength in altogether different sources, including, above all, the multitudinous peaceful activities of a normal civic life. In doing so, it has departed not only from totalitarian practices but from the violent practices of most other revolutions. Some people have questioned whether the Polish opposition movement really amounts to a revolution. Inasmuch as it has not overthrown, or even sought to overthrow, the state, it might be said to have fallen short. Yet, as though to make up for that deficiency, it has been all the more thorough in other areas of life—the social, the cultural, the moral, and even the spiritual. In no area, however, has it been more thorough than in the area of its own practices, which constitute nothing less than a new chapter in the history of revolution. In that respect, it is not just a revolution; it is a revolution in revolution. The revolution began, suddenly and spectacularly, in August of 1980; then, in December of 1981, Solidarity, its organized arm, was outlawed and driven underground; since then, the revolution has bubbled up again in many forms, sometimes more vigorously than ever, though without again achieving dramatic organized expression at the national level. The revolution's ultimate achievement for Poland has yet to be revealed, but for the world at large the chapter of political history that has already been written is the record of an abundance of inventions and discoveries in political and moral life which no subsequent events can erase. Poland still paces up and down in its geopolitical cage, but through the bars it has already passed these inestimable gifts to the rest of us.

Among the voices that speak to us from Poland today, the most important may be that of Adam Michnik. He offers a prediction and some advice:

> I . . . believe that the totalitarian dictatorships are doomed. By now, no one gives credence to their mendacious promises. They still have the power to jail and kill, but almost no other power. I say "almost" because (alas) there still remains their ability to infect us with their own hatred and contempt. Such infection must be resisted with our whole strength, for of all the struggles we face this is the most difficult.

Michnik now sits in a jail belonging to the totalitarian regime, yet his first concern—and herein lies one of the keys to his thinking, and, one should add, to his character—is with the quality of his own conduct, which, together with the conduct of other victims of the present situation, will, he is sure, one day set the tone for whatever political system follows the totalitarian debacle. His essays are the most valuable guide we have to the origins of the revolution, and, more particularly, to its innovative practices. Michnik was born in 1946, in

Warsaw, to parents whom he has described as "Polish Communists of
Jewish origin." In prewar Poland, his father had spent time in prison
for political activities. From early adolescence, Adam proved to be an
irrepressible political activist—though of a strikingly different bent
from his parents'. (By 1977, the father had become enough of a sup-
porter of the son's anti-communist activities to join a hunger strike in
a church in support of an appeal for the release of Adam and others
from prison.) At fifteen, he founded a political club called the Seekers
of Contradictions but known informally to many Poles as the Revi-
sionist Toddlers. (Later, the regime, seeking to give the Toddlers a
more fearsome aspect, began to refer to the club as the Commandos.)
At eighteen, he was arrested for the first time, for involvement in the
writing and disseminating of a letter called "An Open Letter to the
Party," which was critical of the regime and was signed by Jacek
Kuron and Karol Modzelewski—men in their late twenties who were
prominent in the budding opposition movement. Kuron and
Modzelewski received sentences of three and three and a half years,
respectively; Michnik was detained in prison for two months. Thereafter, his life became a round of political activities alternating with
prison terms. In 1964, he enrolled in the History Department of
Warsaw University, and in 1966 he was suspended for participating in
a discussion in which the philosopher Leszek Kolakowski criticized the
regime. In 1968, he helped organize a protest against the closing of the
play "Forefathers' Eve," by Adam Mickiewicz, the revered nineteenth-
century Polish poet, and was expelled from the university on the
order of the minister of Higher Education. Protests against his expulsion were mounted at the university; so was an official campaign,
tinged with anti-Semitism, against the protesters. In February of 1969,
he was sentenced to three years in prison for belonging to an underground organization that was trying to overthrow the state, although

in fact no such organization existed. After serving a year and a half, he was released, and took a job at the Rosa Luxemburg factory, in Warsaw, which produces light bulbs. In 1971, he left his job, and eventually he entered Poznan University as an extension student, and he remained there until 1975, when he received an M.A. in history. In May of 1977, he was arrested again, but this time he was released, along with others, only two months later, following widespread protests in the intellectual community against the arrests. In the late nineteen seventies, he helped to found the Independent Publishing House, and he also helped to found the so-called Flying University, which offered uncensored lectures in people's apartments, among other places. In August of 1980, he and several others were arrested again, and this time the workers in the shipyards in Gdansk made these prisoners' release the final condition of a historic agreement with the government—the agreement under which Solidarity was legalized. After martial law was imposed, he was imprisoned once more (this time without trial), and he was held for more than two and a half years. Six months after his release, he was rearrested, tried, convicted, and given a sentence of three years, which he is now serving.

Michnik is not a political philosopher—and certainly not a "political scientist"—nor is he a proponent of any ideology or system of political thought. His writings, like the Federalist papers of Madison and Hamilton, or the articles and letters of Gandhi, are not only reflections on action but a form of action themselves. With equal justice, one might say that his actions—together with those of countless others in Poland—are a kind of writing, for action, when it is creative, has a power to disclose new possibilities which is as great as that of any book. Michnik's writings, then, both mirror and help to shape the new possibilities that have been and are being brought into existence by the Polish people. An ability to write about events and to participate in them at the same time is unusual. Writing, by its nature, requires solitude, whereas political action, by its nature, requires perpetual association with others. This dilemma was apparently resolved for Michnik by the authorities when they repeatedly threw him in jail. In his essay "Letter from the Gdansk Prison," written in the spring of 1985, he notes that in his recent six months of liberty he had been unable to write, but when he found himself in jail again literary production resumed immediately and, with characteristic irony and good humor, he offers to the general who had him locked up "gratitude for your thoughtful watch over my steps and for providing proper direction to my meditations." (One of the pleasures of Michnik's essays is that they combine gravity of purpose with lightness of style.) At large, Michnik stirs up so much trouble for the regime that it finds it must lock him up; but once he has been locked up he starts to write, and his letters, smuggled to the outside, are read all over Poland, and abroad, and cause, if anything, even more trouble for the regime. It's one more of the quagmires—and not the least of them, either—that the regime is at a loss to fight clear of.

The Czech writer Milan Kundera has remarked that the best novels do not merely confirm what we already know but uncover new aspects of existence. The same can be said of Michnik's political writing. He is never merely adding decibels to one side or the other of an existing argument, never merely engaging in verbal gunfire from a fixed position. Perhaps as a result of this, his essays, though produced in the midst of political struggle, are models of balance and fairness. He is concerned with deepening his own and others' understanding, and therefore he cannot afford the luxury of distortion for partisan reasons. His literary bent also militates against tendentious renderings. Of a writer whose portrait of the contemporary scene he finds too narrowly politicized, he asserts that the man misses "the whole dramatic aspect of the social and political reality . . . the fascinating panorama of defeat mixed with hope, reason with naïveté, fear with bravado." Once, when Solidarity was functioning at its peak, an enraged mob in the city of Otwock surrounded a policeman who they believed had severely beaten up two drunks. Michnik, among others, was summoned to the scene, and, introducing himself as an "anti-socialist element," he helped calm the crowd and save the policeman from harm. The same spirit of unwillingness to see injustice done, even to those who are doing injustice to him, permeates his essays. Unwilling to bend before any regime, he is equally unwilling to surrender the independence of his mind or conscience to any rival faction or orthodoxy. In action and in word alike, he reminds us that although liberty can and probably must be guaranteed by institutions human freedom is always ultimately an achievement of the individual spirit.

In 1976, four years before Solidarity came into existence, Michnik wrote a prophetic essay called "A New Evolutionism," wherein he recommended a new direction for the political opposition, which at the time was small and relatively weak. The essay is written against the backdrop of Poland's "obligation to its friends"—one of many euphemisms used in reference to the prime fact of political life in Poland, which is the overwhelming power of the Soviet Army and the often demonstrated resolve of the Soviet Union to use it to keep its Socialist satellites under its political domination. (In no part of the world does the phrase "our friends" have a more ominous ring than in the nations of Eastern Europe.) If this threat were somehow to disappear, it seems safe to say, the Polish Communist government would fall immediately. (In actuality, of course, the disappearance of the threat is about as unlikely as any event could be in our world.) To be sure, domination by a foreign power, and by neighboring Russia in particular, is hardly a new experience for Poland: it was partitioned for more than a century—from 1795 to 1918—between Austria, Prussia, and czarist Russia, and against these military opposition was nearly as hopeless as it is against the Soviet Union now. In our day, a new factor tightens the vise in which Poland finds itself—the presence in the world of nuclear weapons. Poland is at the very heart of that part of the world which is frozen in immobility, militarily and diplomatically, by the nuclear stalemate. In the past, even though rebellion was unavailing, Poland could dream of rescue by foreign armies, or by some drastic realignment of the international order as a result of war; and, in fact, in our century Poland was twice liberated by war from its oppressors—first when it achieved independence, in the aftermath of the First World War, and then when the Nazis were driven from Poland, only to set the stage, unfortunately, for Soviet domination of the country. Today, however, Poland has to recognize what all of Europe recognizes: that in the nuclear age the map of Europe is unlikely ever to be redrawn by marching armies. The likely alternatives offered by our time are nuclear stalemate and nuclear annihilation, and in neither is there any hope for the rescue of Poland. In sum, the Poles are kept in subjugation by a triple weight: at the local level, the totalitarian regime in Warsaw; at the national level, the threat of direct Soviet invasion; and, on the international level, the militarily paralyzing influence of nuclear weapons, which holds the whole unhappy arrangement firmly in place.

To most postwar observers, this combination of circumstances meant hopelessness, and they unhesitatingly pronounced any dramatic improvement in the situation of Poland to be impossible. Because Poland had no chance of defeating the overwhelming military and police forces arrayed against it, the argument ran (when anyone even bothered to spell out something so self-evident), any resistance was doomed to fail. It was Michnik's genius to separate the two halves of the proposition, and to accept the first (the impossibility of defeating the armies and the police forces) and reject the second (the hopelessness of all resistance). If there is an advantage to be gained from facing overwhelming adversity, it is the death of illusions: mind and body are saved from wasting themselves in pursuit of the impossible. Historically, the Poles have been the most romantic of peoples, much given to the pursuit of the long chance and the distant dream, but not even the most fevered dreams of military resistance could survive the discouragement of nuclear weapons piled on the two hundred divisions of the Soviet army piled on totalitarian rule. Final acceptance of that verdict cleared the way for new investigations, and a new kind of thinking. Abandoning, for the time being, all hope of a jailbreak, the members of the Polish opposition began to examine more closely the cell in which, it appeared, it was the country's fate to live for an indefinite period; that is, realizing that there was no salvation for Poland in our time in the movements of armies, they began to scrutinize the minutiae of their local environment. Soviet troops, it was plain, could not be driven out of Poland; but what if ten people gathered in someone's apartment and listened to an uncensored lecture on Polish history? The Communist party could perhaps not be dislodged from its "leading role" in affairs of state; but what if a group of workers began to publish a newsletter in which factory conditions were truthfully described? And what if millions of people, casting off fear, began to take local action of this sort all over the country? The new ferment, in the words of Irena Grudzinska-Gross in *The Art of Solidarity*, would be "an effort to overstep the limits of the political horizon while remaining inside the same geographical borders."

Perhaps the most acute mind training the lens of its political microscope on these questions was Michnik's. In "A New Evolutionism" he surveys the political scene and proposes a new path of action. He works from the assumption that "to believe in overthrowing the dictatorship of the Party by revolution . . . is both unrealistic and dangerous." He yearns for full independence for Poland but accepts the fact that any project for attaining it in the foreseeable future is hopeless. Nevertheless, he discerns opportunities for action of a kind that he believes can be highly successful. Between the rock of Soviet power and the hard place of contemporary Polish life, he discovers a space. In the conventional view, the interests of the Soviet Union and those of Polish society are unalterably opposed across the board. Michnik arrives at a startlingly different conclusion. "The interests of the Soviet political leadership, the Polish political leadership, and the Polish democratic opposition," he writes, "are basically concurrent." They are concurrent because for all three of them Soviet military intervention would be a disaster: for the Soviet leadership because it would suffer huge and lasting losses in its global political prestige; for the Polish leadership because it would lose the limited sovereignty it now enjoys and, furthermore, might be "dethroned"; and for the Polish opposition because of the bloodshed and the increased rigors of direct Soviet rule. Such an invasion would precipitate "a war that Poland . . . could not win on the battlefield but that the Soviet Union could not win politically." The concurring interests of the three parties, he concludes, define "an area of permissible political maneuver . . . the sphere of possible compromise."

Approaching the question of what can be done, Michnik canvasses past efforts, and it is wholly characteristic of the spirit of his writing that even when his final judgment of one effort or another is negative he gives generous credit for whatever good was achieved. Michnik is anything but a Hegelian dialectician—anything but a believer in blind forces of history acting behind men's backs—but he always keeps an eye on the larger historical story of which any particular initiative is a part, and is keenly aware that the inch of progress made in one decade, though inadequate in itself, and perhaps based on false premises, may make possible the next inch in the next decade. In Poland's recent past he identifies two schools of reform: the revisionists, who sought to soften and liberalize communist rule by invoking the humane aspects of Marxist and other socialist theory; and the so-called neo-positivists, a Catholic group that rejected communism in principle yet sought as a matter of pragmatic policy to moderate it by cooperating with it, even to the extent of participating in the Polish parliament. Revisionism, Michnik writes, was "faithful to the Bible [that is, to Marxism], although it interpreted it in its own way," while neo-positivism "adhered to the Church [that is, the actuality of the communist government], hoping that it would sooner or later disappear." Both were techniques of working within the system—of appealing to "the rational thinking of the Communist Prince"—and for a while both brought limited positive results, often in the form of books and articles and a slightly freer intellectual atmosphere. Yet both schools had to pay the price that is always paid by those who choose to work within the system: they were required, in order to maintain their influence, to renounce ties with people dedicated to changing the system from without. The fatal crisis for each school came, therefore, when protest from without boiled over: for the revisionists in 1968, when the student movement in favor of liberalization of intellectual life arose, and was crushed by the closing of some university departments, the expulsion of students, and reprisals against their parents; and for the neo-positivists in 1976, when workers demonstrated against an announced rise in food prices, and the government took extremely harsh reprisals. At those moments, any opposition that hoped to retain its standing in the society at large had to declare which side it supported—"that of the beaters or that of the beaten"—and because neither reform movement was able to do this both lost the public's confidence.

Michnik's analysis of the failure of the efforts to change the system from within leads him to make a pivotal recommendation: "I believe that what sets today's opposition apart from the proponents of those ideas of reform in the past is the belief that a program for evolution ought to be addressed to independent public opinion, and not to totalitarian power. Such a program would offer advice to the people regarding how to behave, not to the government regarding how to reform itself." The suggestion was simple, but its implications were radical. The change in the venue of action entailed a change in substance. Those who took the route of working with the Prince depended on the decisions and whims of the Prince to achieve any results. But those who took the route of working in and with the society could act directly. Then it was up to the government to react. The first method, based on the belief that the government, by holding a monopoly on the instruments of force, also monopolized political power, viewed cooperation with the government as the only way to share in power. The second method, based on the belief that there were sources of power elsewhere, in public opinion, sought to develop those. And yet Michnik, unlike many people in other times and places who had given up on the government in power and turned to the public for redress, did not seek the overthrow of the government. Rather, he wanted the society immediately and directly to take over its own destiny in certain realms of life, and only then to turn to the government—for negotiation. The eventual result, he hoped, would be a "hybrid," based on a compromise in which the government, while holding on to state power, would acknowledge and accept other, independent institutions in the society. Michnik enumerates the groups in society that he hopes will advance "a new evolutionism." First, and most important, are the workers, whose participation is "a necessary condition for the evolution of public life toward democracy." The key event, he foresees with uncanny accuracy, will be the foundation of independent "institutions representing the interests of workers." Second is the Catholic Church, which has always remained independent but has recently shown an increasing interest in defending the independence and the rights of others, including the workers. In the Church, Michnik notes, "Jeremiads against 'Godless ones' have given way to documents that quote the principles of the Declaration of Human Rights." Third is the intelligentsia, whose duty it is to think through alternative programs while defending fundamental moral and political principles.

Michnik acted on his own advice, and was soon busy organizing and participating in a host of independent groups. One deserves special mention: the Workers' Defense Committee usually known as KOR—the acronym of its Polish name. KOR did not agitate politically, or otherwise address the government. Instead, it set out to render concrete assistance—financial, legal, and medical—to workers and their families who had suffered in one way or another from government repression. Indeed, the committee explicitly declared its purposes to be not political but social, and it restricted its activity to what Jan Jósef Lipski, one of its founders, who has written an excellent history of the organization, refers to as "social work." But what in the eyes of KOR might be considered social was considered by the government definitely political, for in a totalitarian system every aspect of collective existence is supposed to originate with the government and be under its management. In this deep reach of totalitarian government into daily life, which is usually seen as a source of its strength, KOR discovered a point of weakness: precisely because totalitarian governments politicize daily life, daily life becomes a vast terrain on which totalitarianism can be opposed. It was here that KOR implicitly pitted itself against the regime. In consequence, the KOR members soon began to suffer the repression against which they sought to defend the workers—loss of employment, arrest, imprisonment, beatings, and, in a few cases, loss of their lives. It was just one of the remarkable qualities of this organization that its members were willing to suffer government reprisal not in the name of some sweeping political program or visionary goal but in order to get some money into the hands of a fatherless family or to arrange for favorable testimony in the trial of a worker. Only great goals might seem to warrant great sacrifices, but the KOR workers were ready to make great sacrifices for modest goals. "In some dissident circles . . . KOR members were sneered at as 'social workers,' " Lipski writes, "but within KOR such a designation by one's colleagues was regarded as an honor."

The adoption of an overall policy of direct action in society entailed the adoption of a number of other policies that were novel in the closed society of Poland. One was the policy of openness. When KOR was founded, in September of 1976, its members wrote a declaration of purpose to which they not only signed their names but also—an act without precedent for an opposition group in Poland—affixed their addresses and telephone numbers. Thereafter, the committee followed as much as possible a policy of open, public action. Closely related to the policy of openness was the policy of truthfulness. In all its statements and publications, KOR strove meticulously for factual accuracy. Characteristically, there was both an idealistic and a pragmatic reason for this policy. The members believed in telling the truth for its own sake, and they also calculated that in a society surfeited with lies an organization that hewed strictly to the truth would win support and gain strength. Another new policy was "autonomy of action." Autonomy was what the opposition wished for Poland as a whole and for every person in Poland. The members of KOR inaugurated it by making it a principle of their own actions. "There was no question of ordering someone by command of the organization to do something he did not want to do," Lipski writes, and he adds, "There was a principle that if what they wanted to do was not contrary to the principles of KOR they should be allowed to pursue their own ideas. And this is why everything that was done was done by people motivated by their own initiative and enthusiasm, and thus produced the best results." It is striking that the activists of the Polish opposition spoke as much of autonomy, which is the capacity of each person for acting freely, as they did of liberty, which is a person's right to do so. (In the West, you might say, we as individuals have great liberty but little autonomy. We have the right to determine the shape of our own future, but we do not bother to avail ourselves of it very much.) Still another policy was that of trust. Ordinarily, we think of the trust we place in someone as more or less a by-product, produced involuntarily in us by the other person's trustworthy actions, and do not think of it as the result of a policy, or even of any intention on our part. But for KOR trust was indeed a policy. One reason for this was the danger of infiltration by undercover police: a decision had to be made regarding what steps, if any, should be taken to guard against this. KOR's decision was to reject suspicion and all the equipment and procedures that go with it, and "to trust everyone within the bounds of common sense."

The policies of openness, truthfulness, autonomy of action, and trust, which together might be described simply as a policy of militant decency, were not elements in any master plan, but they were of a piece. They equipped KOR not so much to do battle with the government as to work around it. Although KOR did not have any designs on state power, it did hope that activity independent of the government would spread by contagion—that there would occur a sort of epidemic of freedom in the closed society. Lipski observes, "The long-range goal of KOR was to stimulate new centers of autonomous activity in a variety of areas and among a variety of social groups independent of KOR. Not only did KOR agree to their independence but it also wanted them to be independent." Its hope was abundantly fulfilled in the years just ahead.

Nothing illuminates the inner spirit of KOR, which strikes me as an exemplary organization for our time, more clearly than its final act. In September of 1981, the members decided that its role was being filled by Solidarity, and voted the KOR organization out of existence. Missing entirely from KOR, apparently, was that compound of personal interest, factional rivalry, and bureaucratic momentum which, acting independently of all external reasons and causes, often supersedes the purposes for which an organization was founded, and transforms it into a dead weight on the world. When KOR's *reason* for existing dissolved, *it* dissolved. To paraphrase George Orwell's comment on Gandhi, "How clean a smell it has managed to leave behind!"

In August of 1980, the stream of KOR flowed into the great river of Solidarity, but had already done much to determine the course of the river's flow. The policies of openness, truthfulness, autonomy of action, and trust were preserved. "The essence" of the movement, as Michnik later wrote from prison, still "lay in the attempt to reconstruct society, to restore social bonds outside official institutions." What ensued was an eruption throughout the society of civic activity of immense diversity, ranging from the trade unions themselves to associations formed to halt pollution and to protect consumers (areas that had been monumentally neglected by the regime). One is reminded of Tocqueville's description of America: "Americans of all ages, all conditions, and all dispositions constantly form associations. They have not only commercial and manufacturing companies, in which all take part, but associations of a thousand other kinds, religious, moral, serious, futile, general or restricted, enormous or diminutive. The Americans make associations to give entertainments, to found seminaries, to build inns, to construct churches, to diffuse books, to send missionaries to the antipodes." (The notable difference, of course, was that whereas the local groups in Tocqueville's America worked more or less in harmony with the national government those in Poland worked in opposition to it.) In this burst of activity, the very ingredients of political life, having been pounded apart by forty years of totalitarian rule, now came together again in new and vital forms. The classic formula for revolution is first to seize state power and then to use that power to do the good things you believe in. In the Polish revolution, the order was reversed. It began to do the good things immediately, and only then turned its attention to the state. In a sort of political and moral version of the hedonist's credo *"Carpe diem,"* the opposition proceeded directly, and without postponement, toward its goals. Its simple but radical guiding principle was to start doing the things you think should be done, and to start being what you think society should become. Do you believe in freedom of speech? Then speak freely. Do you love the truth? Then tell it. Do you believe in an open society? Then act in the open. Do you believe in a decent and humane society? Then behave decently and humanely. In Michnik's words in "A New Evolutionism," "every act of defiance permits us to build right now the framework of democratic socialism, which should be not just a legal and institutional structure but, what is even more important, a real, day-to-day community of free people." And, as he puts it in the same essay, "in their struggle for truth, or—to quote

Leszek Kolakowski—'by living in dignity,' the opposition intellectuals are striving not only for the proverbial better tomorrow but also for a better today."

Timothy Garton Ash, the author of *The Polish Revolution: Solidarity*, has aptly noted that the opposition's style has been to act "as if " Poland were already a free country. And once those in opposition began to act that way something unexpected happened. As soon as they started to act "as if," the "as if " started to melt away. Then they really *were* defending the worker (and often with success), or giving the lecture, or publishing the book. It wasn't "as if " it were a book, it *was* a book, and soon people were really reading it. Of course, in the country at large the "as if " did not melt away. That became clear when the book was confiscated, or the lecture was broken up by a government goon squad, or the innocent worker was sent off to prison in spite of the opposition's best efforts to defend him. Nevertheless, in the immediate vicinity of the action—and that vicinity expanded steadily as the movement grew—the "as if " was no pretense. There a small realm of liberty was created. And "liberty, when men act in bodies," Burke wrote, "is *power.*" Thus a second surprising discovery was made by the opposition —the discovery that merely by fearlessly carrying on the business of daily life it grew powerful. But the power gained was not power that had been wielded by others and had now been wrested from them; it was new power, which had been created where there had been none before. The program, then, was not to seize political power from the state but to build up the society. In 1970, demonstrating workers had been brutalized by the police, whereupon some of them marched to Party Committee buildings—known in Poland simply as Committees —and burned them down. Later, Jacek Kuroń offered a piece of advice that gained renown and foreshadowed the future course of events: "Don't burn down Committees; found your own."

The distinction between "society," which was to be renewed by the movement, and "power," which was to be left to the state, became common currency within the opposition, and was the subject of much discussion. While no one really expected the government to "wither away," as in the old Leninist dream, a certain contemptuous indifference to it did develop among the members of the opposition. This indifference showed itself radiantly in the extraordinary personal courage demonstrated by people at all levels of society, who at times acted as if there were no repressive government in Poland, and it also showed itself, less happily, in the utter failure of the movement to anticipate the imposition of martial law: that took the leadership of Solidarity by surprise almost the way Solidarity had taken the government by surprise sixteen months earlier. Just as society had massed its millions for action without being noticed by the government, so the government now massed its soldiers and police for action without being noticed by society. It may be that the two sides underestimated each other's strength so drastically because they possessed different *kinds* of strength, and each side judged the other on the basis of its own kind: to the government the opposition looked weak because it lacked military and police power, while to the opposition the government looked weak because it lacked public support. According to the "realistic" laws of the government's existence, the Solidarity movement was an impossibility, but equally, according to the more "idealistic" laws of Solidarity's existence, martial law was impossible. Michnik has characterized the difference memorably:

> The mighty and spontaneous social movement, deprived of examples, changing from one day to the next amid incessant conflicts with the authorities, did not possess a clear vision of piecemeal goals or a well-defined concept of coexistence with

the communist regime. It allowed itself to be provoked into fights over minor issues, into inessential conflicts; it was full of disorder, incompetence, unfamiliarity with its enemies and the enemies' methods. Solidarity knew how to strike but not how to be patient; it knew how to attack head-on but not how to retreat; it had overall ideas but not a program for short-term actions. It was a colossus with legs of steel and hands of clay; it was powerful among factory crews but powerless at the negotiating table. Across from it sat its partner, which could not be truthful, run an economy, or keep its word, which could do only one thing: break up social solidarity. This partner had mastered this art in the thirty-seven years of its rule. This partner, the power elite, was a moral and financial bankrupt and was unable, because of its political frailty, to practice any type of politics. . . . The Polish communist system was a colossus with legs of clay and hands of steel.

What was perhaps most surprising about the imposition of martial law was the surprise itself. In less than a year and a half, Solidarity had made its "ideals" enough of a "reality" so that the effectiveness of time-tested tricks of repressive rule like martial law had been all but forgotten by a whole country. Solidarity lived by trust and it died by trust. Certainly this costly inattention to the government's plotting was a failure of the movement, yet it was a failure that had a certain definite grandeur.

In *A Warsaw Diary*, Ryszard Kapuscinski writes, "Here everything is based on a certain principle of asymmetrical verification: the system promises to prove itself *later* (announcing a general happiness that exists only in the future), but it demands that you prove yourself now, *today*, by demonstrating your loyalty, consent, and diligence. You commit yourself to everything; the system to nothing." The opposition worked in exactly the opposite way. It proved itself *today*, and let *later* take care of itself. In so doing, it offered a new approach to one of the most intractable problems of all political life: the endemic discrepancy between evil means and good ends in politics—between the brutal and mendacious methods commonly accepted as a necessity of politics and the noble or visionary ends toward which these means are directed. In the direct action in society practiced by the opposition movement in Poland, means and ends were rolled into one. Every means was an end, and vice versa. For example, each of the "means" of KOR—openness, truthfulness, autonomy, and trust—was also an end. A courageous act or a truthful word was a good "end"—in itself, it enriched life, made life better—and a redressed grievance or an improvement in a factory's production was a good "means" to further accomplishment. To reform the adversary might take some time, but in the sphere of one's own actions the just society could be established right away. It followed that evil means could no longer be employed to attain good ends. If the journey and the destination were the same, it made no sense to spoil the conveyance in which one was riding. Here, I believe, is the source of the movement's nonviolence, which was especially striking for being practiced even more rigorously than it was preached—a discrepancy far more attractive and more unusual than the reverse discrepancy. The use of violence, spoiling means and ends at the same time, would have polluted the source of both the movement's virtue and its strength. The elements of the movement's style of action—its direct approach to society and its problems, its local emphasis, its rejection of violence and lying and other base means of striving for noble ends—formed a self-consistent whole. If you wished to act locally, then what could be more local than yourself? And if you wished to produce results *today*, then what area of life was more ready to hand, more thoroughly within your grasp, than your own actions? And if, accordingly, you made yourself and your own actions your starting point for the reform of society, then how could you permit those actions to be degraded by brutality, deception, or any other disfigurement? While this style of action was nonviolent, "nonviolence" seems both too restrictive and too negative a term with which to describe it: too restrictive because, along with being nonviolent, the movement was nondeceptive, nonsecretive, and non many other obnoxious things; and too negative because the deepest source of its strength was not any form of abstinence but, rather, the positive, energetic, open pursuit of a free and just society through incessant public action of the kind advocated by Michnik. The genius of the movement lay in its having seized upon a method of action that did not depend on violence and whose strength would have been undercut by the use of violence. A little violence would probably have been as harmful to Solidarity as a little pacifism would be to an army in the middle of a war.

The opposition movement's nonviolence was almost certainly a precondition for the strong support that the movement received from the Catholic Church—support that, by all accounts, was indispensable to it. Most observers agree that the national spirit that gave rise to Solidarity was born more than a year earlier, in June of 1979, when Pope John Paul II, the first Polish pope, returned for the first time to Poland. Shortly after the visit, Michnik described the crucial inner change in the mood of the public which it brought about:

> Julian Stryjkowski's phrase "Poland's second baptism" keeps coming to mind insistently. Indeed, something odd did happen. The very same people who are ordinarily frustrated and aggressive in the shop lines were metamorphosed into a cheerful and happy collectivity, a people filled with dignity.

The police vanished from the main streets of Warsaw and exemplary order reigned everywhere. The people who had been deprived of their real power for so long all of a sudden regained their ability to determine their fate. This is how the social consequences of John Paul II's visit-pilgrimage can be sketched.

A movement born in a "second baptism" must remain faithful to its spiritual origin or lose its strength, and this movement's ability to remain faithful was made possible by the new style of action it had adopted. In modern times, the introduction of spiritual, or even purely moral, purposes into political life has been justifiably regarded with deep suspicion. The City of God and the City of Man, the argument runs, are in essence based on principles so different that for either to adopt the principles of the other will prove ruinous. The danger for the City of God is that by associating itself with the evil means that are supposedly intrinsic and necessary to political life it will be brutalized and lose its spiritual purity. The danger for the City of Man is that by adopting principles of pacifism, or even of mildness, that are embodied in such teachings as the Sermon on the Mount it will be enfeebled, and collapse, or else that in the attempt to wed the evil means of political life to the pure ends of spiritual life the evil means will be given even greater license than usual, and fanaticism and violence will increase. (The course of events in present-day Iran, where otherworldly purity is pursued with this-worldly brutality, shows that the danger is as real in our time as it has been in any other.) In view of these perils, many wise observers have suggested that the two Cities be kept apart; yet separation also has a cost. The moral teachings of religion lose half their field of operation if it must be acknowledged that right at the heart of human affairs there is a realm—the political—

to which they have no application. At the same time, political life is set adrift morally if the moral standards that apply to private life are excluded from it. It is always possible to try to frame moral standards that apply to the political world alone, but every time someone makes a really thoroughgoing attempt—Machiavelli's writings are perhaps the most prominent example—we find that our private standards are violated, and we are repelled. This ancient opposition between the spiritual and the political realms is, at the very least, eased if in the political realm a method of action is adopted that does not cite noble ends as justification for evil means, or even distinguish between means and ends. Then spiritual and moral energies can flow into the political world without necessarily being corrupted. The two Cities then rest on a common foundation; namely, respect for the dignity and worth of the individual person, whose degradation "today" for some noble purpose "in the future" is rejected. This is not to say that political life can henceforth proceed to perfection—that the fulfillment promised by Utopian revolutionaries can materialize forthwith—but only that the actors in the political realm invite judgment of their actions by the same standards that everyone accepts in private life. Political life, then, will be no closer to perfect than private life is, but it will no longer be singled out as a realm in which certain evils are in principle necessary and therefore justified.

Ever since Gandhi led India to independence through nonviolent action, it has become something of a cliché to say that nonviolence could succeed only against a parliamentary democracy like England —that it would have failed against a totalitarian power, such as Stalin's Soviet Union or Hitler's Germany. Inasmuch as Poland has not attained its independence—or, for that matter, even aimed at it— this assumption still holds. And it seems only reinforced when one reflects that the regime in Poland today, though brutal, is far more moderate than the regime of either Stalin or Hitler. Nevertheless, it is now a matter of record that by far the most effective resistance movement ever launched against a totalitarian regime was completely nonviolent. Nonviolent action, far from being helpless in the face of totalitarianism, turns out to be especially well suited to fighting it. Hence it would be misleading to suggest that the Poles made a free choice of nonviolence over violence, as though they had been offered an opportunity to overthrow the regime by violence but had turned it down on the ground of moral principle in favor of nonviolence. Rather, from the outset violence was recognized by almost everybody to be completely useless to the movement. Addressing the question of why the movement adopted nonviolent means, Michnik writes, "No one in Poland is able to prove today that violence will help us to dislodge Soviet troops from Poland and to remove communists from power. The U.S.S.R. has such enormous military power that confrontation is simply unthinkable. In other words: we have no guns." The decision against violence, then, was made not so much by the Poles themselves as by their historical situation. The greatness of the Polish movement lies not in a decision to renounce violence— although the self-discipline required to flawlessly maintain a policy of nonviolence in the heat and anger of the struggle deserves great credit—but in its discovery of peaceful means that still offered hope.

Historically, violence has usually been regarded as the *ultima ratio*—the final arbiter, to which people turn in the last, desperate hour, when all peaceful means have been tried and have failed. "Hallowed are the arms where no hope exists but in them," Livy writes. But when those hallowed arms fail, people have believed, all that remains is the silence either of submission or of death. In Poland, that sequence appears to have been reversed: the futility of violent means—a futility so evident to all that such means did not even have to be tested—was what led to a recourse to nonviolent ones. It was as though beyond the traditional means of last resort new, peaceful ones had been discovered. The government declared a "state of war," and, employing its monopoly of the means of violence against an unarmed society, it "won" the war. (In Michnik's mocking account, "General Jaruzelski has glorified the name of the Polish armed forces by capturing with a flanking movement the building of the Polish Radio and Television, not to mention the telephone exchange.") In the traditional scheme of things, that would be the end of the story; the last resort would have been exhausted, the last card played, and the population would resign itself to defeat. But this has not happened. It seems, Michnik writes, that "the Polish nation does not think it has been defeated." Failing to think it has been defeated, it fails to act as if it had been defeated, and, failing to act defeated, it is not defeated. "What I saw after my release"—on August 4, 1984—"exceeded not just my expectations but even my dreams," Michnik reports. "I found that the people of Solidarity were wise, determined, ready for a long struggle." The government crackdown has taken its toll, but the spirit of opposition is alive. Repression and activism continue side by side. The arrests are made, but people are not intimidated. They live now in what may be the most curious conditions to have developed in Poland so far: autonomy without liberty—freedom together with jail.

Poland's unfinished experiment in nonviolent action is of particular interest in a world in which violence in the form of the weapons of mass destruction threatens the ultimate self-defeat of man. While the Polish revolution may appear to have little to do with the nuclear question, it seems to me that there is an interesting parallel to be drawn between the plight of Poland under Soviet domination and the plight of the world in the nuclear age. For both Poland and the world, sane thinking must begin with the recognition that the use of violence is futile, self-defeating, and thus "unthinkable." (Michnik's use of this word seems significant.) Both Poland and the world are therefore driven to search for nonviolent solutions to their dilemmas. On this point, realism and idealism coincide, and nonviolence, so often regarded exclusively as a choice of idealists, is supremely realistic. And both Poland and the world have been advised by expert opinion that their plights are inescapable, and they should accept the status quo; anything else, both are told, would "destabilize" the existing situation. Yet Poland has, at the very least, found a path to follow, and in this there is hope for the world, too. We are led to wonder whether in the realm of international affairs and diplomacy there may not be a solution as unlikely in the eyes of the experts as Solidarity was—some ultima ratio beyond violence which the world is driven to employ, for reasons both pragmatic and idealistic, precisely because violence, the old ultima ratio, is now useless and bankrupt. If such a solution should be found, and if it should be employed to reunite a divided Europe, then it would be not only a counterpart of the Polish movement but a complement to it. Then Poland and the world would escape from their plights along the same path.

It is tempting to sum up by saying that the Polish revolution practiced a politics based on life, in which political power, assuming the form of public consent and public support, is the natural and spontaneous extension of human beings' ability to act together to build and create, whereas the government practiced a politics of death, in which political power, assuming the form of fear, is an extension of human beings' ability to tear down and destroy—ultimately, to kill one another. But Michnik, it seems to me, might bridle at such a description, finding in it the seeds of what, in his essay "Maggots and Angels," he calls the political sin of Manichaeanism, in which one assigns all evil to one's foe and all good to oneself. Michnik rejects political Manichaeanism wherever he sees it, but he finds it especially inappropriate for Poland. Acknowledging, as he does, that Soviet power is irremovable from the Polish scene for the foreseeable future, he recognizes that everyone, even the most courageous, must accommodate this reality in one way or another. That being so, it is impossible to divide Poland cleanly into two hostile camps, one evil and the other good. Instead, evil and good are distributed widely and subtly. They will be found in one balance in the government official who has to decide whether to be a little more ruthless and ideological in his decisions or to be a little bit more humane and pragmatic, in another balance in the professor who has to decide just how truthful to be in a certain monograph; and in yet another balance in the jailed activist who has to decide whether to sign the "loyalty oath" that the government has put before him as the price of his release. The first may be a largely greedy and self-interested person; the second may be basically decent but frightened; the third may be heroic but wavering. But in all of them good and evil are present, and in each case Michnik would like to see the good prevail—or, at least, advance a little. In this vision of society's betterment, no one can be wholly written off as a "maggot" and no one granted exemption from the human condition as an "angel."

The epithet "maggot" is not Michnik's own but was used originally by the contemporary writer Piotr Wierzbicki, in a satiric essay called "A Treatise on Maggots," in which he lists the various rationalizations that selfish or hypocritical or weak-willed people use to evade their responsibility to oppose the regime. Michnik responds by engaging in a novel exercise. He sorts through Polish history, asking which people, by Wierzbicki's criteria, would have to be called maggots, and concludes that many of the most highly honored figures would at some point in their careers have qualified. Michnik's purpose is not to discredit the heroes of Polish history but, rather, to encourage a more tolerant understanding of the compromises of the present day. History is often consulted by those seeking to assemble a list of grievances or to draw up an indictment. Michnik's intention is just the opposite: he uses history to forgive the present. Central to his argument is a recognition that the need for compromise had its origin in those political situations "where foreign domination of the Polish nation was chronic, while all hope for armed defense of national values was completely illusory; where compromise with a partitioning power became indispensable for saving the very existence of the nation." In such circumstances—which, of course, are also Poland's present ones—arguments for compromise with the regime, or even participation in it, can never be dismissed out of hand. While it is true that "full acceptance of the compromise formula would lead to moral compromise and spiritual capitulation," it is also true that "full rejection of this formula would lead to a more or less heroic isolation." Using historical examples, Michnik shows that different—and even seemingly opposite—stands could all have merits of their own. Those on the inside might found institutions—a railroad, a university—of real and lasting importance to the country; those rebelling against the regime on the outside might be defending the country's honor and inoculating it against occupation at some future time. The eminent figures who made these choices debated fiercely, and often bitterly (Michnik offers fascinating accounts of the debates in his historical essays), but now Michnik seeks what he calls, quoting the writer Antoni Slonimski, "angerless wisdom," in which the contributions made by those figures whose choices differed are acknowledged, and might inspire more tolerance and cooperation among people who face the same choices today. In this vision, understanding, toleration, and forgiveness are the watchwords for each person's dealings with others, yet there is still a realm in which exacting judgment is called for—one's dealings with oneself. Michnik implies as much in an eloquent passage whose direct point is that no one can make a moral choice for another.

Aleksander Wat wrote somewhere that there is only one answer to the question of how intellectuals who live in countries ruled by Stalin should behave. It is the Shakespearean answer: they should die.

Perhaps it is the true answer. But I believe that this is an answer that one can give only to oneself, a measure that one can apply only to oneself, a sacrifice that one can ask only of oneself. Anyone who demands an answer to this question from others is arbitrarily giving himself the right to decide about others' lives. And this usually ends badly.

Michnik does not say that he is ready to die, but then he feels no need to say it, since he has no advice to offer anyone else on the subject. In any case, when it comes to sacrifice, actions speak louder than words. Michnik counsels us to refrain from demanding self-sacrifice from other people, but frequently he offers that counsel from jail.

Throughout the history of political affairs there flows an unending stream of human blood. Sometimes it swells to a torrent, bearing all before it, and sometimes it slows to a trickle, but it has never dried up completely. In our time, it threatens to overflow its banks once and for all and sweep away history itself. Some may reluctantly accept bloodshed as a necessity of political life, some may deplore it, and some may embrace it, but all who enter the political world must come to terms with it in one way or another. The Polish opposition movement, for which and about which Michnik writes, did not add a single drop to this stream, except that which flowed from its own members' veins.

And, while the movement has so far been unable to restrain the violence and repression of its antagonists, the positions it has staked out in the fight—fearless readiness to act in support of one's convictions; unwillingness to lower one's standards, in the name of effectiveness, to the level of one's antagonists'; readiness to make unlimited sacrifice in pursuit of limited goals; respect, in practice as well as theory, for the dignity of each person; readiness to die but unwillingness to kill; and unwavering resolve to live one's beliefs in the moment, so that even in supposed defeat something of beauty and value is left behind in the world—are among the most honorable, the most original, and the most fruitful of which the world has record. From within his prison cell, defying his captors, Adam Michnik writes, in words that will sound down the decades:

> To these people, with their lifeless but shifting eyes, with their minds that are dull but skilled in torture, with their defiled souls that yearn for social approval, you are only raw material with which to do anything they please. They have their own particular psychology: they believe that anyone can be talked into anything (in other words, everyone can be either bought or intimidated). To them, it is only a matter of the price to exact or the pain to inflict. Although their actions are routine, your every stumble, your every fall gives meaning to their lives. Your capitulation is no mere professional achievement for them—it is their raison d'être. And so you find yourself engaged in a philosophical debate with them about the meaning of your life, about taking the meaning away from their lives, about giving meaning to every human existence. You are engaged in the argument of Giordano Bruno with the Inquisitor, of the Decembrist with the czarist

police superintendent, of Walerian Lukasinski with the czarist angel of annihilation, of Carl von Ossietzky with the blond Gestapo officer, of Osip Mandelstam with a member of the Bolshevik Party dressed in a uniform with the blue piping of the N.K.V.D.; you are engaged in the never-ending argument about which Henryk Elzberg once said that the value of your achievement cannot be gauged in terms of your idea's chances for victory but rather by the value of the idea itself. In other words, you score a victory not when you win power but when you remain faithful to yourself.

The Unconquerable World

FINDING GOD IN POLITICAL ACTION

IN THE FIRST years of the twentieth century, the chief elements that made up Gandhi's outlook on the world hung together uneasily, if they hung together at all. Shortly, under the pressure of events, they were to rearrange themselves convulsively in his mind. The crisis, which spanned three years and amounted to a kind of full-scale revolution in the life of a single man, swept together his social program for his local community, his personal spirituality, his political activity on the South African stage, and his view of the British Empire and the world.

The revolution in Gandhi's local community came with the creation of Phoenix Farm, in November of 1904. Gandhi took nothing in this little community as given, but subjected everything, from the activities of daily life (how to brush your teeth, how to clean the latrine) to the most general and fundamental structures of politics and faith, to scrutiny and revision. Because this scrutiny took the form of experimentation, not obedience to any fixed scripture or dogma, the revision was endless. It included an aspect of his life that has baffled and often repelled many of his admirers—his lifelong tinkering with his austere diet and his Christian Science–like home cures, to both of which he directed great attention.

The turning point in Gandhi's personal life came in 1906, while he was leading his ambulance corps during the Zulu War. It struck him that only someone who was pledged to celibacy and poverty could lead a life of unfettered public service. He "could not live both after the flesh and the spirit," he decided. At the time, he wrote later, he had begun to ask himself some questions: "How was one to divest oneself of all possessions? . . . Was not the body possession enough? . . . Was I to destroy all the cupboards of books I had? Was I to give up all I had and follow Him?" Forthwith, he became celibate—renouncing sex even with his wife, though he remained married—and poor, and remained so for the rest of his life.

Vows of poverty and celibacy were, of course, no novelty. Priests and monks had been taking them throughout history. It was the use to which Gandhi put the life thus disciplined that was new. In the religious traditions of both East and West, holy vows have usually been accompanied by a withdrawal from the world and especially from politics. Gandhi proceeded in exactly the opposite direction. He took his ascetic vows in order to free himself for action.

Significantly, Gandhi likened the common British soldiers—the "Tommies"—he met in the Zulu War to Trappist monks. "Tommy was then altogether lovable," he wrote, and went on to compare them to Arjun, the hero of the Indian epic the Mahabarata. "Like Arjun, they went to the battlefield, because it was their duty. And how many proud, rude, savage spirits has it not broken into gentle creatures of God?" Gandhi's admiration for soldiers was lifelong. Like a monk, he would devote his life to God; but like a soldier he would fight for his beliefs in this world. Of his pursuit of God, he said, "If I could persuade myself that I should find Him in a Himalayan cave, I would proceed there immediately. But I know that I cannot find Him apart from humanity." The aim of his life would be to "see God," but that pursuit would lead him into politics. "For God," he said, reversing centuries of tradition in a short sentence, "appears to you only in action."

To the question of whether political power alone might win out over military power, Gandhi answered without equivocation that it could. His answer, however, raised another question that was of the first importance for the future of nonviolent action. If politics was to be free of violence, must it become religious? The objections to the wedding of secular and spiritual power are of course ancient, dating in the East as far back as Gautama Buddha and in the West as far back as Jesus, another religious activist who lived and taught in a backwater of an empire. Universal Christian love, expressed in the sayings "Love your enemy" and "Forgive those who trespass against you," is the spiritual underpinning of his advice of nonviolence to Simon Peter, "Put up thy sword." Certainly, faith in God and ethical responsibility toward others were inseparable for Jesus. On the other hand, although Jesus was caught up in the politics of his time and place, he conspicuously stopped short of rebellion, nonviolent or otherwise. He steered clear of any claim to political leadership (refusing to accept the title "King of the Jews," which his crucifiers affixed to his cross), and he advised payment of taxes to the Roman authorities, saying, "Render unto Caesar what is Caesar's." In other sayings, too, he seemed to place the realm of faith apart from the realm of politics. When Pilate asked him whether he claimed to be a king—a claim that would have been an offense to Caesar—Jesus answered that he was not "a king of this world." If he had been making a claim of temporal power, he went on, his disciples would have used violence to release him. That they did not showed that his kingship was otherworldly. His prophecy that the world would end soon and the kingdom of heaven come also drew a line of separation between Christian love and politics. What need was there to prescribe a rule for a political realm that was about to be destroyed? It was on the basis of these sayings that the disciple Paul and, much later, St. Augustine founded their far sharper separation of the City of God from the City of Man.

To these Christian ideas we may contrast a few of Gandhi's. As he began a nonviolent campaign in 1930, he declared of the Raj, "I am out to destroy this system of Government. . . . Sedition has become my religion." Gandhi admitted no distinction between the City of God and the City of Man. He installed a political conscience in religion and a religious conscience in politics, and called the two the same.

The objections to such a union have come over the years from both saints and politicians. Faith, saints have said, is a domain of purity that is in its nature unworldly, and will be corrupted and destroyed by association with politics, which is in its nature brutal. Rule, politicians have added, is a rough pursuit that will be enfeebled by any introduction of spiritual rules of conduct. (An object lesson—in the eyes of the eighteenth-century historian of ancient Rome Edward Gibbon— was the Christianization and fall of the Roman Empire.) Or else politics, which requires a spirit of tolerance if its natural, ineradicable violence is at least to be moderated, may, if inspired by faith, become fanatical, and even more brutal than it has to be.

To these objections, Gandhi proposed explicit or implicit answers. The most important was nonviolence itself, which he called ahimsa— literally, non-harm, or harmlessness—in Hindi. If the ardor of the spiritual, with its tendency toward absolute demands, was to be permitted to inspire political action, then it had to be purged of violence. The spirit must check its guns at the door, so to speak, before entering the saloon of politics. Otherwise, saints would prove more murderous than sinners. He required the intellect, meanwhile, to undergo a parallel renunciation. It had to rid itself of dogmatic certainty. Shedding dogma was the counterpart in the intellectual world of nonviolence in the physical world: it was mental disarmament. Only if the faithful were ready to open their minds to the worth and validity of other faiths were they likely to be able to hold to the vow of nonviolence. The test of the "absoluteness" of faith became not adherence to the exact prescriptions of any sacred text—what today we call fundamentalism—but the willingness to make sacrifices, including the sacrifice of one's life, for one's admittedly fallible beliefs. Sacrifice and suffering without violence ("self-suffering," as Gandhi put it), not doctrinal purity, was the evidence and "proof" of faith.

These were all ways to permit spiritual love to fuel politics; but they did not answer the question of whether politics, in order to be nonviolent, *required* a spiritual basis. The issue is important, because such a requirement would obviously restrict the appeal of nonviolence. It seems almost in the nature of things that only a small minority can ever take Gandhi as a model for their lives—just as only minorities have ever been drawn to the priestly or monastic life. In particular, Gandhi's asceticism—and especially his vow of celibacy even within marriage—which he regarded as essential to the practice of satyagraha, seems unlikely to serve as a model for very many. The question is what it is about religious faith that enables it to serve as a foundation for nonviolence and whether, outside religion, there may be other foundations.

SOMETHING STRANGE HAPPENS

The transformation in Gandhi's political program in South Africa came just a few months after his vows of celibacy and poverty during the Zulu War. In August of 1906, the Transvaal Legislature announced a so-called Asiatic Law Amendment Ordinance. Its main provision required all Indians above the age of eight to be registered with ten fingerprints and to carry a residency permit thereafter, on pain of fine, prison, or deportation. In combination with other restrictions already in place, the act in effect reduced the Indian community to the status of criminals. Its acceptance, Gandhi believed, "would spell absolute ruin for the Indians in South Africa." In response, Gandhi led the South African Indian community to cross the line from petitioning or otherwise seeking redress within the law to nonviolent lawbreaking.

On September 11, 1906, some three thousand Indian men met at the Empire Theater, in Johannesburg. Gandhi writes, "I could read in every face the expectation of something strange to be done, or to happen." On the agenda was an item resolving that the members of the Indian community would go to jail rather than submit to the Ordinance. One man, Sheth Haji Habib, suggested that the meeting should not only vote for the resolution but publicly vow before God that they would abide by it. Gandhi supported the suggestion in a speech. Such a vow was far different from a mere resolution, he said. It could not be enforced by majority vote; each person had to decide for himself whether to take it and abide by it. But, having once taken the vow, each person was obligated thereafter to keep it, no matter what others did, for "a man who lightly pledges his word and then breaks it becomes a man of straw." All present rose and took the vow.

The "strange" thing had happened. Gandhi knew, he said later, "that some new principle had come into being." Before a year was out, several hundred Indians had gone to jail. This revolution in action, significantly, was born in action. "The foundation of the first civil resistance under the then-known name of passive resistance," he wrote later, "was laid by accident. . . . I had gone to the meeting with no preconceived resolution. It was born at the meeting. The creation is still expanding."

Gandhi was dissatisfied with the term "passive resistance" for what the Indians were doing, and as an alternative came up with the new coinage "satyagraha," which combined the Sanskrit word *sat*, meaning "that which is," or "being," or "truth," with *graha*, meaning "holding firm to" or "remaining steadfast in." It is usually translated as "truth force" or "soul force"—terms that, without further elucidation, are almost as mysterious to the English reader as "satyagraha." Concretely described, satyagraha is direct action without violence in support of the actor's beliefs—the "truth" in the person. The philosophy of satyagraha prescribes nonviolent action in which the actors refuse to cooperate with laws that they regard as unjust or otherwise offensive to their consciences, accompanied by a willingness to suffer the consequences. For the Indian community in Transvaal it meant deliberate violation of the Amendment Ordinance and a commitment to fill the local jails.

SERMON ON THE SEA

The final step in the revolution in Gandhi's life in these years—the reversal of his appraisal of the British Empire—came in 1909, after he had spent several months in England at the head of an Indian delegation fruitlessly pleading with the imperial government for relief from Boer repression in South Africa (which was now about to become the Union of South Africa). Gandhi had already led one delegation to London, right after the passage of the Ordinance, and on that occasion Lord Elgin, the colonial secretary, had played a trick on the Indians. He had informed them that the imperial government would disallow the legislation. Halfway home, they discovered to their joy that it had done so. When they arrived, however, they learned what Elgin had known all along—that the Transvaal would shortly be granted "responsible government," and would then be permitted to adopt the act at will, without imperial challenge, as it soon did.

The second visit was no more productive. The imperial government wished to uphold the appearance of liberalism without paying the price. From the Indian point of view, the problem was not autocratic or arbitrary use of the empire's strength but default and weakness. Notwithstanding the empire's victory in the Boer War, its power in South Africa was waning. Lord Morley, the secretary of state for India, told the Indians that the empire—which, he startlingly said, was "miscalled an imperial system"—could not "dictate to the colonies." The English strategy in South Africa was to shore up overarching imperial power by yielding increased grants of authority to the local whites. For the Cape of Good Hope, like Egypt and the Sudan, was one of those "roads to India" that had to be defended at all costs. Global power politics took precedence over the grievances of the local black majority and the Indian minority, which were hardly a speck on the great imperial horizon. "I have now got fed up," Gandhi wrote home in *Indian Opinion* toward the end of his 1909 visit. "I think the reader, too, must have grown tired of reading uncertain news." At the Empire Theater, Gandhi had broken with the Boers. Now his patience with the British was coming to an end.

The historical predicament faced by Gandhi and other Indian leaders, barred from influence and power in South Africa as well as their own country, was, in its broadest outline, similar to that facing the leadership of all the colonialized countries: how to oppose domination by a foreign state wielding the incomparably superior weapons of the modern West. India's "Omdurman" had been the battle of Plassey, fought in 1757 between English forces under Robert Clive, and those of Siraj-ud-daulah, the nawab of the Mogul Empire. Clive's victory was one of the earliest to show the extreme imbalance that would become such a regular feature of modern imperial war. The nineteenth-century British military historian Colonel Malleson was not exaggerating when he wrote, "The work of Clive was, all things considered, as great as that of Alexander." For after the battle of Plassey, with its loss to England of a handful of soldiers, the power of England over India was not to be seriously challenged again until Gandhi's time.

The power of imperialist Europe presented the Eastern countries with a dilemma that was cultural and psychological as well as military and political. Everywhere in Asia, nascent movements to resist Europe were national, just as, earlier in the century, the European resistance to Napoleon had been national. However much these movements battened on enthusiasm for their own cultures, the most obvious solution to the crisis in which Asia found herself was to abandon her ways and adopt those of the powerful, dangerous West—in short, to "modernize." Nor could this adoption be half-hearted or superficial. The foundations of traditional society, it seemed, had to be uprooted.

In China, the Ottoman Empire, Japan, India, and elsewhere, innumerable variations of this solution to the dilemma were tried out. Science, evidently, was a source of Western power. Why not, then, learn science, and graft it onto Eastern society, combining the strength of the "material" West with the wisdom of the "spiritual" East? Such was the thinking of early Chinese reformers, who, however, soon noted what Clausewitz had discovered—that democracy, too, was a source of Western military power. "Science and democracy" then became the rallying cry of an important school of reformers. Chen Duxiu, a moderate, wrote, "The basic task is to import the foundation of Western society, that is, the new belief in equality and human rights." These Chinese, goaded by their country's humiliation, were perhaps the first anywhere, East or West, to understand and clearly state that at the base of modern power were the scientific and democratic revolutions. But in the early twentieth century it became obvious to them that neither revolution could grow in a vacuum. Both had roots in the emancipation of the individual. In order to be strong, China would have to alter its culture, even its family structure—the very things that, according to earlier reformers, China had been seeking to protect by adopting science. The further one went in Westernizing in order to protect China, it turned out, the less of "China" there was to protect. Not far down this path lay the wholesale condemnation of Chinese tradition that would be expressed by the Chinese Communist Party. The Asian nations, in order to survive in the social Darwinist, adapt-or-die war system that Europe had imposed on the world, seemed to be faced with a choice between watching Europeans destroy their traditional societies or doing the job themselves. It was hard soil in which to grow what later came to be called "national identity."

On a steamer back to South Africa in November of 1909, Gandhi, writing in his native tongue of Gujarati, poured out the longest and most inflammatory political pamphlet he would ever write, *Hind Swaraj: Indian Home Rule*—also called *Sermon on the Sea*. It dealt head-on with the issue of Westernization. If violence is truly the midwife of revolution, as Marx said, then this pamphlet was the closest Gandhi ever came to preaching it. He portrayed the civilization of England and her empire as an unmitigated evil. Gone now was the praise for Queen Victoria, gone the praise for British justice, gone the vision of a harmonious union of "different sections of one mighty empire." The larger villain of the story, however, was not England herself but modern technical civilization, of which England was only one representative. He anathematized it with fundamentalist fury. "This civilization is irreligion," he declared. "According to the teachings of Mahomed this would be considered a Satanic Civilization. Hinduism calls it the Black Age. . . . It must be shunned." To imitate this civilization, as Japan had done and China was trying to do, would be madness. "The condition of England at present is pitiable. I pray to God that India may never be in that plight." He excoriated modern ways. Railways only enabled "bad men [to] fulfil their evil designs with greater rapidity," he said, with primitive logic. English prime ministers had "neither real honesty nor a living conscience." The English Parliament was "a prostitute." The civilization of modern Europe as a whole was a mere "nine-days' wonder" that shortly would destroy itself; one had only to wait.

Indian civilization, he now found, was the opposite of all this. "The tendency of the Indian civilization is to elevate the moral being," he claimed, "that of the Western civilization is to propagate immorality. The latter is godless, the former is based on a belief in God." The foundations of Indian civilization arose, he insisted, from religious roots, when her great religious men had established pilgrimages to holy places, such as the Ganges.

Gandhi's rejection of the West and embrace of his own land was more radical by far than that of other anti-Western leaders of the time. The idea that the East should protect her spiritual treasures by means of a judicious borrowing of Western material techniques had been the stock-in-trade not just of the Chinese and Japanese but of Indians as well. For instance, the religious leader Vivekananda, who in other ways foreshadows Gandhi, said, "It is . . . fitting that when the Oriental wants to learn about machine-making, he should sit at the feet of the Occidental and learn from him. When the Occident wants to learn about the Spirit, about God, about the Soul, about the meaning and the mystery of this universe, he must sit at the feet of the Orient." Gandhi, by contrast, turns his back entirely on Western material techniques, placing his faith in Eastern spirituality alone.

Gandhi's sweeping rejection of modern technology, let us note, was never put into practice in India, except by himself and a few of his followers. And even Gandhi, though remaining true to his belief, did not propose a wholesale program of deindustrialization, and at times confessed that certain industries might be necessary, as long as they were strictly devoted to the benefit of the people. It is in the arena of nonviolence that Gandhi's repudiation of technology has so far proved historically fruitful. By associating technical progress with violence and both with the West and, on the other hand, technical simplicity with nonviolence and both of these with India, Gandhi and his colleagues forged a nationalistic pride in nonviolence that was to endure from about 1920, when the Congress Party adopted Gandhi's program, until 1948, when India gained independence. Thus was nationalism, which usually feeds on self-aggrandizement and militarism, wedded in India to a principle of self-restraint. (Once independent, the Indian state promptly abandoned nonviolence and immediately went to war with the newly created state of Pakistan over the territory of Kashmir; and it now possesses a large military establishment and a nuclear arsenal.)

Gandhi's embrace of nonviolence provided an escape from the discouraging choice between imitation of the West and defeat by the West. Nonviolence was a method for fighting the West *without* imitating her. As Gandhi put it in *Hind Swaraj*, "My countrymen . . . believe that they should adopt modern civilization and modern methods of violence to drive out the English. *Hind Swaraj* has been written in order to show that they are following a suicidal policy, and that, if they would but revert to their own glorious civilization, either the English would adopt the latter and become Indianized or their occupation in India would be gone."

The idea that India possessed a priceless, spiritually superior civilization was a welcome salve to the injured pride of a people that had been taught for some two hundred years to regard everything English as superior. In the words of India's first prime minister, Jawaharlal Nehru, Gandhi wrought in the consciousness of India "a psychological change, almost as if some expert in psychoanalytic methods had probed deep into the patient's past, found out the origins of his complexes, exposed them to his view, and thus rid him of that burden." In Gandhi's Manichaean celebration in *Hind Swaraj* of one civilization and condemnation of another, there is a note of chauvinism of a kind he later avoided. (Although he never repudiated *Hind Swaraj*, he would declare, "East and West are no more than names . . . there is no people to whom the moral life is a special vocation.") Yet we note at the same time a new clarity and firmness of tone in the pamphlet. Anything of the Uncle Tom that may have clung to the frock-coated, silk-hatted Gandhi as he made the rounds of the ministries of the British Empire has been purged. Soon he would adopt the simplest Indian dress. The disparate elements that composed the worldview of this rootless, much-traveled, English-trained, Esoteric Christian, immigrant to Africa, had fused in a new unity. The verbal "violence" of *Hind Swaraj* was perhaps the violence needed to rend the emotional tie with the empire. Gandhi had discovered a way to serve as a true son of India—at one, he was sure, with the spirit of his forefathers.

THE POWER OF NONVIOLENCE

There was practical as well as moral calculation in Gandhi's satyagraha. The West possessed means of violence that India could not hope to match. Gandhi later said, "Suppose Indians wish to retain by force the fruits of victory won through satyagraha. Even a child can see that if the Indians resort to force they can be crushed in a minute." Sensibly, he did not want to play a losing hand. As he explained, "The Whites were fully armed. It was clear that if the Indians were to come into their own, they must forge a weapon which would be different from and infinitely superior to, the force which the white settlers commanded in such ample measure. It was then that I introduced congregational prayer in Phoenix and Tolstoy Farm as a means for training in the use of the weapon of satyagraha or soul force." In 1909, contemplating the might of the British Empire, he wrote:

> You [British] have great military resources. Your naval power is matchless. If we wanted to fight with you on your own ground, we should be unable to do so, but if the above submissions be not acceptable to you, we cease to play the part of the ruled. You may, if you like, cut us to pieces. You may shatter us at the cannon's mouth. If you act contrary to our will, we shall not help you; and without our help, we know that you cannot move one step forward.

Gandhi's nonviolence, too, is a chapter in the story that began with Clausewitz's Prussia, which, faced with the superiority of the French revolutionary armies, had embarked on its policy of conscious imitation of the French innovations, and continued with the attempts of so many nations to "catch up" with more "modern" powers.

By the time Gandhi wrote *Hind Swaraj*, he had in effect nationalized the principle of nonviolence. He brought it down from the ether of universal beliefs and gave it a terrestrial home—India. Violence, meanwhile, seemed to have taken up residence in the modern West.

But where, if anywhere, in Gandhi's newly moralized geography did his *prime* virtue, civil courage, now reside? Previously, he had found it mainly in England, and scolded his countrymen for lacking it. In *Hind Swaraj*, it seems to have been left geographically homeless. Inspiring his countrymen to take active responsibility for their own social and political lives was *the* Gandhian program, yet since India had been defined as the home of the spirit, courage in her case must not take a martial shape (brute force) but must be of a nonviolent kind (soul force). So just when Gandhi's diatribe against the Satanic West reaches its highest pitch in *Hind Swaraj*, as if to justify and prepare the way for anti-Western violence, the restraining hand of nonviolence seems to reach in and turn the criticism and toward the passivity of his own countrymen. Psychologically speaking, we can almost watch the anger at the hated "other" being checked and directed back toward the self, which is excoriated with double fury.

Whatever pleasures of national pride Gandhi may have offered his countrymen when he called their ancient civilization the most godly of all he now more than took back. He dashed the sweet cup of national self-congratulation from the thirsting lips of the humiliated Indians. It is in the passages explaining England's domination of India that *Hind Swaraj* began to chart new political territory. Gandhi held Indians, not Englishmen, responsible for India's colonial dependency. "The English have not taken India," he wrote, "we have given it to them." He explained:

They came to our country originally for purposes of trade. Recall the Company Bahadur. Who made it Bahadur? They had not the slightest intention at the time of establishing a kingdom. Who assisted the Company's officers? Who was tempted at the sight of their silver? Who bought their goods?

History testifies that we all did this. In order to become rich all
at once we welcomed the Company's officers with open arms.
We assisted them.

Gandhi later elucidated his point:

It is because the rulers, if they are bad, are so not necessarily
or wholly by reason of birth, but largely because of their environment, that I have hopes of their altering their course. It is
perfectly true . . . that the rulers cannot alter their course
themselves. If they are dominated by their environment, they
do not surely deserve to be killed, but should be changed by a
change of environment. But the environment are we—the
people who make the rulers what they are. They are thus an
exaggerated edition of what we are in the aggregate. If my
argument is sound, any violence done to the rulers would be
violence done to ourselves. It would be suicide. And since I do
not want to commit suicide, nor encourage my neighbors to
do so, I become nonviolent myself and invite my neighbors
to do likewise.

Liberal-minded people have often held that society's victims are corrupted by a bad "environment" created by their privileged masters.
Gandhi was surely the first to suggest that the victims were creating a
bad moral environment for their masters—and to preach reform to
the *victims*. Even allowing for a certain raillery and sardonicism in
these passages, there can be no doubt that Gandhi is in earnest. Here
we touch bedrock in Gandhi's political thinking. All government,
he steadily believed, depends for its existence on the cooperation of
the governed. If that cooperation is withdrawn, the government will

be helpless. Government is composed of civil servants, soldiers, and citizens. Each of these people has a will. If enough of them withdraw their support from the government, it will fall.

This idea had admittedly occurred to political thinkers in the past. For instance, the sixteenth-century French writer Étienne de La Boétie had observed of tyrants, "the more is given them, the more they are obeyed, so much the more do they fortify themselves," and therefore "if nothing be given them, if they be not obeyed, without fighting, without striking a blow, they remain naked, disarmed and are nothing." The philosopher of the English enlightenment David Hume likewise believed that all government, even tyranny, rested on a kind of support. "The soldan of Egypt or the emperor of Rome," he wrote, "might drive his harmless subjects like brute beasts against their sentiments and inclination. But he must, at least, have led his *mameluks* or *praetorian bands,* like men, by their opinion." And James Madison once wrote, "All governments rest on opinion."

Gandhi, however, was the first to found upon this belief a thoroughgoing program of action and a radically new understanding of the relationship of violence to politics. The central role of consent in all government meant that noncooperation—the withdrawal of consent —was something more than a morally satisfying activity; it was a powerful weapon in the real world. He stated and restated the belief in many ways throughout his life:

I believe and everybody must grant that no Government can exist for a single moment without the cooperation of the people, willing or forced, and if people withdraw their cooperation in every detail, the Government will come to a standstill.

Gandhi's politics was not a politics of the moral gesture. It rested on an interpretation of political power and was an exercise of power. From his surprising premises Gandhi drew a conclusion more surprising still:

> The causes that gave them [the English] India enable them to retain it. Some Englishmen state that they took and they hold India by the sword. Both these statements are wrong. The sword is entirely useless for holding India. We alone keep them.

Gandhi does not merely say that English rule is made possible by Indian acquiescence; he goes a step further and charges that Indians "keep" the English, almost as if the English were struggling to get away and the Indians were pulling them back. Gandhi's claim flies in the face of the one conviction on which everyone else in the imperial scheme, whether ruler or ruled, agreed—that, in the words of the *London Times*, it was "by the sword that we conquered India, and it is by the sword that we hold it." (We cannot prove that Gandhi had read the *Times* editorial, but the similarity in wording of the passage above suggests that he had.) Some enthusiastically approved of this supremacy of the sword, some bowed to it, and some despised it, but only Gandhi denied that it was a fact. Not only was force, in Gandhi's thinking, not the "final arbiter," it was no arbiter at all. What arbitrated was consent, and the cooperation that flowed from it, and these were the foundation of dictatorship as well as of democratic government.

More Active Than Violence

Governments do not normally fall simply of their own weight. Action is required. The obligation to act, in Gandhi's view, took precedence over even the obligation to remain nonviolent. "Non-cooperation is not a passive state," Gandhi said, "it is an intensely active state—more active than physical resistance or violence." Satyagraha was *soul force*, but equally it was soul *force*.

Asked to choose between violence and passivity, Gandhi always chose violence. "It is better to be violent, if there is violence in our breasts," he said, "than to put on the cloak of nonviolence to cover impotence. Violence is any day preferable to impotence. There is hope for a violent man to become nonviolent. There is no such hope for the impotent." "Activist" is a word that fits Gandhi through and through. "I am not built for academic writings," he said. "Action is my domain." Indeed, if he was a genius in any field, that field was action. "Never has anything been done on this earth without direct action."

In 1917, soon after he returned to India, he would say, "There is no love where there is no will. In India there is not only no love but hatred due to emasculation. There is the strongest desire to fight and kill side by side with utter helplessness. This desire must be satisfied by restoring the capacity for fighting. Then comes the choice." In 1918, he would shock his followers by enlisting as a recruiting sergeant for Indian troops to fight for the British in the First World War. How, his colleagues wondered, then and later, could the advocate of nonviolence recruit soldiers for this war—a mechanized slaughter of millions that surely had to rank as the prime exhibit in Gandhi's indictment of modern technical civilization for its "violence of the blackest sort"? His campaign, which proved almost fruitless, can be explained only by his belief that what India needed even more than nonviolence was the will and courage that would propel its people into action—even if this meant serving in war under the British.

Intuitively, nonviolence appears to have a restraining or crippling influence on action. To Gandhi, however, nonviolence appeared in exactly the opposite light. Nonviolent action had nothing to do with quietism or passivity. Noncooperation was, Gandhi believed, supremely energetic. "Another remedy [to injustice] there certainly is, and that is armed revolt," he acknowledged, but "Civil disobedience is a complete, effective and bloodless substitute." If Gandhi embraced nonviolence, it was not because, in the interest of an ideal, he accepted a competitive disadvantage. Satyagraha was not some pale sister of violence, embraced for her virtue alone. For Gandhi such acceptance would have constituted an unacceptable abdication of responsibility.

But how could someone who checked his energy be called more energetic and more powerful than someone who unleashed it without restraint? Weren't Gandhi's two dictates—that one must *act* directly, unhesitatingly, and fearlessly and that one must do so nonviolently— at war with one another? The kinship of action and violence, indeed, seems natural, and it's tempting to see Gandhi's nonviolence only as an attempted remedy for the danger. In this view, nonviolence would be seen as a reduction of freedom in which a certain passivity and loss of energy is the price paid for keeping the peace. And certainly Gandhi did see nonviolence as a cure for the danger inherent in mass action. He often said that in his time the rising tide of action would irresistibly occur whether leaders like him encouraged it or not, and that his job was to help guide it into peaceful channels. "A new order of things is replacing the old," he wrote as he embarked on a campaign of satyagraha on behalf of mill workers in his home city of Ahmedabad. "It can be established peacefully or it must be preceded by some painful disturbances. . . . I presumptuously believe that I can step into the breach and may succeed in stopping harmful disturbances during our passage to the new state of things. . . . I can only do so if I can show the people a better and more expeditious way of righting wrongs." He adamantly denied that the price of restraining violence entailed a reduction of energy and power. On the contrary, he claimed that satyagraha, far from being a restriction on action, was action at last unrestricted and unbound—action grown to the full height of its potential. "Nonviolence," he said, "is without exception superior to violence, i.e., the power at the disposal of a nonviolent person is always greater than he would have if he was violent."

Any action, Gandhi knew, called above all for willpower—for the sort of courage that was especially conspicuous in soldiers. But nonviolent action required even more courage of this sort. Gandhi was fond of a statue of Charles Gordon, a British general of imperial fame, which shows him carrying a mere riding crop instead of a weapon. Gandhi commented:

> The practice of *ahimsa* calls forth the greatest courage. It is the most soldierly of a soldier's virtues. General Gordon has been represented in a famous statue as bearing only a stick. This takes us far on the road to *ahimsa*. But a soldier who needs the protection of even a stick is to that extent so much the less a soldier. He is the true soldier who knows how to die and stand his ground in the midst of a hail of bullets.

Action, moreover, flourishes, Gandhi believed, in freedom; and nonviolent action, precisely because it requires the highest possible degree of courage, exhibits the largest freedom. Violence, although initiated in pursuit of political goals, can take on a life of its own, which distracts from the original goals, and may eventually compete with them or supplant them entirely. On the local scale, this leads to vendetta, which can outlast by generations any political or other purposes that gave rise to a quarrel. On a much wider scale, the logic of war can, as Clausewitz warned with such clarity, entirely supersede the political purposes that lend war whatever sense it may have. On each of these levels, the actors surrender their freedom of action to a process over which they have lost control.

The nonviolent actor exhibits the highest degree of freedom also because his action originates within himself, according to his own judgment, inclination, and conscience, not in helpless, automatic response to something done by someone else. He is thus a creator, not a mere responder. It is not digressive to recall a passage from a writer who might at first appear to be pretty much a polar opposite of Gandhi yet also associated nonviolence not with weakness but with a superabundance of energy and power. Friedrich Nietzsche, asking himself whether such a thing as a Christian turning of the other cheek was really possible, said that, if it were, it would be for only the strongest natures. He wrote:

> To be incapable of taking one's enemies, one's accidents, even one's misdeeds seriously for very long—that is the sign of strong, full natures in whom there is an excess of the power to form, to mold, to recuperate and to forget. . . . Such a man shakes off with a *single* shrug many vermin that eat deep into others; here alone genuine "love of one's enemies" is possible —supposing it to be possible at all on earth. How much reverence has a noble man for his enemies!—and such reverence is a bridge to love. . . . In contrast to this, picture "the enemy" as the man of *ressentiment* conceives him—and here precisely is his deed, his creation: he has conceived "the evil enemy," "THE EVIL ONE," and this in fact is his basic concept, from which he then evolves, as an afterthought and pendant, a "good one"—himself!

If such magnanimous characters—free alike of fear and lust for revenge, and braver than soldiers—had not found an appropriate arena for their kind of activity, they might have passed through history without leaving any mark but the admiration of a few people around them. Their arena could not, of course, be war. In fact, it was the arena of nonviolent action, soon to be strewn with the debris of the world's empires and some of its mightiest and most violent regimes.

THE SHADOW

That lesson, however, is in fact a secondary one. When Gandhi arrived back in India in 1915, he knew he faced not only the evil of British rule but also the mountainous social ills of India, most of which had predated the Raj and would outlast it. The most important tasks, he believed, were providing a decent life, including adequate food, shelter, and sanitation, for India's "dumb millions," establishing a system of active self-government in the country's seven hundred thousand villages, ending the Hindu system of untouchability, raising the status of women, and making and keeping peace among Hindus and Muslims. Although *swaraj*—"self-rule"—included ejecting the English, he always believed that addressing these ills was its deeper and more important task.

Noncooperation, taken by itself, was useless for this purpose. It could do nothing to feed the hungry, to relieve the oppressed, to make peace among India's quarreling ethnic and religious groups. For these purposes, positive action was required. Gandhi gave it the unostentatious name of "the constructive program." Non-cooperation embodied the obligation to reject participation in oppression. The constructive program embodied the obligation to actively pursue social betterment—"truth." As such, it was closer than noncooperation to the central meaning of "satyagraha," which is "to hold fast to truth." The story of Gandhi's satyagraha has traditionally concentrated on the three great noncooperation campaigns; but his most persistent efforts were his unceasing work in support of the constructive program. It's notable, for instance, that all of his "fasts unto death" (from each of which he was released by progress in solving the issue about which he was fasting) were launched in the name of one plank or another of the constructive program—of bringing justice to the workers of Ahmedabad, of ending untouchability, of making peace between Hindus and Muslims. "Satyagraha," he said, "is not predominantly civil disobedience, but a quiet and irresistible pursuit of truth. On the rarest occasions it becomes civil disobedience."

A constructive program to address social ills may seem so elementary as scarcely to be an idea; yet few things caused more controversy in the Congress Party than Gandhi's dedication to it. In one of the lulls between noncooperation movements, Gandhi joked that in Congress "I stand thoroughly discredited as a religious maniac and predominantly a social worker." Most of the Congress leaders wanted to concentrate first on winning power and only then on addressing India's social ills. Gandhi reversed this order of business. He wanted Congress to address India's ills immediately and directly without regard to the English and their Raj. (The similarity between this program and the strategy of people's war is clear. In Gandhi's scheme, noncooperation was the nonviolent counterpart of guerrilla war while the constructive program was the counterpart of the Vietnamese *hiérarchies parallèles*.)

His thinking on the relationship of the constructive program to power was revealed in an answer to a letter from a reader of his journal *Indian Opinion* in 1931. The reader had written to protest that his constructive work was getting in the way of the attempt to take political power. "To me," the reader wrote, "political power is the substance, and all the other forms have to wait." Gandhi answered that "political power is not an end but only a means enabling people to better their condition in every department of life." Therefore, "Constructive effort is the substance of political power [while] actual taking over of the government machinery is but a shadow, an emblem." Five years later, at a time when he was devoting himself almost entirely to the constructive program, he wrote:

> One must forget the political goal in order to realize it. To think of the political goal at every step is to raise unnecessary dust. Why worry one's head over a thing that is inevitable? Why die before one's death? . . . That is why I can take the keenest interest in discussing vitamins and leafy vegetables and unpolished rice. That is why it has become a matter of absorbing interest to me to find out how best to clean our latrines.

If the goal was the renovation of India, why not proceed to it directly? Why not pick up a broom and sweep a latrine—as Gandhi in fact did at the first Congress meeting he attended, in 1915. If one concentrated too much on seizing the means of betterment, he feared, one might forget the goal. And in fact when India did achieve independence, this, in Gandhi's view, is exactly what happened. The Congress leaders took power but forgot what power was for. On October 2, 1947, when offered birthday congratulations, he answered, "Where do congratulations come in? It will be more appropriate to say condolences. There is nothing but anguish in my heart."

This is by no means to say, however, that Gandhi did not value political power, or did not believe in winning it or exercising it. He aimed at both throughout his life, though never as a government official. He did not say that the Congress Party should not take power; rather, he said that this was inevitable. Power might be only a "shadow"; on the other hand, there never was a thing that lacked its shadow.

He frequently suggested, indeed, that the constructive program was as effective a path to political power as noncooperation. Political power, he wrote, would in fact increase in "exact proportion" to success in the constructive effort. Whereas noncooperation drained power away from the oppressors, the constructive program generated it in the hands of the resisters. "When a body of men disown the state under which they have hitherto lived," he said in 1921, "they nearly establish their own government. I say nearly, for they do not go to the point of using force when they are resisted by the state."

Gandhi's view that winning state power, though necessary, should not be the supreme goal of India's political activity was also expressed in his arguments against adopting independence from England as the primary aim of Congress. As late as 1928, he opposed—successfully —a Congress independence resolution in response to the appointment by the English of a Statutory Commission for India. He had made his reasons clear as early as the publication of *Hind Swaraj*. Independence meant expelling the English and taking the reigns of government. But did India want "English rule without the Englishman"? Gandhi rejected this vision, as was not surprising for someone who at the time regarded the condition of modern England as "pitiable." He explained, "My patriotism does not teach me that I am to allow people to be crushed under the heel of Indian princes if only the English retire."

Independence meant dissociation—a merely negative goal. *Swaraj* meant building up something new. "Not only could *swaraj* not be 'given' to Indians," he said, "but rather it had to be created by them." Gandhi wanted action by Indians to better their own lives, not concessions or grants of authority from foreigners. *Swaraj*, as distinct from independence, must proceed from within each Indian. "Has independence suddenly become a goal in answer to something offensive that some Englishman has done?" he asked. And he went on, in simple words that seem to me to come close to the core of this arch-innovator's view of action and its proper place in the scheme of life, "Do men conceive their goals in order to oblige people or to resent their action? I submit that if it is a goal, it must be declared and pursued irrespective of the acts or threats of others." For Gandhi, ending untouchability, cleaning latrines, improving the diet of Indian villagers, improving the lot of Indian women, making peace between Muslims and Hindus—through all of which he believed he would find God—were such goals.

BEFORE A DROP OF BLOOD WAS SHED

John Adams, who appointed the committee that wrote the Declaration of Independence, served as the first vice president and second president of the United States, and was called "the colossus of independence" by Thomas Jefferson, penned some reflections late in his life that form a perfect complement to those of Washington, Paine, and Burke. If these three had defined negatively what could *not* decide the outcome of the revolution—namely, force—Adams defined positively what it was that *did* decide it: the combination of noncooperation and a constructive program now familiar to us.

Adams, in his late seventies, lacked the time and strength, he said, to write a history of the revolution; and so he offered his reflections only in letters to friends. He was prompted to write by the news that one Major General Wilkinson was penning a "history of the revolution," which was to begin with the battle of Bunker Hill, in 1775. Wilkinson, Adams wrote, would "confine himself to military transactions, with a reference to very few of the civil."

Such an account, Adams protested, would falsify history. "A history of the war of the United States is a very different thing," he claimed, "from a history of the first American revolution." Not only was Wilkinson wrong to concentrate on military affairs; he had located the revolution in the wrong historical period. The revolution, Adams claimed, was over before the war began:

> General Wilkinson may have written the military history of the war that followed the Revolution; that was an effect of it, and was supported by the American citizens in defence of it against an invasion of it by the government of Great Britain and Ireland, and all her allies . . . but this will by no means be a history of the American Revolution. The revolution was in the minds of the people, and in the union of the colonies, both of which were accomplished before hostilities commenced.

To his correspondent, Thomas Jefferson, a former political antagonist, he made the point emphatically: "As to the history of the revolution, my ideas may be peculiar, perhaps singular. What do we mean by the revolution? The war? That was no part of the revolution; it was only an effect and consequence of it. The revolution was in the minds of the people, and this was effected from 1760 to 1775, in the course of fifteen years, before a drop of blood was shed at Lexington."

Adams described an event that for him was a true turning point in the revolution. The English crown had decided to pay the judges of the Massachusetts Supreme Court directly. The colonists were indignant, and, at the suggestion of John Adams, voted to impeach the judges in the Massachusetts House of Representatives. The crown ignored the impeachment. Then came the decisive step. Jurors unanimously refused to serve under the embattled judges. Adams, who likes to use military metaphors to describe great deeds of peaceful noncooperation, remarks, "The cool, calm, sedate intrepidity with which these honest freeholders went through this fiery trial filled my eyes and my heart. *That* was the revolution—the decisive blow against England: In one word, the royal government was that moment laid prostrate in the dust, and has never since revived in substance, though a dark shadow of the hobgoblin haunts me at times to this day."

Adams's gallery of heroes are all civilians, his battles nonviolent ones. When he learns that Congress has appointed a national painter, he recommends paintings, to be executed in the grand style, of scenes of protest—a painting, for example, of Samuel Adams, his cousin and a sparkplug of the revolution, arguing with Lieutenant Governor Hutchinson against standing armies. "It will be as difficult," he remarks lightly, "to do justice as to paint an Apollo; and the transaction deserves to be painted as much as the surrender of Burgoyne. Whether any artist will ever attempt it, I know not."

Acts of noncooperation were one indispensable ingredient of what Adams calls "the real American revolution"; acts of association were another. At their center were the Committees of Correspondence, through which, beginning in the mid-1760s, the revolutionaries in the colonies mutually fostered and coordinated their activities. "What an engine!" Adams wrote of the Committees. "France imitated it, and produced a revolution. England and Scotland were upon the point of imitating it, in order to produce another revolution, and all Europe was inclined to imitate it for the same revolutionary purposes. The history of the world for the last thirty years is a sufficient commentary upon it. That history ought to convince all mankind that committees of secret correspondence are dangerous machines." Here, plainly, is another predecessor of the *hiérarchies parallèles*.

The decisive revolution, according to Adams, was thus the process by which ordinary people withdrew cooperation from the British government and then, well before even the Declaration of Independence, set up their own governments in all the colonies. The war that followed was the *military defense* of these already-existing governments against an attack by what was now a foreign power seeking to force the new country back into its empire. In his view, indeed, independence was nothing that could be *won from* the British; it had to be *forged by* the Americans. "Let me ask you, Mr. Rush," he wrote to his friend Richard Rush in April of 1815, in phrases that startlingly resemble Gandhi's later denial that Indian independence could be "given" her by England, "Is the sovereignty of this nation a gift? a grant? a concession? a conveyance? or a release and acquittance from Great Britain? Pause here and think. No! The people, in 1774, by the right which nature and nature's God had given them, confiding in original right, assumed powers of sovereignty. In 1775, they assumed greater power. In July 4th, 1776, they assumed absolute unlimited sovereignty in relation to other nations, in all cases whatsoever; no longer acknowledging any authority over them but that of God almighty, and the laws of nature and of nations."

In a recent description of the process Adams described, the historian Gordon Wood has written, "The royal governors stood helpless as they watched para-governments grown up around them, a rapid piecing together from the bottom up of a hierarchy of committees and congresses that reached from the counties and towns through the provincial conventions of the Continental Congress." On May 15, 1776, Adams notes, the Continental Congress declared that "every kind of authority under the ... Crown should be totally suppressed," and authorized the states to found "government sufficient to the exigencies of their affairs." "For if," Wood comments, "as Jefferson and others agreed, the formation of new governments was the whole object of the Revolution, then the May resolution authorizing the drafting of new constitutions was the most important act of the Continental Congress in its history. There in the May 15 resolution was the real declaration of independence, from which the measures of early July could be but derivations." James Duane, a delegate to the first congress, called this process "a Machine for the fabrication of Independence." Adams responded, "It was independence itself."

It is interesting to observe that another very notable authority on American political history also located the foundation of the Republic before July 4, 1776. "The Union is much older than the Constitution," Abraham Lincoln said in his First Inaugural. "It was formed in fact by the Articles of Association of 1774."

If we accept Adams's view, then both the overthrow of the old regime, laid in the dust (as Adams said) through a series of acts of noncooperation, and the foundation of the new one, accomplished the moment the Americans set up governments to govern themselves, were, like the overthrow and the foundation in 1688–89, nonviolent events, and the war that followed could be seen as a war of self-defense. In that war, Adams wrote to Rush, "Heaven decided in our favor; and Britain was forced not to give, grant, concede, or release our independence, but to acknowledge it, in terms as clear as our language afforded, and under seal and under oath."

THE EXPLOSIVE POWER OF LIVING IN TRUTH

What Michnik called a new evolutionism or building civil society Havel called "living in truth"—the title of an essay he published in

1978. Living in truth stood in opposition to "living in the lie," which meant living in obedience to the repressive regime. Havel wrote:

> We introduced a new model of behavior: don't get involved in diffuse general ideological polemics with the center, to whom numerous concrete causes are always being sacrificed; fight "only" for those concrete causes, and fight for them unswervingly to the end.

Why was this living in truth? Havel's explanation constitutes one of the few attempts of this period—or any other—to address the peculiarly ineffable question of what the inspiration of positive, constructive nonviolent action is. By living within the lie—that is, conforming to the system's demands—Havel says, "individuals confirm the system, fulfill the system, make the system, *are* the system." A "line of conflict" is then drawn through each person, who is invited in the countless decisions of daily life to choose between living in truth and living in the lie. Living in truth—directly doing in your immediate surroundings what you think needs doing, saying what you think is true and needs saying, acting the way you think people should act—is a form of protest, Havel admits, against living in the lie, and so those who try to live in truth are indeed an opposition. But that is neither all they are nor the main thing they are. Before living in truth is a protest, it is an affirmation. Havel, who sometimes makes use of philosophical language, explains as follows:

> Individuals can be alienated from themselves only because there is *something* in them to alienate. The terrain of this violation is their essential existence.

That is to say, if the state's commands are a violation deserving of protest, the deepest reason is that they disrupt this *something*—some elemental good thing, here called a person's "essential existence"— that people wish to be or do for its own sake, whether or not it is opposed or favored by the state or anyone else.

This is the point, it seems to me, that John Adams was getting at when he said that the American Revolution was completed before the war, and that Gandhi was making when he suggested that, if independence is a goal, then "it must be declared and pursued irrespective of the acts or threats of others." Like them (and like Nietzsche), Havel rebels against the idea that a negative, merely responding impulse is at the root of his actions. He rejects the labels "opposition" and "dissident" for himself and his fellow activists. Something in *him* craves manifestation.

Of those labels he writes:

> People who so define themselves do so in relation to a prior "position." In other words, they relate themselves specifically to the power that rules society and through it, define themselves, deriving their own "position" from the position of the regime. For people who have simply decided to live within the truth, to say aloud what they think, to express their solidarity with their fellow citizens, to create as they want and simply to live in harmony with their better "self," it is naturally disagreeable to feel required to define their own, original and positive "position" negatively, in terms of something else, and to think of themselves primarily as people who *are* against something, not simply as people who are what they are.

For Havel, this understanding that action properly begins with a predisposition to truth—often considered a merely private or personal endowment—has practical consequences that are basic to an understanding of political power:

> Under the orderly surface of the life of lies, therefore, there slumbers the hidden sphere of life in its real aims, of its hidden openness to truth. The singular, explosive, incalculable political power of living within the truth resides in the fact that living openly within the truth has an ally, invisible to be sure, but omnipresent: this hidden sphere.

Havel is describing, in words that anticipated the fall of the Soviet Union before that event had occurred, a secular variant of what Gandhi had called "truth force." If Michnik's words anticipated the sudden rise of Solidarity, Havel's bore fruit in the rise of the resistance movement in Czechoslovakia called Charter 77 and in the "velvet revolution" that put an end to communist power in Czechoslovakia.

Konrád offered what might be called a Hungarian version of living in the truth. Having witnessed the slow but surprisingly broad liberalization of the Hungarian system in the 1970s and eighties, he hoped that the changes under way in society would infect the communist functionaries, who would come to see "that their interests were better served by forms of government other than dictatorship." Konrád, who in such passages obliquely debated his Polish and Czech contemporaries on how change might occur, urged "confidence in this growing complexity—in the fact that a society can gradually slough off dictatorship, and that the prime mover in that process is a growing middle class." In his scheme, this liberalization, called "goulash Communism" by some, would gradually turn into goulash decommunization. Konrád wanted society to "absorb" the regime in a "ripening social transformation." He wanted the "iceberg of power . . . melted from within." He cited the historical precedent of the surrender of the dictatorial, right-wing regime of Francisco Franco in Spain to democratic forces in the 1970s. "Proletarian revolution didn't break out in any country of southern Europe," he commented. "If it had, the military dictatorships would only have hardened."

In all three of the Eastern European movements, the strategy was to bypass the government and tackle social problems directly, as Gandhi had done with his constructive program. But whereas "social work" presented no challenge to the Raj, it did challenge the Soviet regime. Within the class of repressive regimes, the Raj was an authoritarian regime, and left vast areas of Indian life untouched. The Raj had no difficulties with Gandhi's constructive program, to which it offered no rival; it was compelled to react only when he practiced noncooperation with the state. To the totalitarian Soviet regime, which sought to control almost every aspect of life, very much including the social, on the other hand, any independent activity looked like the beginnings of a rival governing power. Gandhi had said that once people disown the state under which they live they have "nearly" established their own government. On rare occasions, leaders of totalitarian regimes have also shown that they also understood the danger. In his memoirs, Khrushchev described his fear of the thaw he had started by his secret de-Stalinization speech of 1956. "We were scared—really scared," he wrote. "We were afraid the thaw might unleash a flood, which we wouldn't be able to control and which could drown us. It could have overflowed the banks of the Soviet riverbed and formed a tidal wave which would have washed [away] all the barriers and retaining walls of our society."

We have noted the central role in revolutions of defections among the troops of the old regime. Under a totalitarian regime, which seeks to mobilize the entire population in support of its ideological cause, the people become a sort of army on whose obedience the regime relies. But the very immensity of this army presents a target of opportunity for the opposition. If the essence of totalitarianism is its attempted penetration of the innermost recesses of life, then resistance can begin in those same recesses—in a private conversation, in a letter, in disobedience of a regulation at work, even in the invisible realm of a person's thoughts. Havel gives the example of a brewer he knew who, putting aside official specifications for making beer, set about making the best beer he could. Such was a brewer's living in truth.

Once the unraveling of the single, indivisible fabric of totalitarianism began, the rapidity of the disintegration could be startling. In Havel's prophetic words, "Everything suddenly appears in another light, and the whole crust seems then to be made of a tissue on the point of tearing and disintegrating uncontrollably." Totalitarian rule made constructive work and noncooperation difficult and costly but at the same time was especially vulnerable to those tactics. The pessimistic stock observation that Gandhi could never have succeeded against a totalitarian regime had an optimistic corollary. If such a movement could ever get going, as it did in the Soviet empire, the unraveling would be sudden and irresistible. The "Salisbury field" of a totalitarian regime was its entire society.

The radical potential of constructive work was implicit in a famous saying of Jacek Kuron, an intellectual adviser to Solidarity, who in the late 1970s counseled angry workers, "Don't burn down Party Committee Headquarters, found your own." And that is what they did, in August of 1980, when a spontaneous strike by workers in the Baltic shipyards spread like wildfire through Poland. Soon something like a general strike was under way, and the regime was forced to come to terms by granting, among other concessions, the right to form an independent trade union. The regime would not collapse for another nine years, but its death throes had already begun.

Even before the rise of Solidarity, Havel had reflected on the potential for developing power by founding new associations and organizations. The natural next step for an individual already trying to live in truth in his individual life, he advised in 1978, was to work with others to found what the writer Václav Benda called "parallel structures." These could be expected to arise first, Havel writes, in the realm of culture, where a "second culture," in the phrase he borrows from the rock musician Ivan Jirous, might develop. The step beyond that would be the creation of a "parallel polis" (another phrase of Benda's). This was the Czech version of Kuron's advice to the Polish workers to build their own headquarters.

In 1980, when Solidarity sprang into existence, it preferred on the whole to soft-pedal these radical possibilities, which, its leaders believed, might well provoke the Soviet Union to intervene, as it had in the past in Eastern Europe. They proposed instead a novel division of functions. "Society" would run itself democratically, but "power," which is to say the central government (and especially that part of it in charge of foreign affairs), would be left in the hands of the Communist Party dictatorship, whose survival would serve as a guarantee to the Soviet Union that its security interests would not be challenged. Long debates within the Solidarity movement were devoted to negotiating and fixing the boundaries of such a compromise. The debates came to an end only with the imposition of martial law, in December of 1981.

The similarities between the Eastern European movements and Gandhi's movement in India are obvious. If there were evidence that Havel had pored over Gandhi's works, we might suppose that his phrase "living in truth" was an inspired translation of "satyagraha"—

a term so difficult to render into other languages. In both movements, we find a conviction that the prime human obligation is to act fearlessly and publicly in accord with one's beliefs; that one should withdraw cooperation from destructive institutions; that this should be done without violence (Gandhi endorses nonviolence without qualifications; each of the Eastern European writers enters some qualifications); that means are more important than ends; that crimes shouldn't be committed today for the sake of a better world tomorrow; that violence brutalizes the user as well as his victim; that the value of action lies in the direct benefit it brings society; that action is usually best aimed first at one's immediate surroundings, and only later at more distant goals; that winning state power, if necessary at all, is a secondary goal; that freedom "begins with myself," as Michnik said, is oriented to love of truth, and only then discovers what it hates and must oppose; and that state power not only should but actually does depend on the consent of the governed.

The differences are also obvious. The Eastern Europeans demonstrated that revolution without violence did not have to depend on religious faith or an abstemious life. Whereas Gandhi's movement was spiritual in inspiration, the Eastern European movements were largely secular (although the Catholic Church played an important role in Poland). Whereas Gandhi called for a strict renunciation of selfish desires in favor of civic obligation, the Eastern Europeans sought to separate the private and other realms of life from political intrusions, of which they were heartily sick after decades of totalitarian rule. (The last thing they would have wanted was a single standard, whether imposed by God, "truth," or anything else, to which people had to subordinate every realm of their existence.) Whereas Gandhi was radically antimaterialistic, the Eastern Europeans were, variously, either only moderately so or hugely interested in material abundance for society. (There can be no such thing as goulash satyagraha.) Whereas Gandhi was an ascetic, the Eastern European leaders tended, in their personal lives, to be *hommes moyens sensuels*. Whereas Gandhi dreamed of a village-based cooperative society unlike any ever seen, then or since, the Eastern Europeans wanted to adopt the kind of parliamentary democracies and free-market economies already functioning in much of the world.

Although nonviolence was not an article of dogma for the Eastern Europeans, it was an essential element of their chosen form of action. "The struggle for state power," Michnik wrote, "must lead to the use of force; yet . . . according to the resolution passed at the memorable Solidarity Congress in Gdansk, the use of force must be renounced." One reason for the choice of nonviolence was pragmatic. The totalitarian state's monopoly on the instruments of violence required a search for some other means. "Why did Solidarity renounce violence?" Michnik asked while in prison after the imposition of martial law. He answered, "People who claim that the use of force in the struggle for freedom is necessary must first prove that, in a given situation, it will be effective, and that force, when it is used, will not transform the idea of liberty into its opposite. No one in Poland is able to prove today that violence will help us to dislodge Soviet troops from Poland and to remove the Communists from power. The USSR has such enormous power that confrontation is simply unthinkable. In other words: we have no guns." But in a comment that adds to our collection of remarks from various times and places claiming that the real revolution has occurred before the fighting (if any) breaks out, Michnik wrote, "Before the violence of rulers clashes with the violence of their subjects, values and systems of ethics clash inside human minds. Only when the old ideas of the rulers lose their moral duel will the subjects reach for force—sometimes."

Also like Gandhi, the Eastern Europeans shunned violence for moral reasons: they did not wish to become like the enemies they despised. The point was not to change rulers; it was to change the system of rule, and the system they opposed had been based on violence. Michnik again: "My reflections on violence and revolution were sparked by my puzzlement about the origins of totalitarianism. I searched for clues in the writings of George Orwell, Hannah Arendt, Osip Mandelstam, and Albert Camus, and I came to the conclusion that the genesis of the totalitarianism system is traceable to the use of revolutionary violence."

Havel concurred. He and his colleagues had "a profound belief that a future secured by violence might actually be worse than what exists now; in other words, the future would be fatally stigmatized by the very means used to secure it." In *Anti-Politics*, Konrád expressed full agreement, and drew an important conclusion. His mention of an active search for an alternative to the traditional ultima ratio is especially noteworthy:

> The political leadership elites of our world don't all subscribe equally to the philosophy of a nuclear *ultima ratio*, but they have no conceptual alternative to it. They have none because they are professionals of power. Why should they choose values that are in direct opposition to physical force? Is there, can there be, a political philosophy—a set of proposals for winning and holding power—that renounces *a priori* any physical guarantees of power? Only antipolitics offers a radical alternative to the philosophy of a nuclear *ultima ratio*. . . . Antipolitics means refusing to consider nuclear war a satisfactory answer in any way. Antipolitics regards it as impossible in principle that any historical

misfortune could be worse than the death of one to two billion people.

Violence, the Eastern Europeans found, was to be shunned for another reason: it was useless—more or less beside the point—for the sort of action they had resolved to pursue. Someone once remarked to Napoleon that you can't mine coal with bayonets. Neither are bayonets helpful for writing a book, cleaning a room, designing a microchip, or dressing a wound. Violence might or might not be useful for overthrowing a state, but Solidarity had renounced this ambition.

WHAT IS AND WHAT OUGHT TO BE

The comments of Michnik, Havel, and Konrád bring into the open a question never far from the surface when people choose nonviolent over violent action. Should nonviolence be chosen more for moral and spiritual reasons or more for practical ones? The issue is important because the believer in nonviolent action seems, to an unusual degree, to be ready to suffer defeat rather than abandon his chosen means. For Gandhi, nonviolence was foremost a moral and spiritual requirement. No mere circumstance—least of all the approach of defeat—could justify abandoning it. That is what he meant when he said that nonviolence was for him a creed, not a policy. For Michnik, by contrast, nonviolence was more a policy. He said he wanted the Russians to know that if they used force to put down the Polish movement, they would find themselves "spitting up blood." These are words that Gandhi could never have spoken. On the other hand, as we've seen, Gandhi's nonviolence was founded in part upon the recognition that in a violent fight with the English, the Indians would be "crushed in a minute." In other words, as Michnik said of the Poles, the Indians had no guns. And Gandhi had used language close to Michnik's when he declared that the Indians therefore must create a weapon "which would be different from and infinitely superior to the force which the white settler commanded." In these words, too, there is a kind of ambiguity. Gandhi sought spiritual victory above all else, yet he wanted to win in this world as well.

With Gandhi, we might say, the moral motive is primary, the pragmatic secondary, while with the Eastern Europeans the reverse is true. Either way, it seems to be in the very nature of principled nonviolent action that it tends to combine moral and practical calculation—just as it seems to be in the nature of violent action that, justifying means by ends, it tends to separate the two. That nonviolent action won more and more impressive successes even in the violent twentieth century has, I suggest, a meaning. Isn't it entirely fitting that, in a time when violence has increased its range and power to the point at which the human substance is threatened with annihilation, the most inventive and courageous people would cast about for something better to use? But the wonder of it is not that they have sought but that they have found. Michnik and his colleagues told themselves that they and others had discovered the political equivalent of the "atomic bomb," and they were right—except that their invention in fact accomplished what no actual atomic bomb could accomplish, the defeat of the Soviet Union. When they began their agitation, the iron law of the world dictated that revolution must be violent because violence was the foundation of power, and only power enables you to storm that citadel of violence and power, the state, and so to *take power*. When they were finished, and state after repressive state had been dissolved with little or no use of violence, a new law of the world had been written, and it read: Nonviolent action can be a source of revolutionary power, which erodes the ancien régime from within (even if its practitioners don't aim at this) and lays the foundation for a new state. If totalitarianism is a perversion of the democratic revolution, then the rise of nonviolent revolution is totalitarianism's antidote and cure, pointing the way to a recovery of democracy and, perhaps, to a deeper and truer understanding of democracy's nature, which is bound up with the principle of nonviolence.

Hanging over these political issues are questions of a more philosophical character, having to do with whether or not people are to suppose that the conduct they require of themselves is patterned upon, or takes its cue from, some underlying order of things, natural or divine, or whether, on the contrary, human beings live in an alien, inhuman universe. The tendency of philosophers at least since Nietzsche has been to take this latter view. Neither Gandhi nor Havel considered himself a philosopher, but both plainly thought otherwise. It is striking, for instance, that both chose the word "truth"—perhaps the key word for philosophy—as the touchstone for their actions. Each had very concrete, even mundane, things in mind—for example, the good beer the Czech brewer wanted to brew or the sanitary conditions in India's villages that absorbed Gandhi so much. But each also occasionally touched on metaphysical issues. Describing the illness and death after a jail term in South Africa of a *satyagrahi* called Valliama, Gandhi said, "The world rests upon the bedrock of *satya* or truth. *Asatya,* meaning untruth, also means non-existent, and *satya* or truth also means that which *is*. If untruth does not so much as exist, its victory is out of the question. And truth being that which is can never be destroyed. This is the doctrine of *satyagraha* in a nutshell." For Gandhi, this "truth" was God. In the essay "Politics and Conscience" Havel, a secular man, wrote in terms that were quite different yet conveyed a similar meaning:

At the basis of this world are values which are simply there, perennially, before we ever speak of them, before we reflect upon them and inquire about them. It owes its internal coherence to something like a "pre-speculative" assumption that the world functions and is generally possible at all only because there is something beyond its horizon, something beyond or above it that might escape our understanding and our grasp but, for just that reason, firmly grounds this world, bestows upon it its order and measure, and is the hidden source of all the rules, customs, commandments, prohibitions. . . . Any attempt to spurn it, master it, or replace it with something else, appears, within the framework of the natural world, as an expression of *hubris* for which humans must pay a heavy price.

To live in accord with this "something" was to live in truth. A similar confidence was expressed in the saying that, in the Western tradition, must be considered the foundation stone of any philosophy of nonviolence, namely Jesus' "They that live by the sword shall die by the sword." The advice does more than prescribe conduct; it makes a claim about the nature of the human world. We cannot suppose Jesus means that everyone who kills will be killed. But we can suppose he means that violence harms the doer as well as his victims; that violence generates counterviolence; and that the choice of violence starts a chain of events likely to bring general ruin. What Gandhi, Havel, and most of the others who have won nonviolent victories in our time believed and made the starting point of their activity was a conviction—or, to be exact, a faith—that if they acted in obedience to certain demanding principles, which for all of them included in one way or another the principle of nonviolence, there was, somewhere in the order of creation, a fundament, or truth, that would give an answering and sustaining reply.

THE UNCONQUERABLE WORLD

Fifty-eight years after Hiroshima, the world has to decide whether to continue on the path of cataclysmic violence charted in the twentieth century and now resumed in the twenty-first or whether to embark on a new, cooperative political path. It is a decision composed of innumerable smaller decisions guided by a common theme, which is weaning politics off violence. Some of the needful decisions are already clear; others will present themselves along the way. The steps just outlined are among the most obvious.

I have chosen them not merely because their enactment would be desirable. They represent an attempt to respond to the perils and dangers of this era as it really is, by building on foundations that already exist. For even as nuclear arms and the other weapons of mass destruction have already produced the bankruptcy of violence in its own house, political events both earthshaking and minute have revealed the existence of a force that can substitute for violence throughout the political realm. The cooperative power of nonviolent action is new, yet its roots go deep into history, and it is now tightly woven, as I hope I have shown in these pages, into the life of the world. It has already altered basic realities that everyone must work with, including the nature of sovereignty, force, and political power. In the century ahead it can be our bulwark and shield against the still unmastered peril of total violence.

In our age of sustained democratic revolution, the power that governments inspire through fear remains under constant challenge by the power that flows from people's freedom to act in behalf of their interests and beliefs. Whether one calls this power cooperative power or something else, it has, with the steady widening and deepening of the democratic spirit, over and over bent great powers to its will. Its point of origin is the heart and mind of each ordinary person. It can flare up suddenly and mightily but gutter out with equal speed, unless it is channeled and controlled by acts of restraint. It is generated by social work as well as political activity. In the absence of popular participation, it simply disappears. Its chief instrument is direct action, both noncooperative and constructive, but it is also the wellspring of the people's will in democratic nations. It is not an all-purpose "means" with which any "end" can be pursued. It cannot be "projected," for its strength declines in proportion to its distance from its source; it is a local plant, rooted in home soil. It is therefore mighty on the defensive, feeble on the offensive, and toxic to territorial empires, all of which, in our time, have died. It stands in the way of any future imperial scheme, American or other. This power can be spiritual in inspiration but doesn't have to be. Its watchwords are love and freedom, yet it is not just an ideal but a real force in the world. In revolution it is decisive. Allied with violence, it may accomplish immense things but then overthrow itself; tempered by restraint it can burn indefinitely, like a lamp whose wick is trimmed, with a steady flame. Under the name of the will of the people it has dissolved the foundations first of monarchy and aristocracy and then of totalitarianism; as opinion, it has stood in judgment over democratically elected governments; as rebellious hearts and minds, it has broken the strength of powers engaged in a superannuated imperialism; as love of country, it has fueled the universally successful movement for self-determination but, gone awry, has fueled ethnic and national war and totalitarian rule, which soon suffocate it, though only temporarily. It now must be brought to bear on the choice between survival and annihilation. It is powerful because it sets people in motion, and fixes before their eyes what they are ready to live and die for. It is dangerous for the same reason. Whether combined with violence, as in people's war, sustained by a constitution, as in democracy, or standing alone, as in satyagraha or living in truth, it is becoming the final arbiter of the public affairs of our time and the political bedrock of our unconquerable world.